VIOLENCE AGAINST THE PRESS

VIOLENCE AGAINST THE PRESS

Policing the Public Sphere in U.S. History

JOHN NERONE

New York   Oxford
OXFORD UNIVERSITY PRESS
1994

Oxford University Press

Oxford   New York   Toronto
Delhi   Bombay   Calcutta   Madras   Karachi
Kuala Lumpur   Singapore   Hong Kong   Tokyo
Nairobi   Dar es Salaam   Cape Town
Melbourne   Auckland   Madrid

and associated companies in
Berlin   Ibadan

Published by Oxford University Press, Inc.,
200 Madison Avenue, New York, New York 10016

Oxford is a registered trademark of Oxford University Press

Library of Congress Cataloging-in-Publication Data
Nerone, John.
Violence against the press:
policing the public sphere
in U.S. history
John Nerone.
p.   cm.
ISBN 0-19-507166-2 (cloth).—ISBN 0-19-508698-8 (pbk.)
1. Journalism—Social aspects—United States.
2. Freedom of the press—United States.
3. Violence—United States.
4. Press and politics—United States.
I. Title.   PN4888.S6N47   1994   302.23'2'0973—dc20   93-22639

2 4 6 8 9 7 5 3 1
Printed in the United States of America
on acid-free paper

Acknowledgments

I began this book in 1982, and many have helped along the way. Among the people who have read all or parts of the manuscript or who have influenced my thinking about this subject are Thomas Leonard, John Pauly, Bill Solomon, John Stevens, Dave Nord, James Baughman, Carolyn Marvin, Maurine Beasley, Richard John, Rajani Alexander, John Crane, Gary Krug, Bish Sen, and Minnie Sinha. I'm grateful to colleagues, past and present, at the University of Illinois for advice and support, particularly Kevin Barnhurst, Sandra Braman, James Carey, Cliff Christians, Thomas Guback, Lou Liebovich, Howard Maclay, and Ellen Wartella. My arguments on this subject were first presented publicly through the intercession of Chuck Whitney; a subsequent version appeared in the *Journal of Communication* with the editorial ministrations of Marsha Siefert, who was also instrumental in bringing this project to the attention of Oxford University Press, where it enjoyed the attention of Rachel Toor, David Roll, Ruth Sandweiss, and Betty Seaver. Tasks associated with this project afflicted many graduate students, including Jon Bekken, Britto Berchmanns, Ron Flynn, Carolyn Glassman, Holly Kruse, Bill Mueller, Gilbert Brinkley Rodman, Phil Sellers, and Steve Wiley. Diane Tipps and Anita Specht were indispensable. I can't say how much I owe to Ivy Glennon, though she would never condone the use of an exchange metaphor in such a context.

Contents

VIOLENCE AGAINST THE PRESS

1

Introduction

Not very long ago, the spiritual leader of Iran proclaimed a death sentence against the novelist Salman Rushdie. Because the Ayatollah Khomeini had already been freighted with anti-American significance, this story played naturally in the U.S. media as a regressive attack on freedom of expression—which in fact it was—and elicited from writers, politicians, government officials, and managers of media businesses dutiful yet luminous recitals of traditional liberal formulations of free-press theory. Suddenly, after a presidential campaign in 1988 that had stooped to moral terrorism over whether school children should be compelled to recite the Pledge of Allegiance to the flag, it was again proper to be a liberal. Liberals were now the courageous targets of Khomeini, not the godless bureaucrats who wanted to jail praying students.

Still more recently, Basic Books decided not to publish a book on the Rushdie affair by Middle East scholar Daniel Pipes that it had contracted for some months earlier. In the meantime, Khomeini had died, an event that threatened eventually to take him out of the headlines but did not produce the hoped-for revocation of Rushdie's death sentence. Did the publisher fear Khomeini's disciples? No, not according to George Craig, chief editor of (then) Harper and Row, the parent company of Basic Books, and itself a subsidiary of Rupert Murdoch's News Corporation. Coincidentally, another News Corporation subsidiary, William Collins (which has since been merged with Harper), had recently canceled another completed book, titled "The Rushdie File," in England, in the wake of a series of bookstore bombings aimed at *Satanic Verses*. Craig was anxious to put to rest rumors that his company had a terror-inspired prohibition against books that might offend Muslims. On the contrary, he insisted, the cancellations were business as usual; both sprang from marketing, not political, reasons. Neither book would have turned a profit.[1]

Ironically, the death threats against Rushdie had catapulted his *Satanic Verses* to the top of the best-seller lists, putting the subtle Indian magic realist in the company of Robert Ludlum and Judith Krantz. The threat of assassination gave a public hearing to an unlikely text. But, within months, it seemed, the opening quietly, seamlessly closed. The ayatollah giveth and the marketplace taketh away.

We must not lose sight of this ultimate irony: Khomeini's death threat prompted a loud affirmation of tolerance and diversity—and rightly so. But the publisher's invocation of market realities shocked no one and relieved quite a few. The publisher was not bowing to terrorists. The publisher was conducting business as usual, in which case it was not alarming that otherwise acceptable manuscripts were declared unpublishable. Almost redundantly, at the same time, Washington, D.C., began to resound with howls of outrage at a Supreme Court decision that struck down laws against flag desecration, saying such laws prohibited what must be considered protected political expression. The public's attention span for the truths Americans declare they hold self-evident, one fears, has often been too short.

What I found most revealing in all the rhetoric of the Rushdie affair involved conflicting sets of attitudes about the status of the word. Novelists and literary scholars have a quite distinct set of attitudes. They are accustomed to treating the word as privileged. They conceive of themselves as working in an autonomous realm of wordplay, and believe that they should have absolute freedom of expression, not necessarily because of conscience—Milton's position in *Areopagitica*, the most famous Western argument for freedom from censorship—nor because of property rights—the core belief, some argue, of capitalist individualism—but because of the privilege due imagination. Rushdie should be free to blaspheme, free to distort and mislead and cause havoc in the world—not to say that he has—because he is a writer. The word is privileged. Utterance may be an act, but it is an act unlike any other. Rushdie himself has phrased this eloquently by referring to the attack on *Satanic Verses* as "an attack upon the very idea of the novel form." The novel represents a way of thinking about the word that is in contradiction to religion: ". . . whereas religion seeks to privilege one language above all others, one set of values above all others, one text above all others, the novel has always been *about* the way in which different languages, values, and narratives quarrel, and about the shifting relations between them."[2] That is to say, although to religious fundamentalists the word corresponds directly to divine reality, to novelists and literary folk generally words are chiefly about words.

Ironically, those who understand books in this way might be the ones who are least prone to be moved to action by words. Those who believe in the autonomy of literature, if you will, are conditioned to think of words as just words, as related to nothing but other words. The belief that words are not real in the common sense of the term takes extreme form, of course, as the belief that words are the only reality. In any form, the belief puts words in a category different from cars. Cars should be licensed, words must not. In this sense, freedom of expression carries with it the corollary that words are not in themselves powerful; the power of any particular expression is derived from the way it is used by people (another familiar argument from *Areopagitica*).

Again ironically, it was the critics of Rushdie—and they came from a broad range of backgrounds—who found his words truly powerful. Some found them powerful because of their effect on world attitudes, what friends of mine meant when they said that Rushdie was guilty of "participating in the discourse of colonialism."[3] And this effect was the result of Rushdie's position in history. If Robert Ludlum or Judith Krantz had written *Satanic Verses*, it would not have had the same impact because the world would not have heard a former colonial participating in the discourse of colonialism. Likewise, had an entirely obscure Indian émigré written the book, the world simply may not have heard. In this argument, again, words have power because of who writes them and who reads them and in what historical conjuncture, but words themselves are historical acts, not privileged, and in the same realm as Khomeini's death sentence, which can then be justified as a countervailing act.

But clearly this was not the justification that Khomeini and his followers used. To them, it seemed, the existence of the word was not historically conditioned. The word was real, and it had a moral nature. The text of *Satanic Verses* was evil, no matter how, when, or by whom composed; the act of composition was sinful, no matter who reads. The word itself is alive: not a dead thing, but having in itself a potency of action (to paraphrase Milton again, this time against himself).

These varying attitudes toward the word underpinned the controversy over *Satanic Verses*, then. To Rushdie's supporters, words were autonomous and privileged; to some of his critics, words were historical acts, to others, words were moral creatures.

The temptation for Western observers was to call pro-Rushdie attitudes "modern" and anti-Rushdie ones "traditional." In doing so, they argued that belief in the moral nature of utterances is primitive, a mark of inexperience, a complex of attitudes that must pass away in modern industrial societies. Modern people know better than to punish expression. The freedom of public utterance that seems essential to "modern" societies comes from a particular conception of the public, the public sphere, and the role of public opinion in governance. Jurgen Habermas illuminates these matters in his influential analysis of the rise of the bourgeois public sphere in European countries in the eighteenth century.

According to Habermas, the rising bourgeoisie created the public sphere as a space between the state and civil society.[4] Inside the bourgeois public sphere, voices could be raised against the government, but only if certain rules were followed. These rules all derived from the opposition between public and private. The private realm was the realm of love and family; it was also the realm of self-interested enterprise. All of these factors—everything to do with the private self—had to be excised from the public sphere. Properly public utterance required a negation of the self. In U.S. history, the best example of this sort of self-negation is in the common use of pseudonyms in printed political discourse in the colonial and revolutionary eras. The *Federalist Papers,* the most famous of all U.S. political arguments, were written by "Publius," a name that best translates as "citizen." Of course readers knew that these essays were written by political chieftains with interests and concerns of their own. But the rules of public discourse demanded that the personalities of the authors be negated; in the public sphere, their arguments must win or lose on their own merits. In the public sphere, reason, not passion, and not personality, must govern. Just as the personality of authors was to be disguised, so was that of audiences. Each author was supposed to be the anonymous voice of reason. Likewise, the audience was imagined as universal—what transpired in public was thought to have the attention of everyone.

This conception of the public sphere seems to be a great denial of sociological facts. At no point in history were speakers so anonymous, audiences so universal, and discourse so rational. But conceptions of this sort don't have to be accurate descriptions to be effective, and in fact the set of notions that Habermas outlines was effective in maintaining a buffer between the state and the realm of the private. The concept of the bourgeois public sphere was one key to the protection of the civil liberties that are considered essential in modern democracies.

At the same time, the eighteenth-century bourgeois revolutions were redefining state sovereignty. The source of sovereignty was no longer God or the good or even the good of the people; it was the consent of the governed. From that point on, governments would have to justify their actions as the will of the people.

Of course, "the people" is every bit as abstract a conception as the public sphere. One might define the people variously as "Frenchmen throughout history" or "the freeholders of England" or all adult males or a majority in the legislature or a randomized sample of 1400 adults. So government by popular consent gave birth to an array of techniques for representing public opinion: the mass meeting, the political assembly, the election, the partisan newspaper, the public opinion poll. Each technique, like the notion of the public sphere itself, is supposed to let the people speak for themselves. And each, like the public sphere, is supposed ideally to eliminate all sources of power or influence besides the truth or reason. The power of truth, the guidance of reason—these are what make states modern. And, although everyone recognizes the amount of idiocy that survives in even the most modern societies, most feel that, say, Salman Rushdie has nothing to fear from one; where else could such a man feel at home? On the other hand, has the modern world really been all that modern?

In the wake of the Rushdie affair, as if history really were written by a bad novelist, U.S. attention focused on other issues of free expression. Even while politicians, jurists, and religious leaders proclaimed warm support of Rushdie, they directed a chorus of outrage against desecration of the symbols of U.S. nationhood. We've already noted the Supreme Court ruling on flag desecration. The same season saw controversy over a student's exhibit at the Art Institute of Chicago that implicitly invited visitors to step on the flag, and disputation over federal funding for controversial art and for documentaries on public television. The list could be extended. The point, however, is quite simple: the U.S. public, as well as U.S. opinion leaders, are not consistently "modern" in their attitudes toward the word. Many liberals have been quite consistent in their support of free expression, of course, but even some of them draw the line at Klan or Nazi rallies. Most U.S. citizens seem to view some words as necessarily moral. Though the punishment to be meted out differs from Khomeini's, the underlying set of attitudes may be quite consonant.

Most people find some things to be unspeakable or unprintable. In the United States, the realm of the unspeakable has often shifted, but it's always there, and its borders are always somehow fortified.

The Rushdie affair allowed the U.S. public to declare itself exceptionally liberal; its realm of the unspeakable is small, with borders loosely patroled. Maybe so. But maybe the public is deceived because so many of the border patrol are not in uniform, so to speak. Perhaps U.S. law seems lax because so many other agencies control expression.[5]

I've already alluded to economic restrictions on free expression. The marketplace is generally not considered a mechanism for control because it is called uncontrolled. Most U.S. liberals consider the market to be the essence of freedom because freedom means the capability to dispose of one's own property, including property in one's talents or expressions. But the market has a tendency to accent the middle, a point that Alexis de Tocqueville made unforgettably in his discussion of the tyranny of the majority in *Democracy in America*.[6] Moreover, the unregulated market can fall victim to various "natural" ailments, the most common and dangerous of which, according to the greatest of the free-market thinkers, Adam Smith, is monopoly. Indeed, the U.S. media are increasingly prone these days to monopoly. Virtually all daily newspapers are local monopolies; virtually all cable systems are regulated monopolies; the Associated Press has a near monopoly as a wire service; broadcast networks and movie production, distribution, and now exhibition companies are oligopolistic; and mergers and buyouts have begun to produce media chains and groups of tremendous size and influence.[7] But this situation is not entirely new. The newspapers of the colonial and early national eras were frequently monopolies; political factions and parties influenced content in a fashion similar to networks and wire services; Hearst in his day had a larger market share of all media than Gannett or Time-Warner today. Media ownership has always been a problem for freedom of expression.[8] To put it baldly, no market is ever entirely free as a market, and no free market is ever free as a marketplace of ideas.

The marketplace restricts ideas according to consumer demand. Historically, a lack of consumer demand has been effective in limiting the range of opinion in mass-marketed publications. A buying audience exists for violent pornography but not for its political equivalent; hence, laws are passed against obscenity more readily than against seditious libel. One may advocate revolution with a minimum of legal restriction these days precisely because there is no market for revolution.

Receptivity, then, also limits expression. This happens not just through the marketplace but also, I would like to argue, in directly inhibiting certain kinds of discussion. As John Stuart Mill points out in *On Liberty*, most people are sensitive to public opinion and shy away from offending it.[9] Furthermore, expression is not really communication unless it is attended to. Inattention is thus an effective way of silencing certain kinds of expression, especially as it is enhanced by the market mechanism.

Another species of control is professionalism. Especially in the news media, certain professional routines are maintained and reinforced by practitioners.[10] These routines have a twin effect: they cause messages to be constructed in particular ways (for instance, by insisting on source attribution and balancing statements), meanwhile delegitimizing messages that are not thus constructed, and they erect barriers to entry by limiting input to qualified professionals. The ultimate effect of professionalism is to exclude the most extreme expressions and to take the edge off all expressions. Imagine, for instance, a professional journalist writing a lead like this: Senator McCarthy lied again today about Communists in the State Department.[11] To submit such a lead, no matter how true, no matter how many colleagues might agree, is to surrender one's standing as a professional by proclaiming an allegiance. Professionalism prohibits such expressions in news reporting.

Thus, beyond the law, in the United States and, by implication, in other Western countries, a complex of mechanisms operates at all times to regulate public discourse. This complex has not always run smoothly, however. When it fails, violence often occurs.

Mark Twain has given us the most famous account of violence against the press in his satire "Journalism in Tennessee."[12] In recounting an afternoon in the employ of the *Morning Glory and Johnson County War-Whoop*, he describes the chief editor's reaction to a pistol shot through the window:

> "Ah," said he, "that is that scoundrel Smith, of the *Moral Volcano*—he was due yesterday." And he snatched a navy revolver from his belt and fired. Smith dropped, shot in the thigh. The shot spoiled Smith's aim, who was just taking a second chance, and he crippled a stranger. It was me. Merely shot a finger off.
>
> Then the chief editor went on with his erasures and interlineations. Just as he finished them a hand-grenade came down the stove-pipe, and the explosion shivered the stove into a thousand fragments. However, it did no further damage, except that a vagrant piece knocked a couple of my teeth out.
>
> "That stove is utterly ruined," said the chief editor. (p. 37)

There follows a duel with "Colonel Blatherskite Tecumseh" (p. 39) and visits from half a dozen outraged gentlemen. "People were shot, probed, dismembered, blown up, thrown out the window. There was a brief tornado of murky blasphemy, with a confused and frantic war-dance glimmering through it, and then all was over" (p. 41).

The hyperbolic violence that characterizes the daily routine of the chief editor of the *War-Whoop* is funny because it is an exaggeration of the familiar. Nineteenth-century editors were expected to encounter violence, and Twain's recollections of his own (later) experiences in Nevada journalism attest to the frequency of attacks on and by newsmen.[13]

Violent reprisal was decreed the appropriate response to printed insults by no less a figure than Benjamin Franklin. In a 1789 essay[14] lamenting the press's habit of "affronting, calumniating, and defaming" (p. 38), Franklin pondered how one might discourage such practices without diminishing the useful freedom of the press. Ultimately, he proposed to do this "by restoring to the people a species of liberty, of which they have been deprived by our laws, I mean the *liberty of the cudgel*" (p. 39). By this he meant simply that if the chief editor of the *Morning Glory and Johnson County War-Whoop* savages you in print, "you may go to him as openly and break his head" (p. 40). But suppose the offense is not against an individual but against the public? Should the offenders go unpunished? No, but then "we should in moderation content ourselves with tarring and feathering, and tossing them in a blanket" (p. 40).

Twain and Franklin joked about violence, but it remained nevertheless a very real phenomenon. And it was not always a laughing matter. In Franklin's day, violence was occasionally the lot of printers engaged in partisan disputes; Twain came of age during the great controversy over slavery, in which dozens of journals were targets of mob violence, in both the North and South. In popular memory, the dark side of antipress violence is symbolized by Elijah Lovejoy, antislavery editor, who died in an attack on his newspaper, and has since been celebrated as the first martyr to freedom of the press in the United States.

Violence against the press, then, is a familiar theme in U.S. history. But it is usually understood as part of the distant and colorful past, a product of antique prejudices and outmoded values, one of the many obstacles overcome on the road to pluralism.

The perspective I offer in this book is quite different. I see violence as being an integral part of the culture of public expression in the United States. In itself violence may seem to consist only of episodes and accidents, but upon analysis I hope to show that violent acts are systemic rather than episodic, responses to recurring crises in an evolving system of public expression.

Here it might be helpful to anticipate some objections to what I will argue about the significance of antipress violence.

1. "Antipress violence was never common." On the contrary, one finds examples wherever one looks. Such violence has been unexpectedly common, common enough to become part of the mythology of U.S. journalism.

2. "Antipress violence no longer exists." Although antipress violence no longer assumes the same forms it did in the nineteenth century, it still appears in attacks on individual reporters, in threats against newspapers, and in "terrorist" acts designed to attract media coverage. And harassment of the nonmainstream press remains common. It is true, though, that the mainstream press is better protected now than before against certain types of violence. Urban crowds no longer riot over daily newspapers. Partly this is because professional standards have cut down on offensive material; there are no more *War-Whoops*. Partly it is because urban police stand ready to prevent and punish riotous behavior, rather than engaging in it themselves.

3. "Only a minority of the population ever participated in such violence." Actual perpetrators may have been a minority, but these people were not, on the whole, cranks. Their attitudes usually conformed with mainstream attitudes, and their actions often seemed neither extravagant nor objectionable to their peers. For instance, politicians expressed dismay over riots against antislavery newspapers but frequently barely concealed their relief and approval, and they balked at sponsoring legislation to prevent future riots.

4. "Violence had little to do with prevailing ideas and attiudes about the press." Often, it is true, occasions of violence prompted vigorous argument on behalf of free expression.[15] But in virtually every case the bottom line was ambiguous: support for freedom of expression was usually qualified by a vague notion of virtue. The press should be free but not licentious. The rubric of licentiousness, of course, can always be tailored to fit whatever subject is at hand. Historically, then, even champions of free expression have usually defined freedom in such a way as to exclude *in practice* some groups or positions on moral if not on legal grounds. Because both violence and legal repression remain evident, we might conclude that statements of support for free expression have been misleading or perhaps even insincere.

5. "Even so, the United States has always been more libertarian than other countries." It's true that expressions of support for free expression have been pervasive in U.S. history. It's also true that within the mainstream during peacetime U.S. citizens have freely criticized their government. On the other hand, there have always been limits, both in law and in practice, both on ideas and on groups. Few Western countries have experienced as much labor and racial violence as the United States, for instance, and a large share of this violence has been directed against expression.

What ultimately impressed de Tocqueville about the United States was its stability.[16] And what's impressive isn't how much "liberty" there's been but how little state intervention has been necessary to maintain order. This is because order has been maintained through other agencies. And when these agencies have failed, violent action has been used to restore order.

It may seem inappropriate to think of violence as an aspect of order. We are accustomed to thinking of violence as an agent of disorder, as a destabilizing factor. Indeed, violence falls outside the law, but violence has often operated in place of law in the United States. The long careers of dueling and lynching testify to this. Antipress violence too has usually been stabilizing in intent, if not always in effect; it has been a unique form of conflict because it has usually been designed to prevent conflict (though some recent forms seem to have the opposite inclination). Violence against expression was used to prevent rhetorical battles from developing into full-scale conflict.

To clarify this point, it will be helpful to sketch out the chief types of U.S. antipress violence. I have identified four basic patterns: violence among individuals, violence against ideas, violence against groups, and violence against an institution. Each pattern has its own chronology.

Violence Among Individuals

Public affairs have often been intertwined with private quarrels, and, at least since the time of the Revolution, political disputes have produced violence among individuals. Editorial dueling is the classic nineteenth-century incarnation of this type of violence. Beginning in the late nineteenth century, personal violence began migrating downward through the occupational ladder of journalism. Editors ceased to hold a monopoly on dueling. Reporters became participants and targets. At the same time, such violence came more and more from invasions of privacy than from public quarrels over public affairs—what we might call the privatization of reputation. At present it seems the most likely targets of personal violence are reporters and photographers covering sports and entertainment celebrities.

Violence Against Ideas

Movements in U.S. history have routinely encountered violence, and this violence has often been directed against their media. Among the movements so assaulted have been, in rough chronological order, loyalism, independence, antifederalism, Jeffersonian Republicanism, Catholicism, anti-Masonry, abolitionism, Mormonism, labor unionism, socialism, and civil rights. Sometimes such violence has indicated a nearly equally divided citizenry, but more frequently it has been directed outward from a unified center against "threatening" ideas. Violence against ideas might thus also be described as "majoritarian."

Violence against ideas is intensified by but not limited to periods of perceived social instability. Such violence was most prevalent in the turbulent 1830s and 1840s, for instance. On the other hand, it is difficult to find periods of U.S. history when people did not perceive a threat to social stability of one sort or another. Wartime has usually been marked by crusades against the nonmainstream whether dangerous or not; war is a good excuse for a general ideological housecleaning.

Violence against ideas has waned in the twentieth century. Four factors seem responsible. First, people have become accustomed to letting the marketplace weed out ideas, confident that dangerous ideas will not be commercially viable. Second, institutionalization in the U.S. media has limited access to audiences for nonmainstream media and has fortified the impression among all groups, mainstream and nonmainstream alike, of an immovable consensus on core values. Third, people seem convinced that ideas in themselves are not really dangerous (and in fact may simply not exist except as expressions of or masks for "real" interests). And fourth, government and police have taken on a large share of the job of idea regulation in the twentieth century, frequently targeting labor and civil rights activism and various forms of radicalism.

Violence Against Groups

In the late nineteenth century, violence against groups replaced violence against ideas as the main form of majoritarian antipress violence. Racial, ethnic, and in some cases class descriptions became more important than ideological ones in determining the right to free expression. At the same time, racial, ethnic, and sometimes class groups came to view the press as a crucial symbol of autonomy and influence. Attacks on African-American, foreign-language, and working-class journals followed.

Such violence persists, though it is less common at the end of the twentieth century than in the 1880s or the 1960s. A chief reason for this decline has been the relegation of minority media to supplementary status. They no longer compete with mainstream media for attention, and they no longer insulate minority groups from the mainstream. Minority groups are in fact among the heaviest consumers of mainstream media, especially television. Furthermore, ethnicity seems to be a less salient characteristic of U.S. cultural and political life than it was at the turn of the century, a development that may be attributed to immigration restriction, the extension of public schooling, the effects of routinization in the workplace, and perhaps the impact of the mass media. Still, groups remain targets of violence, hate crimes appear to be on the rise, and experience leads one to anticipate future cycles of especially racial violence. Attacks against minority media will no doubt figure in these.

Violence Against an Institution

Twentieth-century Americans refer to the media as to a monolith. Grammatical miseducation alone does not explain the use of the word *media* as a singular rather than a plural noun; Americans say "media *is*" because it is apparent to them that the media "is" a singular entity. The expression "media is" will always grate on some ears—mine included—but it is here to stay, it seems, because it accurately reflects the public perception that the media constitute a single institution. Media is as media does.

The perception of institutionalization is borne out by some palpable facts. Most newspapers are monopolies; most news comes from official sources; most news media convey the same news diet; most reporting is done by professionals in a style meant to convey and reinforce their professionalism. These are real barriers to entry into the marketplace of ideas, and it is clear to readers and viewers that they do not live in the same world as the news or the people who report it. Some are angry about this.

It has become common for some people to try to force the news to include them in its world. Frequently the attempt will be violent. "Inclusionary" violence is a recent phenomenon, and we might expect it to become more common.

The chronologies of the different forms of antipress violence converge at two points. One is the later nineteenth century, loosely speaking, the time of the industrial revolution. At this point violence against ideas yielded to violence against groups, and personal violence shifted from editorial duels and fights to assaults on reporters. A second moment of convergence is the early to middle twentieth century, when violence against ideas became quite uncommon and violence against the media as an institution emerged.

These two moments of change are also, not coincidentally, crucial moments of change for the system of public discourse in the United States. The industrial revolution changed printing from a craft to an industry characterized by factory production, division of labor, and mass distribution. The life of the newspaper became intertwined by ownership and through advertising patronage with other industrial concerns as well. All of this deeply influenced the ways messages were channeled. Likewise, the early to middle twentieth century was characterized by fundamental changes in the way the media operated. Newspapers were obliged to split markets with radio and film; reporters accepted and created different standards; the federal government became a much more important producer of information. As far as the press was concerned, the upshot of all this was an institutional revolution as dramatic and far-reaching as the industrial revolution.

In both industrialization and institutionalization change proceeded on several levels. One level was the development of material production: the technologies of communication, the techniques of manufacture, the organization of sites of production, the division of labor, the hierarchy of tasks, the relations of ownership, and so forth. On another level were the sets of ideas and values attached to communication, or what we might call the culture of the press.

My interest in antipress violence comes from an interest in the culture of the press. The great question of communications history, I think, revolves around how people make sense out of things. This entails reconstructing mentalities that no longer exist, assumptions that are no longer commonly held. The main tools for such reconstructions will have to be the things people said and wrote about what they thought. But these documents will always be inadequate because it is precisely the things that people take most for granted that they are least likely to give expression to. For such deep structures, one can't trust what people said about themselves. Instead, one might look at what people did. Hence the usefulness of antipress violence; read attentively, it should tell us how people made sense out of the media. It should help reveal the culture of the press.

The culture of the press differed depending on one's position in the communications process. News *professionals* had an occupational ideology that changed over time but tended to remain distinct from notions current among the *public*. A third position with its own form of press culture was occupied by *insiders*, members of the public, like politicians, government officials, and experts, who are privileged participants in or observers of the news. A fourth group might be called *theorists*, articulate thinkers who devote their attention specifically to the process of communication. Within the culture of the press, then, we see several distinct but overlapping arenas of discourse.

In normal situations, it's hard to detect discontinuities between neighboring discourses. The press culture of professionals, for instance, might seem consonant with that of the public. But when violence occurs, discontinuities are thrown into high relief. In some cases, for instance, violence is an expression of public fury at professional behavior, and signifies a real difference between public and professional ideals. Violence also tends to accent moments of change. Often a violent action is an attempt to preserve traditional values—public, professional, or insider—in the face of change. Violent episodes can thus be quite revealing.

What Is a Medium?

Before concluding this introduction, it's necessary to deal with the abstract question of the nature of a medium. The term has a commonsense obviousness that is really quite misleading because when we talk about a medium, we are actually calling to mind several different kinds of things.

As a starting point, consider the *Morning Glory and Johnson County War-Whoop*, or rather its twentieth-century equivalent. One might point to an individual copy of the *War-Whoop* and say, "This is a newspaper." Though this would be true, it wouldn't be the entire truth, because there are, say, a quarter of a million copies of the same edition. Then one might shift one's attention from the commodity—the individual copy, the unit that is bought and sold—to the text: the words and pictures that constitute any particular issue. The text is also the newspaper, but not the entire newspaper because yesterday's text *of the same paper* was quite different. How is it that the text changes but the newspaper remains the same? Quickly, one might answer that it's because there is some continuity in the organization that produces the different texts. In addition to being a commodity and a text, a newspaper is also a system of producing commodities and texts. Thus we can point to the printing office of the *War-Whoop* and say, "There's the newspaper." Again, though, we have not told the entire truth. Not all of the organization that produces the paper is in the *War-Whoop* printing office. The wire services and features syndicates and advertising bureaus that are so crucial to creating the text of the paper are elsewhere, as are, in many cases, the printing facilities. And besides all of the people and things that contribute to the construction of the paper prior to its publication, there are also people and things equally essential to the life of the paper who begin to interact with it only after it's been published. Most obviously there are the paying readers. There are as well all the others who take notice in some fashion: the officials who construe the paper to be "public opinion," the shoppers who clip coupons. Thus we have the (also somewhat true) truisms that "a newspaper is its readers" and that "a newspaper is nothing without the public's trust."

What, then, is a newspaper? It is a structure that produces *and consumes* commodities, texts, meanings, and audiences.[17] And that structure is not a thing so much as it is a network of relationships. At root, the word *medium* refers to something in the middle, an intermediary between or among things. In modern usage, a medium is a structure of connections between and among newsmakers, journalists, advertisers, civic organizations, readers, voters, shoppers, and so forth.

This understanding of the nature of a medium gives us a radically different perspective on what a medium does in the arena of public expression. Consider the commonsense understanding of the power of the press. The press is thought to have power when editors, journalists, politicians, or advertisers direct a message at an audience and produce a desired reaction. But if we think of media as networks of relationships, we can see that each of the actors in this transaction have been constructed historically. In a single instance a message affects an audience, perhaps. But the network of relationships that is a medium is acting all the time. Its existence is intimately bound up in all that its clients do. Its power is thus not manifested so much in persuading voters to elect Mr. Deeds as it is in reinforcing the definition of citizens as voters in the first place. It is not important so much in marketing Philboyd Studge to the public as it is in reinforcing the definition of the public as consumers.

But it is foolish to argue that the media create the world they exist in. The media didn't define citizens as voters; majoritarian politics did that, and then the political parties created media to support the system that resulted. Likewise, the media didn't define the public as consumers; the rise of a market economy did that, and then the suitable media were called into existence to support the resulting economic system. The media are historical constructs too, and they have been constructed or modeled in different and sometimes conflicting ways in the course of U.S. history. But what does this have to do with antipress violence?

Antipress violence marks moments of struggle over the definition of media as networks of relationships. Violence was common during the Revolutionary period, for instance, as newspapers were called on to serve as advocates of a movement and as ideal surrogates of public opinion. Violence was also common in the antebellum period, when reform editors set out to accomplish the nation's moral reconstruction, and in the process savagely denounced the conventional press as servile to the interests of the parties and the marketplace. And violence was common when minorities claimed the press as a voice of their own.

Distinct models for the media have competed for dominance in U.S. history. Each of these models arose at a specific historical conjuncture, and each has an ideology, implied or explicit. I'll close this chapter by discussing some of these models, by way of establishing a rudimentary vocabulary to be used in the chapters to follow.

The newspaper of the colonial and Revolutionary periods was modeled as a kind of town meeting. It was produced by a supposedly impartial "publick printer" who conceived of himself or herself as an artisan or "mechanick." The virtue of the printer was in the quality of the printing: the printer was neither an editor nor a journalist, though the printer did have the authority and responsibility to police the content of his or her paper, rejecting items that were "scurrilous" or "licentious." The purpose of the paper was to allow citizens irrespective of class or party to communicate freely and deliberate rationally. Such a medium was meant to be a tool of "rational liberty." Although often striven for and sometimes approximated, this model of a medium was clearly utopian. But it spawned a set of conventions that colonial and Revolutionary newspapers observed faithfully, the most obvious example being the use of pseudonyms. Even while maintaining the conventions of rational liberty, however, newspapers of the period were often conducted so as to serve specific interests and preserve definite mercantile and political relations.

The rise of partisan and commercial papers weakened and, by the 1830s, displaced the newspaper of rational liberty (which bequeathed most of its ideological assumptions to the reform press). Partisanism and commercialism were distinct but compatible models of and ideologies for newspaper conduct.

Partisanism appeared as early as the struggle over the ratification of the federal Constitution but was not firmly entrenched in press ideology until the rise of the second party system, a process that climaxed in Andrew Jackson's successive campaigns (really one continuous campaign) for the presidency in the 1820s. The ideology of partisanism was loosely based on notions of competition contained in the metaphors of the courtroom, the military, and the marketplace. Appropriately, partisanism emphasized the editor—often a lawyer—over the printer and the personalities of candidates—often military heroes—over issues. Readers were modeled as interested and disciplined voters rather than as selfless rational citizens.

Commercialism defined the newspaper as a product competing in the marketplace. A newspaper succeeded by selling itself to an audience and then selling its audience to advertisers. Commercialism emphasized the entrepreneur over the editor and modeled readers as consumers.

Commercialism and partisanism persisted in the media throughout the nineteenth century and well into the twentieth. Both were modified by the industrial revolution of the late nineteenth century, however. Newspapers became big businesses like other big businesses, and production and distribution were rationalized and consolidated. Part of this process was the creation of new tasks, to be filled by the reporter and allied news organizations like wire services and features syndicates. Reporting had its own ideology in these early days. Reporters were wordsmiths whose virtue consisted in the creation of lively salable copy; they were not supposed to be objective dispassionate observers. But this early "authorship" ideology was already at odds with the dry truncated style of the wire services, and by the turn of the century journalists were seeking to define themselves as expert public servants—professionals, in a word.

The twentieth century has seen the growth of the media as an institution. In this final model, readers as "the public" are dependent on the media for information. But there is far too much information in the complicated world; therefore the media must not passively transmit information, as in the model of rational liberty, nor may they pass along only what party or commercial interest dictates. Rather, they must actively select and digest precisely the information that will allow people to act intelligently. The media have great authority, and hence great responsibility, because they are modeled as encompassing all of society's legitimate competing constituencies. The assumption is that the media aren't aligned with any one or few of these constituencies, unlike in the days of the partisan press. This claim to neutrality is supported by the absence of overt competition among the media. The public sees media wrangle about as often as it sees physicians wrangle; otherwise, we could hardly regard either as professional. Reporting is expected to be fair and accurate, and editorial positions to be balanced and moderate.

I have outlined five models of the press in U.S. history. These are, in order, rational liberty, partisanism, commercialism, industry, and institution. Some models haven't been discussed. Most obviously, I've neglected nonmainstream media. But this outline is meant to be suggestive, not exhaustive.

In this discussion, I have implicitly argued that media ideologies are rooted in media practices. This is not to say that ideologies reflect practices; indeed, often their role is to obscure them. But any real historical model will call forth an ideology, a perfect image of itself, and this ideology will stand between practices and the awareness of them, and will allow people to discuss practices and debate their goodness. Ideologies sometimes change as practices change, but sometimes ideologies persist long after the practices they were created to explain have passed away. Ideologies sometimes produce changes in practices also because people feel the need to remake the world to fit the images in their heads. But this is not a general rule either, nor do I think there is any general rule to describe the interaction between ideology and practice, except that it happens.

Finally, let me emphasize that the models I've presented are in no way meant to be taken as stages in the development of the media. Although each has a moment of origin, none has ever really ceased to exist. The media in the United States have never yet been uniform, and while in some periods a particular model has been dominant, there have always been alternative models. This point is especially important on an ideological level, for each ideology is itself not monolithic. Each ideology takes on a different cast for its various constituencies; for instance, the public has a different notion of what professionalism means than either insiders or professionals have. Furthermore, the ideologies aren't mutually exclusive. Professionalism obviously borrows a lot from rational liberty, though it confines the talents of observation to an occupational class rather than assuming they are shared by all citizens. Again, the ideologies of partisanism and commercialism clearly coexisted in newspapers throughout the nineteenth century.

This outline of media models is meant to illustrate the point that media are defined historically. Media are networks of relationships that can be constructed, reconstructed, and deconstructed in various ways with varying implications for where power is located and how it is exercised. Violent activity is often involved in the process of definition. The violence described in the pages that follow should be understood not as a collection of colorful episodes in the career of a sometimes disreputable calling but as a bright indicator of how groups and individuals have struggled over the continual recreation of the press.

2

The Press and the American Revolution

As an ideological event, the American Revolution has been unparalleled in U.S. history. The independence movement forced British North Americans to formulate fundamental notions about society and government. To explain and justify their actions, and to elicit the public consent they felt they needed, the Revolutionaries fashioned ideologies out of whatever raw material was ready to hand—religious texts, English political traditions, Enlightenment ideas, common sense—making it up as they went along. Some of their formulations became institutionalized. Contemporary rhetoric is deeply imprinted with Revolutionary phrases and slogans.

But this is not to say that Revolutionary ideologies have been transmitted intact. On the contrary: the formulae crafted then became attractive abstractions to be redeployed later in different circumstances by different actors with different agendas. The formulae are so durable because they are so malleable, because they are not limited by original intent. Their "inner" or "real" meaning *as texts* changes depending upon who uses them for what. That's why there have been so many arguments over these formulae, so many debates, for instance, on who the "men" are in "all men are created equal."

The most durable formulae of the Revolutionary period center on the term *liberty*. In the popular memory, the Revolution was fought for liberty, and in the rhetoric of the Revolution, liberty was almost certainly the most frequently used abstract noun. But what the Revolutionaries meant when they used this term is far from clear.

Historians have long disagreed on the ideological import of the Revolution. In recent years, three distinct but overlapping positions have developed. Some historians say that ideology was crucial and articulate and that the characteristic ideology was "republican." Others agree that ideology was significant but maintain that the characteristic ideology was "liberal." A third group downplays the significance of ideology and points instead to social conflict as being the key to the Revolution.

The discovery of "republicanism" was one of the great events of the 1960s and 1970s for U.S. historians. One reason for this was that republicanism seemed to be a truly nonmodern way of thinking about politics, society, and the indidivual; the Revolution could then be understood as a criticism rather than an endorsement of, say, market society. Another reason is that the historians of republicanism also claimed strong effects for ideology, about which more later.

The so-called republican synthesis presents the Revolutionary movement as driven by an ideology that came to North America by way of England's eighteenth-century country opposition politics and seventeenth-century Whig tradition, but that may have had its origins in the categories established for political theory by Renaissance thinkers like Machiavelli. This Whig thought considered the story of history to be a battle between liberty and power. Power seeks to expand itself at the expense of liberty. It does this by corrupt means. Corruption strikes at the virtue of officeholders, who pursue private interests rather than the public good, and scheme to deprive citizens of their independence and drive them into slavery. Independence is attacked by undermining citizens' rights, especially the right to property, which is the chief bulwark of true political independence. Other targeted rights are those to freedom of speech, press, and conscience.

Whig thinkers believed that this vocabulary accurately described recent history. They believed that England's Stuart monarchs in the early seventeenth century and the Walpole administration in the early eighteenth century had behaved in just such a vicious manner, trying to subvert the rights of free Englishmen and reduce the population to slavery. Their schemes had been defeated by a virtuous and vigilant republican citizenry.

Revolutionaries believed that rights were again threatened by selfish, vicious officeholders. They again looked to the citizenry to prevent the slide into slavery. The citizenry could accomplish this only through a stoic dedication to the public good; Whig or republican thought placed a heavy emphasis on civic virtue.[1]

The republican synthesis has been sternly criticized by historians who assert that the characteristic ideology of the Revolution was not republicanism but classical liberalism. Liberalism's distinguishing characteristic is individualism. The individual is thought to be the fundamental fact of society, to have existed before the state, and to have created the state by contract—following Locke—for the sake of protecting the interests of individuals. The natural and proper attitude of the individual is self-interest, not civic virtue—though that may be a function of enlightened self-interest. Republicans would have predicted anarchy from citizens behaving in this manner, but liberals discern an underlying order in self-interest. As in Adam Smith's model of the free market—published providentially in 1776— political liberals find the invisible hand of natural law balancing interests, so that millions of atomic individuals rationally seeking private goals will inevitably promote the public good. The Revolutionaries were liberals, these historians argue, and they fought the Revolution to free up all the private energies and activities that they believed the Empire stifled.[2]

Liberal and republican histories have a lot in common. Both emphasize the Revolutionaries' preoccupation with rights and concern to limit the activities of the state. Moreover, both identify an ideology as the crucial motivating factor. The essential disagreement involves the limits of self-interest on the one hand and civic virtue on the other. Did Revolutionary thought model the citizen as a rational individual pursuing self-interest, or as a virtuous member of a body politic devoted to the public good?

Clearly, this controversy bears on the question of freedom of expression. If the characteristic thought of the Revolution was republican, then we should expect the Revolutionaries to endorse moral limits on expression consonant with the concept of civic virtue. If it was liberal, then we might expect Revolutionaries to condone untrammeled expression, even when it is motivated strictly by concern for personal, not public, welfare. Was the right to free expression thought of as conditional on virtuous conduct?

There are other historians who view the Revolution more as a social conflict than as an ideological movement. In this camp, theorizing was the domain of a leadership caste dominated by merchants and lawyers. These leaders were caught between two groups: the British on the right and the "people" on the left. The people—farmers, artisans, sailors, laborers—had other interests and values. Perhaps they held quite different attitudes about property rights. Perhaps they held values quite alien to the "typographical" culture of the Revolution's propagandists.[3]

The social history of the Revolution also poses questions about attitudes toward public expression. Was an abstract commitment to freedom of expression a class value, confined to an elite? Indeed, if the press served only those with the wherewithal to own or hire a press, then why expect everyone else to support its privileges?

This brief overview, then, has suggested two basic questions about the press and the Revolution. First, were attitudes toward the press republican or liberal? That is, did Revolutionaries think it proper to regulate conduct on the basis of "civic virtue," or did they condone conduct that deviated from their idea of the public good? Second, were there class divisions in attitudes toward the press? Did popular attitudes conform to the doctrines formulated by Revolutionary elites?

To avoid suspense, let me state at the outset that I've found attitudes to have been more republican than liberal. I've also found considerable evidence of class conflict.

A second debate calls for attention here. Students of U.S. legal history have argued for three decades about the Revolution and the law of the press. Leonard Levy has been the chief provocateur, maintaining that even libertarians in eighteenth-century England and North America never abandoned the notion that words can in themselves be seditious. To them, freedom meant freedom from prior restraint—Blackstone's position—not freedom from punishment. Eighteenth-century thought was thus quite different from twentieth-century libertarianism, which holds that utterance alone cannot be seditious, and that the state has no grounds to punish expression of any sort.[4]

Levy's critics have been numerous. They have not been especially successful in finding twentieth-century libertarian thought in eighteenth-century texts. Seditious libel was a crime in law and theory. But, contrary to what we might expect, the law seemed helpless to prevent actual seditious utterance. Patriot publicists criticized the British administration pretty freely, proclaimed their criticism to be perfectly justified, and found the authorities in almost every case unwilling or unable to punish them.[5]

Certainly, there were several different positions on the virtue and legality of public criticism of government.[6] Still, the existence of extensive public criticism of government does not demonstrate a consensus either among printers or the public that public criticism is in itself a good thing. It shows only that certain types of criticism had defenders. Sometimes these defenders employed quite global language, but one must suspect that this language is a rhetorical nicety, unless one can actually find them using the same arguments to support their enemies' right to free expression. Otherwise the ideology could hardly have been deeply felt or clearly formulated.

Indeed, there are reasons why eighteenth-century North Americans should not have developed clear formulations on liberty of the press. First, the subject of press regulation arose only sporadically, largely because enforcement was difficult, but also because colonial printers were habitually inoffensive—anxious not to alienate any constituency in the community, lest they endanger their precarious commercial viability.[7] Occasionally, a printer like John Peter Zenger would take a partisan stance, but usually the stance was transitory, and always it was with the backing of a faction sufficiently powerful to protect him, if not from prosecution, then certainly from onerous punishment.[8] Colonials found few occasions to argue about freedom of the press.

Second, a tradition of comfortable pronouncements was available. Eighteenth-century North Americans read *Cato's Letters*[9] and followed the trials of John Wilkes with sympathy. They had no trouble echoing the sentiments from these British sources that the press was a valuable instrument for exposing corruption and hence was a bulwark of public liberty. These sentiments, however, do not depend on a coherent theory of the acceptable limits of public expression and press regulation. Their meaning was luminous—self-evident, in Jefferson's phrase—and hence was never explored. Because everyone concurred in these sentiments, few bothered to theorize further.

Third, the "public" is not an intellectual body. Public attitudes have a logic to them, but it is demographic and historical and linguistic more than it is theoretical. Public attitudes are mobilized around events and situations and metaphors, not syllogisms. Consistency is not to be expected.

As far as the Revolutionary period is concerned, then, attitudes toward freedom of the press are not thoroughly defined. Freedom of the press was not one of the grand issues of the Revolution; those were taxation, property rights, and representation.[10] And freedom of the press was not a thing in itself but a feature of "liberty" broadly (and fuzzily) conceived. Hence, in Arthur Schlesinger Sr.'s enduring phrase, Revolutionaries justified limits thus: "They simply contended that liberty of speech belonged to those who spoke the speech of liberty."[11]

Although there was no consistent theory behind attitudes toward the *legal right* of freedom of the press, there was a coherent ideology about the *moral duties* of printers. This essentially occupational ideology would, on more than one occasion, provide the justification for suppressing unruly papers. Further, the ideology would itself act as a brake upon press behavior.

Press ideology centered on several key concepts. We may begin with the opposition between liberty and licentiousness. John Adams, writing as "Novanglus" in 1775, expressed this forcefully:

> License of the press is no proof of liberty. When a people is corrupted, the press may be made an engine to compleat their ruin: and it is now notorious, that the ministry, are daily employing it to encrease and establish corruption, and to pluck up virtue by the roots. Liberty can no more exist without virtue and independence, than the body can live and move without a soul. . . . [A]nd the freedom of the press, instead of promoting the cause of liberty, will but hasten its destruction as the best cordials, taken by patients, in some distempers, become the most rancid and corrosive poisons.[12]

Licentiousness is freedom without virtue, then, and hence destroys true freedom. True freedom must be rational, based on the healthy functioning of the will.[13]

To promote rational liberty, printers must be impartial. Newspapers were to be open channels of public communication, and "publick printers" were to be just that: printers, not editors. This impartiality was itself one meaning of the term *liberty of the press*. Thus William and Thomas Bradford argued in defending themselves against libel charges in 1766: "We are only the printers of a free and impartial paper, and we challenge . . . the world to convict us of partiality . . . , or even an inclination to restrain the freedom of the press in any instance."[14] Likewise, "SON OF LIBERTY" criticized the *New Hampshire Gazette* for not publishing a reply to an anonymous letter, arguing that it is "the office of every public Paper impartially to deliver the debates on both sides of any moral or political subject," and attributing the *Gazette*'s failure to do so to "the *undue influence of some in power*."[15] Here we also see the characteristic Whig suspicion of conspiracies in high places against public liberty.

The press was the great palladium of liberty because of its impartiality. Party spirit was always an enemy of liberty in Whig or republican thought, representing a compact or conspiracy to restrict comment and discussion. Press ideology of the Revolutionary period defined freedom as the free, rational, public-spirited activities of individuals. Party spirit was thought of as licentious and dangerous to the common good.[16] Patriots were quite sensitive about betrayal of the common good. Their most hostile reactions were against officials like Massachusetts Governor Francis Bernard and Thomas Hutchinson, whose private correspondence with English officials was felt to embarrass the colony's interests. These men were accused (in a phrase that echoed Cato) of "treason against the people."[17]

In addition to being impartial, a free newspaper must also be impersonal, avoiding personal abuse. Thus printer Benjamin Towne promised in the initial issue of the *Pennsylvania Evening Post* (24 January 1775) "to preserve inviolate the Liberties of the Press, and cautiously avoid all illiberal Reflections upon Individuals." "An Independant," responding to "Bostonian" in 1770, accused him of "very illiberal reflections, wicked misrepresentation, and unjustifiable *personal* abuse."[18] Indeed, this was one area where the printer was expected and required to exercise editorial control.

The common use of pseudonyms is an aspect of impersonality. Among other things, a pseudonym announced that a message was not to be confused with its author. It was to have an independent authority. Reason should reflect on measures, not men. Of course, on the practical side, pseudonyms also protected authors from retaliation, legal or otherwise, and printers often suffered violence for their reluctance to disclose the identity of the author of a controversial publication.

This ideology of rational liberty was shared by printers and the public throughout the colonial and Revolutionary periods, and pervaded all commentary on the press. It consisted well with the conditions and practices of the colonial era: sporadic partisan conflict could be accommodated while maintaining an artisanal independence from "faction." But the Revolution called forth new practices. The press was expected to be an active promoter of a movement, not a passive neutral carrier, and the newspaper conductor was called upon to affiliate himself or herself with the movement's leaders and institutions and to exercise continuous editorial control.[19] These new conditions and practices led to contradictions between activities and traditional values. And these contradictions helped produce an upsurge in antipress violence.

The Emergence of Antipress Violence

Traces of antipress violence can be found before the Revolution. In Philadelphia in 1725, for instance, James Logan's house was mobbed after he published remarks attributing economic hardships in Pennsylvania to moral failings on the part of the people.[20] John Peter Zenger in New York was threatened with caning in 1734.[21] In Charleston, South Carolina, printer Peter Timothy's criticism of the governor's statements on Indian relations prompted an anonymous threat to crop his ears in 1755.[22] But no coherent pattern of intimidation emerged until the Stamp Act crisis.[23]

Much has been written in the past twenty years about the violence of the Revolutionary period, especially the crowd actions.[24] This research has shown that, by and large, Revolutionary violence was not irrational but goal-directed, and moreover part of a long Anglo-American tradition of extralegal political activity as a recognized corrective to the imperfections of government and society. The crowd was a consensual institution, so to speak. But the crowd was also a feature of social conflict, a form of reaction against perceived changes in the social order. Scholars disagree on the extent to which the crowd of the Revolutionary era was independent of or opposed to the Whig leadership. But in any case it is clear that violence was not random or anarchic; rather, it expressed values that were supposed to be those of the "people," and thus had claims to be a natural and proper exercise of public opinion. Such action was itself a text.

The Revolutionary pattern of crowd action took form during protests against the Stamp Act in 1765.[25] The movement that took off at that point included diverse social elements—merchants and lawyers as well as artisans and farmers—and it seems that the Whiggish elite elements did not always see eye to eye with patriots from the lower ranks of society. But the movement felt an ideological need to present an image of unanimity. In terms of eighteenth-century political thought (whether republican or liberal), the key argument of the "patriots" was that British taxation was tyrannical, depriving colonials of their rights, and tending to reduce them to slavery. The people had a right to resist. But such resistance would not be legitimate if it came from only the most interested classes of the population. Then it would signify an attempt by a class to avoid a tax rather than an assertion of constitutional rights. Partial resistance couldn't be principled; thus the movement's opponents seized on every opportunity to portray it as the work of a conspiratorial faction.

The movement also needed to portray itself as constitutional. It called taxation unconstitutional, and claimed to resist it in a legally defensible manner. It was not, it insisted, riotous, above all not riotous. Thus "Mourner," in announcing a symbolic funeral procession for liberty to be held in Newport, Rhode Island, on 1 November 1765—the day the Stamp Act was to take effect—concluded: "His [Liberty's] Children inform the whole World, that they will take proper Notice of every Motion of Disorder and Riot, either before, at, or after the Funeral and prosecute the Offenders."[26] Ideologically, riotousness would seem a violation of those rights, especially the right to property, that the movement declared it protected. Practically, too, riotousness could and did provoke a harsh response from the administration, including the posting of British troops. Patriots were aware of the British posture in Ireland; they did not want to be treated like the Irish.

The movement depended on its depiction. It must seem both unanimous and orderly, not just to colonials but especially in the eyes of Britain's Parliament. Patriot leaders were aware, for instance, that colonial officials frequently enclosed copies of colonial newspapers with their official correspondence. Moreover, they seemed to think of the press as a universally public record that must be kept clean. Hence a pattern of press manipulation and intimidation appeared with the Stamp Act crisis, climaxing in 1769 with the Boston mobbing of John Mein.[27]

Ironically, the first printers targeted by the resistance movement were its supporters. As the date on which the Stamp Act was to take effect approached, printers prepared to halt publication rather than print on stamped paper. Some of these printers were threatened with reprisals unless they continued to publish, among them John Holt of the *New York Gazette and Post Boy* and Andrew Steuart of the *North Carolina Gazette*.[28] David Hall's *Pennsylvania Gazette* was threatened for not printing "spirited papers" against the Stamp Act.[29] But printers were almost universally opposed to the Stamp Act anyway, so why the threat of violence?

Two old habits inhibited printers from attacking the Stamp Act the way patriots wanted them to. One was the habit of avoiding trouble with the law. Violating the Stamp Act by publishing on unstamped paper could bring punishment; if a printer was disposed to violate it, evidence of coercion could be helpful in his defense. The second habit was impartiality. Printers were unaccustomed to promoting a political cause in print, much less taking political action. In some cases, they had to be made to see that this was not an issue with two sides. Impartiality had to be made irrelevant.

Patriots reinforced their point with symbolic violence against those who complied with the Stamp Act. Stamped newspapers from Halifax or Barbados were

burned or hung in effigy.[30] Printers and pamphleteers were also effigied.[31] The most
remarkable examples of symbolic violence during the Stamp Act crisis were directed
against Martin Howard of Newport, Rhode Island, the author of "A Letter from a
Gentleman in Halifax," probably the best-known pro–Stamp Act production in the
colonies. The Halifax Gentleman was hung or burned in effigy throughout the
colonies, but most thoroughly in his hometown of Newport in August 1765. The
newspaper description of the effigy is full of striking details:

> M--t-n H-w--d, with an *S* [for stamp] on his Forehead, and on his Breast, *That
> fawning, insidious, infamous Parricide, Martinus Scriblerus.* His neck . . . con-
> nected with a Rope, to which was appended a paper with this inscription, *We have
> an hereditary, indefeasible right to an Haltar; besides, we encouraged the Growth
> of hemp you know.*—In his right hand he held his Halifax letter, and on his right
> arm inscribed, *The only filial Pen.*[32]

A few things stand out from this description. First, in diction, the effigy's
inscriptions indicate a thorough awareness of the Halifax letter, the grand literate
offense that sparked the demonstration. Second, the inscriptions harp on the themes
of filial ingratitude and familial violence, especially parricide. Howard is depicted
as a traitor to his family, an even more unnatural crime than political treason.
Finally, the violator of the bonds of family is depicted suffering violent punishment. The halter around his neck indicated hanging, and afterward the expired effigy
was burned.

That this violence could be more than symbolic was proved the next day.
Howard was seen strolling through town with customs collector John Robinson
when an angry man accosted Robinson. Howard came to his defense, haranguing
the crowd of onlookers that gathered. Later that evening, a mob formed and attacked
Howard's house, moving on afterward to the houses of other members of the Junto,
as Newport's clique of leading merchants and lawyers called itself, as well as the
house of the stamp distributor. The mob roamed the city all night.

The next day the Whig leaders moved to disassociate themselves from the
riotous proceedings. They handed over as scapegoat John Weber, described as "a
foreigner, lately transported from England," who was committed to jail. It's not
clear whether Weber or the leadership was responsible for the mob's violent proceedings, but obviously the leadership felt the need to condemn lawless activity
publicly.[33]

Much of the violence of the late 1760s was personal as well as political.
Colonials had always been sensitive about personal reputation,[34] and the swelling
chorus of print controversy was bound to offend some finely tuned ears. In one
celebrated case, in 1769, John Robinson, the erstwhile companion of Martin
Howard, took offense at a letter written by James Otis and published in the Boston
papers. When the two met at the British Coffeehouse, the preferred tippling spot
for the friends of England, to discuss their differences, Robinson accused Otis of
"scurrilous treatment," pulled Otis by the nose, and began to cane him. Otis fought
back, Robinson's friends joined in, and finally Otis was beaten senseless. Though
Robinson had prevailed in the coffeehouse, he lost in the courtroom. Otis eventu-

ally won a judgment of £2000, which he forgave in return for a public confession and apology from Robinson.[35]

The Robinson-Otis fight shows the kind of personal animus that was involved in political debate. Participants were anxious to preserve their personal honor and dignity, and seemed to have trouble detaching themselves from their public personae. The importance of personal honor in politics is underscored by the habit of deference that remained a feature of politics throughout the Revolutionary period and well into the nineteenth century. Reputation was a supremely valuable political asset. The personal was also political.

Much of the personal animus directed against printed comments was deflected by the use of pseudonyms. Men who felt themselves unjustly criticized were unable to find the responsible parties; instead, they turned their anger against the printers. William Goddard, the printer of the *Pennsylvania Chronicle*, in 1767 was beaten in the British Coffeehouse in Philadelphia for refusing to give an author's name.[36] Similarly, in 1768, John Mein, printer of the *Boston Chronicle*, angered at comments critical of his paper that had appeared in the *Boston Gazette*, visited the printing office of that paper, demanded to know the author's name—he suspected it was James Otis—and, being denied this information, beat printer John Gill with a club.[37]

At issue in these cases was the ability of private citizens to offer public criticism anonymously. "Populus" styled Mein's attack a "Spaniard-like attempt . . . upon the Freedom of the Press," and urged an outpouring of popular support for Gill: "If we suffer the Printers to be abused . . . [by] those who endeavor to force them from their Duty, we shall soon find the Press shut against us."[38] Indeed, why would a printer prefer to suffer continual beatings rather than refuse to publish anonymous contributions? "Secrecy" was, like impartiality, an important feature of traditional press ideology. The attack on secrecy in these cases was another symptom of that ideology's malaise. Significantly, neither side was willing to concede the right of secrecy to its opponents' publications. Loyalist John Mein was a vigorous critic of the use of pseudonyms, but patriots too reviled pseudonymous contributions as smokescreens for "a few idle, jacobitish tory scoundrels."[39]

Attacks on printers escalated in the late 1760s because legal remedies became impractical. Customs officials, soldiers, and other targets of patriot abuse were unable to satisfy their sense of outrage in court because juries were reluctant to convict and grand juries and legislatures unwilling to bring charges against "libellous" publications. As tensions mounted, Britain's colonial representatives became more likely to seek immediate satisfaction. Ben Franklin's law of the cudgel was invoked more often. Meanwhile, the tide of patriot broadsides, pamphlets, and newspapers continued to rise. In some cases, frustration led to fighting over these publications. For example, in New York City in January 1770 scuffles broke out between citizens and soldiers when the latter tore down broadsides condemning employers who hired soldiers instead of inhabitants as laborers. The scuffling led to the fatal riot known as the Battle of Golden Hill.[40]

So far, then, we have identified several reasons for violence against the press in the late 1760s. The conflicts and contradictions between traditional press ideology and the novel behavior of printers sparked outrage. The perceived need for apparent unanimity on the part of patriots prompted them to force printers into line. The common colonial touchiness about personal reputation introduced a violent edge into public controversy. The frustrations felt by loyalists and officials at their inability to silence their patriot adversaries through legal means inclined them to resort to extralegal means. Both sides were well equipped with motives and justifications for violence. On the whole, patriots seemed more willing than Tories to commit violent acts against printers, though ironically they were also more apt to invoke freedom of the press as a value.

The Chain of Events

The Stamp Act initiated the cycle of resistance. It was repealed in 1766, and for a time colonial protests waned. But Britain's national debt did not go away, and Parliament again moved to raise revenue in the colonies in 1767 with new duties on colonial imports of paint, paper, glass, lead, tea, and other items—the so-called Townshend Duties. Once again colonials expressed outrage at being taxed by a body in which they were not represented. They resolved to avoid the taxes by not importing the taxed articles, and formed nonimportation agreements to enforce their resolve.

Nonimportation had to seem unanimous to succeed. Theoretically, any importation of a taxed article would signify surrender on the constitutional issue of Parliament's right to raise revenue in the colonies. Of course, total compliance was impossible. Patriots expected some merchants to continue importing and selling taxed articles; it would be unnatural for all colonial merchants to forsake profit for patriotism. But merchants also stood to gain from resistance in the long run, and most were willing to comply with nonimportation for a season or two.

The trick for patriots, then, was to make noncompliance seem deviant. They did this by announcing nonimportation agreements at public meetings of merchants modeled on town meetings and by encouraging, sometimes rudely, as many merchants as possible to sign the agreements. They reinforced the impression that the agreements were consensual by identifying a few dissenters and holding them up to public indignation. Should dissenters come to seem more numerous, and less despised, patriots knew the nonimportation agreements would quickly fall apart.

Intercity rivalries also worked to undermine nonimportation. The agreements were local affairs, and each city's merchants had every reason to jealously scrutinize what other cities were up to. If Philadelphia's merchants resumed imports, for instance, their competitors in other cities would hasten to follow suit, and the agreements would collapse like a row of dominoes. Further, each city's merchants were strongly motivated to suspect other cities of covert imports. Thus patriots were strongly motivated to minimize the perceived level of importation in their own cities.

Note that *seeming* was here more important than *being*. Unanimity was improbable. But the appearance of unanimity might convince Parliament that revenues from colonial taxes would be meager indeed and not worth their cost in ill will and disaffection. Patriots set out to *seem* unanimous. They developed rituals of unity.

It was during this period that tarring and feathering became a common punishment for customs informers.[41] This treatment was brutal but not fatal; mostly it was for display. The victim was made ridiculous, then carted around town for all to see. The victim was an object upon which the public could focus its anger; he was also a visible warning to those who might be tempted to do likewise. Tarring and feathering was more brutal than hanging in effigy, but was similar in that it was not really aimed at the victim but used the victim as a *medium* to express a community sensibility. There is no doubt that loyalists got the message. They truly feared the moral authority of the mob, which was the whole point of being a mob in the first place.

Thus the effort to maintain nonimportation was in large part a battle over public image. The press was a central battlefield. Patriots sought to eliminate public evidence of disunity and create in print the unanimity they failed to create in hearts and minds, knowing that, for some purposes at least, the image would be as good as the reality. The best-known casualty in this campaign was John Mein.

The Unhappy Career of John Mein

> And what is John Main printer from Scotland after, in raking up the ashes of the dead and publicly charging twice a week the body of merchants with impudence, lying, injustice, and folly, &c., &c.—did he design to give us the most striking specimens of insolence and ingratitude, or is it not rather to favor the designs of the [customs] Commissioners and the cabal, to whom he is a cat's paw, by exciting an abused people to acts of violence; if the latter, I hope they will still be disappointed.[42]

Why was John Mein so odious? Partly it was for his politics, partly for his personality, partly his religion, his ethnicity, his actions. Ultimately, he came to embody for patriots the sum of the misuses of the printer's craft, and was driven from the continent.

Mein was a native of Scotland. He'd been a bookseller in Edinburgh before emigrating to Boston in 1764, where he opened a bookstore and ran a circulating library. In 1766 he opened a printshop with another Scotsman, John Fleeming, who imported four journeymen from Scotland to assist them.[43] In 1768 Mein and Fleeming began publishing the *Boston Chronicle*. They were successful, claiming a circulation of fifteen hundred by the middle of the year, an impressive figure for those days.[44] The *Chronicle* featured longer essays and more self-consciously literary material than the other Boston papers; it ran eight pages per issue rather than four; and, at least initially, its material was impeccably Whiggish—Dickinson's *Farmer's Letters*, essays by Voltaire and Rousseau, anything about John Wilkes.

But Mein ran afoul of the nonimportation movement. In the issue dated 25 May–1 June 1769, he published an unsigned item that declared "from undoubted authority" that "21 vessels" had imported goods from England for "190 different

persons, many of whose names appear in the subscription for non-importation."
This evidence of dissimulation was controversial, but, with the merchants assuring the people that an explanation would be forthcoming, calm was maintained.[45]
The respite was brief.

In early August, Boston's merchants, at a meeting characterized by "Harmony and Union," according to the published report, condemned violations of the non-importation agreement and issued a list of violators. John Mein's name was on the list.[46] Mein responded in an editorial on 17 August. He admitted importing goods from England used in printing and bookselling, saying that his business, which employed seventeen hands, would otherwise have failed. Besides, he stated that other merchants not identified on the list as violators but considered staunch patriots were deeply engaged in importing taxed items. To back up his claim, he printed first the nonimportation agreement with its list of forbidden articles, and then cargo manifests, listing forbidden articles imported by patriots.[47] Among the merchants indicted in this and subsequent manifests, for instance, was John Hancock.

The Merchants' Committee scurried to publish a rebuttal, meanwhile urging the public not to jump to conclusions. In the interim, individual merchants published advertisements vindicating themselves. By the end of the month, the merchants had released a point-by-point refutation of Mein's manifests, claiming that some items were incorrectly listed, and that the whole affair was rooted in personal animosity and political duplicity.[48] The bickering over details continued for months as Mein published new manifests weekly and merchants responded by citing inaccuracies.

Meanwhile Mein challenged the legitimacy of the nonimportation movement. In a series of editorials—a rare practice in colonial newspapers—he accused the Merchants' Committee of using the nonimportation agreement as a tool for intimidating competitors while they themselves clandestinely cornered the market on forbidden goods. Nonimportation was nothing more than a conspiracy to enrich a few at the expense of the many.[49] The conspirators had singled Mein out for punishment because of "private enmity" and "the black passions of envy and malice."[50] Note how Mein used the language of Cato to attack the self-styled Whigs.

The merchants responded in the same terms. "A MAN" accused him of "consummate hypocrisy, prevarication, and falshood . . . peerless malevolence";[51] "Humanus" accused him of "ingratitude" and "calumny," and called him the "*trumpeter* of a rascally Cabal."[52] The Boston town meeting denounced his publications as "sallacious and scandalous . . . scurrilous and abusive."[53]

Mein was being arraigned in the court of traditional press ideology. He was not impartial; rather, he was the tool of a wicked faction. He was not impersonal; rather, he directly attacked the reputations of leading citizens. He was not public-spirited; rather, he promoted his own interests at the expense of his neighbors. He did not behave as a public printer should; rather, he used his paper as a vehicle for his own advancement. Ironically, the main texts in all this controversy, the cargo manifests, were unimpeachable examples of the kind of publication that traditional press ideology called for. They were raw lists offered up for the perusal of a candid public. Patriot rage thus seems, even to a sympathetic observer, to have been disingenuous; that's why they felt the need for so many adjectives.

Mein responded to this counterattack with more invective of his own. He denied that he had any partisan motivation, and accused the merchants of it. He commenced a "Catechism," in which he asked pointed questions about the merchants' motives and methods. Most dangerously, he began to respond to the merchants' personal invective with his own sarcastic attacks on character, often in thinly veiled allegories. This last tactic especially seemed to rile the patriots. They had not published lists of the members of the Merchants' Committee, presenting that body instead as the selfless and unanimous representative of the entire community. The violators of nonimportation *were* named; this was because they were pursuing private interest rather than the public good. When Mein "named" the committee, he rhetorically sought to reduce them from "the people" to an identifiable faction.

The controversy turned on the question of liberty. Patriots claimed to be defending colonial liberty from British tyranny, but they also accepted the curtailment of personal liberties for the sake of a greater liberty. A letter sent to the *Boston Evening Post* put it thus: "Every man has a right to pursue his own happiness by every means in his own power consistent with the common good."[54] In the same vein, "Determinatus" queried the readers of the *Boston Gazette*:

> Have you not a right, if *you please*, to set fire to your own houses, because they are *your own*, tho' in all probability it will destroy a whole neighborhood, perhaps a whole city? When did you learn that in a state or society you had a right to do as *you please*? And that it was an infringement of that right to *restrain* you? This is a refinement which, I dare say, the *true sons* of liberty despise. Be pleased to be informed that you are *bound* to conduct yourselves as the society with which you are joined, are *pleased* to have you conduct, or if *you please*, you may leave it.[55]

In regard to freedom of the press specifically, the Merchants' Committee granted that everyone has a right to publish, but one "who adopts the weapons of fraud and imposition, to destroy a country and blast the reputation of its inhabitants, does at once forfeit that right and abuse that freedom."[56] Freedom of the press, like all freedom, was bounded by virtuous conduct and the public good.

Mein disagreed, but not entirely. He too believed printers should be virtuous and loyal, not partisan but devoted to the exercise of public reason.[57] He declared his exposure of the Merchants' Committee to be "owing to the Glorious LIBERTY OF THE PRESS."[58] He also claimed to be defending property rights in attacking a movement that curtailed the freedom to buy and sell goods. As "Martyr," in a letter to the *Chronicle*, sardonically asked, "Shall we tamely behold every natural, civil, religious, and national right thus horribly invaded, and usurped by one subject over another, and still pretend to talk of LIBERTY, PROPERTY, and RIGHTS without a blush?"[59] "Bostonian" advised the merchants "at least in policy to show some regard for the LIBERTY of the PRESS."[60] Indeed, Mein wrote, the merchants rivaled "the compleatest Proficients, from the schools of Loyola" in their ability to twist logic.[61] He concluded that it was the patriot press that needed restraint. As "HARPAX" remarked, newspapers must be "restrained from establishing the interest of a few mercenary individuals at the expence not only of the public good, but of public tranquillity."[62]

Mein and his critics talked a lot about freedom of the press, and they used the same vocabulary. Both tried to present their conduct as virtuous according to traditional press ideology, and both argued that the other had violated the accepted limits of freedom. Both accepted the notion that freedom was allowed only within limits established by consensual interests. One suspects that neither side had "freedom of the press" high on its agenda, but that both were glad to invoke it as an ideal whenever opportune.

Patriots had good reason to lay aside their avowed attachment to freedom of the press in this instance. Mein's publications were taking effect. The Merchants' Committee had said all along that Mein's intention was to "prejudice the minds of the Merchants in other Colonies, against the Merchants and Traders here."[63] As summer turned to fall, Boston's papers reprinted condemnations of Mein from other colonies, especially New York.[64] Mein was attracting a lot of the wrong kind of attention too. Merchants in Philadelphia and New York were divided on nonimportation, and Mein's publications (the manifests were later issued in pamphlet form) no doubt hastened the abandonment of nonimportation in those cities in early 1770.[65]

Perhaps someone else would have gotten away with tweaking the collective nose of Boston's patriot elite. But Mein seemed especially hateful. Why?

Part of the hatred was nativistic. Mein's foreign birth was repeatedly mentioned. The Merchants' Committee's August rebuttal castigated him as a "stranger, who came among us for his own private emolument," who repaid the kindness of the public with betrayal, and used "falshood and malicious insinuations, against the most respectable characters."[66] "Alfred" was incredulous: "Shall a stranger dare to be a tool of this Cabal . . . ! What a degree of intollerable vanity and insolence is here!"[67] Indeed, Mein's Scottishness was held against him. The Scots ranked low in popular esteem throughout the nonimportation crisis because Scots merchants had advanced easy credit to colonial shopkeepers so that they could circumvent the merchants' boycott. Mein was also associated with the despised Scots religious sect, the Sandemanians.[68]

Next to his foreign birth, the characteristic most often mentioned about Mein was his insolence. Merchant Francis Green's comments are typical: "What an unparallel'd Stock of Assurance and Self-Confidence must this contemptible Fellow be possess'd of, to imagine himself entitled to call, Time after Time, upon one and another of his Superiors for answers to the most pert and saucy Questions that ever issued from the conceited, empty Noodle of a most profound Blockhead!"[69] Mein's inquiries were improper invasions of the social hierarchy. In a society characterized by deference—though this was not unchallenged among patriots, to be sure—a mere craftsman, the tool of a faction, no less, was surely not entitled to treat with Boston's merchants on a footing of equality. Indeed, Boston's other printers, perhaps mindful of their proper station, did not engage in editorial fulminations. They printed "contributions" but never personally assumed a belligerent stance. The very fact that he wrote editorials made Mein an insolent printer.

His fellow printers had always been ambivalent about Mein. The Fleets, who printed the *Evening Post*, had contracted to distribute Mein's *Chronicle* as well,[70] but this arrangement was strictly business, and otherwise Mein was an outcast. His shop full of Scots immigrants must have seemed threatening to Boston's other print workers. And he was suspected of unethical business practices. Isaiah Thomas reports a rumor that Mein and Fleeming printed books with a fake London imprint, hoping to dupe the public into paying a higher price.[71] He was also accused of not paying his debts,[72] and his loose finances were to cause him serious trouble later.

Mein's unpopularity, coupled with his dangerous publications, made him a prime candidate for violent treatment. And there was a rising tide of violent patriot activity at that time. The papers were full of accounts of tarring and feathering,[73] and Boston was still humming from the "riot" surrounding the customs proceedings against John Hancock's sloop *Liberty*.[74] Loyalist Peter Oliver later recalled that "the civil Power of the Country was not sufficient to protect any one who was obnoxious to ye. Leaders of the Faction."[75] This must have been an overstatement, but it reflects some of the tension that was felt by those who opposed the patriots.

The city was braced for a riot. Troops were stationed in town, put there, patriots believed, because of exaggerated reports of disorder in Boston in the letters of royal officials like Francis Bernard and Thomas Hutchinson, both veterans of the Stamp Act riots. Indeed, patriots suspected that Mein's purpose was to provoke a riot that would justify harsher measures. They urged the people to stay calm.[76]

By the end of October it was clear that calm was not to be expected. In mid-October, in two cases of mistaken identity, men resembling Mein were clubbed in alleyways.[77] Mein began carrying pistols with him when he left his shop.

On 28 October things came to a head. While a crowd was gathering to tar and feather an informer, a group of men encountered Mein and Fleeming on King Street. This group, about twenty in number, many of them, like William Molineux, victims of Mein's publications, and many respectable gentlemen, proceeded to "catechize" Mein. Finally, one of the gentlemen struck a blow with his cane; Mein drew his pistols and retreated to a guardhouse with a larger crowd—maybe two hundred—chasing him, screaming, "Kill him!" A shot was fired, probably by Mein, Mein was hit by a spade—the sequence isn't clear here—and Mein took refuge with the British troops.

The crowd, grown to its full size of more than a thousand, then turned to the evening's main event, the tarring and feathering of customs informer George Greyer. While carting Greyer past Mein and Fleeming's office, though, shots were fired from within. The mob burst in, discovering two guns but no people.[78] Mein was charged with assault for firing his pistol during the riot, but the indictment was quashed. Meanwhile he wisely kept himself from public view.[79]

The most raucous occasion of the year in Boston in those days was Pope's Day, the celebration of the foiling of the gunpowder plot, held on the first Saturday of November, partly in mockery of the Catholic All Saints' Day. Traditionally, the pageantry centered around an effigy of the pope. In 1769 Mein's effigy was substituted for the pope's.[80] This was truly an honor.

Soon Mein fled North America.[81] He took with him a debt of £2000. Ironically, John Hancock bought the notes for his debt and had Mein confined to debtor's prison in London, where he stayed until 1774. Later, Mein resumed his career as a publicist, writing under the pseudonym "Sagittarius" in the London *Public Led-*

ger. His letters were among the most vicious and effective arguments in support of the administration's punishment of Boston after the Tea Party of 1773.[82]

Mein's flight was the climax but not the end of patriot hostility toward "enemy" publications. Even after the flight, the *Chronicle* was not safe from reprisals,[83] though it did continue to publish under Fleeming's direction. Seemingly intimidated, it kept its silence about controversial issues for a time, then, after a month, it resumed publishing manifests. Patriots responded with threats of violence.[84] Sentiment was summed up by "Philadelphos": "[T]he time will come . . . when those men who for their own *private advantage* have disturbed the repose of their Sovereign, and fomented discord between the subjects in Britain and America, shall be made PUBLIC EXAMPLES, in terror to others."[85] Mein's punishment was meant to have a chilling effect.

Even before the mobbing the patriots had taken steps to end Mein's career as a printer. A boycott had been instituted: patriots tracked down subscribers and urged them not to pay, and circulation outside Boston was especially targeted.[86] Mein's other printing revenue, the publication of pamphlets and especially of religious tracts and sermons, was cut to practically nothing.[87] The *Chronicle* was no longer economically viable, and finally succumbed in June 1770. An unmistakable attitude of timidity marked its last months, no doubt in response to the anger that prevailed in Boston after the Massacre of March 1770.

Mein's mobbing became a minor *cause célèbre* among defenders of the British administration. They pointed to it as evidence of patriot duplicity, of the patriots' lack of respect for the liberties they claimed to honor. Patriots resorted to traditional press ideology and convenient elision of memory to defend themselves. Typical of this sort of rationalization is the account of John Adams, writing as "Novanglus" in 1775:

> There never was before, in any part of the world, a whole town insulted to their faces, as Boston was, by the Boston Chronicle. Yet the printer was not molested for printing, it was his mad attack upon other printers with his clubs, and upon other gentlemen with his pistols, that was the cause of his flight, or rather the pretence. The truth was, he became too polite to attend to his business, his shop was neglected, procreations were coming for more than 2000 sterling, which he had no inclination to pay.[88]

This tissue of half-truths cannot conceal the simple facts: Mein's printing was considered intolerable; he was targeted for violence by patriot leaders, or at least some of them; he was driven from the continent; and a campaign of intimidation and economic warfare forced his paper out of circulation. Patriots throughout voiced support for something called "liberty of the press," but it was a liberty not to be used against "the public good." And who may define what that is?

To Independence

Britain and the colonies had a brief rapprochement in the early 1770s. Parliament repealed most of the Townshend duties, leaving a token tax on tea. The sense of urgency behind patriot activity in the later 1760s disappeared for a while. Some of the organizational machinery of the movement kept functioning, though: committees of correspondence continued to maintain the links that had been forged between like-minded people in the various colonies. But little by way of dramatic conflict occurred.

This relative quiescence was broken with the Tea Act of 1773. Patriots again organized to prevent importations. When Bostonians dumped an unwanted cargo of tea into Boston Harbor—an act also performed elsewhere—Parliament retaliated in 1774 with harsh measures. Colonials responded locally by forming committees of safety or of observation—de facto local governments in many cases—and later statewide committees to replace royally influenced provincial governments. They also called the Continental Congress, which legitimized the committees and drafted articles of association, calling among other things for nonintercourse with Britain. In 1775 King George III declared the colonies to be in rebellion, and urged loyal subjects to come to his aid. His loyal subjects, though, had already come under the scrutiny of the committees.

To loyalists and royal officials, it seemed as though a revolution had already occurred. Already "constitutional" government and social institutions had been made irrelevant. Thomas Gage, then acting governor of Massachusetts, complained in 1774 to the Earl of Dartmouth of "the usurpation and tyranny established here by edicts of town meetings, enforced by mobs, by assuming the sole use and power of the press, and influencing the pulpits; by nominating and intimidating of juries, and, in some instances, threatening the judges."[89] The patriots had taken over the instruments of local government and the mechanisms of popular opinion as well, including the press. A writer in Pennsylvania asked, "Where was the Printer who had the virtue or courage to publish one sober remonstrance against their outrageous career?"[90] To loyalists, it seemed that patriot intimidation had been quite effective.

Britain's response was to redouble its efforts to win the hearts and minds of colonials. Impressed by what it saw as the influence of the patriot press, it offered liberal support to loyalist pamphleteers. Indeed, in the years 1774–1776, more original loyalist material was published than at any other time, including the great pamphlets of Daniel Leonard ("Massachusettensis"), Thomas Bradbury Chandler, Samuel Seabury, Charles Inglis, and Joseph Galloway.[91]

While loyalists sought to discredit patriots, patriots sought to project unity of sentiment. They knew quite well that they could not win all of the "hearts and minds" in this battle, but they believed that they could present to the world a picture of unanimous public sentiment on the legitimacy of patriot institutions like the Continental Congress and on the illegality of British measures. They believed that exiling Tory sentiment from the arena of public discourse was essential to establishing the "constitutionality" of the new Revolutionary bodies. Hence in fact if not always in law loyalist public utterance was declared treasonous.

The committees of safety and observation were crucial organs in this phase of the movement. After 1775 Congress and the other Revolutionary governing bodies delegated to the committees the duty of detecting and punishing loyalists.[92] Long before this, however, local committees had begun to single out loyalist printers and pamphleteers for condemnation and symbolic punishment.[93]

Loyalists were furious. Adopting classic Whig language, they attacked the committees as tyrannical. As Major Benjamin Floyd challenged the Smithton Committee of Observation, "Do you really mean to immure the Colonies in Popish darkness, by suppressing the vehicles of light, truth, and liberty? Are none to speak, write, or print, but by your permission? . . . A free press had been the honour and glory of Englishmen. . . . But we are become the degenerate plants of a new and strange vine."[94] Loyalists thus accused patriots of establishing a most un-English inquisition.

Committees and town meetings showed little respect for loyalists' freedom of expression, but by and large their actions were symbolic and not directly violent. They issued condemnations of pamphlets and sometimes their printers,[95] and in many cases tarred and feathered pamphlets or burned them at the stake.[96]

This was all part of a larger pattern of Tory harassment. Even before committees assumed the force of law, popular action was common.[97] Examples are numerous. In one of the more famous cases, Anglican minister Samuel Peters was mobbed several times in Connecticut in September 1774 because he was suspected of writing "treasonous" letters to church officials in England that would ultimately be printed up to discredit the patriots.[98] Anglican divines were often targets of patriot mobs—not surprisingly, because many of them were effective Tory propagandists.[99]

Patriots considered these activities to be orderly and constitutional. For instance, in a report published in a patriot newspaper of a crowd action against two men overheard in a tavern making loyalist remarks, we find this formulaic disclaimer: "Not the least violence was offered, but the whole was conducted with the utmost regularity."[100] Claude Van Tyne, writing from a more critical point of view, has remarked that "everything was done, though roughly, as if with legal sanction."[101] Even while loyalists painted lurid pictures of mob rule, then, patriots sought to deport and depict themselves as orderly.

Tory pamphleteers and outspoken loyalists were unambiguous targets, and patriots wanted simply to silence them. But printers were a more delicate problem. Here again traditional press ideology was a factor. Printers were accustomed, indeed required, to print "contributions" in their papers with impartiality, but sometimes these were offensive to patriots. So patriots pressured printers to turn down certain kinds of contributions. One clear case of this occurred in 1775 when Lieutenant Governor Cadwallader Colden of New York sent printer Hugh Gaine an account of the skirmishes at Lexington and Concord. Gaine first accepted it, then declined to publish it, though Colden had agreed to let it be published under his name as an "official" account, the sort of thing that colonial printers usually savored. Colden thought he knew why Gaine changed his mind: "Hancock and Adams came to Town on Saturday, and were probably consulted by some of the Party here, and with them determined still to suppress every account but their own."[102] Such editorial advice seems to have been more the rule than the exception.[103]

Pamphlets were a problem too. Colonial printers accepted job printing on commercial, not ideological, grounds. They would thus be prone to print any pamphlet that might bring in money without resulting in a lawsuit. Patriots wanted to discourage this habit too. The most remarkable example here is that of Samuel Loudon.

Samuel Loudon was a patriot printer, and was to remain, along with John Holt, an important press conductor for the New York Provincial Congress and Committee of Safety. But in 1776 he undertook to print a pamphlet refuting Thomas Paine's argument for independence in *Common Sense*. New York City's Mechanics' Committee, the guiding body for that city's radicals, resolved to prevent this publication. After a visit from the leader of the committee, during which Loudon refused to name the author of the pamphlet or to stop publication, a mob visited his office, destroying what had been printed up.[104] Loudon, believing himself not to be out of favor and considering the question of independence to be still an open one, appealed to the provincial government, including in his argument an impassioned plea for liberty of the press, which, he said, "is now insulted and infringed, by some zealous advocates for liberty. A few more nocturnal assaults upon printers may totally destroy it."[105] Loudon's petition was dismissed.[106]

This affair indicates some division—perhaps along class lines—between the Mechanics' Committee and the more conservative Committee of Safety and Provincial Congress. An observer sympathetic to the Mechanics' Committee noted that the attack had "given great Umbrage to several of our pretended Friends, but they are forc'd to pocket the Affront."[107] The Whig leaders seemed more concerned than the Mechanics' Committee with maintaining the appearance of order and due process. They also seemed to be more concerned with appearing to protect freedom of the press. But this concern may have been strictly tactical; it may not indicate a genuine attachment to the ideal of free expression. Otherwise, we might have expected the assembly to indemnify Loudon.

Of course the British were also engaged in a campaign for press control. We've already noted Britain's support for loyalist pamphleteering. As independence approached, Tory propagandists retreated to the key port cities of Boston, New York, and Philadelphia, where they were protected by British forces. Meanwhile, British troops and leaders undertook to intimidate patriot printers. In mentality and behavior, British troops were similar to the crowds or mobs that patriots deployed. On occasions like the Boston Massacre and the Battle of Golden Hill, the conflict between British troops and patriot crowds was a contest of equals, rather like the "battles" between the North-end and South-end mobs in Boston in the 1760s.

British troops threatened printers on more than one occasion.[108] In one notorious military action, Lord Dunmore sent troops to confiscate the press of John Hunter Holt, printer of the Norfolk *Virginia Gazette*, no doubt in retaliation for some very sharp criticism of Dunmore but also in order to use the equipment to put out his own stuff.[109] This action was cited by patriot radical leader Isaac Sears as provocation and justification for the most famous antipress action of the period, the raid on James Rivington's *New-York Gazetteer*, discussed below.

This was a battle for hearts and minds, as John Adams pointed out later. And such a battle had to be fought with words. But the strategy of both sides involved fighting the other's words with fists and guns, not just with words. If the realm of public discourse could be swept clean of opposition, the hearts and minds might be persuaded by whatever was left. Even if not, it would seem to observers that "public opinion" was in line, since the press was the main mechanism for representing public opinion. Loyalists, not surprisingly, complained that patriots had "engrossed the press"[110] and destroyed "the liberty and secrecy of the press."[111]

The Rise and Fall of James Rivington

The printer most widely identified with the loyalist cause was James Rivington of New York. Rivington was a London stationer who came to the colonies after gambling debts and lawsuits for copyright infringement and fraud had forced him into bankruptcy. In the 1760s he opened bookstores in New York, Boston, and Philadelphia. Marriage to a well-to-do widow helped clear his finances, and by 1773 his New York business was prosperous enough to enable him to begin issuing a newspaper.[112] The *Gazetteer* quickly became one of the chief newspapers of the colonies, boasting a circulation of thirty-six hundred in 1774.[113] In the meantime, Rivington had earned the jealousy of his fellows in the print trades through his haughtiness, his (suspected) unfair trade practices, and his loose observation of nonimportation.[114]

Rivington's paper appeared just before the upturn in Revolutionary politics triggered by the Tea Act. Despite Rivington's repeated claims of impartiality, the *Gazetteer* quickly became a focus of controversy.[115] Meanwhile, New York was acquiring a reputation as a stronghold of pro-British sentiment, an impression that was supported by its complex, even bizarre political system of competing family coalitions.[116] Rivington may not have intended the *Gazetteer* to be the organ of New York loyalism, but that's what it became.

Rivington's profession of impartiality had the force and resonance of traditional press ideology. Was he sincere? Or was he using impartiality as a cloak? First consider his own position. All of the other New York papers, and almost all of the papers in the colonies, were committed to the patriot cause. An item in the *Gazetteer* put it thus: "The pulpit and press are become subservient to the infernal schemes of these diabolic assemblies, and are used as the great engines to destroy the peace and tranquility of the devoted nation."[117] Anyone who dares contradict the patriots must live in fear:

> Dare the poor man impartial be,
> He's doom'd to want and infamy. . . .
> Precarious lives in constant dread,
> Tar, feathers, murder haunt his bed; . . .
> Alas, vain men, how blind, how weak;
> Is this the liberty we seek![118]

"Anti-Licentiousness" stated that the animus against Rivington was simply rage that "some of your correspondents presume to think for themselves."[119] The upshot was that Rivington presented his newspaper as not merely fair but as the only properly run paper in the region. His colleagues, or competitors, were therefore licentious violators of the values of rational liberty.

Indeed, the *Gazetteer* did present contributions from both sides of the great issues of the day.[120] But Rivington's claim to stand above the fray was disingenuous. He continually slid toward the British side, and gradually evinced more and more hostility for the patriots. Patriots too became more irate.

This spiral of outrage began with the Tea Act. Rivington printed contributions arguing in favor of submission to the Tea Act, though these were generally carefully balanced by patriot rebuttals.[121] But on all matters involving nonimportation and resistance to taxation, patriots were most anxious to appear unanimous, and Rivington must have known that he was making that impossible. But even more offensive than his publications was his actual participation in the tea trade. Charles Lee was astounded at Rivington's gall in publishing ads for tea; everybody, he was sure, "is astonish'd that the miscreant Rivington is suffer'd to heep insult upon insult on the Congress with impunity."[122] He would have been even more astonish'd to learn that Rivington had himself imported tea, and had (incredibly) sent four chests to his quondam business associate Henry Knox in Boston to sell. Knox refused, turning the tea over to Boston's Merchants' Association.[123]

Rivington's ties to the friends of Britain grew closer through 1774 and 1775. By February 1775 he was reported to be hosting a "club of Tories," including Dr. Myles Cooper, an Anglican minister and president of King's (later Columbia) College, as well as a number of British officers.[124] On a more official level, in 1775 his paper was brought under the supervision of James DeLauncey, acting under the aegis of the Royal City Council. That spring, he was brought to the attention of Secretary Pownall and was appointed His Majesty's Printer for New York with an annual stipend of £100.[125] Rivington kept his appointment a secret. Still, patriots were convinced that he'd been bought out. They continually referred to his "prostituted press," called him a "ministerial hireling," and criticized him for his "love of sordid pelf."[126]

Perhaps more offensive to patriots than Rivington's *Gazetteer* were his other printing activities. From his press came the most noteworthy loyalist pamphlets of the long ideological battle of 1774–1776, including the writings of John Vardill as "Poplicola," of Charles Inglis as "A Farmer," and of Samuel Seabury as "A Westchester Farmer." Seabury's pamphlets criticizing the Continental Congress especially caused an uproar. Local committees began a campaign against Rivington's press, and copies of the pamphlets were tarred and feathered or burned at meetings throughout the colonies because of their "pernicious and malignant tendency . . . calculated to deceive and mislead the unwary, the ignorant, and the credulous" and "to destroy that union so necessary for the preservation of our *American* constitutional liberty."[127] Most prevalent in these committee resolutions were references to patriot unity. They were full of phrases like "faction and discord" and "disunite and divide."[128]

Were patriots right to fear these pamphlets? Probably they had some effect in supporting loyalism in areas of New York like Seabury's Westchester County.[129] But more important was the impression the pamphlets gave that there was a legitimate difference of opinion in the colonies on questions like the legality of the Continental Congress. This explains in part why patriots were concerned not just to condemn them and prevent their circulation but also to "discover" their authors to the public.[130] Patriots were keen to show that "A. W. Farmer" was really not a farmer at all but an Anglican minister. Better yet had he been a customs officer. But in any event it had to be shown that legitimate colonial opinion was undivided on the key issues. Such was the common sense of the matter: "It is the opinion of almost everyone in this place that the Acts of Parliament would have been repealed, had it not been for the encouragement given Administration by this place [New York], that the colonies would break their union."[131]

The campaign against Rivington began in late 1774 and gained momentum throughout spring 1775. We have already noted the condemnations by local committees. These usually included a call to boycott Rivington's paper, bookshop, and printing establishment. A county meeting in New Jersey, for instance, resolved "that, by all lawful means in their power, they will discourage the circulation of his Papers in this County."[132] The boycott spread quickly through the middle colonies and seemed to embarrass Rivington's finances seriously.[133]

This economic attack was complemented by the usual tactics of public display and intimidation. Copies of the *Gazetteer* were tarred and feathered and burned as far away as Boston. Rivington himself was threatened with tar and feathers. Patriots spread joyful rumors that he'd been attacked by a mob. Rivington himself reported his hanging in effigy "by some of the lower class of inhabitants at New Brunswick."[134]

Rivington consistently claimed that his opponents were of the lower class. Indeed, one special enemy of his was the leader of the New York "mob," Isaac Sears. Sears was an upwardly mobile man, a ship captain who had a successful career in privateering. Such men were especially admired by the sailors who worked under them. Sears's popularity along the waterfront made him an effective radical leader in New York City throughout the 1760s and 1770s.[135] Rivington and Sears were men of opposite background, temperament, and political allegiance. They came into conflict early, and their quarrel lasted beyond the War for Independence itself. In August 1774, in letters signed "A Merchant" in the *Gazetteer*, Sears was parodied as "Sir Francis Wronghead." Sears responded by citing such letters as examples of licentiousness.[136] Later, in April 1775, Sears was parodied again as "Simpleton Sapskull."[137] For his part, Sears freely accused Rivington of being responsible for New York's apparent Toryism, "for his press hath been . . . the very life and Soul of it."[138]

But Rivington's quarrel was not confined to Sears and the mob. He had also enraged the more moderate elements of New York's patriot leadership by publishing reports of conflict among patriot factions over the selection of delegates to the Continental Congress. New York's Committee of Observation sent John Jay and Philip Livingston to get Rivington to name his sources. He said his news came from "common report." This did not satisfy the Committee, which issued a harsh condemnation of such irresponsible journalism.[139] Rivington responded by printing a letter signed "Anti-Tyrannicus" that accused the Committee of actions "subversive of the very idea of freedom" in holding its sessions in secret and stifling a free and impartial press.[140] New York's Committee's scrutiny was not an isolated event: committees and assemblies throughout the colonies took notice of the *Gazetteer*.[141]

In April 1775 the tone of the controversy changed with the battles between colonial militiamen and British troops at Lexington and Concord. In New York City, news of the fighting arrived on 23 April. The populace was baffled and furious, especially so because for the past few days rumors of reconciliation with Britain had been circulating. Rioting erupted, and for a week the mob ruled the city. Sears and a party of men seized the city's armory, armed themselves, shut up the customs house, and roamed the streets. Rivington was so terrified that he published a "confession" and pledged never again to print Tory tracts. His conversion was too little too late.[142]

On 10 May a mob formed and set off in search of the "odious six," as they called the cadre of loyalist propagandists that centered around Rivington. They attacked the home of Myles Cooper, but found that he had fled. They then turned to Rivington's home and office, forcing him to flee as well.[143] He took refuge on board the British man-of-war *Kingfisher*, then moored in the East River.[144]

From this vantage point, Rivington could clearly see that the British were unable to protect his interests. He appealed instead to the patriot leadership. He printed a notice "To the Public," in which he asserted that "nothing I have done, has proceeded from any Sentiments in the least unfriendly to the Liberties of this Continent, but altogether from the Ideas I entertained of the Liberty of the Press, and of my Duty as a Printer." He pledged in future to "conduct my Press upon such Principles as shall not give Offence to the Inhabitants of the Colonies."[145] He then petitioned the New York Committee of Observation, which referred his petition to the Continental Congress. In the petition he insisted he'd been trying to operate an impartial press according to traditional press ideology. He acknowledged his offensiveness, and promised to avoid future transgressions. He called attention to his sixteen employees, hands that would be idled if his press was not protected from the mob.[146] The Continental Congress referred him to the New York Provincial Congress, which granted his petition.[147] Richard Henry Lee remarked, "I am sorry, for the honour of human nature, that this man should have so prostituted himself in support of a cause the most detestable that ever disgraced mankind. But he repents, and should be forgiven."[148]

The mob had shut down Rivington's press, but the leadership seemed to concur, if not on the means employed, at least on the underlying principles. Patriot leaders did not accept Rivington's claims of impartiality, and seemed unmoved by his appeals to liberty of the press. They did seem a little embarrassed by the petition itself, no particular body wanting to identify itself as the mob's sponsor or patron. The incongruity of the final decision—that he have liberty to publish only in the cause of liberty, and only by the special license of the government—was not commented upon.[149]

Thus Rivington became a patriot printer. But his conversion lasted only until royal government was reestablished in New York City with the arrival of Governor Tryon. Soon the *Gazetteer* was again publishing bold loyalist contributions.[150]

In November Isaac Sears had his revenge on Rivington. A short while earlier Sears, disappointed with the lack of urgency in New York's patriot leadership, had moved to Connecticut and organized a militia outfit. On Thursday the twenty-third he arrived in New York City at the head of a troop of horsemen and went immediately to the *Gazetteer* office, where he confiscated all the printing material he could carry and destroyed the rest. A crowd of more than a thousand spectators gathered and gave three cheers as Sears and his men rode off.[151]

The motivations of Sears and his raiders were manifold. Partly they were personal, the fruit of a long-running feud. Partly they were ideological. Governor Tryon attributed the raid to "the freedom of Mr. Rivington's publications, & especially his last paper."[152] But even read closely, Rivington's final issues before the raid seem inoffensive compared with those of just a month earlier. In fact, he'd seemed to have toned down his editorial presence just prior to the raid.

The main motive for the raid was military rather than personal or ideological. Sears did not condemn Rivington's journalism as irresponsible or suspect; instead, he identified Rivington's press as a weapon wielded by a foe. He captured this weapon and disarmed the foe. Further, he did so in self-proclaimed retaliation for a similar military action: Lord Dunmore's confiscation of John Hunter Holt's press.[153] To Sears and his men, the printed word was not privileged; it did not exist in a realm removed from other forms of action.

Historians have noted that this action produced a storm of outrage among New York's moderate patriots.[154] Pomerantz has implied that this reaction was in essence a defense of the abstract ideal of liberty of the press.[155] Was it so?

Consider the initial reaction of key leaders. Alexander Hamilton, for instance, writing to John Jay, conceded "how dangerous and pernicious Rivington's press has been, and how detestable the character of the man is in every respect," but still could not "help disapproving and condemning" the raid. His grounds for condemnation were not exactly libertarian, however. He expressed fear that the "state of passions" of the "multitude, who have not a sufficient stock of reason and knowledge to guide them," might lead to "anarchy." After all, Sears's raiding party lacked "any proper authority." In fact, the raid seemed an instance of New York's "potent neighbors" (i.e., Connecticut) "making inroads at pleasure." Hamilton feared that this would excite "ancient animosities" between New York and New England, breed "division and quarreling," and make New Yorkers seem "disaffected to the American cause." All in all he was pleased that "Rivington will be intimidated," but wished that Tories could have been overawed in some more regular way, like the stationing of troops among them.[156]

John Jay's reaction to the raid was similar. He disapproved, but didn't mourn Rivington's press. His chief regret was that "if it was to be done, I wish our own people, and not strangers, had taken the liberty of doing it." He noted cautiously that New York's honor "cannot be maintained without some little spirit being mingled with its prudence."[157]

Jay's and Hamilton's private letters did not dwell on freedom of the press, then. Official reaction was more attentive to the rhetorical climate, and occasionally mentioned freedom of the press, but not as a paramount concern. The General Committee of the City and County of New York, in its petition to New York's Provincial Congress regarding the affair, invoked the "peace and harmony of each Colony" and "the general union of the Continent," and insisted that no future raids occur "without the direction of the Continental or this Congress, or the Committee of Safety, or of the Committee of the County into which such inhabitants may come, or of the Continental Generals, unless there should be an invasion into this Colony."[158] One is amazed at the number of bodies that the committee would allow to authorize such a raid. Likewise, New York's delegates to the Continental Congress wrote New York's Committee of Safety that the raid was a "high insult to your authority" and might encourage a "fatal spirit of jealousy."[159] The New York Provincial Congress *did* mention freedom of the press, but only at the bottom of a long remonstrance to Governor Trumbull of Connecticut that mainly concentrated on the issue of authority (Sears had acted "without any authority from the Continental or this Congress, or their Committees") and of the raid's "manifest tendency to interrupt . . . harmony and union." When the remonstrance appealed to freedom of the press, it was only after a disclaimer: "We believe you will not consider this requisition as an attempt to justify the man from whom the types were taken."[160] Moreover, the remonstrance was passed by a divided vote—hardly a ringing endorsement of the abstract principle of freedom of the press. Even so, Connecticut's government did not respond for six months, a tardiness that cannot be fully explained by embarrassment.[161]

Indeed, one might explain patriot allusions to freedom of the press in the aftermath of the raid as feeble responses to ongoing British criticism of patriot restraints. "Coriolanus" (John Vardill) in an article in the prestigious *Gentleman's Magazine* portrayed Rivington as a martyr to "the cause of constitutional freedom."[162] Lord Lyttelton stated the case thus to the House of Lords: "Have they not gone so far as to stifle all free discussion in print, and overthrown that great palladium the liberty of the Press, in the person of *Rivington*, whose only crime was that he published the thoughts of men who ventured to disapprove of the measures they were pursuing?"[163] Lyttelton's phrasing was that of Cato and Wilkes. Sears had given the British a martyr to liberty. Even Rivington's demise was gall to the patriots.

Rivington left the colonies in January 1776. He returned after the British occupation of New York City, and in 1778 commenced the publication of the *Royal Gazette*, the foremost pro-British newspaper in the colonies. He remained odious to patriots, and will return to our narrative at the end of the war.

Wartime Measures

The Declaration of Independence changed the definition of opposition printing. To promote obedience to the king or reconciliation with Britain was now necessarily subversive of the sovereignty of the states. Laws were passed defining sedition, treason, and misprision of treason as crimes. Wartime disruptions, popular sentiment, and the common sense of printers reinforced the laws, so that during the years of the Revolutionary War (1776–1783) no opposition prints appeared in territory occupied by either British or patriot troops or administrations. It was because these factors eliminated print opposition that antipress violence diminished in significance during the war itself. Of course, the relative absence of overt violence did not signal increased tolerance.

Patriots were frankly intolerant of loyalism and anything similar to it, including pacifism. The press was full of anti-Tory fulminations, even in areas where loyalism was not a problem.[164] Printers in New York received cautionary messages warning of "death and destruction, ruin and perdition," if they printed loyalist matter.[165] Anti-Tory vigilante movements appeared throughout the war.[166] For the most part, such hostility was gratuitous because loyalism was rarely a political threat after independence.

In some areas, anti-Tory sentiment seems to have been a vehicle for older animosities. Anti-Quaker hostility in Pennsylvania, prominent throughout the war,[167] was partly ideological: the Quakers' exotic pacifism seemed selfish and antirepublican. But much of the animus came from resentment of Quakers as an elite group. Likewise, Pennsylvanians expressed anger at lawyers who defended Quakers and others accused of disloyalty on ideological grounds, but also because of a traditional resentment of lawyers as a privileged group.[168] It is in the nature of war to unleash such emotions.[169] And there is no doubt that all of this had a chilling effect.[170]

The political context of anti-Tory activity changed too. As regular governing bodies were formed, a flurry of state constitutions were drafted, most with declarations of rights explicitly guaranteeing political freedoms, among them freedom of the press. At the same time, the new legislatures enacted laws for punishing seditious utterances, prescribed test oaths of loyalty, authorized imprisonment and confiscation for loyalists, and denied loyalists the right to vote and hold office.[171] Meanwhile, state committees of safety were called upon to regulate Tory sentiment.[172] And the army also took a hand in battling loyalism, often to the consternation of civilian authorities.[173]

These authorities maintained a potent oversight of printers also. In early 1777, Samuel Loudon undertook to publish excerpts from the loyalist press in his newspaper. A member of the New York Provincial Congress found out and told him not to. Loudon complied—his loyalty was not in question—but inadvertently issued some copies of the paper containing the loyalist excerpts. In punishment, he was reprimanded by the Committee of Safety and lost his printing contract with the state.[174] Printers were more than usually dependent on official favor during the war, and, despite the heady rhetoric of liberty, remained genially compliant, sometimes even servile.[175] The angry public response when James Humphreys, Jr., not an ardent patriot, printed insinuations about the motives of Pennsylvania Committee of Safety members led him to discontinue his paper.[176] Clearly, the American governments did not expect the press to be an independent fourth estate.

But governments recognized the need for printing, and in some cases showed extraordinary latitude toward printers. The Georgia legislature, for instance, confiscated loyalist printer James Johnston's equipment, then offered him the state printing contract, then, when he refused, attainted him of treason. Johnston left the colony but eventually returned with the British army in 1781 to print the *Royal Georgia Gazette*. In 1782 the patriots retook Savannah and banished Johnston for life. In a few months they relented, and again offered him the state printing contract.[177] Johnston might have been treated differently, of course, if a more orthodox printer could have been lured to darkest Georgia. Meanwhile, the British accepted Hugh Gaine's conversion to loyalism in New York, and Benjamin Towne managed to switch sides more than once in Philadelphia.

The British press delighted in discussing patriot restraints on the press. Rivington's *Royal Gazette* ridiculed patriots' "Prostituted presses"—using the same term that patriots had applied to his own *Gazetteer*—and "Aristides" declared that "there are *no freemen* in America, save the few tyrants who, by delusion, fraud and force, have usurped the powers of the new States."[178] This, of course, from a newspaper printed with a subsidy and under the supervision of the British army.

Just as intrusive as popular sentiment, politics, and policy were matters of wartime exigency. Printers fled opposing armies, sometimes had their equipment confiscated, and always had to contend with disruptions in supplies, distribution, and, alas, payment of subscriptions. The war neatly halved the number of newspapers published in the states. Both armies gave opposing printers cause for fear. Christopher Sauer III was arrested by the Continental army. The British arrested Peter Edes, son of Benjamin Edes, printer of the *Boston Gazette*, and questioned him most uncomfortably. The patriot army regularly burned handbills and pamphlets, and on one occasion Charles Lee's aide-de-camp horsewhipped a newspaper critic.[179]

Perhaps it is unsurprising that the war saw attacks on opposing presses by citizens, governments, and armies on both sides. History has seen few examples of tolerance toward enemy apologists in wartime. But who was the enemy? Did Americans tolerate *loyal* dissent during the war? Or was any critic an enemy?

In fact, the tactics of silencing "enemy" critics were used on loyal patriots from time to time. For example, in Philadelphia in 1779, a series of letters signed "Cato" attacking Thomas Paine appeared in Benjamin Towne's *Evening Post*. Paine's supporters among Philadelphia's artisans were outraged. Led by Charles Willson Peale, they visited Towne and demanded Cato's identity. Towne initially refused but relented when the crowd clarified its intentions by placing a noose around his neck. He then identified Whitehead Humphreys, owner of a steel furnace and intimate of Philadelphia's more conservative political circles, as "Cato." Humphreys too was visited by the crowd, and summoned to defend himself the next morning at the Coffee House, which served at the time as a sort of town hall. What happened there is unclear: it seems that Humphreys gave a lecture on liberty of the press and received one on the proprieties of political debate. A few days later, at a public meeting, General John Cadwalader rose to denounce this whole affair and defend freedom of expression but was shouted down by several hundred of the "lower orders." In response yet another meeting was held, this time explicitly to reaffirm freedom of the press.[180]

This confrontation is compelling for a number of reasons. First, it shows how the mechanisms of the politics of loyalty could be redirected at internal critics. The crowd used the very tools—the public meeting and symbolic violence—that had been so integral to the attack on loyalism. Second, the confrontation clearly was along class lines. Paine's and Peale's followers were radical artisans, while Towne's and Humphreys's supporters were led by establishment figures from Philadelphia's government and mercantile elite. In part, this class division resulted from Philadelphia's unique social and political history, but only in part. Indeed, a similar class division was evident in attacks against Rivington, Loudon, and others. Third, the victims responded by using the familiar rhetoric of liberty of the press, while the attackers deployed traditional press ideology to describe their target as licentious.

What isn't clear is whether any group had a real allegiance to the ideology it espoused. Were artisans more prone to use licentiousness as a justification because they maintained traditional corporate values in the face of rising liberalism? Was liberalism the ideology of the mercantile elite? Or were both positions consensual, so that either group would have eagerly used the other's arguments if the positions were reversed? Was liberty of the press a class idea? These issues can best be explored in the most famous cases of antipress violence during the war, the attacks on William Goddard in Baltimore.

William Goddard

The most dramatic attacks against the press during the war itself were directed against William Goddard's *Maryland Journal*. In 1777 and again in 1779, Goddard was attacked for publications that were basically impolite. Goddard's loyalty was not an issue; he was well-known as a patriot and founder of the continental postal system. But his haughtiness and conservatism made him obnoxious to local radicals.

Goddard's biography is intertwined with other characters already mentioned here. During his childhood in New London, Connecticut, his minister was Samuel Seabury, the Tory pamphleteer. In New Haven he was apprenticed to James Parker, later a defendant in the long legal struggle over Alexander McDougall's criticism of the New York Assembly. He was a partner of John Holt, New York's leading patriot printer, and was the clandestine publisher of the *Constitutional Courant* during the Stamp Act crisis. In 1766 he was drawn into an infamous partnership with leading Philadelphia conservatives, most notably Joseph Galloway, in the publication of the *Pennsylvania Chronicle*. Goddard broke with his backers and in 1773 started the *Maryland Journal* in Baltimore. He gradually distanced himself from the *Chronicle*, which was left to Benjamin Towne, and at the same time began promoting his postal scheme. Because this required frequent travel, he left the *Journal*'s day-to-day operations in the hands of his sister, Katherine Goddard, who, like their mother, was an accomplished printer.[181]

Meanwhile controversy brewed in Maryland over the treatment of loyalists. The new state government was not aggressive in punishing Tories; the independence movement had won out in Maryland, and the state's Committee of Safety saw no need for an anti-Tory campaign. But local committees of safety, especially Baltimore's, were harsher, being more responsive to the sentiments of local citizens and radicals.[182] In Baltimore antiloyalism went beyond constituted authority to spark a vigilante movement calling itself the Whig Club, which acted by serving notices of expulsion signed "Legion" on those it identified as Tories.[183]

Goddard ran afoul of the Whig Club in 1777. What triggered this confrontation was a letter in the *Journal*, signed "Tom Tell-Truth," responding to a British peace overture with sarcastic lavishness: "My soul overflows with gratitude to the patriotic virtuous King, the august incorruptible Parliament, and wise disinterested Ministry of *Britain*. I am lost in the contemplation of their private and public virtues."[184] The Whig Club claimed that this would be read not as sarcasm but as an outpouring of genuine emotion.[185] In a sense, this fear of misreading, though condescending, is understandable because the language of the letter was not extravagant by the standards of Tory literature. A good parody must first be a good imitation, after all. And, in the ensuing controversy, no one denied that the sentiments of "Tom Tell-Truth," absent the element of parody, were unprintable. Still, patriots had used parody freely before. One suspects the Whig Club must have wanted to take offense at Goddard.

The Whig Club then moved to punish "Tom Tell-Truth." First, on 3 March, it sent a delegation to ask Goddard to identify the author (who was actually Samuel Chase, then a delegate to Congress. It is unclear whether the Whig Club suspected Chase's authorship, and whether the members were partly motivated by political rivalry with the aristocratic future Federalist. It is clear that they saw Goddard as the ally of an aristocratic faction.) Goddard declined and was then summoned to appear at the club's next meeting, a summons he refused, by his own account, "after ridiculing the mock Patriots."[186] He was then taken forcibly to the meeting, and again refused to name "Tom Tell-Truth." The Whig Club then voted to banish him, and gave him a day to leave town.[187]

Goddard did leave town, but he didn't accept banishment. Instead, he went to Annapolis and petitioned the state legislature. He then returned to Baltimore and published an initial edition of his account of the affair, a pamphlet called *The Prowess of the Whig Club.*

Goddard's arguments against the Whig Club in this pamphlet were full of the rhetoric of the Revolutionary movement. He referred to his accusers as a "lawless ambitious *knot*" (p. 10) and accused them of losing "sight of the *public* interest" and becoming "*judges* and *executioners*, in their own *personal* quarrel" (p. 6).

Goddard also used the rhetoric of class. He called the Club "a motley crew of *extortioners, military pettifoggers*, and *petty clerks, amphibious heroes*, and *deluded artists*." He denied any animus against "mechanics," but argued that "when a man who is only fit to 'patch a shoe,' attempts 'to patch the State,' fancies himself a *Solon*, a *Lycurgus*, and usurps the executive power, he cannot fail to meet with contempt" (p. 7 and footnote). Goddard amplified his class argument in later editions of the *Prowess* by publishing as an appendix a list of key members of the Whig Club broken down by occupation. The list was meant to show that the club lacked respectability, and consequently described naval officers as "Mariners &c." and lawyers as "Pettifoggers &c." This points up an interesting fact that no one denied: the Whig Club's chief constituency was the mechanics and militia of Baltimore, men who believed that though he may have been a patriot, Goddard was no democrat.[188]

The Whig Club was deeply offended by Goddard's pamphlet. On 25 March a mob took Goddard with a clear intent to tar and feather him. Katherine Goddard went to fetch the militia, but they were loath to act, probably because they sympathized with the rioters.[189] Goddard was not tarred and feathered, but was sent out of town.

This time Maryland's authorities took more decisive action. They condemned the activities of the Whig Club and ordered its dissolution. Indeed, after April, the Whig Club was little heard of, probably because the state's militia companies were ordered to battle, and many of the Club's members were also in the militia.

Was the state's vigorous action a triumph for liberty of the press? Only somewhat. It was a firm declaration that due process should be observed. Governor Thomas Johnson's proclamation dissolving the Whig Club declared it an illegal assembly,[190] and the House of Delegates resolved that all citizens were "entitled to the benefits and protections of the laws."[191] But it seems that this action was prompted more by concern to assert jurisdiction than by love of free discussion. The Whig Club and, to a lesser extent, the Baltimore Committee of Safety had been irritants for months now; their treatment of Goddard was a welcome excuse to put them in their places.

Goddard's defense and vindication did not rest on freedom of expression. Even the *Prowess* argued on the basis of due process, not the "marketplace of ideas," and "Tom Tell-Truth" was defended as parody, not as protected political expression. The authorities didn't condemn restrictions on the press, they condemned the Whig Club's imposing them. All concerned no doubt would call freedom of the press the "palladium of our liberties," and freedom of the press was specifically guaranteed in the Maryland constitution's declaration of rights, but whether this was anything but formula is unclear from Goddard's skirmish with the Whig Club.

In 1779 Goddard again aroused the crowd's anger, this time over a set of "Queries" condemning political disfranchisement and the Tory witch-hunt, and criticizing the cult of personality that had grown up around George Washington. The anonymous "Querist" dwelt on Washington's (lack of) military genius, and defended General Charles Lee, who had been dismissed from command when Washington questioned his conduct in battle. The "Querist," *mirabile dictu*, was in fact Charles Lee, and Goddard was the only printer he could find to publish his "Queries."[192]

The "Queries" appeared on 6 July 1779. On 8 July, a crowd led by army officers angered at the criticism of their commander burst into Goddard's home and summoned him to a meeting the next day—an invitation he couldn't refuse. Before the meeting he visited Baltimore's magistrates in their homes but failed to get a commitment from them to maintain law and order. The next morning, confronted with a crowd armed with the tools of humiliation—cart and rope, tar and feathers—Goddard caved in and named the author of the "Queries," apologized for publishing them, and promised to print a retraction.[193] Goddard's apology was printed on 14 July 1779. In it he admitted that the "Queries" were "derogatory of the French Nation, tending to distract the minds of the people; and in particular aimed at the reputation of the Commander in Chief of the American Army." They were "replete with the nonsense and malevolence of a disappointed man." In publishing them he had "transgressed against truth, justice, and my duty as a good citizen."[194]

Again, though, Goddard counterattacked. He appealed to the state government to censure Baltimore's magistrates for failing to prevent the crowd action.[195] A hearing was held, and everyone was asked to behave in future, but no real action was taken.[196] Meanwhile, 150 citizens of Baltimore published a notice condemning Goddard and promising to boycott the *Journal*. Goddard's partner, Eleazer Oswald, challenged Col. Samuel Smith, the leader of the mob, to a duel.[197] But Baltimore calmed down and Goddard continued to publish.

The "Querist" affair showed the limits of free expression in patriot America. Washington and the Continental Army, as symbols of emergent nationhood, were outside the realm of licit criticism. Lee could not insult them nor Goddard publish his insults with impunity, and even though Goddard soon repudiated his apology and claimed a victory for freedom of the press, he still refused to publish more "Queries," as in fact did every other printer Charles Lee contacted.[198] Some things were simply unprintable.

Goddard's problems also show the survival of traditional press ideology. Controversy provoked anger, and anger was justified by labeling its target as licentious. Goddard proved, if only in the eyes of a class of opponents, that licentiousness could exist within patriot ranks.

Changes in Press Status and Ideology

The exigencies of the Revolutionary period forced changes in the press. Most obviously, a style of advocacy was invented, one that required more active editorial control than the colonial printer had been accustomed to. The printer was expected to be a combatant.[199]

The new role of advocacy elevated the status of printers. They thought of themselves as important players in the conduct of public discussion. After the Revolution, printers tended to drop the note of servility that one finds in the colonial period. And during the Revolution, printers began to show a new note of resentment toward outside pressures and government interference.[200]

But in asserting their elevated status printers did not reject their traditional responsibilities. Instead they developed an inflated view of their own importance, and became more morbidly concerned with the proprieties of press conduct.[201] Printers began to assume that press discussion *was* public discussion—that the realm of public debate was bounded by the press—and that therefore the press had enormous power.

At the same time, after the Revolution, the press became much harder to control. During the war control had been effected by a number of means—government subsidy, military and judicial policing, the patriotism of press conductors, and in extreme cases violence—that could be deployed because the war, it was said, made unanimity necessary. After the war, some of these means remained but many did not. And the number of newspapers, always low during the war because of logistical difficulties, began to climb dramatically.

In this situation, newspapers inevitably broke the rules. Especially in places where multiple newspapers were printed, especially in capital cities, printers aligned with factions and published personal attacks. But these partisan practices were not sanctioned. Instead, such newspapers were condemned as "sewers of scandal" deserving "contempt and disgrace."[202]

The state of press ideology can be most charmingly gleaned from two mock "apologies" of unfaithful printers that appeared at the end of the war. The first was written by John Witherspoon for Benjamin Towne, Philadelphia's infamous opportunist, who managed to switch sides safely several times in the conflict. Towne asked Witherspoon to write something in Towne's name to return him to the good graces of the patriots after one such switch. Witherspoon's "The Recantation of Benjamin Towne" is a minor classic of Revolutionary wit, but Towne declined to publish it because he thought it too self-effacing. It later turned up in the patriot press.[203]

In the "Recantation," the printer pleads his own insignificance as an excuse for his infidelity:

> I never was, nor ever pretended to be, a man of character, repute, or dignity. ... Had a Hancock or an Adams changed sides, I grant you they would have deserved no quarter, and I believe would have received none; but to pass the same judgment on the conduct of an obscure Printer is miserable reasoning indeed.

This is, of course, the classic "mere-mechanic" line. The apology goes on in the vein of traditional press ideology:

> I do hereby declare and confess, that when I printed for Congress, and on the side of Liberty, it was not by any means from principle, or from a desire that the cause of Liberty should prevail, but purely and simply for the love of gain. I could have made nothing but tar and feathers by printing against them as matters then stood. ... They are pleased to charge me with hypocrisy in pretending to be a Whig when I was none. This charge is false. I was neither whig nor tory but a Printer.

This is, of course, the traditional claim to run an "open press" so that anyone may have the freedom of the press, and makes a mock virtue out of the colonial printer's habit of deference to the powers that be, in this case including the power of the crowd.

> Finally I do hereby recant, draw back, eat in, and swallow down, every word that I have ever spoken, written, or printed to the prejudice of the United States of America, hoping it will not only satisfy the good people in general, but also all those scatter-brained fellows, who call one another out to shoot pistols in the air, while they tremble so much they cannot hit the mark.

So Witherspoon/Towne closes with a bow to the ultimate technique of press control, direct violence, which he sought to avoid by rhetorically depicting himself as too lame a character to merit a duelist's attention.

The "Recantation" reads superficially as a vindication, but its tone of parody makes it actually self-abasing. Witherspoon/Towne's claims to impartiality and artisanal virtue were made ridiculous, just as they must have seemed ridiculous to patriots anyway, because Towne lacked the crucial element of true virtue in that precise moment: patriotism. The last passage quoted is poignant for just that reason: Witherspoon's Towne tries to fend off with humor the violent punishment he expects patriots will think appropriate.

Also at the close of the war a parody apology appeared for James Rivington.[204] The defense of pseudo-Rivington closely paralleled Towne's. First he claimed to have been doing his printerly business:

> [I]t was my lot to remain with a people who had power in their hands and money in their purses. In this situation it was the part of a wise man to evade the power and possess as much of the money as possible. This I have endeavoured to do.

The printer, he pointed out, was only a *medium*, not an author: "Alas! Alas! I AM BUT A POOR PRINTER, subjected, by my vocation, to the disagreeable task of bringing into the world the monstrous conceptions of disordered fancies." And so, as a mere mechanic, he printed "tory news, tory lies, and tory essays." Yet he remained virtuous because he kept his press open:

> But will anyone say I have refused to publish whig news, whig lies, and whig essays? I challenge all Philadelphia to produce a single writer who ever sent me a whig piece for publication, which I refused or neglected to print.

And ultimately all of this printing caused no harm because the "outrageous lies" that came from Rivington's press were believed only by Tories in London and New York. Honest Americans had too much common sense to take the *Royal Gazette* seriously, he supposed.

These two antiapologies underscore the impact of the Revolution on press ideology. Patriots lampooned the traditional defenses of printers that they were but passive conveyors of public debate and that they were simply obeying market forces. During the Revolution, a printer who was not a patriot had no right to print; after the Revolution, press conduct could not be justified simply by a printer's claim to being a humble artisan. Printers had acquired the status of opinion leaders and would have to live up to it.

Patriots could be quite unforgiving toward printers who had strayed during the war. Despite the best intentions of responsible political leaders, spasms of anti-Tory violence ran through the states at the close of the war.[205] One of the victims of such violence was James Rivington.

Rivington intended to stay in New York City and continue printing after the war, but New York's radicals objected. In December 1783 he was visited by Isaac Sears, John Lamb, and Marinus Willett, who demanded he abandon his business in New York City. There followed a series of attacks: a beating by Nicholas Cruger on 11 January 1784 in reaction to a wartime aspersion; a nocturnal assault on Rivington's house by Sears and company on 14 January; and a threat to attack again the next day.[206] Rivington gave in. Years later Alexander Hamilton recalled that a movement in the state legislature to "discountenance" these actions was stymied by Sears, Lamb, and Willett, all of whom had just been elected to the Assembly.[207] Treatment of loyalists was a partisan issue, with the left wing of New York's Revolutionary leadership seeking revenge, urging intolerance.

Conclusion

The practices of the Revolution included the suppression of unpopular ideas. Loyalism was clearly beyond the boundaries of acceptable printed discourse. Other positions—pacifism, internal political opposition—were on the borderline. Dissent in any form was undesirable, even embarrassing, and dissent in print was considered improper, and in some cases punishable by official or extralegal means. The press, more than other institutions, was expected to display patriot unity on key issues. Perhaps factional divisions were acceptable among committee members or in legislatures, but they should not find their way into the newspapers.

The Revolution was also a period of change in the situation of the press and printers. Newspapers occupied a more cherished spot in thought about government than ever before. They were seen as crucial arenas of public information and discussion, and came to be called essential to self-government. Printers were expected to fill a leadership role in the post-Revolutionary republic. They retained the responsibilities of traditional press ideology and acquired new ones.

The Revolution was a period of ideological ferment. Patriots consistently invoked ideals of liberty, virtue, and reason, and pondered what these terms meant in practice. They produced immense rhetorical resources in their deliberations over justifications for independence, for local sovereignty, for constitutional authority. All of this rhetoric had implications for the press.

Practice and rhetoric looked at together indicate that the Revolutionary press was not governed by a liberal ideology in the minds of printers, insiders, or the general public. The arena of printed discourse was not looked upon as a marketplace in either of the two senses in which the marketplace of ideas has been thought of: patriots did not think it proper for printers to obey market forces, and patriots did not think the unrestrained competition of ideas for public support would further the general welfare. They believed in "Liberty," to be sure, but liberty was the province of the virtuous. True liberty was public-spirited; self-regarding activity was not liberty but licentiousness. Rather than a marketplace of ideas, the Revolutionary generation believed in a commonwealth of ideas.

This corporate notion of liberty was in keeping with both elite and popular conceptions of society and government. But it seems from the activities of Revolutionary crowds that artisans, militiamen, and others of the "lower ranks" were less likely to tolerate press misconduct than their social betters. I cannot, however, conclude that this demonstrates an ideological rift between social classes, though it might signal one, for several reasons. First, the pronouncements of both elite and popular figures about the press seem to share the same republican ideology, even though their behavior differed. Second, there is reason to believe that the "lower orders" were not particularly concerned with the press on a day-to-day basis—circulations remained small, and subscriptions were out of the range of wage earners. Still, newspapers were read aloud at taverns and other public places, and no doubt had much larger readerships than their circulations; moreover, on several occasions noted above, urban crowds were outraged over newspaper items. Finally, it might be that popular antipress activity was more pronounced than elite activity because elites had more avenues of redress open to them. Elites had easier access to courts, legislatures, and opposing papers; they could put economic and social pressures directly on printers; and, if all else failed, a gentleman could challenge a printer to a duel. In short, the view of the press from the top down was likely no more liberal than from the bottom up.

But there were forces for change present in both practice and ideology. Newspapers multiplied and began to interact with nascent political parties in new ways. Notions of corporate responsibility were increasingly strained by the ideological aftermath of the Revolution, especially egalitarianism and individualism in politics, religion, and the marketplace. In the next half century, the working out of the Revolutionary impulse was to produce an opening up of public discourse, though it was to be an opening up with its own barriers and boundaries.

3

Antipress Violence and Politics in the Early Republic

Revolutionary ideology emphasized unity, not division, in the body politic. At every point in the series of events leading to the break with England, patriot apologists invoked a luminous public interest, a mythical cause of liberty, with the rhetorical implication that there was *one* interest, *one* liberty, for all patriots. When patriots disagreed among themselves, it was concealed, if possible. Disagreements happened, and patriot leaders were no virgins when it came to politics, but ideologically they were ill equipped to justify partisan activities.

This changed in the early Republic. By the end of the 1820s, politics came to be characterized by permanent nonideological partisan divisions, and politicians praised political competition as a healthy means of promoting the public good. In the process, a realm of public discourse was created for peaceful combat among interested parties. Within this realm, "licentious" press conduct ceased to produce majoritarian violence; instead, editors and politicians stood ready to punish personal insults by fighting or dueling. Outside the realm of acceptable partisanism, of course, majoritarian violence persisted, with rioting and vigilantism flaring up, especially in the 1830s. The public learned to tolerate a certain range of political differences, then, even while tremendous social dislocations continually redrew the line between tolerable and intolerable expression and behavior.

The First Amendment and Attitudes Toward the Press

The Revolution itself did not produce a popular habit of political tolerance. But it did produce constitutional guarantees of freedom of the press, the most famous of which was the First Amendment to the federal Constitution. Because the First Amendment is such a key document, it will bear quotation in full:

> Congress shall make no law respecting an establishment of religion, or prohibit-
> ing the free exercise thereof; or abridging the freedom of speech, or of the press;
> or the right of the people peaceably to assemble, and to petition the government
> for a redress of grievances.

Like the declarations of rights included in state constitutions, the First Amendment is a catalog of personal liberties. Oddly, press freedom seems out of place;[1] all the other freedoms are inherent in the individual, and could be made to fit the formula of the Declaration of Independence: "endowed by their creator with." But the world has never seen someone endowed by one's creator with freedom of the press, because no one has ever yet been born into a state of nature with a printing press. This is quite unlike the "natural" freedoms of religion, of assembly and petition, or of speech.

How did the generation of founders think of the press that they would include it in a catalog of natural personal liberties? The wording and punctuation of the First Amendment imply that it is an extension of freedom of speech, and hence a prop-erty of the person of the author; because every person is a potential author, then, freedom to print is a natural right, and freedom of the press is the property of the people.

This way of thinking is subtly different from twentieth-century attitudes. Free-dom of the press is now seen as a special preserve of the press, and the press is understood as the media, not as the printing press, an actual physical implement. The media look upon the First Amendment as a sort of official charter, and the public looks upon it is a kind of license for the media, at least insofar as freedom of the press is concerned. And, since this implies that the First Amendment was meant to protect printers, it seems impossible that its drafters could look upon printers as enemies of freedom of the press. But in a way they did.

Jefferson and Press Ideology

The Revolutionary period produced a mountain of political reasoning of all sorts. Some of it was hardheaded: legalistic justifications and explanations of what had been done—details of constitution writing, debates over what was to be retained from English common law now that the states were no longer British. But much of it was more speculative. In the final analysis all of the hardheaded pragmatic elucidations rested on, or at least implied, utopian visions. In the margins of the practical the founders scribbled metaphysics.

The most interesting of the thinkers in this period of the working out of the Revolution was Thomas Jefferson. Still a young man when the Revolutionary crisis came, he yet served in Congress and as Virginia's governor during the War of Independence. After the war he was ambassador to France (during the years lead-ing up to the French Revolution), secretary of state under George Washington, vice-president under John Adams, and president for two terms. He was at the center of U.S. politics for over thirty years, first as one of the leading promoters of the Revolution, then as leader of the opposition to the Federalist administrations of the 1790s, and then as leader of the governing party. He was the principal author of the Declaration of Independence, and died on the semicentennial of its signing.[2]

Jefferson is also known as a champion of freedom of the press.[3] He authored some of the most memorable liberal aphorisms, and was one of the leaders in the fight against the Sedition Act of 1798, the first federal legislation targeting libels.[4] Jefferson's position in the pantheon of free press rhetoric seems secure.

Underlying Jefferson's rhetoric was a clearly utopian vision of the press. This "newspaper fantasy" was widely shared, and was the chief inspiration behind the great proliferation of newspapers in the early Republic. Still, there was a wide gap between this fantasy and the realities of the early press, so that the fantasy also inspired some of the harshest criticism of the press that has ever appeared, criticism that in fact seems overdrawn to the modern reader. Much of the criticism too came from Jefferson's pen.

Jefferson's most famous passage about the press occurs in his letter to Edward Carrington, written in 1787 on the occasion of Shays' Rebellion in Massachusetts:

> The way to prevent these irregular interpositions of the people is to give them full information of their affairs thro' the channel of the public papers, and to contrive that those papers should penetrate the whole mass of the people. The basis of our governments being the opinion of the people, the very first object should be to keep that right; and were it left to me to decide whether we should have a government without newspapers or newspapers without a government, I should not hesitate a moment to prefer the latter. But I should mean that every man should receive those papers and be capable of reading them. I am convinced that those societies (as the Indians) which live without government enjoy in their mass an infinitely greater degree of happiness than those who live under European governments. Among the former, public opinion is in the place of law, and restrains morals as powerfully as laws ever did anywhere. Among the latter, under pretence of governing they have divided their nations into two classes, wolves and sheep. I do not exaggerate. This is a true picture of Europe. Cherish therefore the spirit of our people, and keep alive their attention. Do not be too severe upon their errors, but reclaim them by enlightening them. If once they become inattentive to the public affairs, then you and I, and Congress, and Assemblies, judges and governors all become wolves.[5]

Here, as it so often does, the grace of Jefferson's writing allows us to accept his thought effortlessly, aphoristically; but there is much to unpack in this brief statement.

Jefferson touches here on two issues of governance: how to prevent anarchy and how to prevent corruption. His solution to both is public opinion.

By public opinion he apparently means a sort of natural consensus that forms when all citizens focus their attention on public affairs. This is not the same model of public opinion that we find in modern survey research—the numerical reckoning of how many lean which way on a specific question posed, which is at root a secularization of electoral politics—but a republican/primitive notion of a public "common sense," not divided according to interest or class but harmonious, not like the nations of Europe—always the model of corruption for Jefferson—but like the tribes of happy Indians. But such public opinion does not exist naturally in large nations. Instead, some artificial means is needed to allow public opinion to come into existence and function properly. That instrument is the press.

In the letter to Carrington, Jefferson stipulates that the press must be universally read. That is, it must be a network of relationships that involves all citizens as readers. In the context of his time and place, this stipulation was patently absurd. U.S. newspapers had small circulations, rarely larger than a few thousand, and especially in the South were available to only a minority. Even in the North, where newspapers were more plentiful, large segments of the population came into contact with them only secondhand, by borrowing them, perusing them at a public house, or hearing someone else recount the news in them. Still, it is clear upon reflection that the newspapers Jefferson lauded to Carrington did not exist in this world.

Jefferson was much less enthusiastic about real-life newspapers. These "present only the caricatures of disaffected minds";[6] their "ordures are rapidly depraving the public taste";[7] their printers "ravin on the agonies of their victims, as wolves do on the blood of the lamb."[8] Note the ironic twist of diction: Here it is the press, not the government, that is depicted as bloodthirsty wolves.

What made the real-life press different from Jefferson's fantasy press? We've already noted limited circulation. But this was only incidental; if the newspapers Jefferson criticized had circulated universally, he would have been even more appalled. The real difference was in how printers modeled themselves and the public in these papers.

In his criticism of the press, Jefferson frequently refers to printers as sowers of discord. His fullest statement is in a letter to Elbridge Gerry, written shortly after Jefferson's victory in the hotly contested presidential election of 1800. Already he'd begun to sting from press criticism of his new administration:

> A coalition of sentiments is not for the interest of the printers. They, like the clergy, live by the zeal they can kindle, and the schisms they can create. It is contest of opinion in politics as well as religion which makes us take great interest in them, and bestow our money liberally on those who furnish aliment to our appetite. The mild and simple principles of the Christian philosophy would produce too much calm, too much regularity of good, to extract from its disciples support from a numerous priesthood, were they not to sophisticate it, ramify it, split it into hairs, and twist its texts till they cover the divine morality of its author with mysteries, and require a priesthood to explain them. The Quakers seem to have discovered this. They have no priests, therefore no schisms. They judge of the text by the dictates of common sense and a common morality. So the printers can never leave us in a state of perfect rest and union of opinion.[9]

Printers transgressed when they interposed themselves between the "text" and the public, just as priests transgressed when they interposed themselves between the "text" (that is, the Bible) and its readers. Rather than being priests, printers should be transparent: a perfectly passive instrument for focusing the public's attention on the affairs of government. But, Jefferson here argues, printers in reality will not be passive, because they stand to make money by taking the political text and "sophisticating" it, by introducing extraneous conflict, by forcing schisms into politics just as priests did into religion.

There are several assumptions behind this tirade. First is the assumption that the text of politics is understandable without interpretation to the public. This implies a rational, intelligent public, and no surprise, because Jefferson's belief in the rationality and intelligence of the common man is much fabled.

Jefferson's second assumption is the artificiality of partisan differences. He implies that, absent self-interested outside agitators, harmony would prevail within the body politic. Partisanism was an intermittent and temporary inconvenience, and should quickly fade. He meant it when he told Congress in his first inaugural, "We are all republicans—we are all federalists." His exhortation to "unite with one heart and one mind," to "restore to social intercourse that harmony and affection without which liberty and even life itself are but dreary things" was no mere rhetorical flourish.[10] Jefferson believed that the body of citizens, operating with no restraint on reason, would arrive at a consensus on political decisions. Hence Jefferson always deplored partisanism in the press.[11]

Jefferson's distrust of partisanism was typical of the post-Revolutionary era. Partisanism, considered as the pursuit of private interest rather than the public good, ran counter to the rhetoric of the Revolution, and seemed a practice more suited to the politics of corrupt England. The press abounded with essays critical of "party spirit," and even party activists participated in the criticism.

There was a contrary position on partisanism. The classic refutation of hyperbolic criticisms of party was Madison's Tenth Federalist, in which he argues that partisanism can be safely tolerated in a large republic because no "interest group" will be able to achieve a majority, and hence the government will be safe from the control of a faction.[12] Madison argued that free republican government would produce a balance of interests.

But neither Jefferson nor the bulk of his colleagues were as yet sanguine about the effects of partisanism, even though many were deeply involved in partisan activities. What separated them from a modern liberal understanding of politics was their belief that political discourse was about the emergence of truth, not the balance of interests. Repeatedly, we run across justifications of free expression that invoke the eventual triumph of truth over falsehood. Indeed, Jefferson explained his laissez-faire attitude toward the abuses of the press during his administrations as a "great experiment," one that he believed had successfully demonstrated the ability of the citizenry to distinguish truth from lies.[13] And although he supposed he'd proven no serious harm could come from a licentious press, he still believed licentiousness to be a most regrettable habit: public reason should not have to triumph *in spite of* the press.[14]

Jefferson's concern with truth and virtue explains the tone of his support for a federal bill of rights. He believed the absence of a bill of rights in the original draft of the Constitution to be a great defect, and based his argument against the Alien and Sedition Acts on a literal interpretation of the First Amendment: *Congress* shall make no law restricting freedom of the press. But he did not deny the authority to make such laws to the states, and in fact explicitly supported state regulation of the press on occasion. To some this seems contradictory.[15] But Jefferson thought it proper that the press be expected to promote truth. He condoned occasional prosecutions for falsehood because he considered the Federalist press especially to be in the hire of a selfish aristocratic faction.[16] And indeed such a press *could* do harm in the proper circumstances. Consider his comments on the British press:

> You know well that that [that is, the British] government always kept a kind of standing army of newswriters, who, without any regard to truth, or to what should be like truth, invented and put into the papers whatever might serve the ministers. This suffices with the mass of the people, who have no means of distinguishing the false from the true paragraphs of a newspaper.[17]

Of course, this mercenary press was harmful precisely because the people were depraved in Britain and even more so on the European continent.[18] Should the American people ever become so depraved, then a licentious press would be just as dangerous, and, one supposes, sterner regulation would be appropriate.[19]

Just what kind of press did Jefferson want constitutions to protect? Consider his instructions from Albemarle County to the Virginia Constitutional Convention:

> In regard to freedom of the press, which certainly is, as mentioned in the Bill of Rights, one of the great bulwarks of Liberty, we think that the Printers should never be liable for anything they print, provided they may give up authors, who are responsible, but on the contrary that they should print nothing without. Many good people have been lately mislead [*sic*] by the artifices of the ingenious, but malicious, interested and corrupt writers. Had their names been published, their Characters would have been the antidote to their own poison.[20]

What I would call attention to here is not the familiar criticism of "malicious, interested and corrupt writers" but Jefferson's conception of the press as a passive medium for writers rather than an active producer of original material. Thus Jefferson thought printers will be amply protected if the constitution guarantees they will not be liable for lies they print but do not compose.

On a federal constitutional safeguard of freedom of the press, Jefferson was slightly less liberal and more realistic. He reassured Madison that "a declaration that the federal government will never restrain the press from printing anything they please, will not take away the liability of the printers for false facts printed."[21] State and local governments may punish printers for the pieces they print, though only if they contain false facts.[22] But Jefferson still was protecting a fantasy press, one where printers are passive instruments of public discourse.

Jefferson, in sum, defended the press *in theory* because he imagined it as something quite different from what he saw *in practice*. He adhered to a widely shared ideology, a mutation of traditional craft ideology brought forth by the Revolution's ideology, that I have called the ideology of rational liberty. This ideology modeled the press as a neutral public forum, modeled printers as public-spirited craftsmen, modeled authors as rational citizens offering rational commentary on public affairs, and modeled readers as the entire public of citizens rationally attending to public affairs. A press operating in such a manner would allow citizens to govern themselves in an intelligent manner, preserve freedom, prevent divisions in the body politic, and make it impossible for a self-interested faction to gain power. This is the only press Jefferson could have imagined taking the place of government.

This ideology of rational liberty was widely shared. One finds it invoked in the prospectus of virtually every newspaper in the decades following the Revolution, paid homage to in Fourth of July toasts, remarked on in private correspondence, and referred to in postal regulations. Its pervasiveness is apparent from the tone of William Cobbett's address to the public when he began *Porcupine's Gazette*:

> Professions of *impartiality* I shall make none. They are always useless, and are besides perfect nonsense, when used by a news-monger; for, he that does not relate news as he finds it, is something worse than partial; and as to other articles that help to compose a paper, he that does not exercise his own judgment, either in admitting or rejecting what is sent him, is a poor passive tool, and not an editor.[23]

Keep in mind that Cobbett was an Englishman, and hence insulated from Revolutionary rhetoric. His comments clearly imply that he is ridiculing the common sense of the day, and trying, as in all his productions, to be outrageous. His paper, like the other partisan papers of the day, were similar to English partisan papers, and looked upon as an alien force by many U.S. readers. The ideology of rational liberty was well entrenched in the minds of the public, printers, and politicians in the early Republic.[24]

While Revolutionary rhetoric produced an ideology of rational liberty, though, Revolutionary practice produced techniques of advocacy, and post-Revolutionary disagreements produced opposing factions that employed these techniques.

The Partisan Press

The post-Revolutionary period produced three grand moments of partisan struggle. The first involved the most basic questions of federal polity and centered on the ratification of the U.S. Constitution in the late 1780s. The second grew out of disputes over the interpretation of the Constitution and intensified in response to global competition between France and Britain in the late 1790s, climaxing in an undeclared naval war with France, and then in the presidential election of 1800. The third moment was again in response to international tensions, focusing on the embargo policy of the Jefferson administration, and climaxing in the War of 1812 against Britain.

Each of these moments saw violent activity against the press; indeed, each produced a significant riot centered on a newspaper. In 1788 the printing office of antifederalist Thomas Greenleaf was mobbed in New York City. In 1799 a mob of troops attacked Republican printer William Duane in Philadelphia. And in 1812 the antiwar tirades of Alexander Hanson's *Federal-Republican* triggered a major riot in Baltimore.

In each case, the rioting fit the pattern of majoritarian violence that had been characteristic during the Revolution. And in each case rioting was part of a larger campaign of political intimidation. This suggests that at least until the War of 1812, during moments of stress, partisan political opposition remained intolerable. At those moments, especially when international affairs were involved, opposing partisans appeared treasonous, and opposing printers seemed to threaten the body politic.

Yet even during these times of perceived crisis, opposition partisans and printers were at work constructing an ideology of loyal opposition. The late 1790s were especially important, for it was then that Republicans, arguing against the Alien and Sedition Acts, formulated statements of principle to justify their continuing opposition to the Adams administration.[25] So by the beginning of the nineteenth century, partisan practice had already begun to produce an ideology to replace rational liberty; still, it did not effectively do so until the 1820s.

The Federal Constitution and Greenleaf's *New York Journal*

The ratification of the Constitution produced one of the most memorable contests in U.S. political history. Nowhere was the struggle to ratify more important and more intense than in New York. There a popular wartime governor dominated state politics and leaned toward the antifederalists, and there one of the few newspapers open to antifederalist contributions was published: Thomas Greenleaf's *New-York Journal*. And, although ten states had already approved the Constitution— enough for it to take effect—before New York made its final decision, still a "no" vote might have forced revisions, or even made a true union impossible because New York occupied a crucial spot on the map.[26]

The debate over ratification is enshrined today in the *Federalist Papers*, the series of essays composed during New York's ratification campaign by James Madison, Alexander Hamilton, and John Jay. Masterpieces of political reasoning, these essays are also models of the sort of discourse that the ideology of rational liberty demanded. They were dispassionate and impersonal, thorough, deeply learned, expecting great competence from the reader, and all written over the pseudonym "Publius," which might best be translated as "Citizen."

The debate was less polite than "Publius" would lead us to believe. Many apologists resorted to *ad hominem* attacks,[27] and most were less, well, rational. In addition, pressure was put on newspapers both in New York and elsewhere not to print antifederalist pieces. Federalists used economic pressure to influence newspapers, boycotting the few that resisted, and some asserted that postmasters were deliberately interfering with the circulation of antifederalist papers.[28]

Printers throughout the Republic seemed disposed to favor the constitution anyway. The printers of Philadelphia and New York, for instance, participated en masse in those cities' great federal processions in July 1788. The Philadelphia parade featured a float carrying a working press printing up copies of odes to America in English and German, followed by fifty marching press workers. In New York, the printers' float bore, among other scripture, the motto "May the Liberty of the Press be inviolably preserved as the *Palladium* of the Constitution, and the Centinel of Freedom."[29]

Because partisanship was frowned upon in press ideology, all of New York's printers claimed to be impartial. Still, Greenleaf's *Journal* was the only New York paper regularly open to opponents of the Constitution, and printed the bulk of antifederalist essays that appeared in the state.[30] So lonely was his position among the state's printers that antifederalists in Albany, feeling shut out of the local *Albany Gazette*, appealed to Greenleaf to send them an apprentice or journeyman to start an opposing paper, a request that was not filled.[31] Greenleaf himself tried to maintain an appearance of impartiality, and printed a fair number of federalist essays, including some by Publius. But his patrons complained that these pieces were readily available elsewhere;[32] the usefulness of his paper was as an outlet for the antis.

The ratification process itself was peaceful. Debate, although often intemperate, produced no remarkable violence; elections for a ratifying convention were held; and the convention surprisingly approved the Constitution without asking for changes. The state was troubled to this point only by occasional brawls—notably one in Albany on the Fourth of July—and a bizarre and bloody antidissection riot in New York City in April.

What finally brought the wrath of federalists down on Greenleaf was his flippant reporting of New York City's Grand Federal Procession of 23 July, timed to coincide closely with the final vote of New York's ratifying convention in upstate Poughkeepsie. On the morning of the procession, a derogatory handbill, rumored to have come from Greenleaf's press, circulated through the city. Then, on the twenty-fourth, the *Journal* carried an account of the parade. Three passages in particular seemed to offend federalists. The first was Greenleaf's ridicule of the "Federal Ship Hamilton," a float designed to look like a ship that rolled around the city for days before and after the procession. The second was his sarcastic account of the collapse of the potters' float: "the poor *Potters* were separated from their *clay*, and no longer had *power over it*; the stage fell! and alas! the *clay* became exposed to the *power* of every passer-by." Greenleaf's phrasing here alluded to the potters'craft motto, "The Potter has Power over the Clay," which was displayed on the float. And, third, he chided the members of Congress, present in New York, who "declined *walking* at the procession, on account of this not being a *ratifying* state: they however accepted a seat at the table" and ate their fill. Greenleaf concluded thus:

> It was really laughable to see the variety of phizzes on this occasion. The poor *antis* generally minded their own business at home; others, who were spectators at an *awful* distance, looked as sour as the Devil.—As for the *feds*, they rejoiced in different degrees—there was the ha ha ha! and the ho ho ho![33]

This account outraged New Yorkers. Not only was it a direct affront to federalists, and especially to potters, but, because the *Journal* exchanged with newspapers throughout the states, the insult was broadcast.

Greenleaf was quick to apologize. In the *Journal* of 25 July, he declared he was "MORTIFIED that any exception should be taken to the paragraphs in yesterday's paper"; the mocking reference to the "potters clay" he dismissed as "innocent humour." But Greenleaf's apology "instead of calming, irritated the feelings of the citizens."[34]

Meanwhile, the Poughkeepsie convention ratified the Constitution. When the news reached New York City on the evening of the twenty-sixth, federalists poured into the streets to celebrate. A crowd of five hundred to a thousand formed, headed by "a few popular leaders,"[35] marched to the houses of key supporters of the Constitution and serenaded them. As the night wore on, the mood of the crowd became uglier and they began to seek out antis. They first visited Governor Clinton's house, but Clinton had not yet returned to town from the convention. Then they turned to Greenleaf's printing office and adjoining residence.

When the crowd arrived, Greenleaf and his family were already asleep. The crowd called for Greenleaf, and he came to the door but refused to let them in. When they moved forward to menace him, he drew pistols and fired once, hitting a rioter in the hand. The second pistol missed fire, and the crowd again moved forward. They stove in the door of the printing office, grabbed what they took to be the offending type, and made a general mess of things while Greenleaf fled to safety.[36]

Who were the crowd? All of the contemporary newspaper accounts agree that the crowd was composed of rank-and-file artisans and others of the producing classes; further, although they may have disliked Greenleaf's paper generally, all accounts agree that the crowd was motivated particularly by Greenleaf's remarks about the procession, especially his slur on the potters. This understanding of the crowd's motivation is supported by the actions of its members: they destroyed only the type they identified as that used to print the offending paragraphs. Greenleaf's mobbing was a popular retaliation for insulting New York's craftsmen.

But was the mobbing a political act? Greenleaf depicted it as one. In his account, he asserted that his reporting of the parade was not the cause but simply a convenient pretext, exploited by New York's federalist powers-that-be "to ruin him with the public, and thereby destroy the usefulness of his paper as a free and impartial one." His real offense was "admitting political pieces into his paper." Greenleaf invoked "FREEDOM OF THE PRESS" as the "PALLADIUM OF LIBERTY," echoing traditional ideology, and argued that the press preserves "liberty" and "virtue" by "disseminating information." The persecution of his paper, which he had always kept "FREE for all parties" and free from "anonimous [sic] scurrility of a private nature," could be attributable only to a scheme to delude and abuse the public.[37]

Greenleaf's suspicion of a federalist conspiracy to silence opposition seems unfounded. The ratification struggle was over, after all, and there was little to be gained by an *ex post facto* squelching of the opposition. On another level, though, Greenleaf's mobbing does tell us something about the limits of acceptable political expression. Although he appealed to the standards of traditional press ideology and of rational liberty, in the eyes of the offended he had clearly overstepped the bounds of decency. By holding up groups to public ridicule, he had justified retribution. The fact that his mobbing was not seen as a great insult to freedom of the press is attested to by the silence of most accounts on this subject. Indeed, many of the newspaper accounts of New York City's celebration of ratification fail to mention the mobbing at all.

Still, Greenleaf's mobbing stands out as something of an anomaly in the ratification struggle. No other newspaper in any state was mobbed—probably because so few of them were antifederalist, but possibly because the conventions of impartiality and rational liberty protected printers from reprisals. Greenleaf alone ventured into territory where the ideology offered no protection.

Greenleaf's paper was forced to cease printing for a week after the riot. He resumed publication, but with a bit more caution. The *New-Hampshire Gazette* noted that "in his paper of the 31st ult. he makes a manly apology for the publication which excited the resentment of his fellow citizens against him—and from the tenour of the several articles in that paper, appears determined to support the Constitution which the people have adopted."[38] Suitably chastened, Greenleaf was welcomed back into the fraternity of printers.

The Federalist Era

The first decade of government under the new federal Constitution produced a division among national leaders on key national issues. They disagreed on the limits of federal power, on issues of finance and economic development, and perhaps most importantly on the direction of foreign policy. Opposition to the administration crystallized in Congress and was spearheaded by Madison and Jefferson; the party in power was led nominally by Washington but practically by Alexander Hamilton. Both factions sponsored newspapers based in the capital—after 1790, Philadelphia. The Federalists supported John Fenno's *Gazette of the United States*; the Republicans patronized Philip Freneau's *National Gazette* and, after it failed, Benjamin Franklin Bache's *General Advertiser*, which later changed its name to *Aurora*.

These partisan papers were virtual wire services for newspapers throughout the country. They provided news and commentary from the center that circulated through the mails to every part of the nation, allowing the creation of opposing networks of papers. National political leaders, clustered at the capital for much of the year, wrote essays for these papers, usually over pseudonyms, and passed on information of political significance.

Still, these partisan networks were preliminary and incomplete. Political organization remained decentralized, as did the partisan press; there were numerous local factions and chieftains, and much of the partisan activity of the period was on a state and local level and did not mesh with national divisions. Furthermore, the populace seemed somewhat detached from national political divisions. Voter participation was not high, and voting behavior tended to be inconsistent, not demonstrating high levels of partisan loyalty. Instead, citizens delegated authority to a class of leaders whose excellence they recognized and to whom they deferred as one does to a superior. This system of politics has been aptly described by Ronald P. Formisano as "deferential-participant."[39]

In this context, the partisan press was the arena for a kind of proxy war among

political leaders. It was an extended public representation—one might say carica-
ture—of behavior in legislatures, with an exaggerated self-consciousness of a substantial public audience. In this arena behavior was often grotesque—the wildness
of Cobbett and Bache are cases in point—distorted by the enthusiasm with which
printers performed for their imagined public, but just as often it was characterized
by a stoic formality that was frequently pompous and sometimes approached vanity.

Party spirit was unusually violent in the Federalist era. There are two reasons
for this, both linked to press ideology. One was the absence of a stable basis for
party competition in either experience or theory. An opposition in a republic was
thought to be by definition grounded in a conspiracy against the commonweal. This
anxiety about the nature of parties was heightened by the common belief that
republics are fragile and have historically been short-lived. This anxiety leads to
the second reason for the unusual animus of Federalist-era politics. People believed
that they were embarked on an experiment in republican government of historic
significance, and that the whole world was watching, mostly in hope of a dramatic
failure. This sense of historic significance was intensified by the U.S. role as a bit
player in the "superpower" competition between France and Britain, a role that
produced continual blows to American pride and equally recurrent accusations that
the other party was a tool of a foreign power.[40]

Both parties played the politics of loyalty. In the controversy over the treaty
that John Jay negotiated with the British, Republicans accused Federalists of being
tools of Britain. Demonstrations were staged throughout the states, much like the
demonstrations of the Revolutionary movement, with hangings in effigy; copies
of the treaty were often burned.[41] In the heat of the moment, the Republican *Independent Chronicle* applied the charge of foreign control directly to the issue of
freedom of the press:

> The Press ought to be free—but not so free as to be the hireling of Foreign nations
> . . . to destroy the freedom of a nation. The pensioners of Britain and the hire-
> lings of Tyranny, may depend upon it, that the people of America begin to awaken
> to their danger, and to discover the execrable intrigues of its enemies.[42]

Notice how the passage invokes the memory of the Revolution in its reference to
British hirelings. Likewise, the *Chronicle* compared Federalist papers to "the infamous papers of Mein & Fleming [*sic*], Rivington, &c."[43] The implication was clear:
these papers deserved the same punishment.

Far more often Federalists accused Republicans of being tools of France.
Especially in the wake of the XYZ Affair, when nationalist passions rose at French
diplomatic slights, opposition seemed traitorous. Abigail Adams said that Republican "abuse, deception, and falshood [*sic*]" would "destroy that Confidence and
Harmony which is the Life, health, and Security of a Republick."[44] Alexander
Hamilton predicted that Republicans would "take ultimately a station in the public estimation like that of the Tories of our Revolution."[45] Opposition was called
subversive; opponents were called disloyal; legal means could be used to silence
them, hence the Alien and Sedition Acts; and extralegal means could be employed
when the law came up short.[46]

In this atmosphere, violence against the press became common. A simple list of printers threatened or attacked includes Thomas Adams of the Boston *Independent Chronicle*; Anthony Haswell of the *Vermont Gazette*; Jacob Schneider of the Reading *Adler*; John Daley Burk of the New York *Time Piece*; the notorious James T. Callendar of the Richmond *Examiner*; and the equally infamous William Cobbett of *Porcupine's Gazette* in Philadelphia.[47]

Benjamin Franklin Bache deserves special notice. First his paper was boycotted by Federalists; then Bache himself was beaten while visiting a federal warship under construction; then a crowd of 1,200 young Federalists, who had just been addressed by President Adams dressed in military uniform, marched to Bache's house and attacked it but were driven off; then, two days later, on a day of fasting and prayer, another crowd attacked Bache's house and broke his windows. Abigail Adams, after all this, predicted without regret that "the wrath of an insulted people will by & by break upon him."[48] Bache had insulted the people with his harsh criticisms of Presidents Washington and Adams and his habitual support of France. He was prosecuted under the Sedition Act but died of yellow fever before his case came to trial.

Bache's *Aurora*, along with his wife and his role as chief Republican printer, passed to his associate William Duane upon his death. Duane had been raised largely in Ireland, and had run his first newspaper in India, before coming to the States.[49] He carried on Bache's vigorous conduct of the *Aurora*, and suffered constant legal and extralegal harassment as a result. He was indicted three times for seditious libel and mobbed twice. In February 1799 he was attacked by a crowd of Federalists while circulating a petition against the Alien Acts.[50] His second mobbing came as a more direct repayment for his journalism.

In 1798 the federal government had passed a couple of revenue measures intended to finance what was then thought to be an imminent war with France. As tax assessors visited areas of rural Pennsylvania, however, they encountered a grassroots resistance that was often armed and violent. When some of the resisters were arrested, they were liberated in a raid led by resistance champion John Fries, a militia captain and staunch Federalist. Fries' Rebellion, as the affair came to be called, was a political windfall for Pennsylvania's Republicans, who immediately offered a resolution in the state's House of Representatives to require an investigation of "the agency of foreign incendiaries, or the seditious views of domestic traitors," using the same language that Federalists had used in arguing for the passage of the Alien and Sedition Acts. Meanwhile, though the tax protests had subsided, Governor Mifflin, at the request of the Secretary of War, had sent the state militia—eight troops of cavalry and five hundred men—to pacify the countryside.

Duane shrewdly exploited this unnecessary military expedition. He published signed affidavits from the "combat zone," documenting the troops' repeated violations of citizens' rights. Even more outrageous to Federalists were the letters of his anonymous correspondent in the area, who charged that the troops had quartered themselves at citizens' expense. All of these charges were couched in terms that invited comparison between the federal government and the British Empire at the time of the Revolution.

Duane suffered a violent retribution. On 15 May, a crowd of militia officers cornered him in his office. They repeatedly demanded the name of his correspondent, striking blow after blow when he refused. Significantly, the first blow came from Joseph B. McKean, the son of a prominent Republican politician, who slapped Duane when he called the visit an "electioneering trick"; McKean's participation made the attack seem nonpartisan. Duane's initial response to this attack was to challenge any officer present to duel; none would accept his challenge. Instead, they marched him down to the street. Surrounded by a ring of militia who held off the gathering crowd, Duane was beaten senseless. He later brought suit against his attackers; over the next seven years he won judgments against some of them.[51]

Duane's chastisement was clearly excessive, but it followed the pattern established for such attacks during the Revolutionary period. The attackers, though motivated by general political antipathy, found a pretext for their attack in a violation of press ideology—in this case, the publication of anonymous accusations. They set up a ritualized confrontation, in which Duane was expected to give some offense to, apparently, McKean's honor—which he did with his "electioneering" remark—that would entitle McKean to deliver a beating. But the passions of some of the attackers gave way, the plan was not adhered to, and Duane suffered a much more severe and much less orderly beating. The attackers thus forfeited their claim to have acted according to "constitutional procedures," which had been a standard element of crowd actions against the press.

The attack on Duane was a failure. His press was neither silenced nor reined in, and his followers were galvanized by this and the other "oppressive" acts of the Federalists. The attack failed because the attackers broke the chief rule of extralegal action, which was to seem more legal than the law.

Ambivalent Partisanism

All involved expected the partisan fury of the 1790s to be temporary. When Jefferson and the Republicans captured national power in 1800, with the removal of the capital to Washington, out of the vibrant but divisive milieu of Philadelphia, and with the arrival of peace with France, it was hoped that partisanism would be laid aside, and the press would return to impartiality. Instead, British transgressions on U.S. sovereignty replaced French insults, and Federalists took the stance of opposition that Republicans had abandoned. Partisanism persisted.[52]

Throughout this period parties engaged in what has been called the "politics of revolutionary center."[53] Each claimed the mantle of Revolutionary legitimacy; each arrogated to itself authority to interpret the Revolutionary experience; and thus each characterized itself as the true U.S. politics, denying this status to the other. With few exceptions, partisans during this period did not think of themselves as partisans.[54]

Accordingly, even partisan printers and editors did not embrace partisanism in the press. All were reluctant to admit that they served a part of and not the whole public. Consider the way the issue of partisanism is tortured in Joseph Gale's inaugural address to the public as editor of the chief Republican organ, the *National*

Intelligencer, in 1810: "It is the dearest right, and ought to be cherished as the proudest prerogative of any freeman, to be guided exclusively by the unbiassed [*sic*] convictions of his own judgment. This right it is my first purpose to maintain, and to preserve inviolate the independence of the print now committed into my hands." This sounds like a profession of impartiality: The editor will maintain the independence of his press from all influences but those of reason and his own convictions of the public good. Such professions of impartiality were common.[55] But, he continues,

> It is not, however, incompatible with this determination, to avow my entire devotion to the republican system ... and to republican administrations. ... Feeling nothing like neutrality on this head, it shall be my constant effort to illustrate and vindicate the principles on which they are founded; to shield enlightened and virtuous men from the aspersions of personal detraction or party virulence; and to defend their measures by a temperate exposure of their motives and tendencies.

Here Gale adopts the unabashed stance of the partisan warrior. Even so, he will be a virtuous warrior, not stooping to personal attacks or "virulence." Likewise, he goes on to promise a "rigid impartiality" in political reporting.[56]

Consistent with this ambivalent partisanism, editors continued to play the politics of loyalty. Republicans accused Federalists of being in the pay of the British throughout the series of diplomatic crises leading to the War of 1812.[57] The concept of a loyal opposition remained hard to grasp. On the other hand, partisan papers developed a more sophisticated internal structure. Editors challenged the traditional autonomy of printers. Remarks in the *National Intelligencer* are to the point: "It is but a short time since mechanical skill was deemed the only necessary qualification of an editor, who was consequently the humble copyist of the crude matter cast in his way by accident."[58] Note how the passage refers to editors rather than printers. A division of labor between material production of a newspaper and control of its content had appeared, with the latter taking precedence over the former. The separation between mechanical and editorial production accelerated in coming years, with deep implications for the culture of the press.

This phase of politics climaxed with the War of 1812.[59] Replaying the Revolutionary crisis in rhetoric, and similar to it in its emphasis on U.S. rights in the face of British encroachments, the war marked the penultimate defeat of Federalism.[60] The war also saw the last serious riot against a major-party paper until the Civil War.

Alexander Hanson and the *Federal-Republican*

The most vocal leader of the Federalists in Baltimore was Alexander Hanson, editor of the *Federal Republican*. After he founded the paper in 1808, Hanson's outspoken hostility toward Jefferson's and Madison's administrations led to a court martial—he was a militia captain—and the threat of tar and feathers during the heated electoral battle of that year. As the nation prepared for war in 1812, Hanson repeatedly accused Republicans of exploiting hostilities for political purposes, charging them with using troubles with Britain as a pretext to initiate a reign of terror against domestic political opposition. Republicans accused him of being in league with the British, and with some truth. He kept in touch with British officials, and went so far as to urge them to adhere to policies that had provoked the Republicans in hope that they would be forced out of office.[61]

Republicans expected that the U.S. declaration of war on Britain of 18 June 1812 would silence Federalist criticism, but Hanson, among others, did not oblige. In his paper of 20 June, Hanson included an editorial attacking the war as "unnecessary, inexpedient, and entered into from a partial, personal, and as we believe, motives bearing upon their front marks of undisguised foreign influence"; again he accused Republicans of planning a reign of "terror and proscription" and an attack on "civil rights." He rounded off his tirade by accusing Madison of being under the "dominion of Bonaparte."

Two days after he published this, Hanson's office was demolished by a gang of thirty or forty, with a sympathetic crowd of four hundred watching. One of the rioters fell to his death from an upper-story window. Subsequently, the crowd sought out Hanson and his partner, Jacob Wagner, but both men had hidden themselves. Hanson left Baltimore, resuming the *Federal-Republican* in Rockville, Maryland, and Georgetown.[62]

This riot clearly fit the classic pattern of majoritarian violence. The rioters claimed to be operating in place of constituted authority, and proceeded directly to their intended goals in an apparently well-planned manner. When Mayor Edward Johnson, a firm Republican, tried to intervene, a rioter—apparently an acquaintance—told him to stand off: "[T]he laws of the land must sleep, and the laws of nature and reason prevail."[63] Hanson was convinced that Republican leaders were involved in the riot, though his suspicions were more than a little grandiose: he pointed a finger at "terrorists on the floor of congress," and declared that the riot produced "ill concealed pomp of rejoicing in the higher circles of Washington." At the same time, in unintended acknowledgment of the tradition of mobbing, he asserted that the rioters were a small knot of conspirators with little popular support, implying that if they had truly represented a community consensus, the mobbing would have been legitimate.[64]

The 22 June mobbing of the *Federal Republican* touched off a spate of rioting in Baltimore that lasted throughout June and July. The mob roamed the streets nightly, striking at British sympathizers and free blacks, and dismantling ships suspected of trading with the British.[65] Hanson was wise to stay out of town.

But Hanson was determined to move his paper back to Baltimore. He considered the mobbing to be both an attack on liberty of the press and an act of political warfare by his Republican opponents; neither could go unanswered. With his allies among the more extreme Federalists—moderates kept their distance, doubting the propriety and wisdom of his stance[66]—he planned his return.

To the Young Turks the move was a chance for glory. With child-like simplicity and enthusiasm they prepared for a bloody battle with the mob. They rented a house and armed themselves; they argued over when to fire on an attacking mob, noting that they must seem to abide by the law, and not to "take into our own hands the sword of justice" unless given ample justification.[67] Secretly, Hanson and his allies moved into the city and occupied the rented house. Then on 27 July they issued the first number of the revived Baltimore *Federal Republican.*

The mob did not disappoint them. Reacting quickly to the paper—which featured a long florid editorial scoring the city's leaders for their inaction in June's rioting—a crowd began to gather in the street outside the rented house. Meanwhile, twenty or thirty men had gathered inside the house, determined to defend it. As evening fell, the crowd grew more hostile, throwing rocks at the building, allegedly in anger after a carriage delivered a load of muskets to the house. Then two shots were fired from an upstairs window—the rifles were loaded with blank cartridges, as it turned out. The crowd fell back, then surged forward, threatening to break in; the defenders fired a volley into the crowd, wounding several men, one fatally.

Now the riot turned into a siege. Some of the rioters armed themselves and fired back at the house; one of the defenders shot and killed Dr. Thadeus Gale, a leader of the mob who was within a few yards of the house. And then the mob procured a cannon and aimed it at the front door. By this time a troop of militia had arrived; their captain prevented a cannonade by standing in front of the barrel, defying anyone to fire it.

The standoff continued all night. Sometime around dawn, Mayor Johnson arrived with more militia, and negotiated a settlement. The defenders would allow themselves to be taken to jail for safekeeping, and the mob would be reassured that those who had fired from the house would be brought to trial. The defenders marched off under guard; as soon as they were gone, the mob destroyed the house.

An uneasy peace prevailed through the day. A crowd milled around the jail, but a military guard kept them in check, and finally sometime before nightfall they dispersed. Militia leaders, thinking the crisis was past, then dismissed the guard. Their action was premature.

After nightfall the crowd returned. Mayor Johnson was called to the scene; he ordered the crowd to disperse, but they refused. In a well-planned maneuver, they convinced the turnkey to open the outside door to the jail, forced two inside doors, and assaulted the defenders of the house. About half the defenders managed to escape into the night, but the other half, in action more violent than any other riot we've discussed, were beaten repeatedly until they showed no sign of life, and then tossed in a heap in the street.[68]

Although more violent than other riots, the crowd action again followed accepted models.[69] The rioters clearly invoked the legacy of the Revolution. They repeatedly called their victims Tories (even though two were military heroes of the Revolution: General Lingan, the sole fatality of the mob attack, and Light-Horse Harry Lee); they tore off coats and shirts of some of their victims and applied tar and feathers; some of the victims were forced to confess and apologize to the crowd.[70]

The mob seems to have been part of a general "majoritarian" movement directed against opposition to the war. This impression is reinforced by the fact that, on the same night, the mob attacked other "Tory" targets, including the post office, where they understood copies of the *Federal Republican* were being mailed out. They also threatened the office of the more moderate *Federal Gazette*. At the same time, the mob was clearly more brutal and less amenable to control than other crowd actions of the day.

The composition of the Baltimore mob seems to have been significantly more downscale than other crowd actions. The chief of the rioters was said to be a butcher named Mumma. Contemporaries noted a large number of recent immigrants, especially from Ireland; in terms of occupation, identifiable members were overwhelmingly small mechanics, and the large number of arrested rioters not listed in the city's directory probably were lower on the occupational ladder. Very few of the rioters, three or four, might be called "professionals." Two of these were involved with the press: Henry Keating, who kept a printing office, and Thomas Wilson, who edited a short-lived paper called the *Baltimore Sun*.[71]

The composition of the mob indicates that it did not represent the Republican leaders of the city's government. The mayor and militia especially were accused of being in sympathy with the rioters and of doing as little as possible to prevent the rioting,[72] and it is hard to believe that they were unaware of the plans to attack the jail. Yet their dismay at the barbaric behavior of the rioters was genuine.[73]

The actions of the mob greatly embarrassed Maryland's Republicans. Baltimore became known as a mob town;[74] the Maryland countryside—and the nation at large—reacted with horror, comparing the crowd to those of the French Revolution; in subsequent elections, Republicans lost control of the state's government. Maryland was to be a Federalist stronghold for the duration of the war. So pronounced was the reaction to the riot that Hanson himself was elected to Congress.[75] The crowd action did silence the Federalist antiwar movement in Baltimore, but this limited accomplishment was hardly worth the political cost. Indeed, the *Federal Republican* continued to publish, though outside Baltimore. On the whole, the riot must be considered a failure.

Two reasons can be assigned for this failure. One was that the rioters did not convince the public that they represented community consensus. Rather, they were looked upon as a factional or class movement, and this impression was strengthened by their brutal behavior. Political officials could not help condemning such a crowd action; Madison referred to the rioters as "barbarians and hypocrites."[76]

Second, the victims of the riot were too clearly tied to the political mainstream. Though Hanson's views were extreme even among Federalists, he was accompanied on this occasion by many local notables—some Revolutionary heroes, as we have seen, and many sons of well-known families. Such an assemblage made the riot look less like a community's self-policing and more like a civil war.

Indeed, the first crowd action against Hanson's paper, the 20 June mobbing, had been successful for precisely the opposite reasons. The crowd had appeared to be orderly and efficient, and Hanson had been made to look like a crank. On that occasion, moderate Federalists were reluctant to come to his aid, whereas they seized on the later mobbing as a great political opportunity.

The Baltimore mobs were not isolated phenomena. Among other papers attacked by Republican crowds were the Savannah *American Patriot* in 1812 and the Elizabethtown, New Jersey, *Essex Patriot* in 1813. Federalists complained of a coordinated campaign to stamp out domestic opposition. But this campaign failed. Federalist opposition remained vocal throughout the war, ultimately producing a virtual secession movement; it seems likely that the war gave Federalism a new lease on life, in fact.

The failure of anti-Federalist crowd actions tells us something about the party system of the early Republic. By the 1810s, a mainstream of partisan discourse had developed. Both Republicans and moderate Federalists occupied this mainstream, and though they still weren't comfortable with the idea of permanent opposition as a part of government, neither could they succesfully engineer majoritarian reprisals against the opposition.

The Press Ideology of the Second Party System

Though partisanism was a feature of national politics in earlier decades, a mature ideology of party competition did not fully develop until the 1820s. The party strife of the Federalist era was so violent, after all, because neither party would accept the other's loyalty. The politics of loyalty eased only with the passing of effective Federalist opposition after the War of 1812. There followed a brief period of single-party rule in national politics—not quite an "Era of Good Feelings," but, at least in terms of press ideology, a time of renewal for the ideology of rational liberty, which press conductors had been unwilling to reject even at the height of partisan strife.

Political papers abandoned rational liberty as an ideal only in the 1820s. With the rise of mass politics crystallized around the successive presidential campaigns of Andrew Jackson, newspapers were integrated more closely into electoral politics. They adopted practices and a culture based on metaphors of permanent competition and pursuit of interests. This new culture of the press legitimized partisan practices—the active control of editors, the hostile competition between editors, the aggressive appeal to voters—all of which rational liberty had condemned. Partisans need no longer deny their partisanism.

Three metaphors were regularly used to describe this new partisanism. All three focused attention on elections as the central moment of democratic government; all three modeled the reader as a voter (rather than a citizen continually involved in rational self-government); all three endorsed some form of passion or interest as a legitimate basis for political action. The ideology of the second party system was thus radically different from that of the first; believers in rational liberty were appalled.

The first metaphor for politics was the military. Politics was described as a series of battles, contests that were essentially military in nature. Armies of voters were organized by lieutenants (in this case, editors) to wage a long campaign (at root a military term, of course), at the end of which office would be captured. Consistent with this metaphor, the ideal candidates were military heroes, or at least were touted as such. In the first forty years of the Republic, only one president out of six— George Washington—owed his fame to military achievement; of the next six elected, four ran as conquering generals. If the virtues of candidates were modeled as military, so were the virtues of voters. Continually exhorted to "organize" and "vote the ticket," their main virtues were loyalty and discipline, not "reason."

The second pervasive metaphor was the courtroom. Editors were modeled as advocates, and the most successful partisan editors were in fact lawyers, as were many legislators. As advocates, they were expected to promote the interests of their clients actively. Here the metaphor is elastic: in some uses, their clients were candidates, and their readers a jury; in other uses, the readers were the clients. In either case, political discourse was expected to be biased and interested, just as the arguments in a trial. Again, citizens were modeled as voters, expressing their judgments at election time only, and otherwise delegating both judgment and expression to "professionals": editors and politicians.

The third pervasive metaphor was the marketplace. Both politics and the press were modeled as markets, with varying interests competing for favor. Even as improvements in transportation and production created a national market economy, citizens and voters were increasingly modeled as consumers; their virtue consisted in a wise pursuit of their own interests. Success for political leaders and for press conductors consisted in survival in the marketplace.

Although this new culture of the press explained and justified a vigorous pursuit of party interest, public estimation of the worth of the press seemed to ebb. No longer were mainstream newspapers expected to create a utopia of rational self-government. Instead, they were looked upon as engines of political commerce, as armaments in political warfare. These papers did not serve up a feast of reason, nor did they enlighten; they fired off salvos, they bombarded one another and a public that seemed to many to be jaded with ever more hyperbolic rhetoric. This is the newspaper press that de Tocqueville described as debased and irrational.[77]

Within the bounds of the second party system conflict was institutionalized, but, unlike the strife of the Federalist era, these metaphorical battles were fought within a consensus on significant issues. A political mainstream was constructed, and differing positions within the mainstream were safe from majoritarian violence. But that doesn't mean that violence ceased to be a routine part of the practice of political journalism. When the crowd ceased to police the party press, personal combat took the place of rioting. The next sixty years were the golden age of editorial fighting and dueling.

Editorial Fights and Duels

Colonial printers rarely fought. They rarely backed positions that could lead to physical violence, and always depicted themselves as detached from the people who patronized their independent and public presses. The Revolution made detachment difficult for printers. Consequently, printers often found themselves physically assaulted, sometimes by fellow printers. Still printers did not embrace physical violence as a part of their profession. But the press ideology of partisanship modeled the press conductor as a fighter and a dueler. Editors entered the lists, or crossed swords, or threw down the gauntlet, or stood on the firing line—all metaphors from dueling. They also exchanged blows in a more literal sense.

Fighting became a standard feature of journalism in the 1830s, and continued to proliferate in the 1840s and 1850s.[78] Even the most distinguished editors of the day fought: James Watson Webb of the New York *Courier and Enquirer* fought with Duff Green, then editor of the Washington *Globe*, in the rotunda of the Capitol in 1830; fought William Leggett of the *Evening Post* in New York in 1833; attacked James Gordon Bennett, editor of the *New York Herald*, on Wall Street three times in 1836; and challenged two U.S. Congressmen to duels.[79] Fighting was not limited to a party or a region; fighting or the refusal to fight did not set an editor off as being of a superior class.

Fighting was always somehow personal. Obviously, a fistfight involved the physical person. Further, fights were prompted generally by attacks on personal reputation. When Webb attacked Bennett, it was over allegations of stock manipulations and improper loans in Webb's personal finances and insinuations that these arrangements were responsible for Webb's editorial support of the Bank of the United States.

But these personal matters were also political. The editors of the day were public men in a way that was new for press conductors. They carefully crafted their presentation of self in their papers, just as they designed the images of the cadidates they promoted,[80] and they imposed their personalities on their copy at every turn. The presence of antebellum editors in their media was every bit as pervasive as that of a modern network anchor; more so because "professionalism" and objectivity did not discourage or conceal the editor's involvement in the construction of news. The "personalism" of partisan editors was quite in keeping with the nature of the second party system.

The nature of competition in Jacksonian politics was personal more than ideological. Parties loosely adopted ideas and issues as tools to attract blocs of voters to candidates, but put ideas on and took them off like cloaks. Despite claims to the contrary, their primary interest was in men, not measures.[81] In lieu of ideology, personality became the most useful carrier of voter loyalty.

At the same time, broader currents of Revolutionary ideology made public men more sensitive to character. Repeatedly warned that republics collapsed when civic virtue failed, the statesmen of Washington's generation were careful to cultivate the appearance of selflessness. This is the logic behind the title of the most notorious of the organizations of the veterans of the Revolutionary War, the Order of the Cincinnati, named after the ancient Roman hero who, called from his plow to command the republic during wartime, relinquished power as soon as the crisis was past and returned to his farm. Though hardly a simple farmer, Washington himself repeatedly invoked the image of Cincinnatus. His image as a stern self-denying republican was remarkably successful—though even Washington's image frayed during the 1790s—and was the pattern for Andrew Jackson's and William Henry Harrison's campaign depictions as hybrid military geniuses and simple farmers.

The public personae of Jacksonian politicos and editors were not simply masks, however. We tend to think of "personality" and "character" as private and internal, inherent in the individual and easily separated from public image. Such was not the case in the antebellum period, at least not for public men. They thought of character as dependent upon its public reception. To put it simply, it did one no good to be an honest man if one was reputed to be dishonest; reputation was more than what others think of one, it was what one was.

The blurring of private and public described here is characteristic of societies based on honor. Antebellum U.S. society was not uniform, of course; honor was more in vogue in some regions than in others. New England, with its history of religious pietism and its relatively advanced mercantile and manufacturing economy, showed less anxiety about honor than the rural hierchical ritualistic South and the evangelistic frontier. These regional differences are apparent in the history of the most formal category of personal combat, dueling.

Dueling and the Politics of Honor

Dueling was a frequent feature of public life in the United States from the time of the Revolution to the end of the Civil War.[82] Said to have been imported by French officers during the War of Independence, dueling enjoyed great prestige among military men throughout the colonies until Alexander Hamilton's death in a duel with then Vice-President Aaron Burr in 1804, when public outcry produced a wave of antidueling legislation. Dueling slipped out of currency in the North then, but remained important in the South, becoming even more so in the 1830s, 1840s, and 1850s.

The first significant duel between editors was fought in Philadelphia in 1786 between Colonel Eleazer Oswald, son-in-law of New York patriot printer John Holt, former partner of William Goddard, and then editor of the *Gazetteer*, and Mathew Carey, a recent Irish immigrant and editor of the *Pennsylvania Herald*. Oswald and Carey came into conflict over politics. Pennsylvanians were engaged in a long-running debate over that state's constitution, a radical frame of government passed early in the Revolutionary War. Carey championed the Constitutionalist party, who favored keeping the constitution; Oswald's paper was the rallying point for those favoring revision. But the rivalry between the two went beyond politics. Carey's paper was supported by recent immigrants and workingmen; Oswald aimed at upscale readers, and consciously adopted an aristocratic tone. It was Oswald's ethnic slurs more than his political attacks that provoked Carey: the chief offending paragraph referred to an Irish organization called "The Adopted Sons of Pennsylvania" as "Such Arabs, such horrible vipers, such gorillas of ingratitude, and so detested by the whole of Pennsylvania, that all Americans ought to treat them with the supreme disgust which is all that they deserve." Carey responded with open ridicule of Oswald in a poem entitled *The Plagi Scurriliad*, published as a pamphlet in January 1786. This constituted the offense to personal honor needed to produce a challenge to duel. The two met and exchanged fire, with Carey taking a pistol ball in the thigh; then, honor being satisfied, they adjusted their differences. Carey published a conciliatory statement. He later intimated that Oswald, who was an accomplished duelist, had aimed to miss, or only to wound.[83]

The Carey-Oswald duel is typical in several ways. It sprang from a political conflict but its immediate cause was a personal insult; it thus represented the personalization of politics essential to dueling. It is also typical in that it ended in reconciliation. Dueling was not supposed to be bloody; it was a form not of conflict but of conflict resolution. It was a means of restoring honor to the combatants.

Dueling was an intimate feature of the culture of honor. Honor is of necessity antiegalitarian. Only an elite could claim honor, and each claimant must demonstrate worthiness through some kind of personal excellence. Honor thus is extremely functional in societies based on personal or charismatic rather than bureaucratic authority, and is useful in preserving the deference due to the leadership class of a hierarchical society. Honor is a concept ill at ease in modern U.S. society but quite at home in the social world of the early Republic, and subsequently that of the antebellum South.[84]

Dueling survived in the South because of that region's specific social and cultural structure. More than elsewhere, power in the South rested on personal prestige: it was supposed to inhere in a person's "quality," and could not be bought in either an economic or political marketplace. Southern society was thus based on an alleged natural aristocracy, and elaborate rituals of display and hospitality were developed to preserve hierarchy.[85] Dueling fit naturally among these rituals.

This culture elicited specific character traits among gentlemen. A man of honor was to be self-possessed and at the same time self-assertive; he should have a large portion of the passion that southerners considered essential to human nature, but should also be able to keep this volatile element under control. His behavior should reinforce the reputation of worth that his position in society required, and he should be prepared to protect that reputation through appropriate action.[86] Appropriate action did *not* include recourse to the courts. A gentleman would be dishonored by suing someone for libel because it would indicate that he lacked the strength of character to recover his honor by himself. Only women and members of evangelical religious groups could honorably sue for defamation; gentlemen could retain honor only by dueling.[87]

Southern attitudes toward dueling constituted a concealed consensus. In public, southerners were reluctant to defend dueling, and southern legislatures yielded to arguments by critics of the practice, both North and South, and passed laws against dueling, including disbarment from public office and even death as penalties. But the laws did not deter duelists because among the significant population of leading gentlemen opinion clearly supported the code of honor. When dueling finally lost currency in the South, it was not because of the laws against it.[88]

Dueling came to be thought of as unique to the South by the 1830s. Northerners thought of it as a "peculiar institution," much like slavery, and antislavery activists associated it with the brutality of the slave system. One of the richest repositories for reports of southern duels is the abolitionist weekly *Liberator*, which occasionally carried a digest of news items called "The Bloody and Oppressive South," for which editor William Lloyd Garrison clipped accounts of fights, lynchings, duels, and other putative evidence of the moral effects of slavery on the white population. The southernness of dueling was underscored by a duel fought between a northern and a southern Congressman near Washington in 1838.

The duel between Jonathan Cilley of Maine and William J. Graves of Kentucky originated in a newspaper dispute involving none other than the famous fighting editor James Watson Webb. Webb's *Courier and Enquirer* had published a column from its anonymous Washington correspondent accusing an unnamed Congressman of corruption. It was widely believed that the column referred to Senator John Ruggles of Maine; Cilley thus spoke out on the House floor to defend his fellow statesman, and counterattacked by accusing Webb of having been bribed by Nicholas Biddle, president of the Bank of the United States, to support the Whiggery. Similar accusations had prompted Webb to attack James Gordon Bennett two years earlier, and Webb felt Cilley deserved likewise.

Webb chose Representative Graves to act as his go-between, and by him sent a challenge to Cilley. Cilley declined the challenge. This constituted a serious problem because, according to the code of honor, a gentleman must accept another gentleman's challenge or be prepared to offer an explanation why the refusal should not be taken as an insult. If the refusal was meant as an insult, then the bearer of the challenge must feel himself insulted, and was required by honor himself to challenge the refuser. Although Cilley did not declare that he considered Webb an unworthy opponent, he failed to deny it. At this point Washington's metaphysicians of the duel were called upon for advice. Those consulted included leading members of Congress like George W. Jones and Henry A. Wise.

In the end, Graves did challenge Cilley. They fought with rifles at eighty paces, and exchanged fire uneventfully twice. After each of these rounds the seconds engaged in animated and apparently sincere debates on whether honor had been satisfied, and tried to hammer out a compromise statement that would end the combat. They failed to reach agreement, and on the third fire Cilley was mortally wounded.[89]

The Cilley-Graves duel caused a furor in Washington and throughout the nation. In an age of sectional politics, the death of a New England Congressman at the hands of a southern legislator offered an occasion for a playing-out of all sorts of other tensions, including the debate over slavery. Petitions on the duel poured in to northern Congressmen;[90] the duel became a topic of partisan debate on the floor of both houses, and bills were introduced to make the issuing or acceptance of a challenge in the District of Columbia a federal offense. The debates over this legislation offer some insight into the social and political significance of dueling. Naturally, no Congressman would outright defend dueling, but several offered qualified justifications for the practice.

Senator William C. Preston of South Carolina argued that dueling prevented unrestrained violence. Though not an ideal measure, "it had mitigated the indulgence of revengeful passions, which taking the milder and more deliberate course, evaporated entirely, or assumed a less atrocious form. Was it not . . . manifestly less outrageous upon receiving offence to send a challenge than to draw a dirk?" Dueling was not a resort to brute force, like the kind of brawling then common throughout the states. Rather, it was "an appeal to public opinion. It is a mode by which public opinion regulates and restrains the exercise of that wild justice" that goes "beyond the justice of the laws."[91]

Dueling was also said to be a deterrent to wanton assaults on reputation. This was a special problem in legislative bodies, where traditional privileges prevented speakers from being punished at law for defamation. Even northern Congressmen were troubled by the way speakers would "lacerate the feelings of each other by wanton and rude personalities."[92] And such attacks on feelings and reputation were no less substantial than an actual physical assault, in the words of Preston again: "Is there but one kind of assassination? But one kind of murder? Are bodily wounds those alone which are felt?"[93]

This line of argument implied that the spoken or written word was real in the same sense that a duelist's bullet was real, and that a reputation was real in the same sense that a human body was real. This mentality fit well with the familiar emphasis on the sacredness of a gentleman's word. Indeed, Senator Ambrose Sevier of Arkansas argued that an antidueling law would come between a man and his word: "He held himself responsible for every thing he said on that floor, and he would not give a vote to take away that responsibility."[94]

The overwhelming reason given for opposing a federal antidueling law was that it would have no effect. The law's jurisdiction could be—and was—easily evaded by leaving the District of Columbia. Furthermore, such laws were rarely enforced. The public had an undeniable taste for combat, and Pierce for one noted how the Senate's galleries were always full when a personal confrontation was expected, though empty for the ordinary conduct of governance.[95]

None of the produeling arguments went unanswered. Proponents of legislation asserted that dueling was a kind of terrorism, designed to stamp out political opposition; Senator Perry Smith of Connecticut argued that it especially posed a threat to northern Congressmen, who might find themselves in violation of a code of honor they didn't understand and be obliged to accept a challenge from a more experienced adversary.[96] He found the Cilley-Graves duel to be an alarming case in point. Webb had never been an observer of politeness in political debate, and it was well known that neither the courts nor the public in the North would offer him satisfaction for Cilley's offending speech. But the peculiar practices of southern gentlemen allowed him to circumvent the courts, so that "this worthless character, who has slandered the whole north, . . . comes here, selects his member of Congress, and places his dagger in his hand." Dueling was not a substitute for law; it was, like slavery, an immoral institution, a vicious substitution of strength for justice. That is why, he concluded, dueling had done far less to prevent defamation in the South than the courts had in the North.[97]

Arguing the relative virtues of dueling and law was fatuous. Dueling, being an intimate part of southern society and culture, was not to be replaced by libel and slander laws nor eliminated by antidueling legislation.

The irrelevance of antidueling laws to southern gentlemen is easily seen in a closer look at practices. One especially revealing case was a quarrel between editorial clans in Richmond, Virginia, that climaxed in preparations for a duel between John Hampden Pleasants, editor of the Richmond *Whig*, and William Ritchie, son of Thomas Ritchie, Sr., editor of the *Richmond Enquirer*.[98]

The affair between the Ritchies and Pleasants grew out of an editorial attack on the elder Ritchie, in which Pleasants sarcastically quoted three stanzas from Lord Byron's *Don Juan*, footnoting them as references to Ritchie. Ritchie construed this *jeu d'esprit* with terrible literalness: the article "styled me an Old Woman—held me as one on whom he could not wreak his resentment—but threw down the gauntlet to all my breed and generation." Ritchie saw no way out for his sons, William and Thomas, Jr. A challenge was now an obligation. "This was outrageous—thus to reduce two generous young sons, just putting their foot on the platform of the world, to the alternative of death or disgrace" (82–83).

To the modern observer, this seems like a stunning overreaction. Granted, the Ritchies were distraught over a recent death in the family, and Pleasants's attack was impolitely timed; still, the elder Ritchie construed it as an action *demanding* a challenge, and felt that the resulting duel must be a fight to the death. Pleasants himself, as events were to show, was not prepared for the challenge, and so must have thought that his piece had come within the acceptable bounds of editorial unpleasantness. But he was, according to the Ritchies at least, no gentleman.

William Ritchie received the offending copy of the *Whig* the night before it was issued, still "wet from the press," and brought it directly to his father's attention. So decisive was the insult that the elder Ritchie awoke the family's expert on the *Code Duello*, his son-in-law Thomas Green, for earnest consultation on how to proceed. Thus began a set of deliberations that spread to include more and more of Richmond's political elite.

The planning of the duel was an ill-kept secret, and this was considered proper. The gentlemen knew—enough of them that well-meaning outsiders eventually managed to broker an adjustment. But the preparations were kept quite secret from the women. Thomas Ritchie, Sr., even left last-minute negotiations on the eve of the duel lest his wife's "suspicions might be increased by my absence" (86). Meanwhile, William, who was to fight the duel, scored points in his father's fond estimation by behaving with normal gaiety at social events and sleeping soundly.

The status of Pleasants was a recurring problem in arranging the duel. Initially, William sought him on the streets, intending to administer a caning, a reprisal considered more appropriate to an insult from a social inferior. Then, on the advice of a local expert, Dr. John Brockenbrough, one of the political allies of Thomas, Sr., in the powerful Richmond Junto, William sent a challenge through a second to Pleasants. Pleasants put off giving a direct answer to the second, then responded by sending a note directly to William. This "extraordinary note" appalled the Ritchies for several reasons. First, it should have come through representatives, not directly. Second, it named a place and time, but not weapons or seconds. More discussions took place to remedy these defects. Ultimately, it was arranged that William and Pleasants would meet at 6:30 A.M. and fight with shotguns at twenty-five paces—a rather barbaric style of combat, and further evidence of Pleasants's lack of breeding.

As the time of the duel approached, the various parties performed their ritual functions. Thomas, Sr., the aggrieved party, and his representatives negotiated earnestly with Pleasants's representatives, and William, the man whose honor was to be tested, "slept sound as a rock until the morning" (86). Finally, a scant hour before the duel was to begin, an agreement was reached whereby both parties issued statements simultaneously, Pleasants renouncing any slight on Ritchie's honor, and William retracting the challenge. Apparently, the negotiations had stuck on the timing of the statements for most of the night, with the elder Ritchie refusing to budge from his demand for simultaneous announcements, something he considered "a very important point of honor," so crucial that, though he "almost despaired of an adjustment," he refused to yield, and actually "listened till 8 o'clock for the sound of musketry—every moment dreading the arrival of some disastrous result" (86). Over such a technicality he was willing to risk his son's life, so urgent was his sense of honor.

The adjustment was a triumph for the Ritchie family honor. "[D]ear Will . . . is now the *Lion* of the City, . . . 'the observed of all observers'. . . . Congratulations are pouring in upon us. The girls are talking of his animated spirits & charming conversation" as he'd awaited the duel, "and the Politicians are auguring the best results for one who has the firmness to support, what he has the ability to write" (87).

Indeed, Virginia's Democratic party elite was pleased with the outcome. Ritchie proposed to bring his sons formally into the *Enquirer* as partners, and mentioned his plan to, among others, Governor James McDowell, who approved (87). Thus was honor rewarded.

The Pleasants-Ritchie duel preparations underscore just how entrenched the practice was in the South. Despite continual attacks by critics North and South, dueling seemed to grow in popularity in the South and in the West in the 1840s and 1850s.[99] Some cities especially acquired reputations as dueling centers, with their own dueling grounds outside the city limits, like Washington's Bladensburg field in Maryland and St. Louis's Bloody Island in the Mississippi River. Other cities, like Nashville, Vicksburg, and New Orleans, were famous for fatal duels involving editors.

When dueling finally did die, it was because of deep changes in practices and attitudes. Even when it was reaching its greatest prevalence, dueling ceased to be limited to the privileged classes. More often participants were ordinary, if ambitious, young men with no special attachment to traditional niceties. These new men were more likely to choose rifles and shotguns rather than the traditional dueling pistols; as a result, duels became bloodier and inevitably less romantic. It is this postgenteel style of dueling that Mark Twain satirized in reminiscences about his early days as a reporter in the West in the 1860s. Clearly, dueling that could be ridiculed in such a fashion bore little similarity to the social ritual so central to earlier southern society.

The death of dueling coincided with southern defeat in the Civil War and the great embarrassment of the traditional planter elite. It is too much to say that the postbellum South was run by the new middle classes, or that the war imposed a new industrial *weltanschauung*, but it is fair to say that the experience of defeat made much of the culture of the old order seem brutal, foolish, and pointless. The South retained a firmer adherence to a culture of honor than prevailed in the North, but the duel as an institution of honor did not survive.

The last noteworthy rash of dueling occurred in Virginia in the 1880s. The participants were editors and politicians; the occasion was the heated political battle over the state debt, which saw old party lines disappear and new coalitions based more on class and race arise. But by then dueling was clearly anachronistic, used partly as a last resort and partly as a romantic invocation of the past. The duelists seemed to take their affairs of honor lightly, and none of the duels resulted in serious injury.[100]

Meanwhile, the press had undergone a vast change that made press conductors less prone to dueling. News reporting had become a more important part of the newspaper, and the personality of the editor had receded a bit from its dominant position of the antebellum years. Reporters could and did duel, but in general were of neither the temperament nor social standing to instigate or be entitled to a duel. Dueling was a creature of the golden age of the editor, and lapsed with it.

Other Forms of Political Violence

Jacksonian America saw an upsurge in riots and crowd actions of all sorts. Partly the result of social disorder resulting from the explosive growth of cities, waves of immigration, and challenges to the republican vision of the Revolutionary generation, Jacksonian rioting was also a revival of the old Anglo-American tradition of popular action that was so central to the Revolutionary experience. The next chapter will analyze the most compelling of the antebellum riots, those directed against abolitionist agitation. Here I will briefly outline the chronology and varities of rioting.

The occasions for rioting were many. Targets included most nonmainstream political and religious movements. I shall not attempt a treatment of anti-Mormon and anti-Catholic rioting, which included a significant element of hostility toward expression but which have been sufficiently discussed elsewhere. Also familiar are the era's frequent race riots. Of the political movements that sparked riots, anti-Masonry stands out. Its attack on Masonry's alleged conspiracy of privilege drew on the traditional rhetoric of republicanism, religious revivalism, and class hostility toward business elites. Part of its appeal involved an attack on the established press, which it accused of being dominated by Masons. Feeling shut out of the mainstream press, anti-Masons responded by establishing their own newspapers—perhaps as many as 124 nationwide. Many of these took the title *Free Press*. Anti-Masonry, like abolitionism, disrupted the political order of stable competition, and its organs came under violent attack. Among the targets of mob violence were printers David Miller and Samuel D. Greene and the offices of the *Maine Free Press*.[101]

Anti-Masonry was a manifestation of a widespread anxiety over the survival of the national polity imagined in republican rhetoric. Symptoms of decline from the envisioned society of independent producing artisans and farmers were everywhere: the appearance of an urban foreign-born lumpenproletariat, increasing religious heterogeneity (especially the rise of "authoritarian" faiths like Catholicism and Mormonism), the decline of traditional craft control in the face of new entrepreneurs and wage labor, the expansion of slavery in the South and West, the rise of immediatist antislavery politics in the North. Along all of these fault lines tremors of violence were felt.[102]

One of the most productive fault lines was ethnicity. In the exceptional fluid-

of the early Republic, ethnic groups established institutions of all sorts, many in competition with "native" institutions, and in some cases virtually achieved the status of a state within the state. Though the major political parties tried to muffle ethnic divisions, competition often resulted in rioting. Brawls between ethnic-based fire companies were common in many cities, for instance.[103]

The most common occasions of ethnic violence were election days. Election-day riots were a feature of the era's politics, and were thought of as a kind of recreation.[104] But during the 1850s, with the collapse of the Whig party and the rise of the nativist Know-Nothing movement as an electoral force, election-day riots became fierce and bloody. Dozens died in riots in St. Louis and New Orleans in 1854, in Louisville in 1855, in Baltimore in 1856, and in Washington in 1857.[105] Election-day rioters sometimes targeted newspapers, as in the attack on the *Baltimore Patriot* in 1848.[106]

All of this sort of violence can best be understood in terms of a long process of defining a social and cultural mainstream. Rioting was never between "ins" and "ins"; disagreements inside the mainstream were left to elections and legislative battles. Rioting was between "ins" and "outs" or between "outs" and "outs." It was often a response to attempts by outgroups to enter the political mainstream, and in not a few cases an attempt to regain control of the mainstream by former insiders. The most striking cases of this kind of reactionary violence were vigilante movements.

Vigilantism dates well back into the colonial period of American history, and the Revolutionary era is full of examples. But the antebellum period was also noteworthy for vigilante movements. Part of the southern response to abolitionism consisted of lynchings and other acts of vigilantism. Vigilante movements were also common on the frontier.

Vigilantism in the nineteenth century was a recurring phenomenon, and not just a series of isolated incidents. As such, it reflected deep currents in mainstream culture. In the abstract, of course, vigilantism was the displacement of the legal system by a popular movement, and claimed a legitimate heritage in the *posse comitatus*. It was similar in some ways to volunteer fire companies and militia companies, in which private citizens also performed the functions of the state, and can be called, blandly, an example of nineteenth-century voluntarism. But this is in the abstract. In practice, vigilantism was a denial of legal process and equity rather than an expedition of justice; and vigilante movements often if not usually represented a faction rather than the entire community.[107]

The most famous vigilante episodes of the period occurred in San Francisco in the 1850s. Once commonly thought of as a justified reaction to criminality, San Francisco's vigilante movement now seems to have been an expression of economic and ethnocultural grievances coded in the ideologically acceptable terms of law and order. The vigilantes succeeded in portraying themselves as more lawful than the law and as representative of all respectable San Franciscans partly through manipulation of the local press.

Incidents of antipress violence punctuated San Francisco's vigilante years, making up part of the disorder that vigilantes cited in taking over power. In 1854, for instance, John Taber of the Stockton *Journal* killed rival editor Joseph Mansfield of the *Republican* in an election-day brawl.[108] And the shooting in San Francisco of editor James King provided the immediate pretext for the vigilance committee. To understand this incident we must look further into the city's politics and society.

Two opposite classes of people moved to San Francisco in the wake of the California gold rush. A class of bankers and merchants moved in to service the needs of miners; but this business class had chronic trouble getting credit from eastern bankers and suppliers and so lacked the confidence of local clients and depositors. Failures were quite common.[109] Meanwhile, a wave of workingclass immigrants arrived. Largely Irish and Australian, they stood apart from the business class ethnically, religiously—most were Roman Catholic—and politically. They tended to vote for the Democracy, while the business class supported the Know-Nothing movement and, after its collapse, gravitated toward the emerging Republican party.[110]

In the 1850s, Democratic candidates were quite successful in San Francisco. This enraged the business class, already upset over economic reversals. Business people attributed their losses to fraud and intimidation at the polls—an exaggerated charge, though one with superficial plausibility because election-day rioting was common and there was a Democratic machine.[111] The forces of reaction were eager to have a reason to react. Asserting that corrupt politics had rendered the police and courts impotent in the face of rampant criminality, a vigilance committee in 1851 usurped judicial proceedings, tried ninety men, and hung four of them.[112] It retired after that year's fall elections but continued to cast a shadow over city politics.

One key Democratic stalwart was John Patrick Casey. Casey was politically ambitious—a member of the County Board of Supervisors—and an editor of the *Sunday Times*. His paper was noted for its outspoken attacks on banks and bankers; his tone was offensive enough to prompt bankers to threaten him with physical violence.[113]

Casey had a worthy opponent in James King, a self-styled aristocrat, a failed banker, and editor of the *Daily Evening Bulletin*.[114] King's editorial strategy was to play on nativist and anti-Catholic sentiments, trying to undermine the Democrats' open ethnic appeal and rhetorically to disenfranchise the Irish.[115] He also labored to repulse Casey's attacks on the banks. Here his strategy was *ad hominem*. In May 1855 he published a long article on Casey, presenting a résumé full of innuendo regarding Casey's less than honorable past. Casey reacted passionately. He immediately visited King's office and demanded satisfaction; King dismissed him, and Casey, still irate, warned King that he would shoot him on sight. Later that day, Casey managed to encounter King on the street, and after more remonstration, shot him, and immediately turned himself over to the sheriff. While King lay dying, the vigilance committee revived and resolved not to leave Casey's fate to a sympathetic Democratic judicial system. On King's death, the committee took Casey and another man awaiting trial for murder, and after a secret hearing, hung them.[116]

The committee's penal activities, which continued for the better part of a year, cloaked another mission, which was to dismantle the local Democratic machine. It succeeded in doing so partly by expelling alleged evildoers and partly by intimidating opponents. Its success clearly hinged on presenting itself as a law-and-order movement and not a coup d'état. It accomplished this by maintaining strict order in its public proceedings, especially at the outset. When Casey was taken from jail to be tried and hung, the vigilantes formed themselves into a grand procession, eliciting from even a hostile observer like William Tecumseh Sherman admiration redundantly superlative: "The day was extremely beautiful, and the whole proceeding was orderly in the extreme."[117]

The vigilantes also controlled the local press. Only one newspaper withheld its approval—the *Herald*—and it was requited with a campaign of economic reprisal—canceled subscriptions and advertising—and intimidation—public demonstrations and burnings in effigy. By using the strategies first refined by their Revolutionary ancestors, the vigilantes managed to present an enduring picture of themselves as selfless champions of public safety, as true representatives of the people overthrowing a corrupt regime. As a final act in their exercise of power, the vigilantes held elections in which a Republican slate of candidates was elected in superficially antipartisan balloting.[118]

The San Francisco Vigilance Committee seems a rather one-sided example of political opportunism. Not all vigilante movements can be so cynically described, of course. Nor were all vigilante movements so successful. To name just one other example that involved violence against a newspaper, the vigilante activities of the "All Good Citizens" committee in Bear River City, Wyoming, sparked an anti-law-and-order riot by railway workers. A key target of the rioting was the pro-vigilante *Frontier Index*, the famous "press on wheels," run by Legh and Fred Freeman.[119]

Vigilantism in the nineteenth century proceeded from a set of tensions between republican ideology, social change, and localism. Republican ideology posited freedom but did not anticipate diversity: citizens were modeled as just that—citizens, not Irish-American citizens or antislavery citizens. So republicanism did not readily accommodate group competition. But with waves of immigration, territorial expansion, urbanization, rising partisanship, and the fading of the Revolutionary experience as a unifying cultural template, the citizenry became ever more heterogeneous and ever more factious. Yet despite the increase in the number of truly urban places, the nation remained primarily a collection of what Robert Wiebe has termed "island communities," places dominated by a notion of local unity that coexisted with and usually did not contradict proclamations of national diversity. Vigilante movements thus could employ republican ideology and invoke town self-regulation and an image of local community to embargo or expel "foreign" elements. These foreign elements could be ethnic groups, or they could be behavior patterns—for example, drinking and the tavern culture that went with it—or they could be ideas.[120] In the antebellum period, the idea that sparked the most violence was abolitionism.

4

The Crusade Against Abolitionism

> Garrison's generation proceeded from the premise that there were no moral issues
> or political differences fundamental enough to paralyze the energies of free
> government. Forgetting its revolutionary heritage, it believed that moral questions,
> like political interests, were matters for adjustment, and that in exchange for
> their promise of good behavior minorities might achieve a majority guarantee
> of fair play. This assumption meant that the American democracy functioned
> effectively just as long as there were no absolute moral judgments to clog the
> machinery.[1]

The development of a system of partisan politics was one grand achievement of
the antebellum period. Partisanism institutionalized competition in U.S. government on every level. It also steered political competition away from fundamental
moral issues. Partisans sought out conflict, but the dynamics of the electoral
system—the requirement that the victor win a majority of the electoral vote—compelled politicians to avoid making arguments that would offend many voters.
Partisanism encouraged politicians to avoid divisive issues in a way that the patri-
cian politics of the Federalist era did not. It became common for politicians to
invalidate one another by calling their opponents "fanatics"; this meant that, in
effect, to be committed to a cause was to be, *ipso facto*, nonpoliticians. Rather,
true politicians must be flexible in their commitments.[2]

The anti-ideological thrust of partisan politics was strengthened by the nationalization of the major parties in the Jacksonian era. As local factions aligned themselves with national parties, it became necessary for local candidates and officials
to avoid alienating any significant segment of the national constituency. This irony
is seen clearly in the controversy over abolitionism. Here northern campaigns would
come to turn routinely on the reactions of southern voters and politicians, who could
punish the national ticket for the indiscretions of local activists. Presidential aspir-
ants in the 1830s and beyond leaned heavily on their supporters to avoid the taint
of abolitionism.

The antislavery movement[3] came to the fore in U.S. politics for the first time in the debates over the Missouri Compromise in 1820. This controversy was a foretaste of the controversies of the 1830s and 1840s, when the specter of abolitionism would haunt politics in much the same way as communism would in the 1950s.

Several trends combined to force attention toward slavery at that conjuncture. A global antislavery movement was achieving major gains, while religious revivalism, the expansion of market relations, and the ideological aftermath of the Revolution nurtured opposition to bondage. At the same time, though, antislavery seemed increasingly dangerous because of the fundamental opposition of the party system, the territorial expansion of the United States, and an apparent decline in social homogeneity and, hence, social order.

U.S. antislavery was part of a broader Anglo-American movement. In Britain, the drive to outlaw slavery in especially the West Indies built up in the 1820s and achieved success in the 1830s. The U.S. movement drew sustenance from the British. In fact, its critics saw it as British in both origin and intent, and part of the appeal of the antiabolitionists was frankly xenophobic. U.S. antislavery activists maintained ties with their British counterparts in the face of frequently violent hostility at home. William Lloyd Garrison and others used the British scene as a podium from which to address the broader world; their travels to England were reported in their own press as triumphant tours, as stunning symbols of legitimacy.

Domestic developments also fostered the antislavery movement. Most apparent is the connection between the leading antislavery activists and organizations and the religious revival known as the Second Great Awakening and its array of national voluntary organizations.[4] In persuasive style, in evangelical fervor, in its arsenal of media tactics, and in its emphasis on personal piety, moral purity, human potential, and community (brotherhood/sisterhood), abolitionism drew on revivalism's resources.

On a more abstract level, antislavery was also encouraged by the extension of market relations. The market seemed to carry its own rationality, in which atomic individuals, similar to each other in economic potential, with property in themselves and in their labor, interacted on the basis of self-interest.[5] The market nurtured a free-labor ideology that distrusted slavery and was generally utilitarian.[6] Ironically, the creation of a national economic system simultaneously strengthened ties between North and South, intensifying the friction between pro- and anti-slavery forces and giving the South added leverage over northern businessmen, who might logically have been most shaped by the liberal influence of market relations. Still, the "free-market" sources of antislavery thought are compelling.[7]

But the most obvious source of antislavery ideology was the Revolution. The rhetoric of Revolutionary propaganda, especially the preamble to the Declaration of Independence, implied an unambiguous commitment to individual liberty. Even given the pervasive racism of nineteenth-century Americans, the notion of property in men seems impossible to reconcile with the clichés of U.S. politics, especially as deployed in the Jacksonian crusade against special privilege. The Revolutionary era did, after all, produce peaceful emancipation in the North. Antislavery activists took their Revolutionary heritage seriously.[8] They were appalled that, over half a century later, the Revolution was incomplete.

Logically, emancipation seems implicit in the modernization of U.S. society.

Clearly the post-Revolutionary generation, including prominent slaveholders like Thomas Jefferson, expected the extinction of the peculiar institution; its gradual disappearance from the North and Northwest suggested an inevitable movement. But the trend toward emancipation reversed itself in the 1820s. Southern politicians made it clear at the time of the Missouri Compromise that they expected slavery to be a permanent institution; they resented discussion of the issue, even while national politics came to focus on slavery more and more.

Territorial expansion continually returned slavery to center stage. Though tamely forbidden in the Northwest Territory in the 1780s, slavery bedeviled later territorial organization, with the issue being the pivot of the admission of Missouri, and later of Texas and Kansas; slavery dominated domestic discussion of the Mexican War, which seemed to opponents to be a war of conquest on behalf of the slave power; and proslavery forces looked hopefully to the Caribbean, and especially to Cuba, for new horizons. Each acquisition occasioned a new and more delicate debate.

The party system, with its allergic reaction to divisive issues, inflamed discussion of slavery. Partisans again introduced the politics of loyalty. Abolitionists were called agents of foreign powers, were said to promote violent insurrection, and were accused of fostering a tyrannical federal authority who sought to subvert the Constitution and, with it, free government. The debate over antislavery, it was said, could lead only to a bloody civil war—and here antiabolitionists were dead right, though they blamed the wrong people. The intensity and novelty of partisanship in the Jacksonian era made this kind of hysterical misunderstanding of abolitionists' goals and arguments at least useful, if not inevitable.[9]

Further animating the debate was an intense sense of social dislocation. By the 1830s, the republican vision of a classless society of public-spirited rational independent citizens was fading. Urbanization and immigration destroyed the precious illusion of social homogeneity and harmony, while attacks on the traditional system of craft autonomy[10] and chronic hard-currency shortages dimmed the prospects of working men and women. But U.S. ideology premised continual progress toward republican utopia. The disjunction between rising expectations and increasingly menacing material conditions encouraged scapegoating. Not just abolitionists but Mormons, Masons, and Catholics felt the sting of the resulting anger.[11]

Just when antislavery activism took an upturn, then, conditions that encouraged greater brittleness among antislavery's enemies also intensified. Moreover, the very nature of the slavery issue made compromise increasingly difficult. People were either free or unfree. Slavery was either immoral and should be extinguished or moral and extendable. Middling positions ceased to exist. Although even "immediate" abolitionists rarely called for immediate, total emancipation through federal intervention, and although the proposals of antislavery politicians became more and more abstract and legalistic (note the difficulty of making sense of the twists and turns of the Kansas-Nebraska controversy), they still all seemed to southerners to be radical, heretical, subversive. Much as Lincoln pledged to leave slavery in the southern states untouched, still his presidency was unthinkable to the South. One could no more be a little bit antislavery than one could be a little bit a slave.

A series of dramatic events that occurred around 1830 underscored slavery's political gravity. In 1829, David Walker, a free-born African-American from North Carolina then residing in Boston, published a pamphlet entitled *Walker's Appeal . . . to the Colored Citizens of the World . . .* in which he called for armed resistance to slaveowners. The pamphlet was a sensation, going through three editions in eight months. In the midst of the explosive and angry reaction, Walker died mysteriously, rumored to have been poisoned.[12] In 1831, as if cued by Walker, Nat Turner led his bloody rebellion in Southampton County, Virginia. The biblical violence of Turner's rebels sent shock waves through the slave states, giving new gravity to old fears of "servile insurrection."

Blame for Turner's rebellion was heaped on William Lloyd Garrison. Garrison had acquired notoriety a year earlier by establishing the weekly *Liberator*, harnessing the techniques of partisan newspapering to the previously more decorous and withdrawn cause of emancipation. As an editor, Garrison taunted and tweaked; he lamented Turner's bloodiness, but his main response was a nasty "I told you so."[13] To southerners, his shamelessness was unbearable. State legislatures responded by putting a price on his head; Garrison, of course, relished the attention.

Garrison's notoriety as an agitator was a bit misleading.[14] The *Liberator* should not be taken as typical of antislavery propaganda. The movement was more diverse and more respectable than Garrison's example allowed its opponents to claim.

The Techniques of Antislavery Agitation

Mainstream forces cherished an image of abolitionists as wild subversives. Part of this alarmist image was a picture of a vast and superlatively effective propaganda machine, utilizing the most modern techniques of persuasion. The New York *Herald* in 1835 summarized it thus:

> *Abolition Movements.*—The Abolitionists of New York have had an immense printing establishment in Nassau-street, constantly engaged in throwing off tracts, newspapers, and pamphlets for gratuitous circulation throughout the United States mails. Three large steam presses are at work day and night. They possess lists of every lawyer, every merchant, every person of consequence in the Southern States. It is supposed that this single establishment circulates by mail more papers throughout the slaveholding states, than the whole domestic press of the region does.[15]

This image of the endlessly churning steam press; the fine-tuned direct-mail campaign; the exploitation of federal services like the post office, funded by taxpayers' money, for demonic ends; the flood of propaganda; and the wily, well-financed headquarters in New York, plotting a fearsome servile insurrection in the South and loathsome racial amalgamation in the North, made the antislavery campaign seem like a dagger pointed at the heart of freedom and democracy.[16]

Such depictions, while having a basis in fact, cynically exaggerated the extent and techniques of antislavery activism. Although agitation was vigorous and made significant headway, and although the printing press and the postal system were exploited by abolitionists, this campaign did not constitute the kind of novel blitz that critics claimed. Other evangelical reform movements, like temperance, had done much the same thing. Nor were the new technologies of communication the most important ones. The camp meeting was more effective than the steam press at winning converts.

Abolitionist agitation was a direct offshoot of the Second Great Awakening. The American Anti-Slavery Society (AAS) was formed on the pattern of the national evangelical religious and charity associations as an umbrella organization of state and local societies. The AAS's style of organization and communication was evangelical in origin. State and local societies were formed at meetings and conventions at which national leaders often were catalysts; "agents" certified by the national organization rode circuit through towns and villages, distributing tracts, giving sermons or lectures, seeking to leave behind a permanent group of dedicated converts—much like the more familiar Methodist circuit riders. This style of agitation was institutionalized by 1834, when the AAS sent forth its famous "Seventy," the corps of agents trained in large part by Theodore Dwight Weld, most charismatic of the evangelical abolitionists.[17]

In 1835 the AAS began a major printing effort. Among the types of material issued were weekly and monthly periodicals, pamphlets, and, for the less literate, pictures. But these were neither as numerous nor as effectively targeted as critics asserted. Elizur Wright, Jr., who organized the print effort in New York, recorded 72,500 copies of four periodicals struck off at a cost of $908.75 in the month of September 1835. This monthly output would yield an annual total of 870,000. Adding in pamphlets and other miscellany, it would seem that the national organization distributed something like a million pieces of literature in 1835. The unit cost for these items, judging from Wright's figures, was slightly over a penny; the periodicals were distributed mainly to subscribers at two cents a copy, and the difference subsidized free distribution aimed at making new converts.[18] This is a significant mass of literature, but it seems dwarfish in comparison with the print campaigns of mainstream evangelicals like the Methodist and Western Methodist Book Concerns[19] or the propaganda output of a major party candidacy. The entire output of the AAS was significantly lower than that of the New York *Sun* or *Herald*, and roughly equal to that of *Niles' Weekly Register*. Moreover, it seems likely that the audience for AAS publications was narrow, essentially limited to converts and not extending far into the general public; the same people no doubt subscribed to several antislavery periodicals. A million copies would have reached nowhere near a million readers.

Unfortunately, the free distribution of print materials was rather haphazard. In principle, the journals and periodicals would have been most effective as supplements to traditional proselytizing and as reinforcements for converts. Agents did hand out free copies and try to sell subscriptions, and rank-and-file members were encouraged to "arm yourselves with these pocket pistols forthwith," and give them to friends and acquaintances.[20] Within the organization, then, the publications were effectively distributed and quite useful. But outside the organization their circulation misfired, fueling alarm rather than winning converts. Some items were mailed wholesale to elected officials, whose response tended to be overwhelmingly hostile. Large bundles were mailed to unconverted clergymen and postmasters, who were asked to distribute them within their localities.[21] These bundles were the most provocative, resulting in post office riots and the destruction of abolitionist tracts in Charleston, South Carolina, and Philadelphia[22] and eventually prompting Postmaster General Amos Kendall to condone local postal censorship.

The national print campaign of the 1830s, then, was more smoke than fire. It was less effective in winning converts than direct contact by an agent or grassroots organizer. Moreover, it provided a valuable whipping boy for antiabolitionist alarmists.[23]

In addition to the national campaign, there were independent antislavery newspapers. I've already mentioned Garrison's *Liberator*, published in Boston; in Cincinnati, James G. Birney established the weekly *Philanthropist* along similar lines. These papers, and others like them, were usually affiliated with state or regional antislavery societies; they circulated by subscription to converts; and they were important buttresses to the movement. Like the national journals, they tended to be limited in circulation. The *Philanthropist* was begun with a subscription list of 700; at the time of its first mobbing in 1836, it had 1,700 subscribers; by 1840 it had about 3,000, which would be about as high as it ever got.[24] The *Liberator* was supported in its early years by the generosity of free African-Americans in Boston and Philadelphia; in 1833 it had only 400 white subscribers. Its circulation never exceeded 3,000, and usually hovered around 1,500.[25]

These papers were less important as persuaders than as tools for organization and as objects of controversy. They acted as conduits and amplifiers for all regional antislavery activities, like speeches, meetings, and conventions. Editors like Birney were also active organizers; Birney himself was credited with helping to establish eighty local antislavery societies.[26] Antislavery papers were also lightning rods for antiabolitionist criticism. They were mailed to key nonsubscribers like Congressmen and governors, and they exchanged with both sympathetic and hostile newspapers, the latter combing them for "incendiary" material to reprint under a scare headline. The *Liberator* alone had an exchange list of over a hundred newspapers, many of them in the South.[27]

Critics made these papers out to seem much more inflammatory than they actually were. Birney's *Philanthropist*, for instance, carried mostly legalistic argument, and featured a "Slave-Holder's Department" in which proslavery opinion was reprinted verbatim. In tone and conventions, the paper drew on the traditional press ideology of rational liberty. Garrison's *Liberator* was harsher, more acerbic, more personal—it adopted the style of the partisan press, of which Garrison was a veteran.

In short, the communication techniques of antislavery agitation were not radically innovative. Abolitionists borrowed from evangelical religion and partisan politics to create a propaganda campaign that was vigorous but hardly as novel, sizable, persuasive, irrational, or un-American as opponents claimed. Modern scholars have often taken this portrayal of abolitionist agitation at face value; they have thus interpreted antiabolitionist violence as a response to revolutionary and therefore threatening styles of argument. They have missed the crucial point. Violence was directed at what abolitionists said, not how they said it.

A Violent Age

The rise of antislavery agitation coincided with an upsurge in political violence. The Revolution had endorsed popular action as a form of direct government (as we saw in the crowd actions of the Revolution itself as well as in later vigilantism). Crowd action was theoretically licit in the early Republic. But the 1830s saw a real explosion of crowd actions, along with other forms of violence. This upturn seemed to threaten to overturn the social order (whereas earlier crowd actions had seemed to stabilize it), which in turn called into question the republican notion of the crowd as the people acting out-of-doors, and caused observers to warn of the dangers of "mobocracy." It seemed that popular licentiousness—as exemplified and encouraged by "party spirit" in politics—would sunder the Republic. Indeed, in republican thought, government by consent made sense only where the people were well informed and virtuous, not motivated by partial or partisan interest. "Mobocracy" seemed a threat precisely because U.S. society seemed (newly) riven by class, ethnic, and racial divisions. Many of the crowd actions, as well as the fear of mobocracy, reflected an overarching movement to "restore" (one might say "create") harmonious if not homogeneous communities.[28]

The objects of crowd actions were diverse but had one characteristic in common: they were all perceived as subversive of social harmony or unity. Riots against banks, common after the Panic of 1837, were justified in terms of the Jacksonian attack on special privilege, and implied a critique of the banks as tools of class or personal interest. Riots against African-Americans in northern cities similarly reflected a majoritarian attack on a perceived threat or obstacle to social unity and harmony.

Nativist riots combined ethnic and ideological resentments. Partly they were prompted by the specter of alien societies with their own institutions being formed in the midst of the Republic; partly they were motivated by concerns that foreign-born citizens adhered to alien ideologies (especially Catholicism) that would prohibit them from behaving as independent virtuous republican citizens. Debates between Catholics and Protestants centered on the question of whether "Popery is compatible with civil liberty,"[29] a concern that reformers and conservatives shared. Birney's *Philanthropist*, for instance, remarked on "how well the Catholic plan of teaching religion consists with the views of the slaveholder!"[30] Even more extreme than anti-Catholicism was the hostility directed against Mormonism, with its sensationally different religious beliefs and practices.[31]

Ethnocultural and economic interests combined in violence against temperance advocates. "Wet" immigrant groups viewed temperance as a veiled attack on customs central to group identity; their anger was harnessed in some cases by "rum-sellers" with a financial stake in resisting prohibition.[32]

Similarly, ideological, ethnocultural, and economic motivations would converge in the crusade against abolitionism. But, unlike other targets of antebellum violence, slavery was also a *sectional* issue.

The South Responds

The South viewed antislavery discussion as an attack on its freedom and its social institutions. Within the South, antislavery discussion was squelched after the 1820s, though proposals for emancipation were seriously entertained in Virginia in the 1830s and Kentucky in the 1840s. Commentary coming from insiders was an act of treason, from outsiders an act of aggression.

Indeed, the states that were to constitute the Confederacy had never welcomed antislavery appeals. Early liberal publications, like William Swain's Greensborough, North Carolina, *Patriot* and John Finley Crow's *Abolition Intelligencer and Missionary Magazine* had been threatened with violence. And liberals like David Nelson in Tennessee, George Bourne in Virginia, and Risdon Moore in Delaware, North Carolina, and Georgia were driven out of the South by violence or the threat of violence. Benjamin Lundy, pioneer editor of the *Genius of Universal Emancipation* and Garrison's mentor, was assaulted and almost killed by a slave trader in the streets of Baltimore in 1828.[33] But this was only a prelude to the reign of terror of the 1830s.

In the wake of the Turner rebellion, and in response to Garrison and other immediatists, southerners moved by statute, police power, and direct action to embargo all discussion of emancipation. Russell Nye reports that except for Kentucky, "every Southern State eventually passed laws controlling and licensing speech, press, and discussion."[34] Though there were pockets of resistance to slavery in the South,[35] liberals were relatively ineffective in preventing the criminalization and eventual extermination of antislavery there. And, not content to stop at the Mason-Dixon line, southerners also sought to influence northern political allies to pass similar laws. Northerners did not follow suit, and instead placated southerners by mobbing abolitionists.

Direct action was practiced in the South also. People suspected of antislavery activism were mobbed and often lynched. To cite a few examples, a man named Robinson was stripped and scourged in Petersburg, Virginia, for endorsing emancipation; two men were lynched in St. Helena, Louisiana, for distributing abolitionist literature in 1835; Amos Dresser was whipped and tarred and feathered in Nashville on suspicion of distributing abolitionist literature; and Aaron Kitchell received the same treatment in Hillsborough, Georgia, in 1836.[36] Such actions did not stop after the 1830s. The *Liberator* reported that "over three hundred white persons have been murdered" for alleged antislavery activities in the southern states by the mid-1850s,[37] a figure that is high but believable and does not include slave and free African-American victims.[38]

The wave of lynchings spawned a network of southern vigilante organizations. Patterned loosely after the Committees of Safety of the Revolutionary period, these groups were actually more akin to post–Civil War organizations like the Knights of the White Camellia and the Ku Klux Klan in that they maintained secret membership and were supplementary to rather than subversive of the existing power structure.[39]

There is little doubt that elected officials condoned such vigilante action. In fact, their active involvement was generally suspected. Moreover, their official actions were often not much different from the deeds of the vigilantes. The most famous example here is the public burning of abolitionist material with the approval of the postmaster at Charleston, South Carolina, an action that U.S. Postmaster Amos Kendall declined to forbid, initiating a period of tacitly approved postal censorship.[40]

Public burnings of abolitionist literature were common in the South throughout the antebellum period. These were often festive ritual occasions, with leading citizens and constituted authorities presiding—much like public executions, though not strictly ordained by law. In May 1838, for instance, the mayor and recorder of Petersburg, Virginia, ordered copies of the *Baltimore Religious Magazine* publicly burned because of an offensive article on "Bible Slavery,"[41] and Angelina Grimke's *Appeal to the Christian Women of the South* was publicly burned in Charleston, South Carolina, in 1836.[42]

Southerners tried to stifle the slavery debate both North and South. The reasons they gave ranged from fear of slave rebellion to defense of the constitutional rights of self-governing states. In the process, ironically, they helped move slavery higher on the agenda of national discussion by looking for implications for slavery's future in every act of the national government and every stratagem of a national political party. They zealously policed their northern political allies, whose response, at least initially, was surprisingly docile. Northern politicians endorsed the southern abolitionist witch-hunt, so much so that antislavery activists would accuse both parties of having sold out to the "slave power."

The North Responds

Northern support of antiabolitionism was rooted in simple practical concerns. On one level, northern partisans were aware that antislavery debate could cause only harm in both the short and long run to their party's chances of winning national office. On a less interested level, northerners were convinced that antislavery agitation would in the long run lead to the dissolution of the Union. Having only recently survived the nullification threat from South Carolina over the Tariff of 1832, national leaders were justifiably concerned that even more vigorous measures would greet northern interference with slavery.

Northern leaders of both parties therefore sought to create a reassuring display of northern public opinion. They used techniques refined by the mass political campaigns of the 1820s—the monster demonstration, the public mass meeting, partisan newspapers, legislative resolutions, state addresses, conventions, and ultimately rioting—to assure the South that responsible northerners were committed to stamping out abolitionism.

Especially noteworthy was a spate of public meetings throughout northern cities in the mid-1830s.[43] Such meetings were usually led by established partisans who, for the sake of appearances, drafted leading citizens to lend their names to the meetings' resolutions. At the outset of such a meeting, a "president," "secretary," and other officers would be chosen, usually by acclamation, and a committee appointed to draft resolutions. All of this would have been carefully prearranged, though the form of the public meeting gave the illusion that the resolutions were a spontaneous expression of public opinion.[44] Afterward, an official report of the meeting, carrying the officers' names and the text of the resolutions, would be published in the city's newspapers, which would in turn be sent out through the papers' exchange networks to give the impression that the city was "correct" in its attitudes on abolitionism. The resolutions of the antiabolitionist meetings of the 1830s make for disturbing reading, especially because they express what civic leaders wanted the world to think of the state of public opinion in their locality. At the extreme, they held abolitionists "worthy of immediate death,"[45] a direct endorsement of lynch law.

These sentiments were demanded by the political system, or so party leaders believed. Especially as the presidential election of 1836 approached, Democratic leaders felt the need to offset rumors that their candidate Martin Van Buren harbored antislavery sentiments. Andrew Jackson's State of the Union Address in late 1835, which called into question the constitutionality of antislavery agitation (as interference in the internal affairs of sovereign states), and New York Governor William L. Marcy's equally hostile annual address, were clearly aimed at preventing a southern bolt from the old Jacksonian alliance. Ironically, in 1840 the Whigs would have the same problem with their candidate, William Henry Harrison.[46]

The antiabolitionist riots of the 1830s were outgrowths, in part, of this attempt at constructing public opinion. Mass meetings usually preceded riots; riots were often led by the organizers—both visible and behind the scenes—of the meetings; occasionally riots were meetings that went critical and could no longer be controlled.

The Flow of Antiabolitionist Violence

In the course of my research, I took note of a total of 134 cases of direct action—almost all crowd actions—directed against real or suspected abolitionists and their meetings and media (see Appendix B). Twenty-four of these, between a fifth and a sixth of all cases, were directed against the press in one form or another. Many more were directed against lectures and lecturers.

Not all antiabolitionist actions were reported. Mobbings of antislavery lecturers, for instance, were noted usually only when the lecturer himself or herself bothered to write to an antislavery newspaper; this was by no means routine. Freshman agents were more likely to report attacks than veterans; when he returned to the field in 1840, for instance, Sereno Streeter wrote to Weld that "I have been obliged to encounter more mobs than when out before." But he went on to say that "I have not reported them to any of the papers because I am tired of [reading] about them and I suppose that you had a surfeit of such notices."[47]

Antiabolitionist violence did not disappear in 1836 or in 1840, even if fewer incidents were reported. Indeed, Jonathan Walker was surprised that the proprietor of the meeting hall in Charlestown, New Hampshire, wanted assurances on damages before letting abolitionists meet there in 1846, "for I supposed the days of mobbing abolitionists had gone by, in this section of the country." In fact, even at that late date—sixteen years after the establishment of the *Liberator*—a crowd harassed the meeting, making noise, throwing rocks and even a pumpkin.[48]

The cases I've found represent only a fraction of all cases of antiabolitionist violence. For a time lecturers and agents entering new territory could expect to encounter at least a volley of rotten eggs, a treatment similar in intent to the more famous tar and feathers. But even in cases where overt violence was not manifested, antislavery agitators were subjected to relentless pressure and abuse. The mainstream press and opinion leaders—elected officials, party regulars, most of the clergy—were unremittingly hostile to the antislavery crusade. In despair, one abolitionist asserted, along with de Tocqueville, that "the only real liberty enjoyed in America, is the liberty to think, and speak, and act, as the prevailing voice of an irresponsible, lawless majority may dictate."[49]

Still, antiabolitionist violence seems to have waned after 1845. After that date, the Mexican War and the question of organizing the territories conquered in it forced antislavery politics onto the agendas of the major parties. Though violence flared up in the North around the time of the Compromise of 1850 and even more so with the Kansas controversy, most of the incidents I've found after 1845 dealt with the borders between North and South rather than divisions within northern society. Meanwhile, many Whigs and a significant number of "Barnburner" Democrats took up the cause of limiting the expansion of slavery while remaining loyal to their parties. When the Whig party fell apart in the 1850s, though, the formation of an explicitly antislavery Republican party with its distinct free-labor ideology again introduced an element of moral fundamentalism that mass politics found a bit indigestible.[50] And more extreme violence attended the rituals of self-government in Kansas at the time, as we shall see in the next chapter.

The Causes of Northern Mobbing

The reasons for northern antiabolitionist rioting have been much discussed by historians.[51] The range of reasons offered is broad and various, including social change, social psychology, and a communications revolution. Many of these causes contributed, as we shall see in studying some of the specific cases in detail. Moreover, the precise motives of rioters differed from case to case. I will not offer a monocausal explanation.

But antiabolitionist rioting had certain shared features, including specific rituals, like the inaugural public meeting, and a chronology, that is, the sharp upturn in 1834 and 1835 and the downturn in 1846, that can be explained only in the context of political development. The rituals of antiabolitionism were rooted in the memory of the Revolution, with its style of direct action,[52] and in the habits of the second party system, with its techniques of inventing and mobilizing public opinion. The timing of antiabolitionist actions was very much rooted in the course of national politics, especially the rhythms of presidential elections. Without dismissing the insights into the social and emotional strains of the period, I want to argue that antiabolitionist violence was not an outbreak of public psychosis but a function of the structure of politics. It was a case of leaders mobilizing an engaged public to police the realm of political discourse. With this in mind, we can review some of the main contributing causes to antiabolitionist violence. There are two types of motives: the reasons that antiabolitionists themselves gave, and the reasons that critics and historians have assigned. These two overlap more than one might think.

One reason that antiabolitionists cited that is not credible is public hysteria. There is no reason to believe that rioting against antislavery agitators was ever much inspired by irrational fears of social upheaval, much as mainstream leaders liked to warn abolitionists. Most crowd actions were well organized and not very spontaneous; participants were generally not swept up against their will in a tide of emotion. Instead, many of these actions—especially eggings and other harassments of abolitionist lecturers—were like team sports to the "mob," a form of recreation, not an eruption of social warfare. The habit of attributing crowd actions to public fury was, just as abolitionists claimed, a tactic in the overall strategy of blaming the victim. "Responsible" leaders insisted that antislavery activities were too provocative in an atmosphere of "inflamed public sentiment," even while they were taking steps to further inflame public sentiment.[53]

Somewhat more believable were claims that abolitionism would lead to disunion and disorder. A letter in the Cincinnati *Whig* at the time of the mobbing of the *Philanthropist* in 1836 put it succinctly: "Are not the lives of thousands and thousands of our citizens threatened? The Government menaced and the union, tottering upon the verge of a dissolution, through the machinations of a few individuals amongst us?"[54] The primal fear was of slave insurrection. Though no direct link can be made between antislavery agitation and slave rebelliousness, and though it seems likely that no such link existed, still the fear of antislavery debate touching off a series of Nat Turners throughout the South was venerable, and understandable.[55] Even after antiabolitionists stopped invoking impending insurrection, they maintained that antislavery agitation would serve only to disrupt the union and lead to civil war. This fear is much more difficult to dismiss as groundless.[56]

Ironically, even while claiming that abolitionism would undermine the Union, opponents insisted that it was an attempt to extend federal authority into areas where it did not belong. Northern antiabolitionists were generally pro-Union, but they also believed in states' rights. They maintained that abolitionists wanted to force the South to free its slaves through federal action, and that this would constitute a dangerous expansion of central power.[57] One special threat of increased federal interference was to property rights. If the central government were to be allowed to confiscate property in slaves, then might it not attack other forms of property as well?[58]

The nationalism of antiabolitionists also surfaced in their suspicion of "foreign elements" in abolitionism. Abolitionists were accused of "doing the work of the Autocrats and lordlings of Europe."[59] This was an especially opportune tack because the working classes of antebellum cities and towns, whose numbers would bulk up antiabolitionist crowds, tended to be deeply suspicious of the British. Indeed, the 1834 New York antiabolition riots started when a crowd gathered to harass a British actor who had been overheard making anti-American comments.[60] Abolitionists made themselves vulnerable by trumpeting the success of their tours of England; Garrison noted the effectiveness of the charge that "we had visited England for the purpose of aspersing the character of America."[61]

A final element of the antiabolitionist rationale for violence was fear of racial amalgamation. Racism was part of the common sense of the antebellum North, especially among laborers and Irish immigrants,[62] and violent hostility toward African-Americans was frequently channeled against antislavery activists.[63] Abolitionists' critics labeled them as proponents of racial amalgamation,[64] a term that evoked horror in a way that is hard to understand. But antiabolitionists were quite explicit; the preservation of white supremacy and racial purity was not a hidden agenda nor a covert motivation.[65]

These arguments combined to form an effective explanation for antiabolitionist violence. This is not to say that all these items of belief were deeply held or that they constituted the true motives of rioters. On the contrary, it is hard to imagine the leaders of antiabolitionist mobs sincerely believing that Arthur and Lewis Tappan wanted the federal government to confiscate their property and force their daughters to marry freed slaves. But taken together, their arguments pushed enough buttons in the public rhetorical switchboard to allow their call for action to reach its intended audience. In other words, antiabolitionist rhetoric provided an effective ideology for promoting violent suppression.

Beyond the concerns that antiabolitionists admitted, there were a number of impulses, conscious and unconscious, that prompted violence. One was the competition between mainstream and evangelical religions, part of the dynamic of the Second Great Awakening. Another was a divergence in social class and mentality. The antislavery constituency was generally middle class: partly the new middle class of professionals, manufacturers, and entrepreneurs; partly but less prominently the old middle class of artisans and farmers. Antiabolitionist mobs were generally composed of an alliance between upper-class merchants and working-class skilled laborers.[66] Abolitionists tended, then, to be more evangelical, more middle class, and more involved in the new market economy than their opponents.

Abolitionists were also less attached to the party system than their opponents. We have already noted the hostility of the major parties toward the slavery issue.[67] Abolitionists made frequent reference to this.[68] They asserted that antiabolitionist violence was so common because the officials charged with protecting the public peace tended to belong to one of the major parties and tended to sympathize with the rioters.[69] Antislavery activists tended to have weak party identification; those who did have electoral ambitions sought to use the slavery issue to "restore their lost influence through a disruption of the political structure."[70] In any event, antislavery presented a challenge to the nonideological discipline that allowed the parties to operate.[71]

Because the parties controlled much of the mainstream press, abolitionism became a frequent target of editorial nastiness too. Abolitionists generally blamed the press for inciting riots, and newspapers rarely condemned anti-abolitionist rioters.[72]

We can thus identify four underlying causes of or explanations for antiabolitionist violence: (1) antiabolitionism was an extension of racial animosity; (2) antiabolitionism was an expression of underlying ethnocultural tensions, involving religion, ethnicity, and mentality, and perhaps rooted in social class; (3) antiabolitionism was an expression of economic self-interest on the part of northern merchants and their dependents; (4) antiabolitionism was a function of the party system, promoted by partisan leaders and through the partisan press. All of these causes and explanations are compelling in their own way; all came into play, as we shall see, in specific instances.

It should be noted that even the combination of an ideological justification for rioting with severe underlying tensions did not make violence inevitable. For every case in which violence greeted antislavery agitation, one could find several in which it did not. Generally, violence was most to be expected when antislavery activists were first trying to organize a society in a particular place.[73] Antislavery newspapers, however, were usually set up in places with well-established antislavery societies. Violence against the antislavery press is even more notable, then. As we shall see, it usually came about as part of an escalating cycle of disagreement, often initiated by a political contest or agenda.

The Antislavery Response

Antislavery activists responded to the violence by invoking liberty. The United States was founded on principles of individual liberty, especially the civil liberties of conscience and expression. The "slave power" and "mobocracy," they insisted, were not just threats to the personal freedom of slaves; they also were insidiously undermining the freedoms of northern whites.

Antislavery activists consistently identified their cause with the cause of freedom of the press. They described the tactics of the southern defense of slavery as a frontal assault on northern liberties. James G. Birney, for instance, defended his publishing the *Philanthropist* against southern critics thus:

> What has slavery acting through the south done for the *freedom of Speech and of the Press*. . . . It has used the refinements of metaphysics and the delusions of sophistry to explain away the obvious meaning of constitutional provisions enacted for their preservation; it has claimed for itself the peculiar favoritism of the Constitution, . . . demanding, with lash in hand, of States sovereign as itself, that all *their rights* should bow in submission.[74]

This was a compelling image: the southern slavemaster demanding obedience from the northern freeman.

Antiabolitionists countered by charging abolitionists with licentiousness, in much the same terms as Tories had been castigated during the Revolution. Thus James F. Conover, editor of the Cincinnati *Whig*, argued in 1836 that "abolitionist papers are licentious and demoralizing, and occupy a ground by no means entitling them to legal protection."[75] An 1836 antiabolitionist meeting resolved that although freedom of speech and press are "among the most sacred provisions of the constitution," yet they must not be used "in such a manner as to injure the acknowledged rights of others." Abolitionist propaganda did just that by inciting slave rebellion and promoting disunion.[76]

Abolitionists firmly rejected the charge of licentiousness. They denied that they were either fanatical or treasonous.[77] Some even rejected the relevance of the standard of licentiousness, calling it "the name by which every man designates more liberty than is agreeable to his own taste.... To make a distinction between liberty and licentiousness is mere cant."[78] For the most part, though, they seemed to agree that licentiousness was a bad thing, and eschewed "extravagance of speech," insisting that the only "door to the heart" was the "understanding."[79]

On the contrary, antislavery activists insisted, it was the mainstream press that was licentious. They noted—correctly—that partisan papers and mainstream religious journals virtually unanimously condemned antislavery agitation and often condoned violent reprisals; even when they condemned violence, they tended to argue that it was the abolitionists themselves who were responsible. To abolitionists, the spirit of intolerance in the press was the same as that of the mob.[80]

Initially, then, the antislavery movement embraced an ideology of rational liberty. Its adherents believed that free intelligent individuals would come to the truth through an honest and impartial investigation of issues in the public arena of discourse. The freedom of the press was a powerful weapon in the arsenal of truth: "Demagogues and slaveholders may dread its influence and tremble at its power, but the friends of rational liberty and public virtue will cherish it as the *surest safeguard of a free government*."[81] This belief explains the animus in Theodore Dwight Weld's stunning outburst after the death of antislavery editor Elijah Lovejoy at the hands of a mob:

> The empty *name* is everywhere,—*free* government, *free* men, *free* speech, *free* people, *free* schools, and *free* churches. Hollow counterfeits, all! FREE! It is the climax of irony, and its million echoes are hisses and jeers, even from the earth's ends. FREE! *Blot it out*. Words are the signs of *things*. The substance has gone! Let fools and madmen clutch at shadows. The husk must rustle the more when the kernel and the ear are gone! Rome's loudest shout for liberty was when she murdered it, and drowned its death shrieks in her hoarse hussas. She never raised her hands so high to swear allegience to freedom, as when she gave the death-stab, and madly leaped upon its corpse! and her most delirious dance was among the clods her hands had cast upon its coffin! FREE! The word and sound are omnipresent masks, and mockers! An impious lie! unless they stand for free *Lynch Law*, and free *murder*; for they *are* free.
>   Where are the murderers of Lovejoy? "Free"....[82]

The mobs and their instigators had completed what the corrupt political parties had started: the disembowelment of true freedom. James Birney argued that "this tendency of the public mind acts as tyrannicaly [*sic*] as any censorship of the press that ever was established by monarchical despotism."[83]

Abolitionists were careful to distinguish between the mob and the people. Aware of the tradition of crowd action, conscious of the justifications of rioting implied in republican ideology, they argued that "popular consent" was meaningful only when the people consented as rational individuals. "To *exercise* one's rights is the business of the *individual*; to *protect* him in the exercise of them, is the business of the *government*." If the government bows to "the wishes of the mass of the people (as is almost always the case), then the community becomes a mob."[84] The mob was the mass acting irrationally; the people was individuals acting rationally; the role of law and government was to protect the people in the exercise of their rights. Implied in this understanding of freedom and government was an embrace of Lockean liberalism and a rejection of the "community-standards" limits imposed on freedom by republican thought. Add the "free-labor" doctrine of property in one's own person and labor, and antislavery's evolution into a general movement on behalf of civil liberties seems inevitable. In the course of time, it would nurture a women's movement as well.

In their condemnation of mobocracy, though, antislavery activists often misstated public sentiment. Weld, for instance, wrote that, antiabolitionists had "swept the sewers to mob down" an antislavery convention.[85] He shared with other reformers a belief that the "people" were sympathetic, that the violent opposition to antislavery came from a narrow class of interested merchants and politicians and a somewhat larger lumpenproletariat. Even while they condemned the "tyranny of the majority," abolitionists clung to the belief that a large but mainly silent majority was on their side. The true enemy was a slave-power conspiracy.

In fact, many of the antiabolitionist actions were quite popular, though others were, just as abolitionists said, arranged by narrow cliques of organizers. But even in these latter cases, crowd actions were inspired by larger structural concerns. As such, they attest to limits to appropriate public discourse that were not random, sporadic, or idiosyncratic. To demonstrate this, it will be necessary to examine some of the more important riots in detail.

The Utica Mob

Utica was strategically located. Though neither a center of commerce or government nor a cultural metropolis, it was nestled in a region noted for its enthusiasm for reform movements. It was also in the home turf of presidential hopeful Martin Van Buren, who had become Andrew Jackson's vice-president in 1833, replacing the intellectual chieftain of the South, John Calhoun.

The campaign against abolitionism in Utica began early in 1834. Abolitionist Beriah Green attempted to evangelize the area, and debated the Reverend Joshua N. Danforth. Public reaction was hardly enthusiastic, however. The Common Council resolved afterward to forbid antislavery agitation as "highly inexpedient" and "little short of *treason*." A few nights later Uticans paraded through the streets with effigies of "anti-slavery" and "temperance," which they burned, dancing around the bonfire.[86]

In late September 1835, New York abolitionists announced plans to hold a convention in Utica. Immediately, the convention became a matter of national controversy, with even the distant Richmond, Virginia, *Enquirer* editorializing against it.[87] The reason for this scrutiny was Van Buren's anticipated presidential candidacy. In fact, it seems likely that the convention was scheduled for Utica rather than the more likely New York City, headquarters of the American Anti-Slavery Society, partly to capitalize on this anticipated controversy.

Plans for the Utica convention went ahead, despite criticism from both Whig and Van Burenite papers.[88] On 8 October, Utica Mayor Joseph Kirkland, a Democrat, presided over an antiabolition meeting. Also present was Democratic Congressman Samuel Beardsley, who was to be rewarded for his service with appointment as state attorney general and later chief justice of the New York Supreme Court. Beardsley stirred the audience by defiantly proclaiming, "These occasions will find a law for themselves. I go revolution when it is necessary."[89]

Despite this highly visible opposition, the Utica Common Council voted on 16 October to allow the antislavery convention to meet in the city courthouse. Antiabolitionists met to protest the next day, with Kirkland and Beardsley again in attendance, along with Augustine G. Dauby, postmaster and editor of the local Democratic *Observer*, who vowed to prevent the convention "peaceably if I can, forcibly if I must," asserting that the abolitionists themselves must be held responsible for the outcome.[90] The Common Council then reversed its decision. In response, a pro-rights "Mechanics Meeting" was called for 20 October to protest the proceedings of the antiabolitionist meeting. This was not an abolitionist meeting; seven hundred people attended. But the meeting was broken up by a mob and its rump hijacked by antiabolitionists, including editor Dauby, David Wager, Democratic candidate for Senate, and R. B. Miller, the district clerk.

The next day, 21 October, abolitionists arrived at the courthouse to find it already occupied by an antiabolitionist meeting. They retreated to the Second Presbyterian Church and commenced their deliberations, but were shortly interrupted by a mob of several hundred, led by Beardsley, who, in an act of symbolic mayhem, seized the minutes of the convention and displayed them as a trophy.[91] The abolitionist delegates were chased out of town, finally reconvening, at the invitation of Gerrit Smith, in Peterborough. The mob then descended on the office of the *Oneida Standard and Democrat*, a Van Buren paper that had supported the antislavery convention, destroying the type and trashing the office. As a result, the first account to reach the nation's newspapers was from Dauby's own paper, which naturally emphasized the "orderly manner" of the proceedings.[92]

Antiabolitionists invoked a doctrine of clear and present danger to justify their actions in breaking up the convention and mobbing the newspaper. Beardsley had argued that abolitionists "endanger the south and our institutions. So a man may contend that he has a right to smoke a cigar in my powder-house. The inevitable tendency is to sunder the union." Likewise, Dauby ridiculed abolitionist claims to the right to free speech as "a right to perpetuate mischief, disturb the peace of society, excite civil commotion, promote insurrection among the slaves, produce anarchy and bloodshed, and to dissolve the union."[93] These were the standard antiabolitionist arguments.

But it is abundantly clear in this case that the cause of the riot was presidential politics. The role of the national Democratic party in instigating the Utica riot, as well as other such "media events" in 1835 and 1836, has been well documented.[94] The antiabolitionist meeting in the courthouse on the twenty-first had proclaimed that "we are conscious that the eyes, not only of the people of this State, but of the whole Union, are fixed upon our Proceedings"; Beardsley had argued that the abolitionist convention was "intended to degrade the character of the city in the esteem of the world."[95] The role of Van Burenite politicos in the riot was uncommonly visible and clearly meant to send a signal to the southern wing of the Democratic party, which was not enthusiastic about Van Buren's candidacy.[96] Indeed, abolitionists claimed that the rank and file of the rioters were "cat's paws" who "would as soon think of attacking the phrenologists as the abolitionists."[97]

On 19 January 1836, Silas Wright of New York took the floor in the U.S. Senate to respond to remarks by John C. Calhoun. Calhoun had insinuated that New York was too tolerant of abolitionists. Wright recounted the events of the Utica riot, including the mobbing of the office of the *Standard and Democrat*, which he attributed to "some disorderly persons," as "evidence of the correct state of public opinion." He assured Calhoun that northern antiabolitionism "has already reached a point above and beyond the law, and, if left to its own voluntary action, [will be] decisive of the fate of abolitionism in the quarter." Calhoun replied tartly by reading the *Standard and Democrat*'s recent endorsement of Van Buren; Wright insisted that its affection for Van Buren was unrequited.[98] Van Buren's own comment on the riot was even more succinct: he told his adviser, William C. Rives, that "we have taken the Bull by the horns."[99]

In terms of national politics, the riot was a qualified success. Van Buren did receive the Democratic nomination, but won only seven of the slave states. Locally, the riot backfired. In 1836 Theodore Dwight Weld, antislavery's most compelling agent, lectured in Utica for fifteen consecutive nights; when he was finished, fifteen hundred people had signed an antislavery petition, and a strong local antislavery society was formed.

The Garrison Mob

On the same day as the Utica riot, a mob attacked an antislavery meeting in Boston, eventually focusing its anger on William Lloyd Garrison. Garrison was easily the most hated of the abolitionist agitators. He had become a target for southerners as early as 1831; bounties were offered for him after Turner's rebellion. His return from a highly visible tour of England in 1833 had attracted mobs in New York and Boston.[100] Garrison feasted on this notoriety.

Humility was not one of Garrison's virtues. He cultivated an acerbic and self-aggrandizing style, promoting himself and castigating his opponents in the manner of the partisan editors of the antebellum period, a style he'd learned as a Federalist newspaperman in Newburyport, Massachusetts. His "studied contempt for his opponents" was grating—he referred to another editor as either a "liar [or] a malignant audacious *ignoramus*;" he called another's essays "mere abortions."[101]

Boston was pulled in two directions on the slavery issue. On the one hand, it nurtured a vibrant reform tradition, and was a hub for liberal theologians and free-thinkers. On the other, it was tied to the southern trade, had a deeply conservative merchant class, and had a long history of Federalism in politics.

Hatred of Garrison flared up in 1834 and 1835. The spark for this resentment came in part from the controversial lecture tour of English abolitionist George Thompson, which Garrison had helped arrange, and which had set off riots throughout the Northeast.[102]

In August 1835 a mass public meeting, attended by over one thousand people, was held at Faneuil Hall. Addressed by stalwarts like Harrison Gray Otis, the meeting adopted resolutions that protested "against the principles and conduct of the few who, in their zeal, would scatter among our southern brethren *firebrands, arrows and death*," condemned "*alien emissaries*," and castigated abolitionists for appealing to "the terror of the master or the passions of the slave" and for furnishing a "pretext" for southern disunionists. Formulaically, the meeting deprecated rioting; this ritual denunciation was either a sure sign that a riot was in the making or a veiled invitation for one.[103] Ominously, a gallows was erected outside Garrison's home shortly afterward.[104]

On the morning of 21 October, a handbill appeared on the streets of Boston headed "THOMPSON: THE ABOLITIONIST!!!" Announcing that Thompson was scheduled to speak at an organizing meeting for a Ladies' Anti-Slavery Society at the *Liberator* office that afternoon, the handbill called on the "friends of the Union" to "*snake Thompson out!*" and offered a $100 reward to "the individual who shall first lay violent hands on Thompson." The handbill had been designed by two merchants and printed up at the office of the venerable *Boston Gazette*.[105]

That afternoon a crowd gathered at the *Liberator* office. There they learned that Thompson's appearance had been canceled. Mayor Theodore Lyman arrived and urged the crowd to disperse; meanwhile, the Ladies' meeting adjourned. When the crowd grasped the situation, they sought a secondary target. First they took the *Liberator*'s sign off the building and broke it to pieces; the mayor permitted this, hoping the crowd would be satisfied. This was not to be; instead, the crowd rushed the building, looking for Garrison.

Throughout all of this action, Garrison had tried to go about his normal duties; in his accounts after the riot, he was careful to call attention to his utter calm. As the crowd surged into the building, though, he was encouraged by the mayor to escape out a back window. He hid in a nearby shop but was discovered by the crowd, which marched him out to the street with a rope around his neck—whether to intimate a lynching is not clear. At this point, constables grabbed Garrison and took him through the crowd to safety at City Hall. He spent the evening in jail and then was smuggled out of town, but he was back at the editorial desk of the *Liberator* within a few weeks.[106]

The mob's constituency was numerous and various. We have already noted that the instigating handbill was drawn up by merchants; the city's political and religious newspapers were also sternly antiabolitionist and disapproved of Garrison; the Whig editors were especially harsh. The Garrison mob was not an unruly collection of mechanics like the nativist mob that had attacked Boston's Ursuline convent the year before; it was the creature of gentlemen of property and friends of order.[107]

The Philanthropist Riot (1836)

The most complete antiabolitionist riot of the 1830s was the mobbing of the *Philanthropist* in Cincinnati in 1836. This crowd action combined political and economic motivations with the added tension of location in a border city with a large free

African-American population. The prelude to riot played out for a year with rising and falling tension, giving all of the key players ample opportunity to elaborate their arguments. The climax was swift and violent but sputtered to an inconclusive denouement, leaving the key conflicts unresolved.

The *Philanthropist* was the brainchild of James G. Birney. Birney was born into a slaveholding family in Danville, Kentucky, in 1792; attended Transylvania and Princeton; became a lawyer, studying under the celebrated Alexander J. Dallas, and a Mason; was elected to the Kentucky legislature several times; then moved to Alabama, where he was elected mayor of Huntsville. But he was hardly an orthodox southern gentleman. In the 1820s he converted from Episcopalianism to an enthusiastic brand of Presbyterianism, became involved in the Bible Society and the Sunday School movement, and began experimenting with various reforms like temperance. He also worked as lawyer for the Cherokees in Alabama. Gradually, he became convinced of the evil of slavery. His first move was to the Colonization Society; he also became an active contributor to the *African Repository and Colonial Journal*. Even his involvement as an agent for the moderate Colonization Society was problematical in Alabama, so he moved back to Kentucky in 1833. But his reading convinced him that colonization would never eradicate slavery. The crucial turning point was a protracted debate among the students and faculty of the Lane Theological Seminary, which Birney followed with intense interest. Converted by the "Lane Rebels" to abolitionism, he became a member of and agent for the American Anti-Slavery Society and resolved to begin an antislavery newspaper in Danville, Kentucky.[108]

Northern abolitionists were enthusiastic about Birney's plans, but his neighbors were less obliging. Mass meetings and threatening crowds confronted him, arguing that his scheme was "wild, visionary, impractical, impolitic, contrary to the spirit of our law, and at war with the spirit of our Constitution." Suspicion was directed at his funding from "persons unknown" in the North. Birney's "wanton disregard of our domestic relations" was said to threaten the "harmony" of this "slaveholding community." All of this was reported in the nation's newspapers, of course. When Birney still refused to yield, the citizens of Danville bought off his printer. Left without the means to proceed, Birney decided to relocate to the nearest northern city, Cincinnati.[109]

Cincinnati's sentiments on slavery were tender. Tied by geography and economics to southern produce and by history and migration to both New England evangelicals and to Virginians and Kentuckians, the city had been torn by the sensational conversion of the Lane Seminary students to abolitionism, and further rocked when the students went into the city's African-American neighborhoods to set up schools. On the heels of this drama, and in the midst of the nationwide outburst of antiabolitionist rioting that included the Utica and Garrison mobs, Birney's intentions were not welcome. As newspapers throughout the South printed condemnations, Cincinnati Mayor Samuel Davies met with Birney and warned him that the law would be unable to protect him from "an explosion of mobocratic elements." Despite appeals to the Ohio constitution's guarantees of free speech and press, Birney agreed to set up his newspaper outside Cincinnati in the nearby town New Richmond. Even so, the 1 January 1836 inaugural issue of the *Philanthropist* elicited angry protests from newspapers and mass meetings in the South. In Cincinnati, a mass meeting led by the mayor and an impressive bipartisan array of local notables condemned the paper and abolitionist agitation in general as "pregnant with injury" to peace, the Union, and the Constitution, and pledged "every lawful effort" to keep the paper out of the city.[110]

In February the *Philanthropist* changed the place of publication on its masthead to Cincinnati; in April it actually relocated its printing operations. In May it affiliated itself officially with the Ohio Anti-Slavery Society. Meanwhile, the city remained tense; a mob burned homes and businesses in the "Swamp," the African-American neighborhood, in April.[111]

The *Philanthropist* itself remained unmolested until July. Then, in a nighttime raid on 12 July, a gang of thirty to forty men entered the printing office, destroying papers and equipment, including a printing press. The next day a broadside appeared on the streets headed "THE DOG DAYS ARE COMING: ABOLITIONISTS BEWARE!"

This action produced the usual struggle over the representation of public opinion. Though a small band and not a mass of citizens, the authorities treated the attackers as though they were a legitimate carrier of public sentiment. Indeed, when Birney and others called on the mayor for justice, he issued a proclamation offering a reward for the perpetrators but at the same time blaming Birney and the abolitionists for the "riot complained of," and urging them to "abstain" from agitation that would "inflame the public mind."[112] While Birney and others warned of a conspiracy to stamp out the *Philanthropist*,[113] letters appeared in the city's press condemning the abolitionists as fanatics and newcomers to Cincinnati who would "destroy her fair character" and invoking the image of the Revolutionary generation as men who "did not deem themselves the slaves of the law."[114]

The leading citizens of Cincinnati[115] next called the customary mass meeting. Convening in the Market House on Saturday, 23 July, the meeting resolved that "while we cherish as freemen the liberty of the press, and of speech," still, these rights must be limited so as not to interfere with the rights of others. Antislavery agitation had a "tendency to excite . . . the negroes of the slave-holding states," and thus to promote disunion and threaten the Constitution. Vowing to use "all lawful means," the meeting asserted that "nothing short of the absolute discontinuance" of the *Philanthropist* "can prevent a resort to violence." In an ominous resolution added from the floor, the meeting again invoked the Revolution:

> *Resolved*, That we entertain the most profound respect for the memories of the venerated Patriots of more than 'Sixty years since' who in the harbor of Boston, *without* the sanction of law, but in the plenitude of the justness of their cause took the responsibility of re-*shipping* the Tea Cargo.[116]

Soon the printing press of the *Philanthropist* would find a watery grave, like the East India Company's tea.

The Market House meeting offers an insight into Cincinnati's antiabolitionist coalition. It seems clear that the city's mercantile and political elite closed ranks to try to drive the *Philanthropist* out of the city, or at least to send a clear message to the nation that they would like to do that.[117] The presiding officers were impressive, including Mayor Samuel Davies; Jacob Burnet, a former state Supreme Court justice and senator; William Burke, a minister and the city's postmaster; and Oliver M. Spencer, another powerful minister. A few of the city's leading citizens opposed the Market House meeting, most notably Charles Hammond, editor of the city's leading Whig newspaper, the *Gazette*.[118]

Economic concerns unified the city's elite. Antiabolitionists repeatedly appealed to the city's dependence on the southern trade.[119] Especially urgent was a planned southern railroad. Cincinnati's business community was alert to the advantages that would result if the railroad stopped there, making the city an intersection of rail and river routes. Apparently, the southern interests involved were not averse to using this as leverage: in February the planners proposed bypassing Cincinnati in favor of Maysville, Kentucky, a proposal that narrowly failed on three votes. This explains why leading citizen Robert Lytle had spoken at such length of the railroad at the anti-*Philanthropist* meeting in January. But Cincinnati's place on the railroad remained precarious. The Cincinnati papers followed the maneuverings with legislatures and citizens' committees that went on through the spring and summer. In July the railroad's boosters met in convention in Knoxville, Tennessee; Cincinnati's Daniel Drake attended and sent back frequent reports. The anti-*Philanthropist* movement coincided with the railroad convention.[120] The connection was clear enough that both the *Philanthropist* and the *Gazette* would object that "pecuniary interest" be placed ahead of constitutional rights.[121]

Compared with economic motivations, partisan considerations were weak. Van Burenites were still concerned to show themselves antiabolitionist, and the city's Democratic papers were more vociferous than the Whig papers,[122] but prominent politicians of both parties supported the Market House meeting.

The Market House meeting appointed a committee to negotiate with Birney over the fate of the *Philanthropist*. The committee, which included a cross section of the city's elite,[123] was unable to convince Birney and the Ohio Anti-Slavery Society to suspend publication. The committee then published a report, washing its hands of the affair.[124]

On 30 July, negotiations having clearly failed, antiabolitionists moved to take more direct action. In the evening, a mob gathered at the *Philanthropist* office, demolished the printing equipment, and took the presses and threw them into the Ohio River. The crowd then moved on to the homes of the city's leading abolitionists, threatening violence but finding none of the key targets at home; they then visited the office of the *Gazette*, the one established daily that had opposed the anti-*Philanthropist* movement. Finally, in a climax to their anger, the mob attacked African-American homes and businesses, enjoying the destruction till dawn. On the next evening, another mob gathered at Birney's house but was turned away.[125]

Dismayed by the rioting, another group of leading citizens, including Hammond of the *Gazette* and Salmon P. Chase, shortly to become the nation's leading antislavery lawyer, called another public meeting to meet at the Court House on 2 August to support law and order. The meeting's organizers were less established and more Whig than the Market House organizers. They represented a nascent civil liberties coalition, though most were not themselves abolitionists, and hoped that the meeting would reaffirm liberty of speech and press. Instead, the meeting was hijacked, and passed resolutions endorsing the Market House actions and condemning the *Philanthropist*.[126] The riot's organizers thus had managed to temporarily put a face of unanimity on the mob's actions.[127]

Even Charles Hammond, the chief liberal spokesman, was induced to follow this line. In a striking reversal, in the face of mob action, he editorialized:

> The abolition movements are wrong in principle, as is every attempt to assert abstract rights against the interests, the feelings, and the present judgments, of a decided majority of a country, or a community. When surrounding circumstances so affect the understandings of men, as to preclude the possibility of their being influenced by argument, sound or unsound, it is always worse than useless to press facts or reasoning upon them.
> . . . It matters not, if the mass labored under prejudice, or misconception. In that case, the *enlightened very few*, ought to have deferred to the wishes of the *very many*, even if that many were in the dark upon the subject. Courtesy and good neighborship required this of them.

Even though Hammond stopped short of approving "mobocratic violence," he had retreated quite a way from his earlier appeal for the rights of the minority.[128] And his was by far the most liberal of the Cincinnati papers. The others were so hostile to the abolitionists that Birney would refer to them as a "sort of moral mob."[129]

Birney's attempts to put a better face on things were unconvincing. Despite the thoroughness with which official public opinion was constructed by the antiabolitionists, its very artificiality seemed to Birney to indicate broad popular sympathy for freedom of the press, if not for abolitionism. When the *Philanthropist* resumed publication in late September, it published page after page of condemnations of the riot from around the country, as well as items asserting that the riot had been the work of a cabal of which the majority of the people disapproved.[130] Birney's optimism seems unrealistic. In fact, most people seem to have considered the abolitionists responsible for the admittedly regrettable violence, at least insofar as they reelected Mayor Davies, who had played such a large role in the antiabolitionist actions. And the antiabolitionist leadership seemed relatively pleased with the results: southern businessmen were satisfied with the city's orthodoxy, the national parties found nothing to regret, and the city's temporary reputation as a mob city was, as everyone acknowledged, not their fault.

The cause of antislavery did get something out of the riot. In the long run, the riot helped energize a set of younger men and women to worry about the future of freedom and, in many cases, to devote themselves to antislavery: Salmon Chase is a good example. Finally, the *Philanthropist*'s printer and the Ohio Anti-Slavery Society took some key rioters to court and three years later won fines of $1,500— a significant sum—in damages.[131] Such judgments against rioters had been rare but became more common in the late 1830s as new laws were passed to try to stem the tide of "mobocracy."

The Death of Lovejoy

The most famous example of antiabolitionist violence was the murder of Elijah Lovejoy. Celebrated now as the first U.S. martyr to freedom of the press, Lovejoy's story has been recounted fully elsewhere.[132] Some features will bear repeating, however.

Lovejoy was editing a religious weekly in St. Louis in 1836 when a shocking lynching took place. An African-American man named McIntosh, accused of murder, was taken out of jail by a mob and burned alive. Lovejoy's comments on this extravagance were strident enough for Judge Lawless (whose name became an easy mark for wits) to refer to in his remarks to the grand jury investigating the affair. Lawless's other instructions deserve attention. He told the jury it must first decide whether the lynching was the work of a few or the many. It would be obliged by law to indict a few, but if the perpetrators were "of congregated thousands, seized upon and impelled by that mysterious, metaphysical, and almost electric phrenzy, which, in all ages and nations, has hurried on the infuriated multitudes," then the crime "is beyond the reach of human law." The jury returned no indictment, following this odd logic. When Lovejoy protested, a mob attacked the office of his paper, the *Observer*, on the night of 22 July and destroyed the equipment.[133]

Lovejoy resolved to reestablish the *Observer* across the Mississippi River in Alton, Illinois. On 24 July, though, the *Observer*'s rebirth was postponed when its printing press was attacked and destroyed on the dock at Alton. This attack was blamed on St. Louisans, however; the town of Alton welcomed the opportunity of hosting a paper as a sign of cultural maturity. A public meeting the next day condemned the violence.[134]

Alton's welcome became a little less warm as Lovejoy began more and more to devote his paper to antislavery. Handbills were printed up and meetings were held, accusing Lovejoy of breaking his pledge to publish only a religious paper. At one meeting plans were made but not executed to tar and feather Lovejoy. Instead, a mob attacked and damaged Lovejoy's press—this for the third time— on 22 August. Now Lovejoy became involved in an escalating cycle of threat and resolve. The citizens of Alton were determined not to host an abolition paper; the Illinois Anti-Slavery Society was equally determined to keep the *Observer* in business. Meanwhile, an ongoing mayoral campaign pushed political leaders to rhetorical extremes: the Reverend Charles Howard, a candidate for mayor, accused of being soft on abolitionism, had disproven those claims by haranguing the crowd. Thus, when a new press arrived on 21 September, incumbent Mayor Krum watched while a mob destroyed it, tossing it into the river. Then state Attorney General Usher F. Linder led a mob to break up meetings of the Anti-Slavery Society. Undaunted by the destruction of four presses, the Anti-Slavery Society and Lovejoy ordered yet another. At a public meeting led by Attorney-General Linder on 3 November, however, the "people" resolved to prevent a reestablishment of the *Observer*. Both sides were armed and prepared when the new press arrived on 7 November. In the ensuing pitched battle, Lovejoy was killed, rifle in hand.[135] In a telling footnote to the tragedy, the defenders of Lovejoy's press, not the attackers, were indicted and brought to trial. They were acquitted.[136]

Lovejoy's death sent shock waves through the ranks of northern antislavery activists. It was not just that Lovejoy had been killed. Rather, he had died fighting. His death violated the principled nonresistance of the early abolitionists; although he was no John Brown, still many of his colleagues were dismayed.[137]

Lovejoy's death also raised the stakes on the issue of northern civil liberties. It was one thing to destroy property to prevent inexpedient discussion or to make a symbolic political statement; if these riots could cost lives, though, then they must be reckoned with. Appropriately, in the year following Lovejoy's death, a young Abraham Lincoln published a lyceum lecture condemning "mobocracy."[138]

Violence after 1840

There is a persistent claim in historical literature that antiabolitionist violence declined sharply after Lovejoy's death and the burning of Pennsylvania Hall in Philadephia the next year. Nye has argued that antiabolitionist violence galvanized proliberty sentiment. Richards has added that abolitionists refocused their activities from open-ended agitation to petitioning and lobbying Congress, and posited that northern anxieties about abolitionism gradually wore down. Richards supports his claim by showing a marked decline in reports of riots in key periodicals after 1837.[139] Certainly, antiabolitionist violence was most plentiful and dramatic in the mid-1830s. But this pattern of violence did not disappear; it remained a major factor in abolitionist agitation and in party politics.

There are good reasons why antiabolitionist violence should have moderated after 1837. One is a general dampening effect that seemed to be associated with the Panic of 1837 and the long depression that followed. One might assume at first glance that the onset of hard times might increase public disorder, but it seems to have had the opposite effect, at least in the short run. Riots of all sorts were fewer after 1837.

A second contributing factor was the ebbing of the tide of evangelical fervor that had lifted abolitionism in the early 1830s.[140] As abolitionists shed their zeal, they became more pragmatic about goals, about forming alliances with mainstream groups. A moderate antislavery movement formed; radical abolitionists split off from this group, and if anything grew more radical, but they were somewhat shielded from popular violence by their more orthodox brethren.

The main reason that antiabolitionist violence became less common was the entry of antislavery into the realm of partisan politics. In 1840, over the objections of many old allies, a Liberty party was formed, and James G. Birney was nominated for president.[141] No antislavery candidate had a reasonable hope of winning national office, but in some states the antislavery forces elected a few officials who, if the two main parties were divided evenly, could shift the balance of power, a fact of great importance when U.S. Senators were often elected by state legislatures.[142]

Antiabolitionism remained significant during the campaigning for the presidential election of 1840. Again, antiabolitionist meetings were held throughout the North, and many violent acts were committed in 1839 and 1840. Just as in 1835–1836, these actions were intended to buttress a candidate's qualifications for southern support—in this case it was William Henry Harrison, the Whig hopeful.[143] After 1840 antiabolitionism became less salient during presidential campaigns, partly because it didn't work—it hadn't prevented the election of either Van Buren or Harrison—and partly because it did work—subsequent major party candidates were unassailable on the slavery issue. At the same time, party strategists must have realized that mass meetings and rioting weren't putting the issue to rest. On the contrary, both parties developed antislavery wings in the 1840s.

It is doubtful that any decline in violence was due to mainstream acceptance of abolitionists' arguments about the right to agitate. Although newspaper reports of riots characteristically deplored violence, they almost invariably blamed the abolitionists, and as a rule called into question the reasonableness of arguing an unpopular cause.[144] Abolitionists developed a coherent set of civil liberties principles, but they did not transform the ideology of public discourse that the major parties adhered to. Their individualist libertarianism competed with the more conservative corporate liberalism of mainstream politics. It was not until the end of the Civil War that the abolitionist notion of individual liberty, adopted by the Radical wing of the Republican party, would be incorporated into national policy in the form of the Thirteenth, Fourteenth, and Fifteenth amendments to the Constitution.

Some of the most important instances of antiabolitionist violence occurred in the 1840s. The *Philanthropist* was mobbed again in 1841, for example. This time the immediate precipitating cause was racial rioting. In the midst of a September weekend of rioting much more violent than that of 1836, a mob of angry whites attacked the paper's office and again threw its press into the river. Once more, the authorities tacitly supported the crowd's action. And once more the riot was buoyed by fear for the southern trade in the wake of an Ohio Supreme Court ruling protecting certain runaway slaves. Ironically, the *Philanthropist*, which was in serious financial trouble at the time, would probably have gone under had the mobbing not prompted sympathizers to send generous contributions.[145]

In 1845 Cassius Marcellus Clay, scion of the notable Kentucky family and a cousin of the illustrious Henry Clay, decided to start a paper devoted to emancipation in Lexington, Kentucky. Clay was a Whig partisan in good standing and of high temper; his motives were a mixture of stubbornness and opportunism. He reasoned that a majority of Kentucky's electorate were white workingmen who did not own slaves and envied the prosperity of northern workers who didn't have to compete with slave labor. His emancipationism was quite unlike Garrison's abolitionism, then. But his social and political "soundness" did not protect him from violence. After a round of heightening tensions, a mass meeting attended by two thousand people and addressed by, among others, Thomas F. Marshall, nephew of John Marshall, resolved that Clay's *True American* presented a clear danger of sparking an insurrection. A committee of sixty members was appointed to pack the press and ship it to Cincinnati. The packing was supervised by Henry Clay's son, in an effort to make the extralegal action seem especially civil. The Committee of

60 was later tried and acquitted of riot, while Clay suffered universal castigation in Kentucky as an incendiary. He resumed his *True American* temporarily from Cincinnati but abandoned it to fight in the Mexican War. A later attempt to start an emancipationist paper in Lexington ended after three issues in 1851 when his surrogate editor fled in fright.[146]

Several less notorious papers were victims of mobs in the 1840s. In 1843 Samuel Davis suspended his *Peoria Register* under threat of mob action; in 1845 editor DePuy of the Indianapolis *Indiana Freeman* was attacked by a mob; in 1847 M. R. Hall's Cambridge, Ohio, *Clarion of Freedom* was mobbed.[147]

In 1847 Gamaliel Bailey, late of the *Philanthropist*, managed through great tact to establish the antislavery *National Era* in Washington, D.C., without provoking a riot. For about a year the *Era* operated unmolested. Then on the night of 15 April two Yankee abolitionists led a daring escape attempt of about eighty slaves. Fleeing on a sloop up Chesapeake Bay, they were captured and returned to Washington and placed in jail. A crowd gathered and marched on the *Era* office but was turned away by police and federal marshals, apparently sent by President Polk through the intercession of Bailey's neighbor Mayor William Seaton. Again the next night a crowd gathered at the *Era* office but was turned away. An offshoot of the crowd then visited Bailey's home but was dissuaded from serious mischief.[148]

In Newport, Kentucky, across the river from Cincinnati, the *Daily News*, run by William S. Bailey, a machinist by trade, was burned down by a mob in 1851. Reestablished, it stayed in operation for years, changed its name to the *Free South*, but was again destroyed by a mob in 1859.[149]

Conclusion

Continued violence against the antislavery press shows that the issue of free discussion of dangerous ideas was not settled in the 1830s. Under the pressures of political expediency and relentless intolerance, antislavery was driven from its proper place at the center of U.S. public discourse. But it refused to disappear. Instead, it continually reasserted itself in new form: not in the simple garb of abolitionism but in more elaborate costumes, as arguments over the organization of territories acquired during the Mexican War, or, in the Kansas territory, as violent disputes over popular sovereignty and electoral fraud. Politics as then practiced refused to deal in a straightforward fashion with slavery. It left that job to war.

5

The Civil War and Civil Liberties

In the 1850s the structure of national politics collapsed. Under the pressure of an increasingly abstract debate over the extension of slavery, the Whig party splintered, sectional allegiances came to prevail over partisan ties, virtual warfare raged in the Kansas territory, and the South threatened secession. Strength of numbers enabled the North to elect a sectional, minority president, and after the failure of statesmanship, the Civil War ensued. The northern victory in the Civil War confirmed the status of the Union and transformed the Constitution from a compact among sovereign states to a fundamental national charter with priority over state constitutions. Though the radical nature of this transformation was obscured by the reactionary drift of Reconstruction politics after 1868, the Civil War era must be seen as marking a basic shift in the conception of national polity.

The legacy of the war era for political discourse is more ambiguous. On the one hand, a civil liberties coalition was formed out of the ideological thrust of the antislavery movement, culminating in the landmark passage of the Thirteenth, Fourteenth, and Fifteenth amendments by a radical Republican Congress. Never before had the argument for individual liberty under the law been expressed so forcefully and inclusively in the arenas of U.S. government. On the other hand, the period was marked by frequent invasions of the right to free expression in practice. In Kansas in the 1850s, newspapers were treated as weapons of war, and came under literal bombardment in the sack of Lawrence. During the war itself, newspapers were targeted for violent attack with unprecedented regularity; extralegal violence worked hand in glove with government policy North and South—justified by military expediency—to punish opposition politics, especially at election time. And in the Reconstruction South, African-American and Republican newspapers were frequent victims of vigilante and terrorist activity. Liberty under the law was not secured by the Civil War.

At the same time, mainstream newspapers were undergoing a crucial transformation. Industrialization began to turn metropolitan newspapers into large and ostensibly less political businesses; the newspapers themselves then acquired immunity from violence by dint of size and distance from the public. Industrialization also enhanced the division of labor. Reporters became a fixture of the culture of the press, with a mythology of their own; reporters also became targets of violence. The division of labor also opened newspapers to the kinds of labor violence that increasingly troubled U.S. industries after 1877. The mainstream newspaper acquired a species of political security by fortifying itself as a business. Nonmainstream newspapers remained vulnerable, of course.

Kansas, the National Public, and the Metaphysics of Antislavery

From 1820 until the 1850s, the Missouri Compromise had governed federal policy toward slavery in territories awaiting statehood. The compromise had drawn a line north of which slavery would not be permitted. In the ensuing years, territories had been admitted to statehood more or less in pairs, one slave and one free, to ensure parity in Senate representation. This stable model of expansion began to fall apart after the Mexican War, partly for practical reasons, partly for metaphysical reasons. In practice, the Mexican War added an immense amount of territory to the United States, including California, which would be admitted as a free state in 1850. The admission of a Pacific Coast state fostered a sense of urgency to organize the territory in between. Inconveniently, relatively little of this territory seemed ready for admission as slave states: the Plains and other territory along the Oregon Trail offered little opportunity for plantation agriculture at the time. Also, most of it was above the line drawn by the Missouri Compromise.

The Mexican War also opened political debate about slavery in the territories. In Congress, David Wilmot of Pennsylvania introduced what came to be known as the Wilmot Proviso: a clause stating that territory taken from Mexico would not be used for the expansion of slavery. In the North this made sense: the Mexican War could not be justified politically if it was seen as a war of conquest on behalf of the slave power. To the South it seemed like a spiteful and unnecessary intrusion. Debate over the Wilmot Proviso, however, begged the metaphysical question of whether the federal government had any right in the first place to prohibit slavery in the territories. This question would seem to reasonable observers to have been settled when the Old Northwest was organized in 1785, and again with the Missouri Compromise, but in this new conjuncture proslavery advocates were impelled to argue that the federal government had no such power, and that the compromise itself was unconstitutional. The logic of sectional politics made this tortured misreading of constitutional law and history into orthodoxy.

The drifting metaphysical debate about slavery, the territories, and federal authority came to a point in the controversy over the Kansas-Nebraska Act. Introduced by the powerful U.S. Senator Stephen Douglas of Illinois, the act repealed the Missouri Compromise, divided the remaining land from the Lousiana Purchase into two territories, Kansas and Nebraska, and provided that the issue of slavery there would be determined by "popular sovereignty." Popular sovereignty was one of those magic phrases that, on the surface, sounded good to everyone but carried,

Trojan horse–like, an army of difficulties. In practice, it meant that slavery would be permitted and even protected by the federal government in territory where it had little use until such time as residents could constitute a government; this in turn meant that forming each teritorial government would entail a protracted battle between proslavery and antislavery forces. Even conservative northerners reacted with outrage to what seemed the latest in a series of concessions to a militant South; northern legislatures responded in part by passing laws designed to prevent enforcement of the stern Fugitive Slave Act of 1850, and northern voters refused to reelect Democratic Congressmen in fall 1854 elections.[1] As it turned out, what seemed to be a fine way of escaping a debilitating congressional debate on territorial organization worked to keep national attention on slavery and sectional turmoil for years, to nurture the growth of antislavery politics, and to end in the ruin of the Democratic party.

The policy of popular sovereignty initiated a scramble between North and South to claim the Kansas territory. In both sections, efforts were organized to send settlers to Kansas, the most famous of these being the New England Emigrant Aid Society, headed by Eli Thayer. The settlement effort was complicated by geography. Kansas was far from New England—still is—and shared a long border with Missouri, a slave state. At election time, Missouri men would cross into Kansas and vote in large numbers; they were encouraged to do this by no less a personage than Missouri's U.S. Senator David Atchison.[2] Popular sovereignty thus turned out to be a chimera. Before "the people" could "decide for themselves," northern emigrants, southern neighbors, Congress, Democratic presidents, and the national public would have struggle to define who "the people" were.

There was a further irony here. It was generally agreed by all parties that slavery would not likely be an integral part of the society or economy of the eventual state of Kansas. Through all the territorial turmoil, there seem to have been no more than two hundred slaves in Kansas. The battle in Kansas was not over slavery itself, then. It was over the slave "system" or the "slave power," formulations more abstract than slavery itself but no less compelling.

The Kansas-Nebraska Act was signed into law on 30 March 1854. The competition to settle Kansas had already begun, and initial territorial elections were held shortly afterward, with proslavery forces dominating in voting marred by widespread fraud in early 1855. Free-state forces centered around Lawrence responded by drafting their own constitution in the fall of 1855 and holding elections for a free-state legislature in January 1856. The territory now had two governments, both of dubious legitimacy: the one based on fraudulent elections, the other clearly unauthorized by the federal government. The refusal of free-staters to recognize the proslavery government was dangerously close to treason.

Throughout this mounting controversy, both sides were attentive to how things played with the national public. As one of the key players, Charles Robinson, later wrote, "The battle-field was the nation."[3] Both sides were quick to establish networks to bring news from Kansas to the nation. Eastern newspapers like the New York *Tribune* and *Times* sent correspondents to send back dispatches over the telegraph, then reaching west of the Mississippi River.[4] At the same time, local newspapers were begun to feed the alternate news network of postal exchanges. The first Kansas newspapers—the Leavenworth *Kansas Herald*, the Lawrence *Herald of Freedom*, *Free State*, and *Tribune*, the Atchison *Squatter Sovereign*—began publishing before they had any significant local public to serve. The *Kansas Herald* printed its first issue before the first building had been completed in Leavenworth. At its height, the *Herald of Freedom* printed eight thousand copies and mailed them all over the North.[5]

Kansas newspapers occupied an anomalous position in terms of the traditional culture of the press. They were not linked with local readerships, and were not designed to be organs for local self-government. Nor were they set up to contend with other local papers over national politics, as partisan papers generally did. Indeed, there was really no local "arena of politics," at least as normally conceived. Local constituencies were not only firmly divided by political allegiance but also divided by geography, with proslavery forces centered in Leavenworth and Lecompton and free-staters concentrated in Lawrence and Topeka. Free-state newspapers aimed more at readers in Boston, Washington, and even Richmond than at proslavery rivals in Leavenworth. Proslavery forces showed their awareness of this situation in their campaign against free-state newspapers.

The free-state press came under attack early in the controversy. The proslavery territorial legislature passed laws against "offences against slave property"; editors were among those arrested under this broadly construed legislation.[6] More direct than this convoluted legal assault were acts of direct violence. As political rivalry deteriorated into guerrilla warfare in 1855 and 1856, newspapers and their editors were among the most visible targets.[7]

The animus behind these attacks can be seen in the mobbing of the Parkville, Missouri, *Industrial Luminary*. The *Luminary* was a free-soil sheet, run by George S. Park and William J. Patterson; Park also ran a hotel that was frequented by free-soil settlers en route to Kansas. As the rush of Kansas emigration began in the spring of 1855, the folk residing around Parkville grew resentful of the *Luminary*. The tension climaxed when Park printed an editorial about the absence of law and order in Kansas, chiding Missourians for illegally voting in the March territorial elections and implicitly challenging the legitimacy of those elections. A response to this journalistic betrayal was prepared. In a well-coordinated action, an advance guard of "10 or 15 of our most respectable country acquaintances" visited the *Luminary* office on Saturday, 14 April 1855, and detained Patterson (Park was, to their disappointment, out of town). Shortly after, at noon, a crowd of two hundred men arrived. The press was quickly taken into the street, where previously composed resolutions were passed declaring the paper a "nuisance" that should be "abated" and its editors "traitors to the State and country in which they live." The mob also resolved against tolerating other free-soil agitators, and declared that "our peace, our property, and our safety require us at this time to do our duty." The mob then topped the press with a white cap and the label "Boston Aid" and tossed it into the Missouri River.[8]

Park, who had not been present at the mobbing, responded in the usual fashion. First, he denied that he was an "abolitionist," pointing out that in fact he owned slaves. He attributed the mobbing to a "large and powerful secret organization," denying that it represented local public opinion. And he appealed to freedom of the press: "Independence of thought and action is inherent in the bosom of every freeman, and it will push up like a perpetual fountain forever!"[9] But Park's vision of the free press was not shared by his critics. The Platte *Argus* was to the point: "The 'freedom of the press' is not for traitors and incendiaries, but for those confining themselves within the bounds of the constitution and the laws." Because Park had abetted the opponents of slavery in Kansas, he had committed treason against the proslavery laws of that state.[10]

This charge of treason seems insubstantial. But with the creation of a rival free-state constitution and government, treason became a more believable accusation. Indeed, the free-state alternate government elected in January 1856 was intended to undermine the legitimacy of the proslavery government elected in 1855. It was with a sliver of cause and a chunk of presidential support that the proslavery government set out to suppress the free-state movement.

The competition between the rival governments exploded into actual warfare in late May 1856. After the proslavery sheriff, Samuel J. Jones, was shot in the back in Lawrence while trying to make an arrest, a grand jury handed down treason indictments against key free-staters and further recommended that the *Herald of Freedom* and the *Kansas Free State* be "abated" as "nuisances" and that the Free State Hotel, which had been built almost as a fortress, be destroyed. Under this authority, U.S. Marshal I. B. Donelson and Sheriff Jones led a posse of four hundred into Lawrence. They met with no resistance as they quietly made their arrests. Then Jones led the posse as it mobbed the two newspaper offices, throwing most of the printing equipment into the Kansas River. In the most dramatic action of the day, the posse went on to attack the hotel, bombarding it with a howitzer and then looting the remains.[11]

The purpose of such actions was clear. Proslavery forces hoped to cut off an important part of the network by which free-state activists communicated with the national public. The target was not a local medium, and although the rhetoric of community responsibility may have been used, it was certainly disingenuous. Free-state newspapers were not attacked because they threatened the welfare or stability of the local community, as antiabolitionist mobs had claimed (again, often disingenuously); free-state newspapers were attacked because they were a vital part of a national political movement.

Proslavery forces in Kansas prefigured the Civil War more than they continued the tradition of antiabolitionism. In passing laws and mobbing papers, they were using tactics that had proven effective in the battle against abolitionism. But abolitionism, understood as the demand for immediate emancipation, had been ruled out of the mainstream with the help of northerners, who were just as appalled as southerners by the radicals and anarchists and revolutionaries—such they pictured the abolitionists to be—who wanted to unleash the uncivilized African-American. Northerners were also racially intolerant, of course. The free-soil cause in Kansas was something else. It was, above all, a white man's cause, a crusade for the rights of the free independent working man and yeoman farmer. It angrily denied any affiliation with abolitionism or Garrisonism. It was part of the northern mainstream. Its attempted suppression by the South looked like an act of war.

Ultimately, Kansas was admitted as a free state. This was not a victory for

African-Americans; they were denied the right to vote, and African-American immigration was outlawed. One might argue that it was a victory for the free press, but the record of the Civil War years themselves raises some doubt. At least four Kansas newspapers were mobbed during the war, two of them by northern troops, and the federally appointed postmaster at Leavenworth not only banned certain newspapers from the mails but, in the tradition of the Charleston, South Carolina, post office riot in 1835, publicly burned them.[12]

The Coming of the Civil War

The Kansas conflict sparked a national partisan realignment. The Whig party had already begun to fall apart, with its likely successor, the so-called American party, basing its appeal on nativism. As a loose coalition of northern and southern former Whigs, Know-Nothings, evangelicals, and anti-Democrats, the American party could not survive the Kansas controversy but quickly split into northern and southern wings. Meanwhile, in the North, the Republican party was founded as a successor to the earlier Free-Soil party. With the collapse of the Whiggery and the breakup of the Americans, the Republicans found the field clear to emerge as the main challenger to the Democrats in the North. In the presidential election of 1856, the Republican nominee, John C. Fremont, made a respectable showing in the North; he could actually have won the election had he carried a few more northern states.

In 1860 the Republicans nominated Abraham Lincoln. Now it was time for the Democratic party to split into northern and southern factions. Partly as a result, the Democrats were not able to challenge effectively in the North, and Lincoln, who was not even on the ballot in the South, carried the North with enough electoral votes to win the election. Southerners cried foul, and in the next few months began to move toward secession. Lincoln's inauguration saw a dismembered union on the verge of war. In April 1861, the first shots were exchanged over Fort Sumter on the South Carolina coast. Lincoln issued a call for troops, and the war came.

The Civil War presented all the ordinary wartime dilemmas for freedom of expression, plus a couple of new ones. First, there was the problem of political opposition. The war began as a partisan crisis, and a large share of northern Democrats opposed it, just as Federalists had opposed the War of 1812 and Whigs the Mexican War. Second, there was the problem of military secrecy, complicated this time by the fact that the war was fought at home, where it was easily observed by the press and others. Third, there was the problem of world opinion. Should key countries—especially Britain—decide to recognize the Confederacy as a nation, the Union war effort would be imperiled, just as French assistance had helped doom the British effort to subdue the American Revolution. An unruly press, it was thought, could hasten such recognition. Fourth, both sides were hampered in their efforts to control the press by their own rhetoric of liberty; newspaper conductors North and South were attentive to the contradictions between government actions and professed ideals. Finally, the standard practice of newsgathering made it easy for propagandists on both sides to plant "misinformation": northern and southern newspapers continued to copy from each other's columns, following the old habit of newspaper exchanges. All of this made it difficult for governments North and South to control the flow of information and opinion.

The North and South followed parallel courses in controlling the press. In both sections, a combination of governmental curbs, official press releases, de facto subsidies, official and unofficial military action, and crowd action was deployed to prevent disaffection from undermining the war effort or the legitimacy of the government. The South was more effective at suppressing dissent, mainly because a strong consensus prevailed there at the outset. In the North, dissent flourished with every battlefield setback, and the response was often heavy-handed.

Government and Military Policy Toward the Press

Both North and South, a variety of governmental and military agencies were employed to regulate the press. In the North, the main office for censorship was the War Department, headed first by Simon Cameron and then by Edwin Stanton. Working primarily through Stanton, the federal government officially suppressed dozens of opposition newspapers under the rubric of military necessity. Sometimes the suppression was temporary; at other times the military seized an issue or two of the paper. At the other extreme, hostile editors were imprisoned under suspicion of disloyalty; often such imprisonment was prolonged because Lincoln had suspended the right of habeas corpus.[13] The War Department also instituted a system of telegraphic censorship.[14]

Perhaps just as important was the action of the postmaster general in denying mailing privileges to newspapers of suspect loyalty. Most newspapers of the day still relied on the postal system for cheap delivery; most still derived their main impact from exchanging through the mails with other newspapers. The chilling effect of postal censorship can be seen in the action of the Brooklyn *Eagle*: after being denied postal privileges, the paper sacked its editor, replacing him with a safer, less partisan one, and had its privileges promptly restored.[15]

Action was also taken further down the federal chain of command. In two well-known cases, federal grand juries in New York and New Jersey issued "presentments" naming newspapers as disloyal. The New York grand jury's presentment resulted in the revocation of postal privileges. In New Jersey, the grand jury called for the "wholesome action of public opinion." Both grand juries acknowledged the right to freedom of the press, but argued that "in a war . . . the press . . . should uphold the existing government, or be treated as its enemies."[16]

Press regulation by the federal government was a continuous fact of the war. In all, at least 92 newspapers were subjected to some form of governmental restriction; of 360 copperhead newspapers, only 225 remained unmolested.[17] The burdensomeness of regulation cannot, however, be weighed apart from other factors. Without governmental action, it seems, an emotional public would have been even more active in attacking newspapers extralegally: government suppression may have dampened the wave of mobbings that we will discuss below.[18] And, compared with the measures taken by the government in earlier and later wars, Lincoln's administration does not seem harsh. It did not call for a federal sedition law, as was the case in 1798 and would be again in 1917. Still, newspaper conductors were made aware that they were not operating in an open marketplace of ideas; they were to behave as if on a battlefield instead. Union generals made this especially clear.

Generals frequently invoked military codes to muzzle editors and leash reporters. The most infamously antipress of the northern generals was William Tecumseh Sherman, who once remarked that "Napoleon himself would have been defeated with a free press."[19] Sherman represented one extreme of a common belief that northern newspapers were open conduits for military information for southern generals.[20] Of course, northern newspapers were also full of misinformation. And, in fact, the argument of military secrecy was often used cynically to stifle political opponents. The most famous case was the (temporary) silencing of Wilber F. Storey's Chicago *Times* by General Burnside in 1863 under General Orders No. 38, forbidding "acts for the benefit of our enemies" and proclaiming that "the habit of declaring sympathy for the enemy will no longer be tolerated," the same article under which he had arrested copperhead leader Clement Vallandigham. Storey's suppression ended quickly when Lincoln was warned by Illinois politicians of a likely electoral backlash.[21]

The union military was not consistent in its suspicion of newspeople. Some generals favored specific reporters; others savored publicity; many were political appointees; and many had political ambitions. Some believed that news coverage could benefit the war effort. Even Sherman thought the press could aid the military, a belief that he expressed most forcefully when his troops sacked southern newspaper offices.[22] But a general hostility toward the press of the Democratic opposition clearly marked the Union military; the strongest evidence for this is the participation of Union soldiers in the mobbing of over forty newspapers.

The newspaper problem in the South was somewhat different. Two generations of solidarity in the face of the antislavery movement had produced a habit of unity in the southern press; the instinct for loyalty was enhanced by the perception that the South was on the defensive in the Civil War. Hence there was much less call for repressive measures: Confederate newspapers and editors, as well as the Confederate Press Association, founded in 1863, were generally cooperative. Nevertheless, the government pursued similar measures to those used in the North: controlling the telegraph, postal censorship, secrecy, occasional imprisonments. Opposition newspapers like William G. Brownlow's *Knoxville Whig* were sometimes suppressed outright.[23] Confederates also made it a policy to plant stories in northern papers, in one case paying Benjamin Wood of the New York *Daily News* $30,000 to print pamphlets and buy arms.[24]

Newspaper conductors both North and South protested against government restrictions. In the South, the Confederate Press Association was active after 1863, making it more difficult for the government to rein in the press against its will, though cooperation remained the rule. In the North, editors protested against abuses of power. Typical were the resolutions of a group of New York editors, convened by Horace Greeley of the *Tribune*. While affirming "the duty of fidelity" and condemning journalists who "incite, advocate, abet, uphold, or justify treason or rebellion," they yet claimed "the right of the press to criticize firmly and fearlessly the acts of those charged with the administration of government" and denied "the right of any military officer to suppress the issues or forbid the circulation of journals" outside areas of military activity. Aimed at actions like Burnside's suppression of the Chicago *Times*, this protest and others like it, coming from clearly loyal editors, apparently were effective in discouraging more vigorous measures.[25]

Union and Confederate governments and military treated newspapers as combatants, then. A legal and regulatory apparatus enforced limits on the press and punished transgressors. But the Civil War was a large and strange one, especially compared with the Mexican War of the 1840s or the War of 1812, and, if one simply peruses the federal paper trail, all of these actions might be understood as unexpectedly benign.[26] But the true nature of such controls can't be read entirely from official actions. Unofficial pressures on the press are much more eloquent.

Mobbings in the North

Crowd actions amplified (and occasionally challenged) government policies. Put in the context of crowd actions, the seemingly mild press regulation of the Lincoln administration assumes a more forbidding aspect. Frequent and well-timed outbursts of crowd activity disciplined the opposition press, while allowing the administration to claim a middle ground between an enraged people and an irresponsible opposition. Without strategic mobbings, northern regulation could never have seemed so lax while actually supporting boundaries on expression that were rather firm.

A simple breakdown of the 111 mobbings and threatened mobbings listed in Appendix C tells a great deal about the chronology and, by implication, the motivations of these events. The greatest number of mobbings occurred in 1861, the first year of the war, and the majority of these occurred in the two months of April and August. The April mobbings followed the firing on Fort Sumter, and were demands, sometimes festive, that newspapers demonstrate their loyalty. In New York and Brooklyn, for instance, mobs roamed the streets at night and forced newspapers to fly the flag.[27] The August mobbings followed the Union defeat at the First Battle of Bull Run; they were considerably angrier, coming as northerners first realized the seriousness of the war. The August crowd actions were sometimes blessed by government officials. Following the mobbing of the West Chester *Jeffersonian*, for instance, U.S. Marshal William Millward confiscated its press and closed its office.[28] Indiana Governor Oliver P. Morton and other leading Republicans privately encouraged the vigilance committee that threatened Joseph J. Bingham, editor of the Indianapolis *State Sentinel*.[29] The troops that mobbed the Bridgeport, Connecticut, *Advertiser and Farmer* appear from accounts to have been on a quasi-official mission.[30]

The 1861 mobbings seem to have begun as spontaneous outbursts of passion and enthusiasm. Coupled with the developing official policy of regulation, they established boundaries to acceptable behavior. As the war entered its second year, these boundaries seem to have been observed; 1862 saw relatively few incidents of violence, and official regulation also seemed to contemporaries to be rather relaxed.[31]

Mobbings increased dramatically in 1863 and 1864. If the 1861 mobbings can be attributed to outbursts of popular emotion, the 1863–1864 mobbings must be looked upon as rationally directed political retaliations. They were clearly not linked to military necessity, nor did they come in the wake of events—like those of 1861—that would naturally trigger spontaneous outrage. They occurred in response to the rise of copperhead sentiment, and were concentrated in areas where Vallandigham had his greatest support; they often involved troops, and seem designed to drive home the point that opposition to the war was illegitimate. The classic case is the mobbing of the Columbus, Ohio, *Crisis* of Samuel Medary by troops under the command of General Burnside.[32] The mobbings were a telling counterpoint to the hotly contested elections of those years, in which northern Democrats staged a significant recovery. The extent of opposition to the war can be seen in the occurrence of a number of attacks on proadministration newspapers by antiwar mobs, most notably in Dayton, Ohio,[33] and in the New York City draft riots of July 1863, to be discussed in more detail below.

After 1864, as the war drew to a close, mobbings ceased. But then one more outburst of spontaneous rioting occurred, following Lincoln's assassination. In San Francisco, a mob formed and attacked five opposition newspapers in succession; similar actions occurred in localities as disparate as Westminster, Maryland, and Bluffton, Indiana.[34]

Meanwhile in the South a similar pattern appeared. Printers who treated Abraham Lincoln as a legitimate candidate were mobbed or threatened in Lexington, Missouri, and Quitman, Texas.[35] In 1861 an initial spasm of popular hostility drove papers opposed to secession out of operation, usually without overt violence.[36] A newspaperman suspected of northern sympathies was mobbed and jailed in Charleston.[37] Opposition to secession and the war virtually ceased within the South for the duration of the war.[38] Editors who criticized wartime measures or leadership from a loyal position still faced the threat of personal violence in the form of dueling. William A. Courtenay of the Charleston *Mercury*, for instance, fought a duel with Captain G. B. Cuthbert and narrowly avoided one with Robert Barnwell Rhett, Jr.[39] In the very few cases where newspapers promoted peace, violence was to be expected, especially in the wake of military reversals. Soldiers who took exception to the peace politics of editor William W. Holden mobbed his Raleigh *North Carolina Standard* shortly after the Confederate defeat at Gettysburgh in 1863. This was one of five "actual, attempted, or imminently threatened mob actions" against the *Standard* in the war years.[40]

Antiwar Violence: The Draft Riots

In a Fourth of July address in 1863, New York Governor Horatio Seymour, a Democrat, struck a premonitory note in his comments about Union encroachments on constitutional freedoms, including the draft: "Remember this, that the bloody, and treasonable, and revolutionary doctrine of public necessity can be proclaimed by a mob as well as by a government."[41] His warning perhaps unintentionally recalls the actions of the antiabolitionist coalition in the antebellum years. The prowar mobs of 1861 in New York City differed from that city's antiabolitionist mobs of the 1830s certainly in terms of agenda and behavior—they were Republican, and they were not very destructive—and probably in terms of social and ethnic composition. The old "mob," workingclass and in large part Irish, would reemerge in 1863.

In 1863, after two years of war, Union army ranks were thinning as a cohort of enlistments expired. To maintain troop levels, Congress on 3 March authorized a draft to take place that summer. On Saturday, 11 July, New York City held its first lotteries. Despite predictions of resistance, there was little disorder.[42] The unhappy calm lasted until Monday morning, when a mob gathered and attacked conscription offices, destroying records and preventing proceedings. Soon rioting became general, and offshoots of the mob began attacking other targets: the Orphan Asylum for Colored Children, African-Americans on the streets and in streetcars, armories, companies that produced war supplies, and, as rioting wore into its second, third, and fourth days, well-dressed men, even Columbia College.[43]

Among the more prominent targets were the city's Republican newspapers, especially Horace Greeley's *Tribune*. On the first day of rioting, a crowd "composed principally of overgrown boys" formed in Printing House Square, eagerly following the bulletins on the progress of the riot as they were posted at the various newspaper offices there. The crowd also "groaned" the editors of "obnoxious" papers and beat whatever African-Americans happened by. As evening approached, grown men joined the crowd, which became more aggressive. At the outset, the Republican newspapers had expected trouble; the *Times* and the *Evening Post* had armed themselves, but Greeley declined to provide for the military defense of the *Tribune*, even though it was easily the most "obnoxious" to the mob. At 7:30, with a barber named James H. Whitten egging them on, the crowd began stoning the *Tribune* building, finally mounting a charge that carried them into the business office of the newspaper. There they destroyed papers and equipment and tried to set the building on fire before being chased out by police. Several times again that night crowds threatened the building but were held off by police.[44]

The actual assault on the building was just one of a series of expressions of fury at Greeley. A mob looted a house thought to be Greeley's residence and beat senseless a neighbor mistaken for Greeley. Another mob attacked a former city editor of the *Times*, shouting, "Here's a damned abolitionist!" and "He's a *Tribune* man! Hang the son of a bitch!" One witness describes a festive bonfire on that first night of the riot, with men and boys dancing around it, shouting, "Bring out Greeley." Greeley and his *Tribune* had become a lightning rod in the center of this storm of frustrations. And the mob's anger did not disappear after the first day; further attacks were prevented only by massive and visible armed defense.[45]

The *Tribune* was easily the most hated of the Republican papers, and New York's was easily the most violent of the draft riots. But neither was unique. In other cities, other mobs attacked other newspapers: in Newark, New Jersey, the office of the *Mercury* and the home of its editor were attacked; in Troy, New York, the office of the *Times* was attacked.[46] In New York City, the *Times*, which itself had felt threatened, intoned against what it perceived to be a general attempt "by violence and destruction of property to dictate topics for public discussion, or to control the sentiments and utterances of the public Press."[47]

The draft riots did in fact mark a resurgence of the same hostilities that had impelled attacks on abolitionist papers. The crowd expressed ethnic, racial, and class attitudes in attacks on African-Americans, on "$300 men" (that is, those who could afford to pay substitutes for the draft), and on the symbols of the Anglo-Saxon establishment. On the second day of the riot, Roman Catholic Archbishop John Hughes wrote a letter for the *Herald*, apparently the preferred newspaper of the Irish working class, perceived to be the core of the rioters, that began with a none too subtle acknowledgment of ethnocultural tensions: "In spite of Mr. Greeley's assault upon the Irish . . . ."[48]

The mob attacked the *Tribune* as a way of attacking all that beset it. The *Tribune* stood for the war; it stood for the sympathy for African-Americans that caused the war; it stood for the self-righteous Anglo-Saxons, too few of whom would die in the war; it stood for all the insults that those Anglo-Saxons had forced more humble folk to endure for a generation. The mob in its actions angrily dissented from the notion that the *Tribune* was a force of independent moral criticism, a conscientious observer of and commentator on public affairs. On the contrary, the mob clearly perceived the *Tribune* as an active participant in a social contest, and was not willing to concede it a privileged place outside the battlefield. The draftees would be sent to war; Mr. Greeley deserved a taste of war himself.

This was similar to antiabolitionist violence, but there was a difference. Abolitionist papers were mobbed in order to prevent a rupture of politics and business as usual. By the time of the draft riots, this rupture had already taken place. When the mob moved to attack Greeley, it was less concerned to shut him up than it was to punish him for his entire history of political blasphemy and bad citizenship. There was more anger and I think more danger in Greeley's position than there had been in Birney's.

The draft rioters clearly were not the same people who had marched in April 1861, forcing Bennett's *Herald* to fly the flag. Phrases like "the New York mob," which historians have picked up from contemporary sources, obscure the true nature of crowd actions. When we talk about mobs in this period, we are not talking about a single group of people with identifiable interests and attitudes but about an instrument of action or expression. Like the press, it was an instrument that could be used by various groups for various purposes. And, in cases like the New York draft riots and many others, it was an instrument that could be directed against the press.

Liberalism and Constitutional Change

The history of Civil War–era antipress violence shows that at least among the public and probably among political insiders the culture of the press was not yet truly liberal in the modern sense of the term. The model of press behavior that peopled the heads of those who accepted mobbings as the natural working of public opinion was not one in which the press—newspapers in particular—constituted a realm of ideas in which individuals competed as in a marketplace. Rather, as we have seen, it was a realm where groups competed as on a battlefield. Newspapers were not seen as quiet voices talking to undifferentiated rational individuals but as commanding officers marshaling troops of committed followers. During the Civil War, the military metaphor prevailed over the marketplace metaphor.

Military and marketplace metaphors had coexisted peacefully in the partisan press. But even at that time there were limits to what was permitted in the marketplace. Abolitionists and others were seen as outside the marketplace and at war with society; they were depicted as dangerous fanatics who must be silenced. In the Civil War era, the range of people and movements identified as dangerous fanatics or mercenaries in the pay of the enemy increased—something we would expect, given the pressures of war and the consequent opportunities for taking political advantage.

In the midst of war, however, constitutional changes were being forged that would incorporate a more complete notion of individual rights on a national level. Abolitionism had served to create a civil liberties coalition. Beginning with the call for freedom for the slave, and countering the various attempts to silence them, abolitionists constructed an argument for the unity of freedom: slavery will conspire against the liberties of free men everywhere, they argued, just as the southern "slave power" had attacked northern free speech, press, and religion, and then free soil. Freedom would not be safe until freedom for all was guaranteed. This theoretical stance appealed to a much wider range of northern whites than abolitionism itself had, and especially after the Kansas controversy had energized a successful party movement. During the war itself, men sympathetic to this civil liberties position had achieved control of the national government, and with the northern victory they were able to implement a program of constitutional change.

Northern victory did not restore the union as it was. In the antebellum period, the Constitution had been construed as a compact among sovereign states, though the limits of that sovereignty were disputed. The limitations on the national government included in the Bill of Rights were not understood to apply to the states. The Constitution stipulated that all the states would have a "republican" form of government, a clause quite vague beyond forbidding the elevation of a king of Kentucky or the like; otherwise, states were deemed free to limit civil liberties in any number of ways, including the southern states' draconian legislation against antislavery agitation.

After the war, the northern civil liberties coalition set about putting an end to the ambiguity in the limits of state sovereignty. In a series of amendments that were ratified by southern states as a condition of readmission, slavery was outlawed and civil liberties, including the right to vote, were guaranteed to all adult men. This amounted to the nationalization of the Bill of Rights,[49] as the key passage of the Fourteenth Amendment states:

No State shall make or enforce any law which shall abridge the privileges or immunities of citizens of the United States; nor shall any State deprive any person of life, liberty, or property without due process of law; nor deny to any person within its jurisdiction the equal protection of the laws.

The implications of this constitutional revolution were far-reaching indeed. In addition to guaranteeing the protection of the judicial system, it guaranteed the right to participate in the political process. It was meant to insure the equality under the law of all men (though this did not necessarily mean social equality, and though it explicitly excluded women).

Embodied in the constitutional revolution was a reconfiguration of attitudes toward the political process. We might summarize this as the triumph of liberalism over republicanism. Where republicanism had seen liberty as a property of a polity, liberalism saw it as specifically a property of an individual. Republican attitudes had emphasized virtue in the individual, and made the maintenance of virtue a condition of free government; liberalism saw this as archaic. Republicanism had supplied since the Revolution at least a language for justifying limitations on individual freedom. The Civil War era had stretched that language to the point where it was no longer believable: the mobbing of virtually a third of northern opposition newspapers was an act of political, not moral, policing.

The constitutional revolution implied a reconstruction of U.S. society, both North and South, on the basis of liberalism, not republicanism. This in turn implied a rethinking of limits on free expression and a reconfiguration of the arena of public discourse. But the triumph of liberalism was muted—perhaps postponed—by the failure of Reconstruction.

Reconstruction

Union military victory, complete as it was, settled less than one might have expected. Issues like the status of the southern states, which legally had never seceded, and the status of African-Americans, North and South—no longer enslaved, but even in the North rarely enfranchised—defied easy resolution, as even among the victors no deep consensus prevailed. All of this was complicated by Lincoln's assassination and the succession of Andrew Johnson, an ill-equipped political outsider whose murky leadership emboldened southern resistance. In response, a Radical majority in Congress superseded Johnson and enacted a program of constitutional reform aimed at enfranchising African-Americans and breaking up the southern-white-Democrat monopoly on electoral power. After battling sporadically with the forces of tradition for a decade, congressional Republicans gave up in 1876–1877, in the wake of a contested presidential election and in the face of a deep and long economic depression. They had achieved some gains, but left southern African-Americans still only marginally enfranchised and increasingly tied to the old masters, now the new landlords, through a system of debt peonage made ironfisted by depression and deflation. Reconstruction was a failed revolution.[50]

In the South, Reconstruction was a time of great violence. Always more prone than northerners to take the law into their own hands, southern whites were impelled first by wartime dislocation and then by their inability to make use of normal legal and police powers to employ an arsenal of violent techniques, ranging from dueling and fighting to rioting and vigilantism.[51] Two groups bore the brunt of this violence: African-Americans and Republicans.

Racial violence reached extraordinary heights during Reconstruction. African-Americans expected autonomy—not necessarily equality—and with Yankee assistance set about negotiating labor contracts with former masters, trying to acquire land, establishing schools and churches, and forming political organizations. All of these routes to autonomy inspired white violence. Sometimes the violence was personal; assault, rape, and murder were common. In Texas, in the years 1865–1868, 373 African-Americans were murdered by whites, a figure amounting to fully 1 percent of the adult male African-American population.[52] Increasingly often, violence was organized. Leftover Confederate soldiers operated as bushwhackers, and later vigilante organizations, of which the Ku Klux Klan has received the most notoriety, mounted a reign of terror against ambitious African-Americans.[53] (The Klan will be discussed below.) Often violence climaxed in periods of rioting. Hennessey has counted thirty-three race riots in the south during Reconstruction involving more than one death, and they seem to follow a pattern of white attack on African-American autonomy. Two-thirds occurred in areas with an African-American majority, more than a third around election time, and more than half began with a white attempt to break up an African-American political meeting. Though often helpless victims, and almost always the losers in rioting, African-Americans usually fought back.[54]

The frequency of election-time rioting underscores the hostility whites felt toward challenges to the hegemony of traditional politics. One of the goals of Reconstruction was to create a self-sustaining Republican party in the South out of the remnants of the southern Whiggery and newly enfranchised African-Americans. Early in Reconstruction, with some federal protection for African-American voters and a large portion of former Confederates disfranchised, Republicans were influential, even dominant, in state governments and constitutional conventions. But beginning with the presidential election of 1868 and intensifying as "redemption" advanced, violence stunted southern Republicanism. White rifle clubs marched in African-American townships, seeking to overawe voters; often fighting broke out. In Eutaw, Alabama, 78 percent African-American, during the 1870 election campaign, whites fired on a crowd of African-Americans, killing five and wounding up to fifty-five.[55]

Republican newspapers were established as part of the Reconstruction experiment. These papers faced extraordinary difficulties: southern merchants declined to advertise in them, most southern whites declined to buy or read them, and a large part of their natural market, former slaves, had been kept unlettered by their masters and were only then learning to read.[56] Still, one finds a fair number of newspapers named *Republican* or, just as revealing, *Tribune* or *Times*, being established in the south during Reconstruction.

Republican papers frequently became targets of white violence. A telling example is the attack on Robert W. Flournoy's *Equal Rights*, published in Pontotoc

County in northern Mississippi. Flournoy was also superintendant of schools for the county, and had become controversial by vigorously supporting African-American education and advocating integrated schooling and admission of African-Americans to the state university at Oxford. Charging that Flournoy's plan was to "put the negro over the white man," night riders affiliated with the Klan in early 1871 began visiting teachers who worked in African-American schools. Flournoy denounced these vigilantes in his paper as "prowlers, robbers, and assassins." On the night of 12 May, his print-shop foreman woke him up and warned him that disguised men were looking for him. Flournoy armed himself, gathered a few allies, including the sheriff and a local magistrate, and went to the street. There they encountered a column of masked horsemen, riding in two-by-two formation. When the sheriff ordered the horsemen to surrender, a shot was fired. Flournoy and his men returned the fire, downing one of the horsemen, who, before dying, confessed to the Klan's role in the action. Even though they'd faced down the attackers, Flournoy felt Republicans could not express their opinions in Mississippi without fear of personal violence. Indeed, threats had driven off his coeditor and some of his teachers.[57]

Flournoy's case is exceptional mainly in the level of support he received from fellow whites, some of them Democrats. He had lived in Pontotoc County since 1856, and was fairly well established as a member of the community. Generally, Republican newspapers were seen as intruding forces of northern aggression and African-American domination.

The centrality of race deserves emphasis here, though the next chapter will focus on it more closely. Reconstruction Republicans were straightforward in their intention to use the enfranchisement of African-Americans to achieve political power. But courting the African-American vote was a portentous move in the southern mentality. Already pervasive violence had greeted assertions of simple freedom, like reluctance to stay on plantations. Traditionally, southern society had rested on a foundation of African-American labor, and in the minds of southerners the advent of African-American political activity meant the eventual collapse of the racial barrier that kept that foundation in place. Any activity promoting autonomy was subject to attack. And, as we shall see, the specter of "social equality," always implying miscegenation, was powerful enough to unite whites of all classes in the South in extralegal activity against African-Americans and their allies. In response, as Reconstruction failed, Republicans in the South increasingly adopted a "lily-white" stance, but even so it was rare that Republicans achieved electoral success in the south.

Conclusion

The Civil War era produced deep changes in several relevant areas. It occasioned a constitutional revolution that might be characterized as the triumph of liberalism. It also occasioned a new racial dynamic in politics, one that will be at the heart of the next chapter. And it enshrined ideas and government practices that would be important components of the period of industrialization that was to follow.

The Civil War era was also a watershed for the press. The spasm of mobbings of copperhead newspapers was the last wave of majoritarian violence against a mainstream position. Subsequent crowd violence would be directed against minorities defined by racial, ethnic, or class characteristics. The trigger to violence would be the specter of group empowerment, not the voicing of obnoxious ideas.

6

Violence and Minority Media

At the base of public discourse in the early Republic was a dialectic between liberalism and republicanism. Republicanism emphasized consensus and civic virtue while liberalism emphasized individual self-interest. The mechanisms of government were constructed according to the laws of liberalism, but citizens and civic leaders often used the rhetoric of republicanism to explain and apply them. There was a built-in possibility for contradiction here: the notion of republican virtue could be used to justify majoritarian limits on individual liberty—as for instance in the crusade against abolitionism.

By the end of the Civil War, republicanism was outmoded. The war fostered a Darwinian view of society, where individual initiative was lionized over social direction, where the virtues of the warrior were emphasized over those of the statesman, at least rhetorically, where the metaphors of warfare were applied with increasing literalness to the realm of production: captains of industry battled armies of employees and so forth. Industrial capitalism replaced republican notions of civic virtue with Darwinian individualism just as it replaced island communities with modern cities.[1] The language of republicanism came to sound increasingly archaic, anachronistic: the phrases had a ritual familiarity, but no longer connected with a vital sense of social reality. No one pretended that General Grant was Cincinnatus.

Two particular types of groups were left out by the now dominant ideology of industrial individualism, however. One was the working class, left out first because industrial individualism justified ruthless employer practices, second because it denied the legitimacy of "class" identity. Republicanism had fostered a "producer ideology" that affirmed the centrality of labor in economics and underscored the obligations of proprietors to their workers. Republicanism also had projected a notion of corporate or civic responsibility, along with traditional notions of just prices, wages, and working conditions. Industrial individualism substituted the amoral mechanism of the market for these older moral controls. At the same time, individualism removed justifications for class action or consciousness (which had been of questionable legitimacy in republicanism too). In the individualist ethos, any combination of individuals (including unions) would have to be seen as a violation of the "natural" order of competition. The only proper course of action for workers would be individual mobility: leaving the ranks of the laborers and joining the managers and owners. This prescription did more than deny the moral fitness of class action; in asserting the mobility of all individuals, it also denied the social fact of class.[2]

A second family of groups left out by industrial individualism were ethnic and racial minorities. Unlike in the case of class, Darwinian individualists did not deny the existence of race or ethnicity. On the contrary, the latter part of the nineteenth century saw the apotheosis of a genetic notion of racial identity. Moreover, ethnicity and nationality likewise came to be seen as racial: Italians were a race, just as Africans were; their cultural and psychological characteristics were determined by bloodlines as much as folkways. Ethnic and racial plurality was an undisputed fact,[3] but the numerous races were not equal. On the contrary, the ethos of individualism insisted on the inherent superiority of Anglo-Saxons, a superiority self-evident in the "natural" order of industrial society, the unique achievement of the Great Race.[4] This kind of racial thinking coexisted easily with mainstream Progressive liberalism—Theodore Roosevelt and Woodrow Wilson alike adhered to a commonsense Anglo-Saxonism.

How might ethnic and racial groups fight the unfairness of Anglo-Saxonism? Individualism offered only a partial answer: individuals might strive for economic and (sometimes) political advancement, but only by abandoning the group, and even then "social" equality (often identified with interracial marriage as much as integrated schooling and public accommodations) was denied by racialism. But promoting group interests—as in Booker T. Washington's program of race advancement—meant defining African-Americans out of the general society and accepting a minority and, in the climate of the times, necessarily inferior position.

But individualism entered a second moment in the course of the twentieth century. Gradually, the commonsense designation of ethnic groups as races became obsolescent. Few people now speak of Italians or Germans as a race, and ethnic identity has come to seem increasingly a matter of individual choice. African-Americans remain an exception, but even here, where identity is generally assumed to be genetic and somatic, the assertion of racial *inferiority* is generally considered inappropriate and offensive. In other words, most groups are no longer considered to be "natural," and "natural" groups are no longer deemed to constitute a "natural" hierarchy—at least in public discourse.

Still, the dilemma of minority groups remains. Either they are real groups, and society is made up of groups of people who are really different (even if not superior or inferior), or they are artificial groups of real individuals, and society is made up of individuals who are really the same (in spite of their accidental historical situations). If society is made up of groups, then there should be different values for each group—a position that I shall call pluralism. If society is made up of individuals, then there should be universal principles that govern all individuals—a position that has been referred to alternately as industrial individualism and liberalism above.

Replacing the old dialectic of liberalism and republicanism, then, is a new dialectic of industrial individualism and pluralism. By pluralism, again, I mean the notion that society is and should be composed of groups that contend with one another, an idea that underpins several familiar uses of the term *pluralism*. In political science, pluralism is usually taken to mean that power is shared among a variety of competing institutions representing different constituencies; power is thus forced to be responsive to more than a single dominant group. Another common usage of the term *pluralism* refers specifically to culture and implies that national culture is and should be a tapestry of various historically distinct "authentic" cultures. In both usages, pluralism is commonly seen as a necessary component of liberal democracy. But there is a fundamental contradiction, one that comes to the surface in debates over affirmative action and over laws against racist speech or hate literature. Industrial individualism or liberalism calls for principles that are, in the cliché, color-blind. No just law, in this frame of thought, can take special account of race. A law that forbids Ku Klux Klan demonstrations, in liberal thought, must also outlaw rallies of African-American nationalists. In what I've called pluralist thinking, however, it's perfectly permissible to outlaw Ku Klux Klan rallies without imposing the same restrictions on African-American nationalists. Pluralist thinking sees the real situation as one of differential power—and therefore unjust oppression—among groups. Because whites dominate African-Americans (and not the reverse), white supremacist speech constitutes a real wrong against African-Americans (and not the reverse).

Pluralism was clearly at odds with the liberalism dominant in the age of industrialization. But that liberalism was not without contradictions of its own. Industrialism emphasized a "value-free" science of management. Bureaucratic organization and expert control—what Alfred Chandler has called the "visible hand"[5]— seemed to have no room for notions of ethnic or racial "character." But at the same time the language of Darwinism became incorporated into common usage, supporting a "scientific" racism that legitimated the rise of Jim Crow laws in the South. Group disputes and group identities highlighted fault lines within liberalism.

Violence Against African-American Media

Violence against African-American media in U.S. history occurred in four distinct but overlapping moments. In the first, centered in the Reconstruction era (1865–1877), African-American media, especially in the South, were attacked by whites, especially during election time, as part of an attempt to regain or reinforce political and economic hegemony over what was perceived as a crucial source of cheap labor. In the second moment, assertive African-American newspapers were attacked, again by mainstream whites, again especially in the South, again for challenging white hegemony; in this second moment, consistent with prolynching arguments, the crucial rhetorical justification for violence was the rape of white women. The newspapers mobbed in this second moment—we shall discuss three specific cases— were obnoxious in numerous ways to whites, but were mobbed only after they had committed the classic faux pas of hinting that white women could desire African-American men. The third moment centered in the wave of race riots that crested in the period following World War I. This marked a turning point in racial violence in that African-Americans could now be expected to use violence to defend themselves against violence. The final moment centered in the civil rights movement of the 1950s and 1960s, and may be said to continue into the 1990s. Here violence was directed not just at African-American media but also at mainstream journalists who publicized momentous events to the nation at large.

It is noteworthy that at at least two points assaults on African-American media paralleled attacks on radical media. In the post–World War I era, racial violence coincided and interacted with the Red Scare; in the 1960s, racial violence was associated with the legal harassment of and extralegal violence against the radical press. Similarly, the World War II–era African-American press encountered significant official hostility and public suspicion on grounds of disloyalty, much like a range of radical publications. The irony here is that despite the high visibility of African-American radicals, most African-American publications have been impeccably conservative on issues other than race.[6] In these cases, African-Americans and radicals shared mainly an apartness from the mainstream.

Most of the specific incidents that follow occurred in the South. That fact alone does not mean that the structures of racial thought that came into play were specifically southern. On the contrary, racial discourse has followed similar lines North and South. Violent incidents of the sort described here were more common in the South for several incidental reasons. The races lived in more intimate contact in the South. African-Americans were more numerous and therefore a more threatening political force in the South. African-Americans tended to be Republican until the second half of the twentieth century, and the Republican party was always seen as an intruder by southern whites. And, in terms of both economic power and electoral politics, southern whites stood to gain by intimidating African-Americans, while northern whites had fewer practical reasons to engage in racial violence. In other words, northern whites were not prompted as often or as powerfully to strike out against the media of African-Americans, and frequently made political hay out of accounts of southern racial violence. This does not mean they were more at ease with African-Americans or their media.

Reconstruction Violence

In the years following the Civil War, in attempts to establish a viable Republican party in the South, African-Americans were enfranchised and recruited by Reconstruction governments. One aspect of this movement was the establishment of newspapers seeking the patronage of freedmen. As part of the general wave of violence that accompanied the failure of Reconstruction, many of these papers were attacked.

The establishment of Republican and African-American newspapers was a real challenge. Readerships were small, limited by the poverty and illiteracy of former slaves. Advertising revenue was minimal because the economy remained white dominated. In general, these newspapers thrived only where Republicans controlled the state legislature and awarded printing contracts accordingly. Even so, African-Americans were keen to establish papers to promote their interests; as the Civil War came to a close, African-American papers turned up in states throughout the South. The eagerness of the former slaves was astounding. White Republican editor Robert Flournoy's comments to a congressional committee investigating the Ku Klux Klan are instructive: "They cannot read. Many of them would have taken my paper, and said to me that they wanted to do so, but neither themselves nor their children could read it. I said to them that it would be foolish to take the paper when they could not read it." It is clear that these papers were more than instruments of information transmission to their African-American patrons. They were vehicles of belonging; they were tangible evidence of freedom; they were a voice, whatever message it spoke.[7]

In the hostile environment of the Reconstruction South, African-American newspapers survived without political patronage only if guided by exceptionally canny editors. P. B. S. Pinchback, the free-born fair-skinned son of a white Mississippi planter, acquired high office as lieutenant governor and acting governor of Louisiana and member of the U.S. House of Representatives, and from 1870 to 1881 edited the weekly *New Orleans Louisianan*. Richard Henry "Daddy" Cain, son of a free African-American man and a Cherokee woman, also a holder of state offices and a member of Congress, bequeathed similar longevity to the Charleston, South Carolina, *Missionary Record*.[8] Newspapers with less august editors were often run out of business or driven away by violence or the threat of violence.

One such newspaper was the *St. Landry Progress*, published in Opelousas, St. Landry Parish, Louisiana. The *Progress* was a bilingual paper, with different editors for its French and English pages; although its operators were both white and African-American, its primary constituency was the freedmen of St. Landry Parish, an up-country agricultural area. It was unabashed about its readership and its politics: it embraced radical Republicanism, placing itself to the left of the moderate Republican movement headed by Lousiana's carpetbagger governor Henry Clay Warmoth.

The split between Warmoth and the radicals involved both political strategy and racial considerations. Warmoth and his colleagues envisioned a healthy Republican party with a strong cohort of conservative native southerners; partly to attract this element, they shunned demands of African-Americans for economic power, political office, and (the most notorious buzzword of the next century) social equality. For the rest, this conservative Republicanism used the rhetoric of liberalism, as is evident in the resolutions of the 1864 Union Republican party convention, invoking the Declaration of Independence ("all men are created equal") and calling for "universal suffrage, liberty and equality of all men before the law."[9] Coming before the end of the war and the passage of the Fifteenth Amendment, these resolutions seem to go a long way toward racial justice. But even so they stop well before recommending any substantive improvement in the economic situation of freed slaves, and carefully avoid advocating social equality. In other words, conservative Republicans aimed to give African-Americans justice but not power. In return, they hoped that grateful enfranchised freedmen would become loyal

Republican voters and at the same time not be so demanding as to frighten native whites. This bid for a consensual political center was not to succeed, either in Louisiana or elsewhere in the South.

Conservative Republicans underestimated both the ambitions of their African-American cohorts and the determination of southern whites to retain the old ways. In the electric atmosphere of Reconstruction politics—featuring the nation's first presidential assassination and only presidential impeachment, as well as the most fervent period of state constitution writing since the Revolution—Louisiana's African-Americans demanded a more active role in Republican party building and in state officeholding. In 1867 and 1868, African-Americans fought with both Democrats and conservative Republicans over the drafting of a new constitution. Using the *New Orleans Tribune* as their chief organ, they set up a newspaper network, formed party organizations, campaigned against "the supremacy of a privileged class" in officeholding, and looked toward the day when "the long-neglected race will, at last, effectively share in the government of the State." Governor Warmoth and his conservative Republican allies saw this as an attempt to "Africanize the State."[10] The reaction of Democrats and white traditionalists was far more violent.

This statewide controversy was reflected in St. Landry Parish in the establishment of the *Progress*. A modest four-page weekly with weak advertising support and more white space than usual for a paper of its era, the *Progress* was established in late 1867 by means of a subscription campaign among the region's African-Americans—testimony to their eagerness to have a tangible voice. Its owners, the Donato brothers, and its French-language editor, Michel Vidal, were men of color.[11] The office of the *Progress* became a regular Sunday meeting place for hundreds of local African-Americans, who gathered to hear the paper read aloud. The paper announced its support for routine Republican measures—"equality before the law," no cotton tax, tariff protection for sugar, and the "harmonization of the races"—but went further in proposing legislation designed to open political and economic opportunities for African-Americans: weekly pay for officeholders, for instance, and an eight-hour workday for hired labor. Moreover, the paper began its career by printing lists of violent acts committed against African-Americans in St. Landry Parish.[12] This kind of exposé was most delicate. It threatened to invalidate claims of gradual, peaceful reform under a conservative Republican administration, to dash hopes of quick normalization of state politics and of restoration of Louisiana's place in the Union, and to prompt calls for indefinite military occupation.

But the record of racial violence in Lousiana's postwar years was indeed frightening. The exposé in the *Progress* identified about three dozen specific incidents of white-on-black violence, many of which were outright murders. Much of this violence seems prompted by a perceived loss of control by whites over African-American labor—not unexpected when masters were obliged to negotiate wages and working conditions with former slaves—but much of it was also more directly political.

Political violence became more pronounced both in Louisiana and throughout the South as the presidential election of 1868 approached. Racial violence had been common since the war; indeed, its extent was staggering, though the violence of the war itself has tended to obscure the memory of postwar turmoil. In Texas, for instance, the number of African-Americans murdered by whites in the years 1865–1868 amounted to a full 1 percent of African-American males between the ages of fifteen and forty-nine.[13] Rioting was common, and some of the riots—especially in New Orleans and Memphis in 1866—were outright armed attacks on a city's African-American population resulting in dozens of deaths.[14] But homicide and rioting were just the most dramatic manifestations of what was actually an organized campaign of terrorism. Practices that mimicked traditions like the "code of honor" and political clubs exploded out of all proportion into constant harassment and intimidation of African-Americans and routine attacks on institutions identified with African-American progress—schools, churches, and newspapers.[15] Much of this violence was election-oriented. But electoral violence reached a crescendo in 1868,[16] partly due to the popularity of a new secret organization, the Ku Klux Klan.

The Reconstruction-era Klan claimed honor and respectability. Its members included local white elites, often within the Democratic party leadership, and its activities were framed within the long tradition of southern vigilantism. It was not a collection of cranks or white trash.[17] Its respectability made its activities all the more frightening. Its attacks on African-American institutions often went unchallenged because local law enforcement officials were often sympathetic. And federal officials, by then appointees of Andrew Johnson, who had grown to like the old planter elite, were also reluctant to take action.[18] Eventually, Congress, still under Radical influence, would take action against the Klan, passing an act against conspiracies against civil rights in 1871. This action severely curtailed Klan activity, but it did not put an end to white supremacist vigilantism. Even during its heyday, the Klan held no monopoly on political intimidation; after its (temporary) eclipse, organizations like the White Leagues and rifle clubs would routinely drill in African-American townships in often successful attempts to overawe African-American activists and voters.[19]

The overall record of Reconstruction racial violence is stunning. So pervasive was violence against African-American activists (and their white allies) that at least 10 percent of all African-American members of state constitutional conventions in the years 1867–1868 were victims of some kind of assault, and at least seven were murdered—without doubt the most severe rash of assassinations in the nation's history.[20] More than a little of the violence was directed against newspapers.[21]

In Louisiana, 1868 was a very bloody year. That year the state reported 784 deaths from political violence; the federal government put the figure at over a thousand. Outright terrorism was probably the reason that only half as many people voted Republican in the presidential election in the fall as had voted Republican in the spring's gubernatorial election.[22] There was also a spate of newspaper mobbings. The *Iliad*, a Republican paper in Homer, Claiborne Parish, edited by newly elected Congressman W. Jasper Blackburn, was mobbed twice; the *Attakappas Register* was mobbed; the *Rapides Tribune*, edited by Mayor William F. McLean of Alexandria, Rapides Parish, was mobbed twice. Noting the mushrooming of paramilitary secret organizations and the pervasiveness of heated rhetoric, Governor Warmoth concluded that "the Republican Party in Louisiana was paralyzed by the violence of the opposition."[23]

In St. Landry Parish, tensions grew throughout the year and came to focus on the *Progress* and its English-language editor, Emerson Bentley, an Ohio-born carpet-bagger then only eighteen years old. Bentley was a gifted altruist and enthusiast. In addition to running the newspaper—his responsibilities there seemed to increase after the French-language editor, Michel Vidal, was elected to Congress in 1868's spring elections—he also ran a school for local African-Americans, was a principal organizer for the Republican party, and was an upstate correspondent for the New Orleans *Tribune* and *Republican*.

Louisianans held two elections in 1868. The first was statewide; citizens voted to ratify a recently drafted constitution, which, if passed, would return the state to the Union. Ballots were also cast for statewide offices, including governor. Then, in the fall, Lousiana voted in the national election for the presidency. The fall election was the more violent, but tensions were clearly apparent in the first.

In St. Landry Parish, a minor controversy erupted in February over Radical Republican meetings. These meetings were generally held on Sunday, a day of rest for field hands and other laborers who were overwhelmingly African-American. On 16 February, the commander of the local post of federal troops in Opelousas and the head of the Freedmen's Bureau interrupted a meeting, remarked that secret meetings of armed men were illegal (though the meeting was not secret and the men were not armed), referred to white fears of African-American insurrection, and advised the Radicals to stop their meetings. Bentley was present at the meeting (which was held in the same building that housed his school), and described the visit in a telegram to the *New Orleans Republican* and in a report in the *Progress* as a blatant attempt at intimidation. He noted accusingly that "after this masterly feat they [the officer and the Bureau man] retired to receive the congratulations of those whom they served to the best advantage." He closed his account with a promise to publish a story "wherein our unfortunate 'Boy' [the officer], the 'booro' [Bureau] man, two public women and a social party will be mentioned."[24]

Bentley's reportage incensed local Democrats. On 22 February, the same day that the *Progress* had appeared, a meeting of the "conservative" citizens of the parish denounced "the persistent and unscrupulous efforts which, for mere party purposes, have been made to create an antagonism between them [local African-Americans] and ourselves—their true friends and protectors." They resolved to "oppose and resist, by all the legal means within our power . . . the subjugation of Louisiana to the dominion of an inferior race, incited and led by unscrupulous demagogues."[25] The local Democratic newspaper hinted darkly at violence: "Fire is called a good servant but a dangerous master. . . . [W]e have an idea, a sanguine hope and an abiding belief that it will prove your master yet, and the instrument of the redemption, regeneration, and disenthrallment of the white race, despite of such impediments as the ex-editor of the 'Progress' and the saintly successor [Bentley] on whom the mantle has so fittingly fallen."[26] As for Bentley's threat to publish embarrassing tales about his opponents, the Democratic paper replied with traditional condemnations of "scandalous insinuations regarding private matters." Further, it threatened, "We don't think you will, as it might result in another *Costley operation*."[27] This last phrase apparently referred to a physical assault on Bentley that had occurred a few days earlier.[28]

It is important that opposing editors argued the proprieties of print discourse with Bentley. When the local Democratic weekly regularly criticized the *Progress* for its style of argument and (usually imaginary) violations of decorum, it was acknowledging that it and the *Progress* shared the same public space. Of course, because the *Progress* had a public printing contract and ties to high government officials, it would have been foolish to treat it as utterly negligible. Still, white southern newspapers did come to ignore competing African-American papers, even well-established ones, even ones with ties to the party in power. In the Reconstruction era, African-American voters and newspapers had not yet been segregated off from the white arena of discussion. Rather, abuse was heaped on the outside agitators who were responsible for deluding the naturally docile African-American masses.[29] African-American newspapers were hardly respected, but they were not yet ghettoized.

Tensions in Louisiana did not erupt in the spring of 1868. In the spring elections, the new constitution was ratified, Henry Warmoth was reelected, and Republicans of one sort or another won a majority of the state legislature. In St. Landry, the constitution was narrowly defeated on almost entirely racial grounds, with 2,277 African-Americans and only 32 whites voting for it, while 2,266 whites and 358 African-Americans voted against. At the same time, in the parish, Warmoth received 2,514 votes, of which probably a third were cast by whites, while the Radical candidate took 649 votes—probably almost all African-American—and the Democrat took 1,187. In the gubernatorial race, then, racial polarization was not yet complete, and Republicans had hopes of maintaining a centrist coalition for the presidential candidate, Ulysses Grant, himself hardly a Radical. The Democrats were determined to carry the parish and the state resoundingly for their candidate, Horatio Seymour. The strategy they adopted for doing so was and would remain a familiar one: to unify white voters and terrify African-American voters through a combination of heated racial rhetoric and paramilitary intimidation.

Throughout the South, whites organized into both secret and public groups in the months leading up to the 1868 presidential election. The most notorious of the secret organizations was the Ku Klux Klan. Although the Klan was certainly an important factor, it was not the only such organization. Also active in Louisiana were the Knights of the White Camellia and the Seymour Knights. These groups drilled on horseback, often fully armed; their activities were clearly designed to terrorize African-American voters, who were already fully familiar with white southerners' capacity for violence, especially following the bloody New Orleans riot of 1866, which had left at least twenty dead after a well-coordinated armed assault on a rump constitutional convention.

As summer turned into fall, the passions of political organizing in St. Landry began to take on an ominous aspect. The Seymour Knights conducted open martial displays, and on at least one occasion confronted a Republican rally. This was in mid-September; the Republicans, mostly African-American, assembled in Washington and paraded to Opelousas. On the road they were stopped by a two-by-two column of hundreds of Seymour Knights on horseback, who then accompanied the parade into town. Such behavior seemed designed to menace African-American voters. That evening, the leader of the Knights called on Bentley, who had addressed the rally, and demanded that the *Progress* print "nothing but the truth" about the day's events. The clearly implied threat of physical violence accounts for the circumspect, even cryptic quality of the account of the affair in the *Progress*.[30] Even so, Democrats found reason to be upset with Bentley's reportage. At a meeting on 21 September, the Knights resolved that the *Progress* had "grossly and falsely reflected upon the conduct of the Seymous Knights," and claimed their right as "honorable gentlemen" to respond to "scurrilous, false, or malicious" articles.[31] Noteworthy here is the reference to traditional values and practices: the indefensibility of "scurrilous" newspaper conduct, and the right of offended parties to call out their traducers. But the Knights had in mind not dueling but more terrifying forms of physical violence. The *Progress* had already noted outbursts of night-riding and other forms of intimidation in the parish; one night, anonymous callers had posted a KKK sign on the door of Bentley's school building.[32]

Democrats and Republicans both recognized the threat of violence. In a late attempt to prevent bloodshed, party organizers agreed on a set of rules forbidding armed men and disallowing inflammatory speeches at political meetings.[33] The détente was brief.

On 28 September, three members of the Seymour Knights, led by Judge James R. Dickinson, visited Bentley in his schoolroom and demanded that he retract an article, Dickinson asserting that his "honor had been assailed." When Bentley refused, Dickinson began caning him. Bentley's students, thinking he was being murdered, ran out and alarmed the countryside. As a result, a crowd of several hundred African-Americans armed themselves and gathered in Opelousas, triggering in turn the mobilization of local troops of Seymour Knights, Knights of the White Camellia, and other whites, who had been told for weeks to expect a race war. Bentley, beaten but still alive, tried to get the African-Americans to disperse peacefully but without success. A shot was fired, and fighting broke out. In the ensuing riot, the African-Americans were disarmed, a dozen of the leaders were taken to jail, and the press of the *Progress* was destroyed. That night, the leaders were taken out of jail and lynched. For three days following, a virtually genocidal campaign resulted in the death of up to two hundred African-Americans, according to reports.[34] In the Democratic press, the whole affair was portrayed as a "negro uprising" instigated by radical provocateurs. The *Planter's Banner* was exultant over the aftermath: "The negroes all over the Parish have been disarmed, and have gone to work briskly. Their loyal league clubs have been broken up, the scallawags [*sic*] have turned Democrats, and the carpet-baggers have run off, and their carpet-bag press and type and office have been destroyed. St. Landry is quiet for the first time since the War."[35]

The riot in St. Landry Parish served its local purposes. It silenced the voice of local Republican and African-American voters. Even though Bentley escaped the carnage, trekking through the bayous for weeks until reaching safety in New Orleans, the *Progress* was defunct, and the hopes of the African-American and Republican voters that it served were likewise dashed. Locally based federal troops did nothing to halt the bloodshed, and Republican voters were understandably intimidated. In presidential balloting, not a single vote was cast in the parish for the Republican candidate, even though Warmoth, a Republican, had carried the parish in the spring.[36]

The fate of the *St. Landry Progress* underscores the tragedy of the African-American press and racial politics generally in the Reconstruction period. White southerners were not necessarily monolithic in their individual attitudes toward African-Americans or Republicans, but Democratic political activists were successful in linking together the idea of racial superiority, the fear of race warfare (building on the antebellum fear of "servile insurrection"), and xenophobic hostility toward Yankees with traditional political values (self-government) and traditional rules of discourse ("scurrility," "honor"), rendering it difficult, if not impossible, for an African-American voice to make itself heard in the political marketplace. In the case of the *Progress*, alleged violations of the rules of gentlemanly discourse were cited as justification for first personal violence—beating Bentley—and then a mobbing of the newspaper. This by-then-familiar circuit of antipress violence was cynically used to clothe a campaign to renew racial domination, the real cause of the mobbing of the *Progress*. The lesson for the African-American press was clear: African-Americans would be free to publish newspapers only so long as their voices were heard primarily by fellow African-Americans and only so long as they did not threaten white supremacy. When these bounds were broken, some violation of propriety would be alleged, and some form of violence would result. Though such violence was illegal, whites would depict it as legitimate.

Lynching, Rape, and Attacks on African-American Newspapers

Among the most powerful justifications for white violence against African-Americans was the sanctity of white womanhood. Always employed as the justification for lynching in the abstract, though actually cited as the direct cause in a minority of all lynchings, the fear of African-American men's raping of white women was widely and deeply held, especially but not exclusively in the South. Behind this fear was a visceral aversion to miscegenation, especially when it involved African-American men and white women, similar to the feelings expressed in earlier anti-abolitionist violence. The fact of pure white womanhood and elemental African-American manhood taking pleasure in each other was unmentionable.[37]

This taboo was used on more than one occasion to justify the mobbing of African-American newspapers. Three cases stand out: the 1885 mobbing of Jesse Duke's Montgtomery, Alabama, *Herald*; the 1892 mobbing of Ida B. Wells's Memphis *Free Speech*; and the 1898 mobbing of Alex Manly's Wilmington, North Carolina, *Daily Record*. Spanning the decades surrounding the introduction of Jim Crow laws in the South, these mobbings point to one very real limit on printed expression. But in each case it was something more than the ideas expressed that provoked the attack. In each case, the specific attack on the newspaper marked the climax of white reactionary violence against recent economic and political gains by African-Americans. The attack on the press was a marker of a broader and deeper attack on African-American power.

The long period between Reconstruction and the beginning of the great migration of southern African-Americans to northern cities in the years after World War I was marked by contradictory developments for African-Americans. On the bright side, there were some advances, following the depression of the 1870s, in the economic situation of some African-Americans, as more came to own farms and businesses. Among African-American—owned businesses were newspapers, growing steadily in number from about a dozen in 1870 to 173 in 1914.[38] At the same time, African-Americans experienced an equally steady erosion of political rights, as the various southern state governments were "redeemed" by Democrats, who passed laws disfranchising African-American voters and segregating schools and public facilities. On the national level, African-Americans saw the Supreme Court ratify these actions, most memorably in *Plessy v. Ferguson* (1896), and the Republican party abandon its efforts to create a southern presence with African-American voters, instead adopting a "lily-white" policy. By the World War I era, the political mainstream had become so insulated from African-American concerns that Woodrow Wilson would screen D. W. Griffith's powerful film narrative of the Reconstruction-era Ku Klux Klan, *Birth of a Nation*, in the White House and praise it. Even more shocking, Warren G. Harding, unlike Wilson a northerner and a Republican, would, also in the White House, be sworn in as a Klan member. Ironically, the disfranchisement of African-Americans did not mean they were left in peace; instead, as C. Vann Woodward has pointed out, "the more defenseless, disfranchised, and intimidated the Negro became the more prone he was to the ruthless aggression of mobs."[39]

Lynchings and disfranchisement peaked at the same time, in the 1890s. Ironically, both the violence and the legal maneuvers toward African-American disempowerment coincided with reform movements, like Populism and Progressivism, whose southern manifestations were always framed within the context of racial divisions. Southern Progressives, for instance, were able to tie corruption to African-American suffrage through a general indictment of machine politics; they were also able to capitalize on the general panic over African-American criminality to promote pet causes like temperance. The period of Populist and Progressive agitation, 1898–1908, was also a high point for racial violence, with forty major riots in the decade, as well as several hundred lynchings and perhaps more than a thousand race-motivated killings each year.[40]

The growth of the African-American press throughout this period meant that African-Americans were acquiring a voice, but it was not necessarily an assertive one. The African-American press still had trouble reaching a large part of the African-American population. Partly this was due to illiteracy, which, while declining, still remained at 30 percent in 1920. Moreover, African-American newspapers had less advertising revenue, less likelihood of government printing contracts, and smaller circulations than their white counterparts. At the same time, especially in the South, African-American papers were reliant on support from white advertisers, and were run by proprietors who were often tied to local white businessmen and mainstream partisan organizations. As a result, especially in the South, the African-American press was often if not always more conservative than the African-American population generally. With the passage of time, some of the better-established northern African-American newspapers, which were often independent of white patronage and partisan ties, and hence less guarded in their discussion of racial issues, promoted their circulation aggressively in the South and acquired a significant presence. Even so, the dominant tone was set by the master politician of the age, Booker T. Washington, who advocated nonconfrontational tactics and quiet self-improvement, and who secretly subsidized a large number of southern newspapers and strongly influenced the National Press Bureau.[41]

The often docile tone of the African-American press was in no small measure due to the threat of physical violence. No overall survey of violence against the African-American press in this period is possible here, but the examples are so abundant as to suggest that, especially in the South, violence was a routine expectation.[42] The most dramatic incidents involved the most emotional racial issue of the day: lynching, and the claim that it was justified by rape.

Jesse Duke and the *Montgomery Herald*

Gilded Age Alabama was the scene of some prominent African-American newspapering, including a statewide Colored Press Association. But the open public sphere of discussion generally excluded African-Americans. When Jesse Duke moved from Selma to Montgomery and began publishing the *Montgomery Herald* in the mid-1880s, his white counterparts seldom condescended to engage him in print. Their policy of neglect toward Duke and other African-American papers was coupled with a profession of friendship toward the race.[43] In other words, white papers implied that African-Americans needed no voice in the public sphere because the white papers served that purpose.

Jesse Duke was a Republican partisan activist. He had held a minor appointed office as a postmaster, and had been an unsuccessful candidate for the state legislature, was on the Board of Trustees of Selma University, and was active in the Colored Baptist Convention; in short, he was involved in all the key institutions of African-American life in the period. Even the *Montgomery Daily Advertiser*, a newspaper that was to play a key role in his downfall, admitted that Duke was "the possessor of unusual intelligence," and remarked on how he "contrives generally to make his presence in the community felt."[44] His assertiveness had already annoyed white leaders, who were prepared to act when Duke printed the sentiments that allowed them to drive him out of town.

Duke's *Herald* on 13 August 1887 carried an editorial on recent lynchings. In it Duke remarked:

> Every day or so we read of the lynching of some negro for the outraging of some white woman. Why is it that white women attract negro men now more than former days? There was a time when such a thing was unheard of. There is a secret to this thing, and we greatly suspect it is the growing appreciation of the white Juliet for the colored Romeo, as he becomes more and more intelligent and refined.
>
> If something is not done to break up these lynchings, it will be so after a while that they will lynch every colored man that looks at a white woman with a twinkle in his eye.[45]

This editorial appeared on a Saturday. Over the weekend white indignation grew; a public meeting was scheduled for Monday. Attended by seventy-five people, the meeting settled on sending a committee to order Duke out of town in eight hours.

It visited the *Herald* office only to find that Duke was not in town. Accordingly, a second public meeting was called for that afternoon to adopt resolutions concerning the affair. To this point, the involvement of the town's white press was remarkable. The article had come to the attention of the white citizens of the town by being reprinted in a white paper; representatives of the white papers were present at both public meetings, and at the afternoon meeting, reporters from the white papers acted as secretaries.[46]

Though some citizens favored more direct action, "cooler heads" at the afternoon meeting secured adoption of what whites considered to be a mild set of resolutions, denouncing Duke's language as an "intolerable insult" and Duke himself as "a vile and dangerous character, who seems bent on inculcating doctrines among his race that are a menace to society and to every white woman in the land." The meeting then resolved: "That the above does not call for an apology on his part or a promise not to repeat it, but stamps him as a scoundrel who has crossed the limit of toleration in this community." The meeting then effectively exiled Duke from Montgomery, and commanded the owners of the *Herald* not to allow any future infractions of a similar nature. The meeting went further, denouncing a movement to bring a partly state-funded African-American college to Montgomery as an attempt to produce "Educated 'Romeos.'" Meanwhile, crowds wandered the streets looking for Duke, who was rumored to be returning to town from Selma. One crowd confronted a leading African-American lawyer named Garner who worked in the same building that housed the *Herald* and commanded him too to leave town.

The response of the African-American community to this attack on their press was characteristically conciliatory. African-American leaders met and passed reolutions distancing themselves from Duke and condemning his article.[47] C. M. Dorsette, an African-American doctor who had been threatened by a crowd, similarly published a card distancing himself from Duke.[48]

By now Duke had returned to Montgomery. The mayor, a white man who had attended the afternoon meeting and had signed the resolutions exiling Duke, had hidden Duke in his home. From these unsuspected quarters, Duke sent an apology to the white papers, but by this time his situation was hopeless. A mob visited his house, putting out the windows, and whites showed no sign of relaxing their anger. Only Duke's exile would prevent a much more widespread assault on Montgomery's African-Americans. Duke left town again, clandestinely, and never returned.

The controversy over Duke was not an isolated affair in Alabama. At least two other editors, Mansfield Bryant of the *Selma Independent* and R. C. O. Benjamin of the Birmingham *Negro American*, were threatened by mobs in the summer of 1887. Benjamin was forced out of town; Bryant survived this incident and another mobbing in 1889 before being indicted for "incendiary utterances" and put out of business. And there were other African-American papers threatened.[49] The frequency of such incidents suggest that they were the rule rather than the exception in Gilded Age Alabama.

But the case of the Montgomery *Herald* was more significant for a number of reasons. It occurred in a state capital; it attracted more attention than usual as a result. Therefore the actors were careful to craft explanations for their actions, to behave in what they could describe as a lawful and orderly fashion, and to involve as much of the white community and as many of its elected officials as possible. The *Advertiser* was especially eloquent in its defense of the white community's response: it claimed justification could come from "the common consent of a community, that some evil or danger which the law cannot remove or avert, must be, on the principle of self-preservation, removed or averted outside the law." Thus the community gathered in, as it were, a committee of the whole and settled on "the exile of Duke"; the action thus acquired the force of law: "We all endorse it and the community is bound by it." The action will remove an existing threat and prevent a future one: "The forced removal of Duke will have a salutary effect, upon any who would hereafter follow in his lead, whether by tongue or pen."[50]

The reasoning was not novel, and most Americans would have assented in the abstract to the propriety of such community action to prevent real harm. The troubling feature is the concrete particular evil. It is apparent that the *invoked* symbolic evil was rape, but no one accused Duke of rape, or of conspiracy to commit rape, or even of encouraging rape. We must entertain the possibility that rape was a bogey for social equality, not just in the Duke case but in the justification of lynching generally. In fact, as antilynching advocates continually noted, rape was the alleged crime in only a quarter of actual lynchings. Duke's actual offense was to have spoken of lynching with irreverence, to have spoken as a social equal.

Ida B. Wells and the Memphis *Free Speech*

Ida B. Wells was born in Mississippi in 1862, and grew up with the wave of ambition associated with the first generation of emancipation. She attended Rust College, an institution supported by the Methodist Freedman's Aid Society, and migrated through the church network to Memphis, the regional metropolis. There she worked as a schoolteacher and freelance writer. A series of letters published under the pen name "IOLA" established her as a figure of some promise in the growing world of African-American letters, and she gradually shifted more and more of her energy into journalism.[51]

In 1889 Wells began her association with the Memphis *Free Speech and Headlight*. This was a church-affiliated paper, long edited by the Reverend Taylor Nightingale, minister at the Beale Street Baptist Church, the city's largest African-American church. Nightingale had moved to Memphis from Arkansas, where he had edited the Marian *Headlight*; controversial editorials had aroused local whites, and he was driven out by mobs. Wells bought a one-third interest in *Free Speech* and became more and more important in its production, writing more of its articles and editorials, and investing a lot of time promoting its sale throughout the region. In 1891 she embarked on an aggressive circulation campaign, traveling through Mississippi, Arkansas, and Tennessee, recruiting subscription agents and setting up a network of correspondents. In that one year, circulation jumped from fifteen hundred to four thousand, and the paper's impact shifted from local to regional. Wells bought out Taylor's share in the paper. She also forged links with the national Colored Press Association and with African-American press magnates like T. Thomas Fortune of the *New York Age*.[52]

Violence and Minority Media   143

As its influence grew, the *Free Speech* and its editors began to arouse more controversy. Wells lost her teaching job in retaliation for items critical of the school board. And Nightingale became the target of scheming after a series of editorials urging African-Americans to resist lynchings. Unfortunately, a split in his congregation gave his enemies an opportunity to have him indicted for assault on a parishioner. Convicted and sentenced to eighty days, Nightingale fled to Oklahoma.[53]

Tension between whites and African-Americans in Memphis came to a head in early spring 1892, in a riot and lynching over a grocery store. Three African-American men—Thomas Moss, Calvin McDowell, and Henry Stewart—had begun a successful grocery store, the People's Grocery, in the African-American neighborhood known as the Curve; by doing so, they threatened a long-established white grocer who'd held a monopoly to that point. One day a fight between African-American and white boys over a game of marbles led to fighting among adults, with the African-Americans prevailing. After the brawl, a rumor circulated that whites were planning to use the fight as an excuse to mob the grocery store. The African-Americans armed themselves, and on Saturday night—a night when the store was usually the scene of socializing for local African-American men—they fired on three whites assumed to be arsonists, who were actually policemen with warrants. The police swept through the neighborhood, rounding up one hundred African-American men and putting them in jail. Fearing a lynching, an African-American militia company guarded the jail for three nights. After the third night, the company was ordered disarmed; on the fourth night, a group of white men was admitted to the jail; they took Moss, McDowell, and Stewart out of town and shot them dead. Then a mob looted and trashed the People's Grocery. The store was shut down, but the three dead owners were buried with great emotion by the African-American community, who turned out in the thousands to form the largest funeral procession in the history of Memphis.[54]

Tension simmered through the warm months of April and May. Frightened and furious African-Americans began to leave the city in large numbers, while defensive whites cited evidence of a wave of African-American violence throughout the South. The *Appeal-Avalanche*, the city's leading white newspaper, printed story after story of lynchings, mostly tied to alleged black-on-white rape.[55] Meanwhile, the paper carried out a protracted debate over the justice of lynching with the northern press, mainly arguing that lynching was a regrettable violation of the rule of law, but one that must be expected when the laws are incapable of preventing African-American criminality, and which the North has no business acting pious about.[56]

Unremarked upon by the *Appeal-Avalanche* were the stinging editorials of the *Free Speech*. Wells was treated by her white counterparts in Memphis as a nonspeaker, not to be taken notice of. But her voice was becoming harder to ignore, especially because she'd acquired a regional audience of African-American subscribers, a national audience of African-American editors, and a northern audience of white liberals. If the white press of Memphis tried to ignore her, the white press of Chicago listened with interest. Locally, she urged her readers to boycott white-owned businesses and to emigrate to Oklahoma. As the spring wore on, African-

American emigration advanced, and the white-owned streetcar company neared bankruptcy.[57] Evidently, it began to occur to local whites that the *Free Speech* must be silenced "in such a way as not to arouse further antagonism in the Negroes."[58]

Wells accommodated the white opposition by printing the magic words. An editorial in the issue of 21 May (which, it turns out, may have been written by her business partner) remarked on the recent spate of lynchings for alleged rape, and called that justification "the old thread bare lie." It then intimated that white women bore some responsibility: "If Southern men are not careful, they will over reach themselves, and public sentiment will have a reaction; a conclusion will then be reached which will be very damaging to the moral reputation of their women."[59] The wording was circumspect, but not circumspect enough.

Shortly after the editorial appeared, Wells left Memphis on a long-planned trip to New York. She was not to return. Public outrage was whipped up over the editorial; white papers suggested that "the black wretch who had written that foul lie should be tied to a stake at the corner of Main and Madison Streets, a pair of tailor's shears used on him, and he should then be burned at the stake."[60] A public meeting was held, much inflammatory rhetoric was indulged. After the meeting, on 27 May, a mob visited the *Free Speech* office, chased the business manager out of town, and trashed the type and presses. Afterward, the sheriff seized the leftover equipment and auctioned it off to pay the paper's creditors. Local leaders let it be known that the paper was not to be revived.[61] Wells stayed in New York, where she traded her subscription list for a share in Fortune's *New York Age*. She went on to become a noted muckraker and critic of lynching on two continents and a founding member of the National Association for the Advancement of Colored People (NAACP).[62]

The forceful suppression of the *Free Speech* was a prelude to defusing the racial crisis in Memphis. In early June, a meeting of white and African-American leaders was held at the Cotton Exchange. Significantly, African-American minister B. A. Imes, in remarks reported favorably in the white press, tactfully repudiated the "unwisdom and rashness" of the *Free Speech* editorial, while insisting that "the author alone must be responsible." He criticized newspapers that "are great on agitation . . . but not . . . appeals to reason," and attacked the "mischievous" doctrine of race conflict, asking for harmony in acceptance of "necessary and natural social distinctions." Imes's speech was endorsed by white General Luke Wright, who remarked in passing on the potential usefulness of the African-American press: "If the colored people had a conservative newspaper published here, devoted to building up the race in morals and general advancment, it would do more than anything else to advance the race."[63] Meanwhile, Wells continued her criticisms through the *Age*, which had readers in Memphis. Again in June, accommodationist African-American leaders, including Imes, were prompted to repudiate appeals "to passion and prejudice" designed to arouse "the spirit of strife." "Virtue cannot be encouraged by sowing scandal broadcast, polluting the minds of the innocent and pure."[64] Note the implication that African-American readers in particular are innocent and naive, easily influenced by "scurrilous" publications.

The Memphis incident, like the Montgomery one, demonstrates that the powerful symbol of rape could be used as a weapon to silence an unruly African-American voice. Like Jesse Duke, Ida Wells had taken positions on the fringe of "accept-able" race relations. Furthermore, she had built an organ of some prominence and influence. Her voice had begun to hurt the local economy and national prestige of white Memphis. Facing prolonged conflict and a possible challenge to white supremacy, local whites seized on an injudicious editorial to silence the paper, obeying the outward forms of orderliness—that is, the public meeting—and co-opting "moderates" among the African-American leadership. As in the Duke case, they literally succeeded in exiling Ida Wells.

The Wilmington Riot of 1898

In the 1890s, economics deflected the normal run of partisan politics. A long depression capped an even longer downturn in the agricultural economy, while industrial unrest also peaked; Democrats and Republicans were hard-pressed to head off challengers from outside the mainstream. Some of the dissatisfaction coalesced into the third-party Populist movement. Though it did not emerge as a successful major party, Populism did alter the partisan equilibrium in many states, and hence was courted by one of the major parties, usually the Democrats, who ran joint tickets by nominating Populist candidates and vice versa. This tactic of "fusion" took a unique form in the South, especially in North Carolina.

The southern version of Populism teetered between the politics of race and the politics of class. Composed mainly of white farmers and farm laborers, southern Populist parties had natural class allies in African-Americans, who had long seen the Republican party as their vehicle for opposing elite-dominated Democratic parties. But the tendency for Populists and Republicans to fuse was countered by resurgent racial animosity. Democrats could appeal to racial solidarity to defuse class challenges. Nowhere was this tactic more successful than in North Carolina.

A Populist-Republican fusion campaign captured the North Carolina state legis-lature in 1895. Immediately Fusionists moved to consolidate their victory by liberalizing voter registration requirements to reenfranchise African-Americans.[65] Support from new voters strengthened Fusion's hold on the legislature in 1897 and helped open a door shut since Reconstruction to African-American officeholding. Part of the problem here was gerrymandering. North Carolina's post-Reconstruc-tion redistricting had created a single congressional district that meandered around to include most of the state's African-American voters; for years, this district's Representative was the only African-American in the U.S. Congress. On a local level, coastal cities with large African-American populations were districted to maintain white rule. Such was the case in Wilmington, whose white population was at or under 40 percent.[66] Fusionists' attempts to redraw these political lines brought cries of corruption from Democrats; and the return of African-American officeholding prompted outrage. The *Wilmington Morning Star* editorialized, "The negro was never as assertive in North Carolina politics as he is now, . . . for he has never before been so recognized and pandered to as he has been by the Republican-Populist combine."[67]

The *Star*'s anger was directed at the reconstruction of Wilmington's political structure. After the Fusionists won state power, the state legislature moved to end white minority rule by revising the city's charter to create a police board, appointed by the legislature, with control of much of the city's budget and patronage. In 1897 further charter changes gave the governor the authority to appoint half the city's aldermen. Naturally, appointees were Republicans; naturally, Democrats challenged the constitutionality of these changes. With the city's charter under question, hotly contested elections in 1897 produced four claimants to the office of mayor; the state Supreme Court upheld the Republican candidate's claim. By 1898 Fusion had brought about significant though not proportional African-American participation in the city's government: three out of ten alderman, plus some justices of the peace, the coroner, and some policemen and firemen were African-Americans.[68] African-American officeholding, coupled with rising African-American ambitions and achievements in business and the professions, made Wilmington's whites fear a coming age of African-American supremacy. They responded by organizing well in advance of the 1898 election to retake power. And their organization was not strictly political. Vigilance committees were arranged on a block-by-block basis, with local businessmen being the most active leaders. At the heart of this movement was a campaign committee of twenty businessmen and a core cadre called the "Secret Nine," hearkening back to the patriot organizations of the American Revolution. Whites held a series of inflammatory meetings, and the white press began emphasizing sensational accounts of black-on-white crime, piquing white anxieties. By autumn of 1898, according to Democrat politico Josephus Daniels (then editor of the Democratic Raleigh, North Carolina, *News and Observer*), "Ministers of the Gospel and citizens of high standing were organized into squads, and every block in the town was patrolled at night by prominent citizens with guns. A reign of terror was on."[69]

Tensions in Wilmington coincided with a statewide "white supremacy" campaign.[70] Again, white supremacy was a rather transparent strategy to deflect attention from class divisions by focusing on race. Thus a first step in this strategy was to demonize African-American officeholding. To this end, Democrats seized on a speech by Congressman White, the African-American Representative from North Carolina's second district, to a Republican convention in July. In a long and rambling speech, White responded to Democratic race baiting by saying, "I am not the only negro to hold office. There are others. There are plenty more being made to order to hold office. We are the most modest people in the world and don't hold as many offices as we will. I invite the issue." To the Wilmington *Star*, White had "openly, defiantly, and proudly" drawn the color line. In a series of editorial responses, the *Star* declared that North Carolina already "has in office more negroes than all the other States in the Union combined," certainly more than hypocritical northern states. Wondering, "Where is this thing going to stop?" the *Star* asserted that the "law of self-preservation" required whites to prevent "negro domination, and to protect the negro from himself." The specter of "saucy" and "mouthy" African-Americans conspiring to wrest political power from whites combined with the fear of economic power: if not checked, "negroes would be the possessors of the land and the farms of the white men."[71]

Democrats claimed that African-Americans were by nature incapable of self-government; as a result, officeholding would yield only corruption and criminality. To support this reasoning, Democratic newspapers filled their columns with exaggerated accounts of crimes and lynchings, manufacturing, as it were, the crime wave that they said was inevitable.[72] Especially at risk, supposedly, were North Carolina's white women:

> Nearly all the white women of North Carolina are Democrats, Democrats both from reason and instinct, for they feel and know that no one is more or as much dependent upon good government as they. There must be good laws for their protection, laws so enforced that they will feel safe going to a neighbor's house unaccompanied by a male protector, and they know that until the present mongrel gang that rule the State are weeded out of power and Democrats put in their place, they will have no such protection of the laws.[73]

The campaign began with these naked appeals to race issues, with the heavy-handed invocation of the fear of crime, especially rape. By midsummer, Democrats were holding "White Men's rallies," had formed a White Government Union,[74] and plans were laid for a White Supremacy Convention, which, when it met, resolved:

> That as a consequence of turning these local offices over to the negroes, bad government had followed, homes have been invaded and the sanctity of woman endangered, business has been paralyzed and property rendered less valuable, the majesty of the law has been disregarded and lawlessness encouraged. . . . It is not our purpose to do the negro any harm. It is better for him as well as for us if the white man shall govern and while we propose to protect and encourage him in all his rights and duties of citizenship, we affirm that North Carolina shall not be negroized. It is of all the states of the union particularly the home of the Anglo-Saxon and the Anglo-Saxon shall govern it.[75]

It had been determined from the outset by the Democrats that the campaign would be fought on the race issue. It had also been determined that criminality, especially rape, would be a focus. Democrats were thus on the lookout for evidence of African-American insensitivity when the leading African-American newspaper in the state obliged them by printing the magic words.

The Wilmington *Daily Record* had become the preeminent African-American newspaper in North Carolina by the late 1890s. Located in the chief city of the state's "black belt," the *Record* was edited by Alex Manly, a fair-skinned descendant of Charles Manly, Whig governor of North Carolina from 1849 to 1851, and his slave mistress. Manly set up the *Record* across the street from the white Democratic *Morning Star*, and delighted in tilting with his neighbors. They rarely tilted back until his editorial of 18 August.[76]

Manly's editorial was a rebuttal to a speech by a white evangelical named "Mrs. Felton" justifying lynching as an extreme measure for preventing rape. Manly complained,

> The papers are filled often with reports of rapes of white women, and the subsequent lynching of the alleged rapists. The editors pour forth volleys of aspersions

against all negroes because of the few who may be guilty. If the papers and speakers of the other race would condemn the commission of the crime because it is crime and not try to make it appear that the negroes were the only criminals, they would find their strongest allies in the intelligent negroes themselves, and together the whites and African-Americans would root the evil out of both races.

We suggest that the whites guard their women more closely, as Mrs. Felton says, thus giving no opportunity for the human fiend, be he white or black. You leave your goods out of doors and then complain because they are taken away. Poor white men are careless in the matter of protecting their women, especially on farms. They are careless of their conduct toward them, and our experience among poor white people in the country teaches us that women of that race are not any more particular in the matter of clandestine meetings with colored men, than are the white men with colored women. Meetings of this kind go on for some time until the woman's infatuation or the man's boldness bring attention to them and the man is lynched for rape. Every negro lynched is called a "big, burly, black brute," when in fact many of those who have thus been dealt with had white men for their fathers, and were not only not "black' and 'burly" but were sufficiently attractive for white girls of culture and refinement to fall in love with them as is well known to all. . . .

Teach your men purity. . . . Tell your men that it is no worse for a black man to be intimate with a white woman, than for a white man to be intimate with a colored woman.

You set yourselves down as a lot of carping hypocrites; in fact you cry aloud for the virtue of your women while you seek to destroy the virtue of ours. Don't think ever that your women will remain pure while you are debauching ours. You sow the seed—the harvest will come in due time.

In summoning up the image of white women enjoying sexual congress with African-American men, Manly gave the Democrats the emotional ammunition to energize whites along race lines. Democratic papers throughout the state reprinted the editorial as evidence of Fusion criminality; the Wilmington *Star* reprinted excerpts daily for the remainder of the campaign under the headline "A HORRID SLANDER: The Most Infamous That Ever Appeared in Print in This State."[77]

As in the cases of Jesse Duke and Ida B. Wells, Manly's editorial seems to have been a useful pretext for white leaders. After all, the editorial, while pointed and undiplomatic, was hardly a direct attack on whites, appearing as it did in an African-American newspaper that whites did not read and that white newspapers rarely took notice of, even to rebut. Without the cynical machinations of Democratic politicians, the editorial would never have come to the attention of the white public. Of course, when it did, the public found in it evidence of that "saucy" and "mouthy" attitude that created the atmosphere of criminality that leaders said was so pervasive among African-Americans. The outrage of the white public was predictable, if not reasonable. But the real target of outrage was not the editorial but the possibility of African-American power and, associated with it, the existence of an African-American voice in the public sphere.

As the controversy played out, the status of the *Record* as a legitimate public voice was a central issue. Democrats, considering the outrageousness of the editorial and its author to be self-evident, focused their efforts on pinning it as firmly as possible on the chest of the Fusion ticket. Fusionists, reluctant to defend the editorial or its author, instead repudiated Manly as a loose cannon and pretended that the *Record* was not an important organ.

Manly began to feel the heat immediately. He received threatening letters and crowds gathered outside his office; the County Executive Committee of the Republican party immediately met to repudiate the *Record* and denounce Manly "as a mischief-making simpleton." On the night of 24 August, in response to rumors of a plan to mob the *Record* office, a crowd of supporters gathered, dispersing when reassured by policemen. The next day's *Star* ran the story under a headline that is a classic in distortion: "RIOTOUS NEGROES: Threatening Demonstration by a Mob . . . NO KNOWN CAUSE FOR IT: Angry Mutterings Against the Whites— Police Inefficient or Indifferent."[78]

There is no question that Manly's supporters were right to expect violence, as subsequent events would prove. But, for the time being, white leaders counseled patience, urging their followers to "not weaken the strong position we now occupy."[79] Their reasons for forebearance were clear. Democrats were involved in a rather complicated game. It was crucial to their strategy to convince African-American voters of the threat of violence, and thus dampen voter turnout, especially in Wilmington, where whites were in the minority. At the same time, they could not give evidence of actual disorder, because that would provide the necessary grounds for Republicans in Raleigh or in Washington to send in troops to preserve order, guaranteeing high turnouts for African-American voters and possibly a Fusion victory. However, Republicans in Washington were also concerned that interference in southern affairs would hurt them in national elections in 1900 and so were reluctant to commit troops. At the same time, Democrats knew that allowing the *Record* to continue publication would only increase outrage among whites, and demonstrate that Fusionists were incapable of handling the "Negro problem." They continued to maintain a state of high tension while avoiding outright violence.

Concurrently, Democrats tried to nail Manly to the Republicans, despite their repudiations, saying Manly "is well-known as a Republican and has held the position of Deputy Register of Deeds under the Republicans."[80] Republicans were in a double bind as Democrats seized on any shred of support for Manly or the *Record* as evidence of his significance to the Republicans and African-Americans, while at the same time they reprinted just as eagerly any Republican criticism of Manly.[81] On the whole, African-Americans were more likely than white Republicans to support Manly, but African-American leaders too were quick to distance themselves from Manly's ill-timed remarks.[82] Citizens, though, were quick to come to the defense of the *Record*, as was shown in the street disturbance that followed the editorial's reprinting, and in the fact that the *Record* was not forced out of business by the defection of white advertisers, pressure from white creditors, or the machinations of fearful Republicans.

The skewering of Manly set the tone for the remainder of the campaign. As summer turned to autumn, Democratic tactics of racial intimidation intensified. "Red Shirt" companies—a cross between the militia and the KKK—began appearing at Democatic rallies, where they made a truly terrifying impression on African-

Americans with memories of Reconstruction-era night-riding. Just as in Reconstruction, the Red Shirts disrupted political meetings and spread terror through random violence. Republican Governor Daniel L. Russell issued a proclamation forbidding Red Shirt rallies but was ignored as intimidation reached the point where he himself was forced to cancel campaign appearances.[83]

In the end, Democratic intimidation was sufficient to overcome the advantages of Fusionist incumbency. The Democrats won four times as many seats in the legislature as the Fusionists, outpolling the Fusion ticket by twenty-five thousand votes statewide. The threat of violence had kept many African-Americans from the polls, and the race issue had driven a wedge between Populists and Republicans.[84] In Wilmington itself, Republicans had declined to run a slate of candidates, fearing violence. Republican leaders urged African-American voters to vote the ticket in state and federal races, then immediately return home to avoid election-day clashes.[85] The election was in fact peaceful, though armed whites stood outside polling places throughout the state.

The election having been won, whites now set about "redeeming" the government of Wilmington, which was still run by a Republican mayor who had not been up for reelection. On 9 November, the day after the election, a mass meeting of the white citizens of Wilmington was held. Presided over by Alfred Waddell, a fiery speaker who during the campaign had pledged to drive out the Fusionists "if they have to throw enough dead Negro bodies in the Cape Fear to choke up its passage to the sea,"[86] and with reporters from the Chicago *Record* and Washington *Star*, as well as representatives of several North Carolina papers, in prominent attendance, this meeting was clearly designed to give the nation the impression that it was the legitimate voice of the "respectable" element of the city. Among the resolutions passed were these:

> 3. That the negro has demonstrated by antagonizing our interest in every way, and especially by his ballot, that he is incapable of realizing that his interests are and should be identical with those of the community.

> 7. That we have been, in our desire for harmony and peace, blinded to our best interests and our rights. A climax was reached when the negro paper of this city published an article so vile and slanderous that it would in most communities have resulted in the lynching of the editor. We deprecate lynching, and yet there is no punishment provided by the laws adequate for this offense.

The meeting further resolved that Manly be "banished" and that the mayor and aldermen resign.[87]

Implicit in these resolutions is a clear statement about the proper role of the African-American press. Key to this notion is the insistence that African-Americans as a group have no interests or rights in conflict with the rights or interests of whites. This does not necessarily imply that African-Americans may not have a press of their own; it does imply that this press must be strictly accommodationist, a means of enhancing group loyalty to the common good rather than a means of intervening in the definition of the common good on behalf of group interests. Manly's infraction in this regard was not simply the insult to white womanhood—a mere violation of manners, albeit one for which the punishment was likely to be severe. Even had Manly not printed the magic words, he was likely to have been the target of hostility and probably overt violence precisely because he ran a newspaper that was a significant voice of group interest. Indeed, in insisting that the *Record* was the preeminent organ of African-Americans in North Carolina, white Democrats were also arguing that the "slander" of white womanhood was inseparable from the running of such an organ; they ridiculed any attempt by African-Americans to condemn the editorial without repudiating the paper. The medium itself and not just its message was the sin.[88]

The mass meeting of 9 November gave Manly a deadline for departure. Manly accepted, but through a series of accidents the committee appointed to oversee his banshment did not receive his reply in time. When the deadline passed, Alfred Waddell led a mob of four hundred men to the *Record* office, which was dismantled and then burned to the ground—supposedly, the fire started by accident. The appearance of this paramilitary force in the city's African-American neighborhood naturally caused alarm, though a crowd leader, James Sprunt, "explained to the negroes that the white men only desired to destroy the *Record* office and neither they nor their homes would be hurt." In the event, fighting did break out. The result was rather one-sided: at least a dozen and maybe as many as a hundred African-Americans killed in Wilmington and the countryside, and three white rioters wounded before the militia and the naval reserves stationed in and around the city were called in to restore order. Republican Governor Russell was induced to call on Wilmington's Republican mayor and aldermen to resign; it turned out that they already had. Waddell himself assumed office as the new mayor. In short, the riot and its aftermath might best be described as a coup d'état.[89]

The Wilmington riot shut the door on Fusion's promise of empowerment for African-Americans. Some key leaders, including Manly, and some key organs, especially the *Record*, were exiled or silenced; the nascent political machine was broken. The new Democratic state legislature, riding the crest of white supremacy, enacted Jim Crow laws and new voting requirements that effectively disfranchised the state's African-Americans. The result can be seen in voting statistics for New Hanover County, including Wilmington: in 1896, Democrats took 41 percent of 5,438 votes cast; in 1900, Democrats took 99 percent of 2,966 votes cast; in 1904, Democrats took 99 percent again, but this time only 1,340 votes were cast.[90] At the same time, the white supremacy campaign secured a place in the lore of southern politics. Hoke Smith, whose campaign for governor of Georgia preceded Atlanta's bloody race riot of 1906, made clear his debt to North Carolina. "On several occasions in the heat of emotion he shouted his willingness to 'imitate' Wilmington."[91]

Progressivism and the Race Issue

The 1890s saw the triumph of Jim Crow in the South. The completion of segregationist regimes was not a simple or automatic process, as we have seen. In cases like that of North Carolina, Jim Crow was established only with the disfranchisement of the African-American electorate, which not infrequently required violence or intimidation. It is not accidental that the triumph of Jim Crow coincided with a peak in numbers and frequency of lynchings.

By contrast to the benighted 1890s, the beginning of the twentieth century is usually dubbed the age of Progressivism and is thought of as a time of liberal reform. Progressivism and its journalistic manifestation, muckraking, did produce some notable achievements in race relations, including an antilynching campaign (which failed to bear fruit) and some classic reporting on the evils of southern segregation (especially Ray Stannard Baker's *Following the Color Line*). But some of the fundamental aspects of Progressivism were actually regressive in terms of race. Two stand out.

First, Progressivism included a strong appeal to moral uplift and the elimination of especially political corruption. One key enemy of Progressives was machine politics. Unfortunately, Progressives often associated the machines with the manipulation of African-American voters. The presence of significant bloc of supposedly undereducated voters was thought to encourage political corruption. Hence Progressivism provided an explanation and an impetus for disfranchisement through literacy tests and similar techniques, which, in practice, were notoriously misapplied. Further, Progressives often tended to associate African-Americans with social problems like drinking, gambling, and prostitution. The upshot was that African-Americans were seen as causes rather than victims of social and political injustice.

Second, Progressivism celebrated science and expertise. In politics this produced a movement toward rationalizing governing bodies and placing more power in the hands of "apolitical" managers; in economics this produced the cult of efficiency and the rise of the "science" of management. Unfortunately, the infatuation with science encouraged the rise of pseudosciences. In the area of race, Progressivism intersected with the widespread popularity of Darwinian terminology to valorize "scientific" racism; notions of inherent racial superiority/inferiority and of race "character" acquired greater intellectual legitimacy, even becoming common sense.[92]

Within the African-American community, the Progressive era saw the solidification of opposition between accommodationists and radicals. The accommodationist position was spearheaded by Booker T. Washington, who mixed calls for the advancement of the race with pleas for moral uplift—ironically reinforcing the white stereotype of African-American criminality—and moderation. The radical position congealed around the formation of the NAACP in 1909 and demanded full equality under the law. This split was reflected in the African-American press. Washington subsidized numerous newspapers, and inflected the tone of virtually the entire African-American press by barraging editors with clippings and other contributions. The NAACP founded a national magazine, the *Crisis*, with W. E. B. DuBois as editor, and also began to feed press releases into the African-American press system. Meanwhile, northern African-American newspapers, especially the *Defender* of Chicago, were becoming more strident in tone and more aggressive in building national circulations.

Southern towns were prone to take action, legal or extralegal, against militant African-American papers. In some cases, the sale of papers like the *Defender* was

prohibited. Mississippi passed a law in 1920 outlawing the printing or circulation of appeals for social equality; the city of Somerville, Tennessee, passed
an ordinance forbidding the sale of African-American newspapers and requiring
African-American citizens to read the (white) *Falcon*. Local agents and correspondents for papers like the Chicago *Defender* and the Philadelphia *American* were
attacked throughout the South. The white animus against northern or radical African-
American newspapers resulted in southern African-American newspapers moder-
ating their tone and stopping the practice of reprinting articles from their northern
counterparts.[93]

Frequently, racial tensions flared into all-out riots. The first decade of the
twentieth century was marked by about forty major race riots, the most notorious
being in Atlanta in 1906. After World War I there was another outbreak of rioting,
featuring an especially bloody battle in Tulsa in 1922. In both Atlanta and Tulsa,
African-American newspapers were casualties.

Race Riots: Atlanta and Tulsa

Atlanta has always been a center for middle-class African-Americans. Already
by 1906, the better-off sections of Atlanta's African-American community were
thought of as showcases for the self-improvement of the race, featuring healthy
businesses like banks and department stores, and community institutions like
churches and schools. The success of the middleclass was a cause of resentment
for whites who had not done so well. But Atlanta's African-Americans were not
all middle-class, and in the city's poorer districts, whites and African-Americans
mixed in a potentially volatile combination. As elsewhere in the South, the vices
of the poor were used as carriers for racial hostility directed against more successful African-Americans.

Atlanta's racial powder keg was ignited by an inflammatory political campaign.
In 1906 Hoke Smith, a candidate for the Democratic gubernatorial nomination who
delighted in populist appeals, began to focus his attacks on the issue of African-
American criminality. Partly as a result, newspapers began to sensationalize reports
of crime, especially rape. In Atlanta, a report of such a crime was enough to warrant
an "extra" edition with banner headlines. Shortly after one such edition hit the
streets, scuffling began on Decatur Street, then Atlanta's chief vice district, which
was more or less integrated. Knots of whites began attacking African-Americans,
gradually merging into a mob of five to ten thousand. A personal appeal from Mayor
James Woodward was ineffective; after nightfall, the mob roamed the streets with
little interference from the police. In this first night of rioting, around twenty
African-Americans were killed; in outlying areas, however, and in middle-class
neighborhoods, African-Americans were armed and ready to fight back. The next
day saw no restoration of order, and on the following night a mob attacked "Dark-
town," the poorest of the African-American districts. The mob was repelled by
gunfire, and elsewhere snipers fired on whites. The rioting climaxed on the next
day, when militia visited Brownsville, a middle-class neighborhood, to disarm the
residents, killing four and arresting three hundred in the process.[94]

Atlanta was home to a periodical called *The Voice of the Negro*, edited by J. Max Barber, who was inclined toward DuBois's position on racial issues. After the riot, it became known that Barber was the author of an article contradicting white accounts of the genesis and conduct of the rioting that had appeared in the New York *World*. Although subsequent investigation by authorities would confirm Barber's account, his authorship was so offensive that the governor's chief of staff summoned him and threatened him with a chain-gang sentence. Instead, Barber fled Atlanta. His thriving journal, which had reached a circulation of fifteen thousand, relocated with him but died a lingering death the next year. Barber quit journalism and became a dentist.[95]

The Voice of the Negro was a peripheral casualty of the Atlanta riot. Though rioters did not target him specifically, had it not been for the atmosphere of violence, Barber may have continued to publish his important periodical.[96] By contrast, in the Tulsa riot, African-American newspapers were direct targets of mob violence.

The Tulsa riot was among the most bloody of the wave of race riots at the end of World War I. Tension between whites and African-Americans ran high in cities throughout the nation as an economic downturn coincided with the Red Scare and the beginning of a large migration of rural African-Americans to the cities. During the summer of 1919 alone, major race riots occurred in Omaha, Washington, Knoxville, and Chicago.[97]

In Tulsa these trends were if anything exaggerated. Through the 1910s, the city had boomed on the strength of its oil industry, growing from a town of eighteen thousand in 1910 to a bulging city of ninety-eight thousand in 1921, the year of the riot. Tulsa's growth was not free of conflict, however. Continual labor troubles culminated in 1917 in a vigilante campaign against Industrial Workers of the World (IWW) activists that included the whipping and tarring and feathering of seventeen men, including a printer, with the passive participation of the police.[98] Likewise, racial tension grew as the African-American population increased to eleven thousand. Tulsa's African-Americans constituted an autonomous and self-conscious community, with a thriving business district and two newspapers, the *Tulsa Star* and the *Oklahoma Sun*.[99] Both papers were partisan; the *Star* supported local Democrats and the *Sun* backed the Republicans. But they were specifically "race" papers; as the *Star* insisted, "We want the world to know that we put the interest of the Colored Race ahead of everything else in the world." And these were relatively large papers too; the *Star* had ten full-time employees and a $15,000 plant.[100] Both newspapers were destroyed in the riot.

The riot began when an African-American youth was arrested for assaulting a white girl. Fearing a lynching, armed African-Americans gathered, facing off against a crowd of fifteen hundred or more whites. It seemed for a time that the situation might be defused, but as the crowds began to disperse, shots were fired, and in the resulting volley ten whites and two African-Americans were killed. The next morning, in what seemed to be a coordinated maneuver, whites attacked "Little Africa," the African-American neighborhood, using machine guns and setting fire to homes and businesses. When the fighting stopped, at least seventy-five and maybe two hundred African-Americans had been killed, along with up to fifty whites. Contemporaries noted the determination with which African-Americans fought back against whites and the heavy toll inflicted on white rioters, and blamed the African-American newspapers for creating the aggressive attitude that led to the rioting.[101]

The Tulsa riot, along with the other riots of the World War I era, marked a shift in patterns of racial violence. Henceforth urban riots would be battles between the races rather than simply attacks by whites upon African-Americans, which had been the case in southern cities since Reconstruction. Meanwhile, in the countryside as well, lynchings tapered off significantly. This did not mean that violence and intimidation were no longer directed at African-Americans and the African-American press; oddly, at the same time, the Ku Klux Klan was reestablished, reaching its zenith in the 1920s. It did seem, however, that violence was not as simple a means of racial "policy" as it once had been, that its effectiveness had come to seem questionable.

World War II and After

The World War II era did not produce a major outbreak of vigilante activity, either in racial and ethnic affairs or in political matters. Domestic violence was seen by government and responsible public officials as something to be avoided at all costs during the war. Conflicts in the home public were defused or postponed as much as possible.

Nevertheless, the war saw frequent race riots. Partly this was the result of an intensified migration of African-Americans to northern industrial centers, where they encountered long-standing barriers in terms of housing and employment. Partly it resulted from impatience and restiveness among African-Americans who couldn't help noticing the contradictions between the rhetoric of antifascism and the still-sanctioned practices of segregation and discrimination. In 1943 alone, there were 242 racial battles in forty-seven cities.[102] In most cases, whites were the aggressors, but in general African-Americans were less willing than earlier to suffer quietly.

This attitude was reflected in the wartime behavior of the African-American press. African-American editors were extraordinarily vigilant in pointing out unfair treatment; none were actually "disloyal," but many were critical of the nation's wartime agenda, which they believed called for disproportionate and unrewarded sacrifices by African-Americans. As a result of this heightened advocacy role, the aggregate circulation of African-American newspapers increased 40 percent. The press was not the only institution that grew at this time; NAACP membership increased tenfold, and the Congress on Racial Equality (CORE) was established in 1942.[103] White leaders were concerned that the African-American press would promote disloyalty and disaffection among its readers, and began an editorial campaign against the African-American press. Characteristic was an article by Virginius Dabney, liberal editor of the Richmond, Virginia, *Times-Dispatch*, attacking the self-interested attitude of African-American editors, and asserting that if whites were to read the African-American press, riots would break out.[104]

As it turned out, no wave of violent reprisals against African-American newspapers materialized. Partly this was because African-American editors moderated their tone in response to criticism, both official and unofficial.[105] Partly it was because, in fact, white people did not read the African-American press, and thus were not in a position to be outraged by it. And partly it was because of the uncommon extent to which leaders frowned upon violence during the war.

World War II marked the high point in influence for African-American newspapers. Shortly after the war, readership for African-American papers was cut into by mainstream media, especially local-monopoly white dailies and, later, television. At the same time, within African-American communities, the press was superseded by more energetic institutions, especially religious ones, as the civil rights movement gained momentum.[106]

World War II also initiated a turn in U.S. race relations. In the years between World War II and the late 1960s, the rules of public discourse were fundamentally altered to make overt racial appeals obscene. After more than a century of success, white supremacy campaigns were finally eliminated; instead, candidates and legislation became careful to present themselves as racially enlightened. The political arena became, in fact, far more responsive to the needs and expectations of African-Americans than the white electorate seemed to be. The federal government especially became active for the first time since Reconstruction in enforcing racial justice.

The reasons for the nation's change in race relations are unclear but obviously manifold. On the broadest level, national changes reflected global changes. The same period witnessed the decline of European colonialism in Africa and the rise of new nations; in the United Nations, the crusade against apartheid began well before the United States, with its embarrassing legacy of segregation, was able to support it. The decline of colonialism was tied to the framing of World War II as a war against fascism. The crusade against fascism reverberated on the home front as well. Both for practical reasons—the need to maintain high levels of wartime productivity and the loyalty of African-American citizens—and for ideological reasons, the Roosevelt and Truman administrations were eager to prevent racial disruptions, and in some ways this meant guaranteeing, both verbally and through institutional measures, like the Fair Employment Practices Commission, the rights of African-American citizens.

Of less obvious importance was the ideological attack on ethnicity.[107] Part of the crusade against fascism was an anxiety over the possibility of totalitarianism taking root in the United States. To reassure themselves and the public, thinkers discovered a bulwark against fascism in the "American character." The American character came out of the "melting pot," a notion that dated back to the turn of the century. After their metaphorical smelting, the American people no longer bore the impurities of European peoples: twisted ideologies and ghettoizing group identities. Instead, the American people were practical, rational, individualistic, and indomitably democratic. Voiced with renewed intensity after a two-decade-long period of immigration restriction, the myth of the American character proved deeply alluring in the World War II and postwar eras. In schoolbooks, in movies, and in public rhetoric, the ethnic dimensions of U.S. history and politics disappeared.[108] In the ideological context of the postwar United States, traditional race relations were more an absurdity than ever.

Yet another contributing factor was demographic change. The great migration of African-Americans to northern cities had intensified during the war. African-Americans had taken industrial jobs and joined unions; the CIO was far more interested than earlier trade unions in recruiting African-Americans. African-Americans had in fact insinuated themselves into the economic and political life of the North. In terms of practical politics, this meant that the African-American vote often represented the balance of power in northern cities; long the preserve of the party of Lincoln, it now became an object of desire for the party of Franklin Roosevelt, whose First Lady soon became a champion of racial justice. For a time in the 1950s and 1960s Democrats engaged in the contradictory practice of courting the African-American vote in national politics while running segregationist candidates in the South; going into the 1990s, the Democratic party still hasn't quite sorted this dilemma out. But by the 1960s, Democratic Presidents Kennedy and Johnson had, to the chagrin of many of their southern compadres, committed the federal government to assisting desegregation in the South.

The immediate cause of change in the postwar era was a massive bottom-up movement among African-American folk. Tired of unequal schooling and housing, of segregation in public accommodations and transportation, African-Americans turned out in large numbers to support bus boycotts and voting registration drives, seemingly pushing rather than being pulled by their leaders.

Voting rights and school desegregation were the immediate keys to violence. Southern whites resisted the U.S. Supreme Court's ruling against segregated public schooling in *Brown v. Board of Education* (1954) with legal and extralegal maneuvers, ranging on the extreme end to rioting and eliminating public schools. And, especially in states like Mississippi, whites fought voting rights with official obfuscation and political terrorism.

Southern African-American newspapers paid less attention than one would have expected to civil rights activism. Even in the hottest centers of the movement, papers like the *Jackson Advocate* in Mississippi, the *Outlook* in Greensboro, North Carolina, and the *World* in Atlanta shied away from printing news stories about protests, much less editorializing in support.[109] As a result, in many cities, new newspapers were begun by African-American activists.

In some cases established African-American newspapers took a more active role and became targets of violence as a result. A good example is the Little Rock *Arkansas State Press*, run by L. Christopher and Daisy Bates, which took a leading position in the fight for school desegregation partly because Daisy Bates was state president of the NAACP. Because of their involvement, they received constant threats, crosses were burned on their lawn, and in the summer of 1959 their home was bombed.[110]

Local African-American newspapers were not the sole, or even the main target of antimedia violence during the civil rights period in the South. Instead, one finds frequent mention of threats and attacks against local white media and especially representatives of national media. During the controversy over desegregation in Little Rock, for instance, three representatives of *Life* magazine, along with an African-American newspaperman, were beaten by an anti-integration mob. In Mississippi, during the Freedom Summer, the moderate *Laurel Leader-Call* was bombed. Northern reporters were attacked along with other "intruders" during freedom rides and voter registration campaigns.[111]

The attention of the national media to the struggles for civil and voting rights prompted violence for several reasons. National media attention was seen as outside agitation in a local or regional problem; reporters were condemned in the same terms as the freedom riders. Indeed, both served the same purpose: to overturn local order by focusing national attention on injustices. But the national media were seen as crucial to the public legitimization of the movement. African-American voices had traditionally been allowed to speak to African-Americans through African-American media; now they were succeeding in speaking to the nation through white media. Pressure was exerted on the white media in return, sometimes with telling effect, as for instance when CBS commentator Howard K. Smith was fired for his vivid account of beatings of freedom riders.[112]

The achievement in the civil rights era of the representation of African-Americans in the mainstream media was a mixed blessing. African-American concerns received far more, and far more sympathetic, attention among the national public. But this attention hastened the erosion of the market niche of African-American media; no longer were they the primary instruments of reporting on race issues. The failure of the old Negro Associated Press in 1965 is telling.

As the media center for race issues shifted from the African-American press to the mainstream media, those media came under attack from African-American activists also. During the Watts riot, for instance, rioters fired on the helicopter of television station KTLA. This must be looked upon as something other than a practical or tactical move, that is, an attempt to prevent news from being conveyed: urban rioters weren't especially publicity-shy. Rather, it expressed anger against media perceived to be an intimate part of the power structure. Hostility toward the media was integral to the whole set of tensions and frustrations responsible for urban unrest.[113]

Hostility toward mainstream media remains high. A vivid demonstration of this came in 1992 following the acquittal of Los Angeles policemen accused of using excessive force in the beating of African-American motorist Rodney King. Rioters attacked the offices of the Los Angeles *Times* and the Los Angeles Times Syndicate, stealing equipment and trying to set fires. In Los Angeles and other cities, notably Atlanta, reporters and photographers found themselves targets of the rioters' anger.[114]

Contemporary Racial Violence

The media continue to experience racial violence, though it seems muted. The Klan, which has periodically threatened African-American papers, especially in the South,[115] has seemed to be experiencing another revival, along with more extreme groups. In recent years, the *Carolina Times*, the Wilmington, North Carolina, *Journal*, the Jackson, Mississippi *Advocate*, and the Klanwatch offices at the Southern Poverty Law Center have all been bombed.[116] African-American journalists still encounter violence on the job.[117] And new white supremacist groups, like The Order and the Knights of the New Order, have targeted both African-American and mainstream media.[118]

Still, the work of African-American journalists and their white sympathizers is less dangerous now than at any point since the Civil War. The reasons for this are manifold. First, African-Americans have by now already entered the realm of politics. Much of the violence of earlier years was intended to prevent African-American political participation: from Reconstruction to the violence of Freedom Summer in Mississippi,[119] terror was used to keep African-Americans from registering to vote, and violence against the press often reflected this basic goal. But the right to vote has been won; furthermore, African-American voters have been incorporated into the strategies and operations of mainstream political parties. Political exclusion is no longer a goad to antipress violence.

At the same time, the African-American media have acquired a different position vis à vis mainstream media. Previously, African-American media spoke to an audience that was insulated from mainstream media. They were truly in a position to present a competing view of reality to their readers. This no doubt made African-American media seem ominous to whites, in much the same way that, say, Catholic priests ministering to non-English-speaking congregations seemed threatening in the nineteenth century. But the African-American public is no longer insulated from the mainstream media; indeed, African-Americans watch mainstream television more than whites, and tend to read local-monopoly daily newspapers with a frequency almost equal to that of their white neighbors. As a result, instead of presenting a competing version of reality, African-American media tend to supplement a mainstream version of reality.

Meanwhile, mainstream media have made efforts to represent African-Americans more fully. Partly, this is the result of the ascendant notion of media responsibility; in the words of the Hutchins Commission on Freedom of the Press, news media are responsible for "the projection of a representative picture of the constituent groups in the society."[120] Although mainstream media have generally acknowledged a responsibility to represent the various groups in society, they have also become aware of the importance of African-Americans as a market. This is especially true for two key types of media: local monopoly daily newspapers and network television. Both types of media are anxious about audience erosion: newspapers see themselves losing circulation to broadcasters, and networks believe they are losing viewers to cable television and VCRs. As a result, both are more eager to court previously neglected African-American viewers and readers.

The acceptance of African-Americans in mainstream society has never been readier. But there are signs that racism and racial violence—along with other kinds of "hate crimes" directed against Jews, Arabs,[121] gays, and lesbians—are resurgent. This violence is often dismissed as the work of extremist groups, but I think at the base is the still unresolved tension in American ideology between groups and individuals.

Other Group Violence

Other groups have experienced violence. One persistent type of antigroup violence is that directed against religious groups, like Catholics and Mormons. This kind of violence was far more common in the nineteenth century, when the nation's specifically Protestant character was a matter of deeper concern to "native Americans," but the twentieth century has seen a fair amount of this sort of activity, most notably directed toward "sects" like the Jehovah's Witnesses. Similarly persistent has been violence against immigrant groups. Such ethnic animosity peaked around the turn of the century and then again during World War I, resulting in immigration restriction in the 1920s.

In part this violence stemmed from a tendency to associate immigrants with political radicalism. This was especially the case in the years of repression surrounding Chicago's Haymarket Riot (1886–1887).[122] The assassination of President McKinley in 1901 by anarchist Leon F. Czolgosz touched off another two-year round of antianarchist and anti-immigrant hysteria, including a series of crowd actions, some directed against periodicals like *L'Aurora*, an Italian-language anarchist paper published in the coal-mining town of Spring Valley, Illinois, and the *Freie Arbeiter Stimme*, a New York City Yiddish-language anarchist paper. These crowd actions are all the more interesting because they paralleled legal and legislative moves to restrict freedom of speech and press on the basis of political beliefs. By coincidence, in Virginia, a new constitution was being drafted in 1901; after the assassination, there was a movement to strike the right of free speech from its bill of rights, on the grounds that free speech had caused the assassination. The movement failed, but meanwhile states began to pass laws outlawing anarchism and anarcho-syndicalism, and the federal government passed laws restricting the immigration and naturalization of political radicals.[123]

It would be a mistake to attribute hostility toward the foreign-born to political belief alone. To native-born Americans, waves of immigration seemed to create vast pockets of strange folk inside but insulated from the great public. Language differences allowed immigrant groups to maintain boundaries, to forestall assimilation. John Higham, the preeminent historian of nativism, puts it thus:

> What was worse than the size and strategic position of the alien population was its apartness. The impulse for unity crashed against the plain, frightening fact that the new immigrants lived in a social universe so remote from that of the Americans on the other side of the tracks that they knew practically nothing of one another.[124]

The existence of cultures within and distinct from the general culture invited the enmity of nativists, who believed that distinctness must be denatured in the great melting pot.

By far the most compelling episode of violence against an ethnic group was the World War I–era attack on German-Americans. German-Americans had experienced hostility during anti-Catholic and antiradical crusades in the past, but during that war they came under assault for the very fact of their Germanness.[125]

German-Americans were perhaps the best-established of the non-English-speaking immigrant groups. By 1900, 8 million first- and second-generation German-Americans, plus another 4 million descendants of German immigrants, lived in the United States, accounting for roughly one-sixth of the entire population. These were mostly well-seasoned Americans too: German immigration had peaked at 250,000 in 1882; in the years 1895–1914, it averaged only 30,000 per year. But German-Americans had never been a strongly unified bloc. They were divided along religious lines between Catholic and Protestant, as well as between religious and secular, and along social lines between rural and urban. There was a National German-American Alliance in the pre–World War I years, but it unified Germans on little besides an opposition to prohibition, always an important symbolic issue for immigrant groups, along with an opposition to women's suffrage (seen as a stalking horse for prohibition), and support for German-language public schooling. It was the war itself that first brought German-Americans together, now to campaign against U.S. entry on the side of the French and British.[126]

The German-language press was as large as and better organized than the German-speaking population. The number of German-language papers in the United States peaked at 894 in 1894, and declined to 488 in 1910—still a very large number. On the eve of World War I, in 1914, German-language newspapers circulated 620,000 copies daily and 1,753,000 weekly. Most of these papers were part of Louis Hammerling's American Association of Foreign-Language Newspapers. The association marketed national advertising for its newspaper members and coordinated editorial policy—often in return for advertising patronage—generally maintaining a pro-Republican line. Thus the German-language press, along with the National German-American Alliance, was well positioned to lobby against U.S. entry into the war.[127] For the three years that the United States avoided entry into the war, despite mounting anti-German sentiment following the sinking of the *Lusitania* and the escalating submarine war, and despite a rising campaign against "hyphenated Americans" that tinged the 1916 presidential election, the German-language press held its ground. Then, in early 1917, with the interception of the Zimmerman telegram (outlining German strategy and war aims in the event of U.S. entry on the opposite side), virtually the entire German-language press, with the exception of some Socialists and a few independent editors, became loudly pro-Allies.[128]

The editorial conversion of the German-language press did not convince the "100% Americans." Former President Theodore Roosevelt, for instance, proclaimed that "while this war lasts we should not permit any newspaper to be published in German or in the tongue of any of the other nations with which we are at war. . . . The leading German newspapers of this country have been scandalously disloyal."[129] The history of opposition to the war gave some support to Roosevelt's suspicions, but still it seems a bit harsh to condemn an entire language group at a time when it was scrupulously loyal in expression for opposing the war before entry, when a tremendous chunk of the English-language press likewise opposed the war. The condemnation of Germanism was not simply pragmatic, not simply based in a concern for loyalty; there was also an irrational suspicion of Germanness. Fantasies of German outrages spawned and thrived; for example, Richard Metcalfe, one of William Jennings Bryan's lieutenants, broadcast stories about teachers in Nebraska's German Lutheran schools whipping students who happened to speak English during recess.[130] The popularity of stories like this, along with frequent indictments of the tyrannical strain of the German national character, reminds one of the proliferation of tales of the abuses of the confessional in antebellum anti-Catholicism. The German language became the focus of these suspicions. It was the German language that allowed disloyal persons to conspire against their nation with relative confidence because they could not be overheard; German-language schools, churches, and newspapers would foster a massive network of subversion. So the language itself must be eliminated. The Missouri Council of Defense stated this eloquently:

> The Missouri Council of Defense is opposed to the use of the German language in the schools, churches, lodges and in public meetings of every character. The Council believes that the elimination of German and the universal use of English at all such gatherings, is essential to the development of a true, patriotic sentiment among all the people.
>
> The general adoption of English by all patriotic German organizations is a national duty and prompt action by all such will be regarded by loyal Americans as the clearest evidence of loyalty and a sincere determination to help and not hinder the American nation in this war.

This sentiment had great impact. In Missouri, for instance, a state with a large German-American population, English was substituted as the language of worship in many churches, some German-language newspapers began publishing half in English while others ceased to publish altogether, and two counties prohibited the use of German on the phone lines.[131]

Missouri's experience during World War I was typical. Some kind of council of defense was set up in most states, and committees of defense or public safety operated on the local level, scrutinizing the loyalty of the citizenry. National volunteer organizations were formed as well: the American Protective League, the National Security League, the American Defense League, and for youth, the Anti-Yellow Dog League. Most of these were in communication with and supported by the Justice Department and the Committee on Public Information, the federal government's official war propaganda arm. Among the targets of suspicion were German churches and schools; in many cases, German-language books were removed from public libraries, and sometimes they were publicly burned.[132]

The press became the focus for much of this public hostility. German-language newspapers and editors encountered a whole array of violent behavior, including threatening letters, officially sanctioned vandalism (in Cleveland, Boy Scouts burned German-language papers), tar and feathers (like the committees of safety, a homage to the Revolutionary era), flag-kissing ceremonies, dousings with yellow paint (yellow being the color of disloyalty at the time), and mobbings (the American Protective League raided the offices of German newspapers in Chicago and Philadelphia).[133] The irony is that the German-language press was no longer a vehicle of dissent. Editors were overwhelmingly loyal or silent.[134] It was not the actual but the imagined dissent or disloyalty of German-speaking citizens that prompted hostility; to avoid violence, German-Americans had to give up their Germanness.

Popular action was matched by government action. We have already noted the measures taken by state and local councils of defense. On the federal level, the German-American press was singled out for scrutiny by the Justice Department, which raided the offices of numerous papers in September and October of 1917, and by the Post Office, which revoked mailing privileges for many newspapers. In

October 1917, Congress passed a law requiring German-language publications to provide verbatim translations of all material dealing with the United States or the war to local postmasters. The simple cost of this measure prompted many papers to suspend operations. Further, inexact translations, even if inadvertent, could lead to prosecution; as a result, many German-language publications avoided printing any war news. In addition, editors, along with other German-American leaders, could be interned as aliens.[135] Congress also obliged President Wilson with the passage of acts regarding espionage and sedition, the first federal legislation in this area since 1798.

Government officials seemed by their actions to support popular intolerance. Officeholders, candidates, judges, and the press often explicitly endorsed the actions of vigilante groups.[136] One could argue that had official action not been taken, popular violence would have been much more extreme. It is hard to credit this argument, however; in practice, it seems that legal intolerance generally serves to exacerbate popular intolerance, largely by legitimizing the attitudes that support intolerance.

The end result of legal and extralegal actions against the German-language press was stunning. Between 1910 and 1920, according to census figures, the number of German-language papers fell from 488 to 152, and their aggregate circulation declined from 3.4 to 1.3 million. The dropoff in daily newspapers was even more dramatic: from 64 with a circulation of 935,000 to 14 with a circulation of 239,000. This decline was concentrated in the war years.[137] It signals nothing less than the disappearance of a highly significant group voice. Even Louis Hammerling's American Association of Foreign-Language Newspapers had had its teeth pulled. In December 1918, after a senatorial investigation had discredited Hammerling, he sold his controlling interest in the association to backers of the corporate-controlled American Inter-Racial Council, who installed assimilationist Frances Keller as its head, and used the association's control of national advertising to flood foreign-language newspapers with patriotic articles and antiradical propaganda.[138] This shift stands as a striking testament to the shift in the social function of the "immigrant press" generally and the German-American press specifically from preserving a separate voice in public discourse to facilitating assimilation into the mainstream.[139]

Conclusion

Groups have had a real presence in U.S. history. Defined both by their apartness from the mainstream and by their internal sense of identity, ethnic and racial groups have been both objects and subjects of action. The United States has been not just a polity of individuals but also a polity of groups.

But U.S. political ideology has always had trouble with the notion of group rights. Proponents of a republican vision of polity were always wary of the machinations of classes and factions, and classical liberals have also condemned group "interference" with individual freedom. The realm of freedom and justice has generally been conceived of as a realm of rational individuals, grounded in a community, perhaps, but not in a group. Although republicans and liberals have often acknowledged the injustices that some groups have suffered—African-Americans, for instance, have not been without white sympathizers—they have generally conceived of the problem and the solution as involving the acceptance of African-Americans *as individuals* into mainstream society.

The gains that nonmainstream groups have made in the post–World War II era have been achieved through the appeal to individual rights. In the civil rights movement, this appeal was phrased most memorably in Martin Luther King, Jr.,'s "I Have a Dream" speech, in which he appeals on behalf of African-American people that all be judged on "the content of our character" and not the "color of our skin." This is to say, we should all be treated as individuals and not as members of a group. This is certainly a reasonable appeal for *standards of judgment*; it does not, however, constitute a formula for determining *who we are*. We may all demand that the law treat us as individuals, yet we all understand ourselves as members of various groups, from the immediate family to local communities, professional and business groups, political groups, ethnic groups, and so forth. Furthermore, we consistently assign people we encounter to groups, whether by occupation or age or gender or ethnicity. We act, and we expect others to act, as members of a group.

This conundrum—the tension between rights defined as individual and identities based on group allegiance; the tension between liberalism and pluralism—is central to understanding violence against the minority media. African-American newspapers have been attacked when they have asserted a group identity and group rights and group power because they represent a group voice in the marketplace, because they define a space apart from the mainstream but with claims to recognition in the mainstream. Violence has diminished *pari passu* with the apartness of African-Americans. The same has been true for other ethnic groups. Violence was common when ethnicity represented genuine apartness, and diminished as ethnicity came to mean mainly food.

A similar trend is evident in labor-related violence. When labor periodicals promoted genuine apartness—class identity and anticapitalism—they were greeted with official and extralegal hostility; when labor interests were identified primarily as wages, violence waned.

7

Labor-Related Violence

Just as there has always been an ideological barrier to the acceptance of racial separatism, so has there been a barrier to class separatism. The agitation of class issues
in the press and the establishment of class-based newspapers has often provoked
violence. This class violence has, moreover, been colored by some unique features
of U.S. labor history.

The United States has had an exceptionally violent labor history.[1] Labor violence has often been obscured in public memory by overriding beliefs in social
mobility and ideological consensus, which produce an impression of unbroken class
harmony and industrial stability. This impression is simply wrong. Compared with
other Western industrial nations, the United States has experienced longer, more
frequent, and more violent strikes and industrial disputes; the United States also
boasts an exceptionally violent history of suppressing left-wing movements. All
of this discord seems evanescent, though, absent class-based politics and the threat
of a "workers' revolution."

The United States has never developed a national labor party, unlike other Western nations. Partly this was a result of political contingencies. Systems of parlia-
mentary government, with their natural openness to a multiplicity of parties, are more
conducive to class-based political movements than U.S.-style majoritarian democracy. Similarly, unlike in England, where the drive to win the right to vote provided
a unifying goal for working-class politics, in the United States universal male suffrage was achieved without a class struggle, simply because it was always in the
interest of the party in power to extend the franchise to win the support
of new voters. In addition, the peculiar social history of U.S. labor limited the
opportunities for working-class politics. Workers were always divided along lines
of race and ethnicity. Also, ironically, labor was usually cut off from a natural base
of support among farmers, who one might argue produced the most effective third-

party movements in the industrial United States in Populism and the Non-Partisan League. And we should not neglect the role of plain repression in stamping out class politics.

Perhaps most crucial, however, was the ideology of liberal individualism. The United States has maintained an individualist ethos quite at odds with labor's implicit mutualism. Thus, during the 1877 railroad strike that inaugurated the modern period of labor strife in the United States, the nation's leading religionist, Henry Ward Beecher, defined the struggle as one between freedom and collectivism:

> The European theories of combinations between workmen and trades-unions and communes destroy the individuality of the person, and there is no possible way of preserving the liberty of the people except by the maintenance of individual liberty, intact from Government and intact from individual meddling. Persons have the right to work when or where they please, as long as they please, and for what they please, and any attempt to infringe on this right, and to put good workmen on a level with poor workmen—any such attempt to regiment labor is preposterous.[2]

Beecher was elucidating the ideology of "industrial freedom" that would be invoked continually by opponents of officially recognized unions. It should be noted that in addition to serving the interests of industrialists, this ideology also expressed the deep hostility of ordinary U.S. citizens and workers to limits on individual freedom, which seemed obnoxious coming from labor activists as well as from "robber barons."

Individualism allowed labor's opponents to characterize activists as un-American. In fact, even the recognition of collective bargaining in federal legislation is premised on individual consent, as Mike Davis remarks:

> American unions have never possessed the corporate rights accorded by European and Japanese legal codes which recognize their integrity as organizational entities. In the United States, collective bargaining is legally derived from a classically liberal concept of individual consent to representation. Despite the mass struggles of the 1930s, the word "union" does not appear in either the Wagner or Taft-Hartley Acts. Because its legitimacy is therefore based on individual consent, the rights of American unions under law are provisional and revocable; anti-union campaigns on the right are always waged in a Jeffersonian language of the "rights of individual workers."[3]

Individualism has always acted to stunt labor activism and class politics.

Whatever the causes, the result has been a disarticulation of mainstream labor unionism and mainstream partisan activism. Unions have worked with parties and candidates on specific legislation, and have been, especially recently, heavily involved in campaign financing—unions invented the political action committee— but they have not tried to move industrial conflict to the center of politics. They have shied away from making class consciousness and class conflict crucial to campaigns. One effect of this has been a remarkable lack of unity among union members when it comes to voting. Especially since 1980, union leaders have had little success in delivering voters to the candidates they support, even while they've delivered money to war chests.

Labor Movements

U.S. labor history is characterized by struggles between left and right among working-class groups as well as between labor and outside forces—capital and the state. In the 1880s, for instance, the Knights of Labor acquired mass membership and stood to represent labor as a whole, though challenged on the left by anarchists and socialists; the Knights' prominence faded quickly in the aftermath of the Haymarket Riot. Then, in the early decades of the twentieth century, the Socialist party on the left and the craft unions that made up the American Federation of Labor (AFL) on the right vied for the loyalties of workers. Both were eclipsed by the wave of reaction that followed World War I; the AFL survived, but the Socialist party was torn apart by internal disputes and external repression. The Great Depression of the 1930s revived unionism as a strategy of national recovery. The National Industrial Recovery Act and later the Wagner Labor Relations Act of 1937 established the right to collective bargaining in federal law and implicitly designated craft and industrial unions—the AFL and, to a lesser extent, the Congress of Industrial Organizations (CIO)—as legitimate parts of a capitalist economy. Meanwhile, on the left, the Communist party grew in influence by organizing marches of the unemployed and establishing a foothold among maritime, textile, and agricultural workers; Communist party members were also active in some of the unions affiliated with the CIO. By the end of World War II, according to the Bureau of Labor Statistics, union membership peaked at just over 35 percent of the nonagricultural work force.[4]

After World War II, labor's vision became less expansive. Several events coincided to pinch the ambitions of activists. Congress passed the Taft-Hartley Act, limiting the rights of union organizers and strikers; the AFL and the CIO merged, creating a dominant conservative bloc; and radicalism, especially the Communist party, was eviscerated by government action. The transition to an "establishment" unionism was made easier by the U.S. position of unchallenged global industrial dominance, which allowed companies like the major automobile manufacturers to trade off wage increases to prevent work stoppages.

In the 1970s and 1980s the position of labor began to erode again. In law and government, the climate turned generally hostile to organized labor, and union membership fell. By the end of the 1980s, the most successful unions were among clerical and white-collar workers, like the American Federation of State, County, and Municipal Employees (AFSCME), while the older industrial unions—the United Auto Workers and the United Steelworkers—were hampered by plant closings and automation and failed to achieve notable successes in negotiations for wage increases or job security. Meanwhile, management practices like the hiring of permanent replacement workers during strikes were rehabilitated with the active support of the executive branch of the federal government, and unions showed an inability to make inroads into the rapidly growing service and information sectors of the economy. One might expect another cycle of radicalism, labor activism, and repression.

Labor and the Press

Mainstream U.S. newspapers have generally been antilabor. Exceptions come quickly to mind: the Scripps newspapers, for instance, and the early Hearst newspapers, made conscious appeals to working-class readers. Even so, the daily press could usually be counted upon to oppose labor activism. The later Hearst press is a classic example. It retained a "populist" tone while waging war on labor organizations, among whom "I Don't Read Hearst" became a rallying cry. Indeed, many of the most "popular" newspapers of the age of industrialization were also the most antilabor: the Denver *Post* and the Chicago *Times*, for instance.

Press hostility cannot be blamed simply on the economic interests of newspaper owners. Although it is true that the industrial revolution affected newspapers as well as other businesses, and that the news industry saw its share of "captains of industry" (positively connoted) or "robber barons" (negatively connoted), and that the craft structure of daily newspapering disappeared and was replaced by a more remote ownership structure around the time of the Civil War, still it was not predetermined that the editorial stance of newspapers would be antilabor. Indeed, one would expect that a tempting market would exist for prolabor newspapers; the fact that many successful left-leaning papers were run out of business only through concerted effort—and in some cases government harassment—should make us wary of the argument that economic forces dictated that the press be antilabor.

Rather, the individualist culture of the press seems to have predisposed newspeople to be suspicious of labor. The same wariness of conspiratorial power that prompted Ida Tarbell to expose Standard Oil's machinations, for instance, inspired Ray Stannard Baker's reporting on the United Mine Workers union in the Pennsylvania anthracite region. In both cases, the story was the same: the independent, the little guy, was being squeezed by the combine.[5] Mainstream journalists distrusted radical organizations like the Industrial Workers of the World (IWW) and the Communist party, which they saw as conspiracies against the public interest on behalf of a class or even a foreign power. The hostility of the mainstream press was one spur to the creation of an autonomous labor press and a wide range of radical periodicals.

Labor newspapers appeared early and often. The "labor press" has never been adequately chronicled, but it is possible to identify several key moments in labor journalism and a few main genres of labor newspapers. The first labor papers were the "workingmen's" papers that began turning up around the 1820s, part of the general ferment of Jacksonian politics.[6] These papers sometimes supported labor organizations, but usually they were aimed at a general public and followed a Jeffersonian rhetoric of popularized enlightenment. They were not, then, labor organs per se. They proclaimed the ideology of rational liberty that informed many of the mainstream early national newspapers, and sought an undifferentiated and perhaps universal public of rational individuals.[7]

After the Civil War, labor organization and a specifically labor press developed quickly. These papers were more likely to figure their audience as a class, a group that shared a position in an industrial production process and therefore had group interests that were in opposition to the interests of other groups with different positions in the productive process. This kind of press might best be seen as the journalistic analog of the Knights of Labor: broad-based and somewhat radical but not strictly organized along craft lines and not yet disillusioned with the dream of wide opportunities for social mobility and the purifying function of republican political institutions.

Many of these papers were embedded in the language and culture of immigrant groups. The "identity" of U.S. workers was never exhausted by reference to class, of course. The labor history of the United States has always been distinguished by the fragmentation of workers along lines of race, religion, and ethnicity. Ethnicity also provided a unifying element among workers in some key locations: the "Polishness" of Chicago's Packingtown workers, for instance, was an important source of their sense of identity. Ethnicity, in every instance, provided a sense of apartness along with a sense of belonging. The apartness of ethnic communities may have been crucial in heightening a tendency toward and a reputation for radicalism: Marxism appealed most strongly to the foreign-born, and movements for immigration restriction always accompanied the nation's recurrent "Red Scares."

The rise of craft unionism and industrial unionism along the lines of the AFL and CIO, especially in the twentieth century, produced union newspapers. These were and are generally national in scope and aimed at a segmented readership; they have tended to carry information of relatively narrow concern, and in no way compete with the mainstream press. The union newspaper has become the dominant form of labor organ.

The long course of labor journalism, then, has been characterized by a movement from a utopian or enlightenment appeal to the rational public to a more specific appeal to a class or ethnic group to a narrowly focused appeal to a specific occupational group. At the same time, a somewhat independent tradition of radical politics and journalism developed.

Radicalism and the Radical Press

The connection between radical politics and labor activism is not entirely secure. The style of unionism that has come to be empowered in the United States is conservative: it does not question capitalism, it works within a framework of large-scale corporate enterprises (and is at odds more often with small-scale entrepreneurs than with Fortune 500 companies), and it is a major factor in the operation of the mainstream political parties. The anticommunism of the AFL has always been notorious. Still, radicalism and labor share many things—primarily, an intended constituency and the historical hostility of the mainstream.

The radical press also has a long history, beginning before the Civil War with the efflorescence of reform papers. Like the labor press, the radical press has featured both organs tied to specific movements—for example, Socialist party newspapers—and relatively independent papers aimed at a general audience, like *Wilshire's*. And, although no adequate general treatment of the radical press exists, it is possible to construct its chronology simply by noting the occurrence of Red Scares, which usually came at the end of periods of radical success. The major scares occurred in 1877, during the great national railroad strike that marked the commencement of the modern phase of labor strife; in 1886, with the Haymarket Riot, which marked the climax of the eight-hour movement and, coincidentally, of the Knights of Labor; in the latter 1890s, rising with the violent Homestead Strike and peaking with the assassination of McKinley by a professed anarchist in 1901, responding to increased labor tensions during a prolonged depression further enhanced by nativist activism and resulting in the first laws aimed at "syndicalism"; in and following the 1910 bombing of the Los Angeles *Times*, reversing a decade of advances in trade-union organizing and matching the growth of the Socialist party; during and following World War I, climaxing in the great Red Scare of 1919, crippling the Socialist party and the IWW and reversing gains by conservative labor unions during the war itself; in the mid to late 1930s, responding to Communist party successes during the Great Depression; in the post–World War II era, symbolized by Senator Joseph McCarthy, destroying the prestige Communists had gained as a result of the World War II alliance with the Soviet Union and ultimately eliminating the Communist party as a force in U.S. politics; and in the 1960s and beyond, responding to the successes of the civil rights, antiwar, and black power movements.

Labor, Radicalism, and Press Violence

Antipress violence figures in the history of labor and radical movements in a number of fashions. Violence has been directed against labor and radical papers. Likewise, mainstream papers have been attacked by labor activists and sympathizers. Finally, labor disputes within newspapers and the newspaper industry have produced sporadic violence.

Not all segments of the radical and labor press have experienced equal violence or harassment. Radical newspapers were attacked often. Because they were generally the most visible feature of any particular radical movement, they became frequent targets for vigilante action and other forms of violence. Gradually, violence became less common as governmental action was formalized and centered within the federal bureaucracy. The underground press of the 1960s, for instance, suffered only sporadic violence but was the subject of a long and intense FBI project of harassment and "counter-intelligence."

Labor papers, on the other hand, were rarely the first target of antilabor violence. First were usually picketers and demonstrators. They were closely followed by labor organizers and orators, and people distributing leaflets and other literature. Labor's newspapers were not usually its most public face, and because violence was most likely to occur within the context of a strike, those most actively involved in strike activities were the most obvious targets.

Not all labor-related violence was directed against labor. AFL unions acquired a reputation for violence early in the twentieth century; labor was more frequently the victim than the aggressor, but acts of violence by labor were trumpeted by antilabor forces and the mainstream press, cementing the stereotypes of union dynamiters and bomb-throwing anarchists. Because newspapers were perceived by labor as powerful enemies, they too were occasionally attacked.

In addition, newspapers as industrial enterprises were themselves sites of labor struggle. Newspaper unionization was blunted by several factors, notably the fragmentation of news workers by craft—printers and pressmen organized separately, for instance—and the decentralization of newspaper production among thousands of different companies and plants. Still, the drive to unionize newspaper production produced both prolabor and antilabor violence; the potential for violence during newspaper strikes was seen most recently in 1990's strike at the New York *Daily News*. At the same time, technological change has always produced tensions in newspaper production, displacing skilled and perhaps unionized workers, who have responded occasionally with acts of sabotage and ludditism.

This chapter presents case studies of different types of labor-related press violence. These cases suggest some constant structural features in labor relations and radical politics, and indicate patterns of change. The reader is cautioned, of course, that this is not—nor is it intended to be—an adequate overview of the development or character of the U.S. labor press. Rather, it is an exploration into the boundaries of public discourse where labor and, more generally, class are concerned. Our starting point will be strike-related violence.

The Course of Strike Activity in U.S. History

U.S. history has been generously peppered with strike activity. Some periods stand out for their intensity:[8] the late 1880s, and the efflorescence of the Knights of Labor; the 1890s, with the struggles over railways and steel, the Homestead and Pullman strikes; the great rise of the AFL in the World War I era and the CIO in the Great Depression and beyond. These periods also featured repressive movements: the Haymarket Riot and its aftermath (1886), the nativist movements of the 1890s, the Red Scare of 1919, and the various anticommunism crusades from the Dies Committee and the Red Squads of the 1930s to McCarthyism in the 1950s.

Not surprisingly, these periods are also notable for cases of violence against labor and radical newspapers, including the organs of striking unionists. It is beyond my resources to give a complete accounting, but examples are readily available. As early as 1810, carpenters in New York City stoned the windows of newspapers hostile to their demands.[9] When large-scale strike violence became a constant feature after 1877, mainstream and labor papers both were attacked. During the Colorado mining strikes in 1903–1904, as part of the general suppression of the Western Federation of Miners, the sympathetic Victor, Colorado, *Record* was raided by militia;[10] likewise, the Huntington, West Virginia, *Socialist and Labor Star* was mobbed by militia during a coal strike in 1913.[11]

One particular area in which labor disturbances were likely to affect the media was the unionization of the print trades. Workers at newspapers, divided as they were into several "crafts" with differing workplace cultures and varying claims to professional status, and affected with differing severity by the introduction of new technologies, approached unionization gingerly. Newspaper proprietors were often successful in maintaining an open shop, and at some key newspapers existing unions were busted in the last decade of the nineteenth century and first decade of the twentieth.[12] Union busting at newspapers made the antiunion attitudes of most editorial pages all the more galling to labor activists.

The Bombing of the *Los Angeles Times*

By far the most famous case of labor-related violence against a newspaper is the 1910 bombing of the *Los Angeles Times*. The bombing was the culmination of a long battle between labor and capital in southern California. The *Times* had successfully broken the unions in its own shop and was the catalyst for antiunion sentiment in southern California. Unionists resorted to terror to chill the hyperbolic rhetoric of the *Times* and to moderate antiunion attitudes. The scheme backfired tragically.

The *Times* and its proprietors occupied a key position in the economic and political life of the region. Harrison Gray Otis, the paper's founding father, and his son-in-law and eventual successor, Harry Chandler, belonged by wealth to the city's elite—Otis personally owned a million acres of land by 1900—and by political affiliation to the Republican coterie that ran city and county politics around the turn of the century. Otis, Chandler, and the *Times* centered the forces that kept Los Angeles an open-shop town.

Harrison Gray Otis had purchased the year-old *Times* in 1882. In the 1880s, southern California boomed on the strength of rising real-estate values and the expected completion of a railroad system. Otis formed strategic alliances with the railroads—always key players in California politics—while at the same time anchoring the fight to improve the harbor at nearby San Pedro. By 1900 Otis and the *Times* had become dear to the area's business community. The circulation of the *Times* outstripped any of its local rivals; at less than thirty thousand, it seemed small by eastern standards, but because of its sizable advertising patronage, the *Times* could claim to be the nation's heaviest newspaper.[13]

One key achievement of Otis was the formation in the mid-1890s of the Merchants and Manufacturers Association. By 1903, 80 percent of the firms in the Los Angeles area were members of the association; through such widespread cooperation, the area's companies were able to exert influence on local and state officials, including judges and police, and to thwart most unionizing campaigns. Of fifty-one local strikes in 1905–1906—elsewhere in the United States a good season for union organizers—forty-two were complete failures, and another four were no more than partially successful.[14]

Otis had such cachet among area merchants and manufacturers partly because he was so successful at fighting the unions in his own shop. In 1890 Otis invited a showdown with the unions at the *Times* over the issue of "deadheading," the use of pretypeset advertising copy, which compositors asserted violated their traditional prerogatives. When workers affiliated with the Los Angeles Typographical Union (LATU) refused to make concessions, Otis locked them out and brought in replacement workers from the Printers Protective Fraternity, a national outfit that eventually came to be housed in the *Times* building. Not only did Otis break his own unions, then, but he also became the patron of an organization that sent scabs to other shops in Los Angeles and around the country. Thus began over two years of running warfare between the *Times* and the LATU, the International Typographical Union (ITU), and the AFL. These bodies instituted boycotts against the *Times* in 1896 and again in 1901; in 1903, the unions lured Hearst to the Los Angeles market, hoping that competition from his *Examiner* would force Otis to the bargaining table; in 1907, a promising boycott of *Times* advertisers was scuttled by a Supreme Court ruling against secondary boycotts and the onset of the economic downturn following the Panic of 1907. Meanwhile, in response to a citywide strike by printers and pressmen as part of a national eight-hour-day movement in 1906, Otis orchestrated the formation of the Employing Printing Trades Alliance, of which 95 percent of the city's print firms were members.[15] In terms of strategy, the unions were right to look upon Otis as their chief enemy.

Otis and his *Times* were also chief molders of the ideology of the open shop, or "industrial freedom." Industrial freedom meant the freedom of individual workers to bargain on an individual basis with employers—this was the freedom of opportunity characteristic of classical liberalism, in which any individual may seek his or her interest without interference from government and without the trammels of group privileges. In its editorials, the *Times* appealed constantly to the image of the sober, industrious, independent worker and demonized unionists as the opposite: vicious, lazy, jealous. Typical is this characterization of strikers in 1910:

> They are mostly of the anarchic scum of Europe. They are envious, idle, brawling, disorderly men who hang about the deadfalls and, between drinks, damn as a scab every non-union industrious worker. They hate law, hate order, and hate the men and the conditions which compel them to work occasionally. Their instincts are criminal, and they are ever ready for arson, riot, robbery, and murder. . . . They combine in labor unions whose honest purpose they pervert . . . to prohibit the skillful and industrious mechanic from accomplishing any more work in a day than the unskillful and lazy man.

These unions are formed by vicious men for vicious purposes, then, and they will, if allowed, prevent any worker from behaving industriously or virtuously. The union movement will pervert the labor marketplace. But it won't be just workers who suffer. The union movement will undermine public liberty too. Invoking the same metaphor of wolves and sheep that Jefferson used in his famous letter to Carrington to justify the freedom of political newspapers (see Chapter 3), the *Times* editorialist questioned the rights of the labor press: "the public journals which directly or indirectly cater to these human wolves are public enemies." Citizens should take steps to protect their vital interests: "Eternal vigilance is the price of order as well as of liberty."[16]

Otis saw to it that the *Times* maintained its vigilance. When Hearst's *Examiner* moved into Los Angeles, the city's labor unions organized an impressive parade. Otis took this as a declaration of war; that evening, he handed out rifles to his staff. Over the next few years, he was to maintain an almost provocative state of preparedness: Bob Gottlieb and Irene Wolt have called him "the compleat soldier"; Mike Davis says he was "the first militarist of space in Los Angeles." He had a cannon mounted on his touring car; he named his homes the Bivouac and the Outpost; he had the *Times* building designed to resemble a fortress; he called his staff the phalanx, and during times of high tension with the labor movement, he had his "soldiers" drill with rifles in the *Times* offices.[17] Much of this was for show, one supposes. But it's fair to say that Otis did not think of the battle with the unions purely in terms of rhetoric and discourse. The battle was a battle.

Through the summer of 1910, it seemed that labor's attempts to organize in Los Angeles might indeed turn into an actual battle. Organizers based in northern California moved into the South. A series of strikes affected industry after industry, most notably brewing and construction. To counter, an injunction was issued against picketing, which was upheld on appeal; the police were sent to enforce the injunction; picketers defied the injunction; fights broke out between picketers and police, between replacement workers and picketers. Through all this, the tone of the *Times* was relentlessly hostile as it printed story after story of labor's atrocities. The building trades unions bore the brunt of the attack as summer turned to fall.[18]

At 1:07 A.M. on Saturday, 1 October, while Saturday morning's newspaper was in press, a blast shook the *Times* building. It was followed by a second, more intense explosion as stored ink and probably leaking gas ignited. Twenty-one people, almost all workers, were killed; Otis and Chandler were out of the building. Half a million dollars worth of damage was done to the *Times* building, which was gutted by the explosions and the fire that followed, but the newspaper didn't miss a day of publication, instead shifting its operations to an auxiliary printing plant.[19]

Instantly, blame was fixed on union dynamiters. The *Times* accused the "Enemies of Industrial Freedom" of the crime, and quoted California Governor Gillett to this effect: "The labor unionists will have to be blamed for the crime until shown they are not guilty."[20] Not that organized labor was without defenders—many believed, with good reason, that the blast was caused simply by leaking gas. Why, after all, should unionists cause so much carnage and not even succeed in silencing the *Times*?

Rhetorically, the reaction of the *Times* was surprising in only one respect: It did not invoke freedom of the press. Instead, it invoked industrial freedom. General Otis stated this best himself: "So the battle must go on and we, who are in the midst of it, are profoundly confident of the ultimate outcome, which will surely be complete triumph for the cause of freedom in the industries, which is altogether as sacred as are political freedom, religious freedom, or personal freedom, none of which can be sacrificed without leading to the final destruction of the republic."[21] The failure to specifically cite freedom of the press or freedom of expression in the outpouring of commentary in the pages of the *Times* in early October may have been a simple oversight. On the other hand, it may be testimony to the fact that labor had already claimed the issue of freedom of expression in fighting injunctions against picketing and rallies, restrictions on expression that the *Times* supported.

Immediately after the explosion, the resources of the Los Angeles police, as well as of private investigators employed by the *Times*, were mobilized to track down the dynamiters. In April of the following year, arrests were finally made. The accused were members of the International Association of Bridge and Structural Iron Workers, including John J. McNamara, secretary-treasurer of the union, and his brother J. B. Unionists were outraged by the arrests. The fact that the McNamaras were virtually kidnapped to avoid lengthy extradition hearings added a scent of suspicion to the whole case. As their trial approached, the McNamaras attracted many of the celebrities of the left to their cause, including Lincoln Steffens and Clarence Darrow, who took charge of their defense. In Los Angeles, public opinion began to sway in their favor, lifting the election hopes of local Socialists, including mayoral candidate Job Harriman, who also signed on as a defense attorney for the McNamaras. Indeed, Harriman's election seemed so probable that the *Times* actually threw its support to the incumbent mayor, George Alexander, a progressive who had always been anathema to Otis and Chandler.

Then, in a stunning development on the eve of the mayoral election, the McNamaras decided to plead guilty. This shocked organized labor, especially the AFL, which had apparently believed in the innocence of the McNamaras and had organized their defense. The aftermath was decisive: the Socialists were defeated in the election, and the open-shop forces emerged triumphant again in the Los Angeles region. Nationally, the AFL and its affiliated unions also lost momentum, and the Iron Workers were decimated by subsequent investigations.[22]

In retrospect, it is as difficult to justify the bombing strategically as morally. The end result was almost as disastrous for the unions as the immediate result had been for the slain workers. Of course, the dynamiters could not have foreseen that the blast, augmented by leaking gas, perhaps, and volatile chemicals, would have been of such magnitude. Still, what did they expect from a lesser blast? J. B. McNamara apparently hoped to intimidate the *Times* in the short run: "It was my intention to injure the building and scare the owners. I did not intend to take the life of anyone. I sincerely regret these unfortunate men lost their lives."[23] Although the blast wasn't meant to produce a mass slaying of nonunion workers, even as a scare tactic it was profoundly stupid. Otis and the *Times* had chosen the rhetorical position of besieged victim well in advance of the explosion, and had reveled in the martial spirit that such a role invited. It doesn't take hindsight to predict the uselessness of dynamite as an intimidator in this case. Nor does it seem believable that the dynamiters could have expected to cause sufficient property damage to put the *Times* out of business. Its position in the area was secure, and the backing of the local business community, as the aftermath showed, could be counted on in any emergency.

The bombing of the *Times* was not an isolated instance. Other newspapers were attacked by persons or groups sympathetic to labor, usually in the midst of some kind of labor struggle. What stand out about the *Times* bombing are the body count and the clandestine nature of the assault. In the second most famous instance of labor-related violence against an antiunion newspaper, the attack came from an enraged crowd and caused only property damage.

The Mobbing of the *Denver Post*

Colorado has seen some of the most violent labor confrontations in U.S. history. Much of the labor warfare was connected with the state's early boom industry, mining; as a result, the miners' unions, especially the Western Federation of Miners, were among the more militant forces in U.S. labor, and the labor movement in Colorado had a distinctive frontier radicalism. Labor strife also colored government and the press in Colorado. Labor activists generally considered elected officials and the mainstream press to be tools of the mining interests and the business element.

The most notoriously antilabor of Colorado's newspapers was the *Denver Post*. Brought to prominence by Harry Tammen and Fred G. Bonfils, the *Post* was sensational to say the least. Tammen and Bonfils painted their editorial office red and called it the Bucket of Blood; they editorialized so much in their news columns that they dispensed with their editorial page. Bonfils especially enjoyed personal combat; in 1907 he beat up Thomas Patterson, editor of the *Rocky Mountain News*, in retaliation for newspaper attacks. Bonfils was brought to trial, where some of the testimony centered on allegations of blackmail by the *Post*.[24] Labor activists considered the *Post* to be hopelessly corrupt; it was frequently cited in Upton Sinclair's muckraking exposé of the newspaper business, *The Brass Check*. The *Post*'s antiradicalism seems incongruous with its position as Denver's circulation leader through the early years of the twentieth century, but its pages were strewn with scare headlines about anarchist bombings and Bolshevik revolutionaries. It printed headlines in bold red ink throughout the post–World-War-I Red Scare, and in the spring of 1920 it eagerly publicized Attorney General A. Mitchell Palmer's predictions about a May Day revolution in the United States.

The days following World War I were tumultuous for labor. Unions had made major gains during the war both in recognition and in wages and hours, but a recession gave momentum to management attempts to roll back these gains. Postwar hysteria about Bolshevism gave labor's adversaries another weapon to use; in 1919 and 1920 major national strikes by coal miners and steelworkers were defeated partly by appeals to an alarmed public.[25]

In Denver, all of these threads were to come together in an outburst of rioting during a street railway strike in the summer of 1920. The Tramway Company strike was basically over wages; the union's demands for a living wage ran counter to the company's desire to cut costs and Mayor Bailey's campaign promise to lower fares to five cents. As the strike approached, the company depicted the union as unreasonable and warned of violence; the union thought that the city administration gave too much encouragement to the company's scare tactics. When Commissioner of Public Safety Frank M. Downer warned against "any radical, violent, or destructive methods," union officials responded that "no foundation exists" for such fears, that "these officials are trying to prejudice the public mind."[26]

The Tramway Company responded to the strike by hiring replacement workers and importing armed guards, and then sending riderless streetcars out on routes simply to show the public that the strike had been broken—actions looked upon as provocative by union sympathizers. Trouble came on the evening of Thursday, 5 August. Angry crowds gathered downtown near the streetcar barns. Apparently, one of the armed guards fired a shot, and general rioting broke out. The crowds attacked streetcars and replacement workers and imported gunmen and police, and then turned their attention to the *Post*. A mob stormed through the *Post* building, demolishing equipment, breaking windows, and starting fires. When firemen came, rioters took their ladders and used them to climb into upper-story windows to wreck more machinery and raid the editorial offices. The crowd took every copy of the paper on hand and tossed them all into the streets.[27]

Though the rioters struck at strategic targets, it doesn't seem that their violence was orchestrated. Denver's unionists had been univocal in calling for no violence, and in fact the officials of the streetcar union were optimistic that city officials were about to help broker an agreement. Of the twenty-three rioters arrested, none were union men.[28] The hostility of nonunion men toward the Tramway Company was no doubt partly rooted in anger at fare increases, but it also must have involved a more general hostility toward the corporate and political interests that ran the city—hence the attack on the *Post*.

In fact, the city's press in general, and the *Post* in particular, were frequently blamed for the riot by those friendly to labor. The *Labor Bulletin* stated the case simply and repeatedly: "The lying and false statements with which a subsidized press has been trying to break the strike for the Tramway Company inflamed the people to mob violence." And again, "[T]he daily papers . . . are making cowardly attacks on organized labor in general, [and] advocate an open shop to please the interests who have subsidized them in this fight." And again, "Another reason for the present riots was the constant propaganda by a subsidized press against organized labor and against the cause of the Tramway men in their controversy with the company. That this is a fact is clearly shown by the action of the mob in destroying the Post." And again, "Those who have given any thought to the labor movement must realize that the greatest struggle facing the workers is the freeing of the newspaper from the blight of selfish and interest control."[29]

The actions of the rioters make it clear that they felt that the *Post* had violated fundamental rules of fairness and decency. Probably they had resented the *Post* for some time. When rioting broke out, when armed guards shot into an unarmed crowd, it presented an opportunity for people to act on a moral judgment that had been formed earlier. This moral judgment, according to all of the prolabor rhetoric that followed the strike, was in accordance with a traditional sense of a newspaper's responsibility to a community's best interests, a responsibility that was violated when newspapers sold their columns to special interests, when newspapers supported the intrusion of outside forces (in the persons of "hired thugs") to solve community problems, and when newspapers repeatedly distorted information in order to pervert public opinion. The rioters more or less explicitly contended that irresponsible behavior resulted—especially in this instance, but also more generally—in concrete harm to the public, who were apt to be impelled to action on the basis of newspaper propaganda. This is the gist of Charles Kelley's reflections: "The public will be fair if it is informed. When it strikes in blind fury at sincere, well-meaning men whose only purpose is to secure decent living conditions . . . it is because it has been fed up on the vicious, lying propaganda of unscrupulous newspapers that serve not the public, but the enemies of all the people."[30]

In the event, both labor and traditional notions of press responsibility suffered from the Denver riot. The riot forced elected officials to take action, declaring martial law and calling in U.S. troops, who disarmed the Tramway's hired guards. Initially, this seemed to work to the advantage of the striking workers. But at the same time the judicial system was at work; in September, a grand jury handed down indictments against four labor leaders for inciting to riot and against about three dozen of the rioters who had attacked the *Post*. Labor activists noted that none of the guards who had fired into the crowd were indicted, though their provocations were more immediate than anything the labor leaders had done.[31] With these indictments draining the strikers' momentum, and with the winter coming on, the Tramway men called off the strike and returned to work in early November.[32]

The bombing of the *Los Angeles Times* and the mobbing of the *Denver Post* are the two most dramatic incidents of labor violence against antilabor news media. Such incidents have not been very common, probably because labor has usually had a strategic interest in promoting freedom of expression. The two incidents discussed here are dissimilar in many ways, including the precise tactics used, the amount of premeditation involved, and the apparent motivations—the *Times* bombing was meant to intimidate; the *Post* mobbing was an act of moral vengeance. There is one chief similarity: in both cases, violence was counterproductive. Attacks against labor and radical media, on the other hand, tended to be more effective.

The Significance of the Labor Press

The labor press of the late nineteenth-century, as noted above, directed its voice in part to the larger community, while serving primarily as an organ of a labor group. David Montgomery describes this kind of labor press as "especially important to strike agitation" because it "carried the strikers' message to the community and to the nation at large, between strikes sustaining a drumbeat of exposures of speedups, long hours, and abusive foremen. So disturbed were mill owners by this activity that their most common way of attacking the labor movement during the early 1880s was by bringing suits for libel against its editors."[33] Indeed, the judicial system tended to work for owners and against workers, both by reinforcing a tradition of individual rather than collective bargaining and by limiting—especially through use of injunctions—the use of many of labor's most effective weapons, including picketing, boycotts, and negative publicity. Late nineteenth-century owners did not always have a free hand in court, however. As Herbert Gutman has shown, older elite groups, suspicious of the new capitalists and disdainful of industrial work relations, could unite with workers to stymie legal action. Gutman notes the example of Joseph P. McDonnel, an Irish-born radical and the editor of the Paterson, New Jersey, *Labor Standard*, who was twice convicted in court but survived with significant support from several sectors of the community to carry on a long and successful career as a labor editor and promoter of prolabor legislation.[34]

This kind of community-centered labor press did not comport well with the conservative unionism of the AFL, which had emerged as the leading sector of the labor movement by the end of the nineteenth century. Rather, conservative union-ism cultivated a style of labor journalism that was narrowly aimed at union mem-bers. At the same time, the realm of news was being colonized by the mainstream press. If they wanted to reach the general public, labor activists would henceforth rely on the reporting staffs of general circulation dailies. Meanwhile, the old elites that had in some instances protected labor editors from the new industrialists were withdrawing or being displaced from public life.

In this conjuncture of simultaneuous change in social structure, in media envi-ronments, and in the strategies of labor activists, two types of violence against labor voices appeared. One was directed against labor papers, designed to cripple them as organizational tools. The other was directed against labor sympathizers in the mainstream media, and was designed to stifle labor's voice in the general arena of discussion. Both types were particularly likely to be exercised during strikes, and especially if the striking workers showed some sympathy for radical ideas.

Accounts of attacks on labor media in the early decades of the twentieth cen-tury are relatively easy to find in the pages of socialist papers or in the early reports of the American Civil Liberties Union (ACLU). Mining was an industry of abundant violence in this era. Attacks on the Huntington, West Virginia, *Socialist and Labor Star* and the Victor, Colorado, *Record* have already been mentioned; in 1910 thugs hired by the Homestake Mining Company mobbed the office of the *Black Hills Daily Register*, a paper that had been founded five years earlier by the Western Federation of Miners;[35] and the Butte, Montana, *Daily Bulletin* was a continual target of violent harassment—in 1920 editor Burton K. Wheeler was attacked by a mob while campaigning for office.[36] Violence was also directed against the distri-bution of labor papers and leaflets. In the mining districts of southern Illinois in the 1930s, the radical Progressive Miners Union was able to distribute literature only by hiring an airplane; even so, the airplane was shot at.[37]

Also common were assaults on reporters. Sometimes the reporters represented prounion or left-leaning news organizations, such as when Boris Israel and Mrs. Harvey O'Connor of the Federated Press were shot at during the Harlan County miners' strikes in 1931.[38] But reporters for mainstream media were also in harm's way. During the violent Gastonia textile strike in North Carolina, a local sheriff severely beat a reporter for the Charlotte *Observer*, and during the Passaic, New Jersey, textile strikes, reporters were singled out as targets by police during clashes with strikers.[39] Attacks on general reporters have been less common than attacks on radical or labor journalists, however, because the mainstream media have rarely committed significant resources to covering labor activities, and because their coverage has usually been antilabor.

As these examples show, even when the immediate target of violence was mainstream, the probability of violence was heightened when there was some significant involvement by the more radical sectors of the labor movement—Socialists, Communists, or the IWW especially. Attacking conservative unionists was risky. Because they tended to form working relationships with mainstream political forces and to support the right to property in its broad outlines, they could usually muster some support from empowered groups. Anarchists, Socialists, and Communists, on the other hand, were connected with the political and economic powers-that-be only by abstract commitments to political freedoms. The consensual acceptance of the right to free expression often proved to be pretty flimsy where radicals were concerned.

Violence Against Radical Publications

Radical publications in the twentieth century have been frequent targets of violence.[40] Often the attacks were carried out by local branches of national organizations like the American Legion and the American Protective League. Often, too, local police organizations condoned or actually carried out assaults, claiming to be exercising lawful authority. Such violence has decreased in the years since World War II as antiradicalism has become the domain of the federal government. Perhaps also a firmer confidence in the remoteness of dangerous class struggle has contributed to the decline of antiradicalism.

Antiradicalism had had a long history in the United States, but it began to take on a new shape in the early years of the twentieth century. The first precipitating event was the assassination of President McKinley. At last two anarchist newspapers, the New York *Freie Arbeiter Stimme* and the Spring Valley, Illinois, *L'Aurora*, were targets of crowd action; in the state of Washington, the anarchist colony Home was also a focus of hostility from neighboring communities.[41] But the level of repression was still modest compared with the outburst associated with the Haymarket Riot.

What distinguished the aftermath of the McKinley assassination from that earlier red scare was the legislative response. Criminal syndicalism laws were passed by state legislatures, and, at the federal level, Congress debated a series of antiradical measures, finally approving immigration-restriction rules that singled out radicals for exclusion.[42] From this humble beginning, the activities of the federal government in fighting sedition and radicalism would become quite expansive in a relatively short time. As a result, violence was less often called for.

World War I

The World War I era has long been recognized as a formative moment for the modern notion of civil liberties. Because U.S. entry into the war was earnestly opposed by large segments of the population, because many were tied by culture and language to the declared enemy, because the institution of a draft was widely unpopular, because the demands of wartime production presented an unexpected opportunity for organized labor to press its demands, because the Bolshevik Revolution sent shock waves through the Western world, and because the harmful potential of propaganda seemed unlimited, intolerance toward domestic radicalism was pronounced. Vigilante action combined with local and federal government action to produce a crisis in civil liberties.

No less a personage than Woodrow Wilson observed on the eve of World War I that should the United States declare war, the people would "forget there ever was such a thing as tolerance." He was not incorrect. The war on the homefront is remembered for its crusade against "hyphenated Americanism," for the (Creel) Committee on Public Information, for the Espionage and Sedition Acts, and for an unprecedented use of the postmaster's authority to regulate the mails—all matters for which Wilson himself must bear great responsibility. Whether the government nurtured or merely responded to the atmosphere of intolerance, the effects were devastating. In terms of newspapers, the years 1916–1920 saw the disappearance of 137 dailies and an amazing 2,268 weeklies. Many of these failures were caused by secular economic trends and by wartime shortages, but left-leaning papers stood a far greater chance of failing than the average publication. Indeed, the World War I years saw the destruction of a large chunk of the radical network that had been built over the past two decades. By the end of the war, fifteen hundred of the more than five thousand Socialist party locals—about one-quarter of the organizational base—had been eliminated. Most of the lost locals were in small communities. The attrition rate for Socialist newspapers was similar; losses there were likewise concentrated in small towns. Nor was the Socialist party the only group so attacked. The IWW was also beset. Although both the Socialists and the Wobblies survived the war and were notably active in the 1920s, neither really regained its strength.[43]

The Socialist party and the IWW were especially vulnerable because of the outspokenness of their opposition to the war and then to the draft. Neither of these oppositions was very unpopular. In fact, it was the extent to which segments of the public seemed to respond to radical criticism of the war and the draft that prompted local and federal leaders to initiate repressive action.

The antiradical campaign was coordinated at the level of Woodrow Wilson's cabinet. Postmaster-General Burleson used his power of denying second-class postal rates to periodicals effectively to bar most Socialist and radical publications from the mails, including such papers as *The Masses*, the *Appeal to Reason*, and the Milwaukee *Leader*. At the same time, Attorney General Gregory declared war on radicals, especially the IWW, and solicited the support of quasi-official citizens' groups, most notoriously the American Protective League (APL). The attorney general's office asserted it was getting between a thousand and fifteen hundred citizens' reports on disloyal activities a day throughout the war. The Justice Department's activities expanded as the war went on, intensifying with the success of the Bolshevik Revolution. Victor Berger charged Justice agents with orchestrating an advertising boycott of the Milwaukee *Leader* during the war. One undisputed legacy of World War I was the rise of the FBI as an institution of domestic antiradicalism.[44]

Federal officials could declare with some justification that their actions were needed to moderate popular hysteria. As Neil Wynn points out, "No matter how severe or repressive the government's measures were to be, local politicians, newspapers, and businessmen called for more extreme action." Indeed, direct federal action was easily matched if not dwarfed by the activities of voluntary organizations like the APL, which claimed 250,000 members in six hundred cities and towns. APL operatives infiltrated labor and radical organizations and bombarded the attorney general's office with reports on disloyal activities. Local units of the APL also conducted raids (under dubious authority) and may have detained as many as 400,000 suspected "slackers," or draft evaders, in the course of the war. Condoned by governments and the mainstream press, such classic vigilante action flourished during the war, and continued to grow after the Armistice with the Red Scare attacks of American Legion locals on radicals.[45]

The attack on radicals was made possible in part by the silence of their erstwhile partners in civil liberties among the conservatives in the labor movement. AFL-affiliated labor unions sensed an opportunity in the war. Despite misgivings, most traditional unionists dropped their opposition to the war and to the draft, did relatively little to oppose the Sedition and Espionage Acts, and concentrated on winning organizing rights and wage-and-hour concessions in industries central to the war effort. This opportunism was encouraged by the federal government, which, faced with an outburst of strike activity in the early months of the war, sought to maintain convivial labor relations. It formed the Presidential Mediation Commission and eventually the National War Labor Board, virtually endorsing rights to collective bargaining, an eight-hour day, and a living wage. In return, the AFL joined with the Creel Committee to set up a labor-based Alliance for Labor and Democracy, with eventually 150 branches, as a counter to the Socialist party. Though much of the wartime gains of labor would be rolled back in 1919–1920, during the war itself, labor could not be counted on to support besieged radicals.[46]

In this heated atmosphere, attacks against newspapers were very common. Some of the targets were relatively mainstream—like the Hearst papers, which had been pro-German before the declaration of war—but the most vulnerable papers were those published by Socialists and Wobblies. Not only were newspaper offices attacked, but individuals distributing papers and pamphlets were also targeted, and in many cases mobs directed symbolic violence against papers by burning bundles of copies in public ceremonies.[47]

The Mobbing of the Pigott Printing Concern

Seattle was the Northwest's boomtown in the early years of the twentieth century. With railroad links to the rest of the nation completed in the 1890s, and with the additional spur of the Klondike gold rush, the city's population increased from around forty thousand in 1890 to almost a quarter of a million in 1910. Then, with the naval buildup that came with World War I, the city's shipbuilding industry took off. Rapid industrialization in the latter 1910s exacerbated already sharp class tensions, and the shipyard workers weren't alone in developing strong unions. By World War I, Seattle's Central Labor Council had effectively coordinated the interests of dozens of AFL-affiliated unions, giving labor a strong voice in affairs.[48] To the left of the Labor Council, the city's Socialist party organization was strong and grew stronger with the long discussion of U.S. entry into the war. Further to the left, the IWW was also well organized and increasing in strength. And each of these groups produced its own newspaper. The mainstream unions sponsored the *Seattle Union Record*, a weekly that was to go daily in 1918; the Wobblies put out the weekly *Industrial Worker*; and the Socialists, after many miscarriages with weekly papers in the 1910s, finally bore the *Daily Call*.

The *Daily Call* was begun in the afterglow of the Russian Revolution by a newcomer to the Seattle area, Thorwald G. Mauritzen. Mauritzen had managed to raise about a thousand dollars, and had contracted with Henry C. Pigott, a printer with a populist point of view, to print the four-page paper. Pigott and Mauritzen figured that with a circulation of ten thousand a day at two cents per copy, they could pay off the newsboys and still have $100 left with which to buy material and pay an editorial staff—utopian calculations, even by the standards of Socialist newspaper conductors. But the paper was surprisingly successful, surpassing fifteen thousand in circulation shortly after its appearance on 28 July 1917. As its readership grew, its content—initially composed almost entirely of clippings from other Socialist papers—was supplemented by increasingly strong original reporting and columns, most notably from Anna Louise Strong (under the pen name "Gale") and Joe and Morris Pass. And the content was controversial. The *Call* printed news of socialist revolutions around the world, and called for the same in the U.S. The antiwar and antidraft sympathies of its staff made it suspect in any case, and at no time in its career was it accorded second-class mailing status by the Post Office.[49]

The strength of Seattle's radical movement made it a frequent target of attack throughout the 1910s. In 1913 controversy over Hulet Wells's political satire *The Colonel and His Friends* (the Colonel was Alden J. Blethen, publisher of the *Seattle Times*) led to the mobbing of two Socialist and IWW halls as well as Millard Price's locally famous Red News Wagon. In 1917 soldiers and sailors in transit attacked prolabor and antidraft speakers, and federal and local officers raided IWW offices and harrassed Socialists.[50] During the war, businessmen recruited and supported "patriot" organizations like the Home Guards, the Minute Men, and the Sons of Liberty. After the war, the American Legion carried on the tradition of patriotic action in attacks on radicals in the Northwest, culminating in the Centralia massacre of 1919.[51]

On Saturday night, 5 January 1918, a mob of about two dozen sailors led by a pair of armed civilians stormed the Pigott Printing Concern, where the *Daily Call* and the *Industrial Worker* were printed. The attackers made the six workers present lie on the floor while they pounded the machinery, spilled typecases, and destroyed as much paper as they could lay their hands on. In addition to wrecking some type for the *Call* ("You've been running some pretty bad dope," one attacker told a worker), they also destroyed type for Red Cross jobs and campaign materials for Ole Hanson (who would later become nationally famous as the anti-Red mayor who broke the Seattle General Strike of 1919). Total damage was said to amount to $15,000.[52]

The attack was immediately condemned by Seattle's labor organizations. They saw it clearly as the work of local business interests, directed against both the radical newspapers and the printer who supported them. They castigated the authorities for moving so slowly against the leaders of the mob, who were easily identified.[53]

The mob's leaders were G. Merle Gordon and J. Fred Drake, both Minute Men. Gordon and Drake were arrested only after considerable pressure had been brought to bear on local authorities by Secretary of War Newton Baker and Secretary of the Navy Josephus Daniels, who feared a work stoppage in the shipyards. Drake and Gordon were hardly the stuff of which heroes were made. Drake had been a notorious strikebreaker. Gordon had earned some minor celebrity as a Red Cross stump speaker whose tales of the German atrocities he'd witnessed on 150 flights over Belgium with the French Aviation Corps were apparent lies. The *Industrial Worker* reported a bizarre incident in which Gordon had addressed an IWW meeting, trying to persuade those in attendance to march en masse to the Red Cross building for a photograph. The *Worker* figured that his scheme was to pass this off as Wobblies mobbing the Red Cross, an act heinous enough to justify severe retaliation. The attack on the printing plant came two weeks later, without any immediate justification. The *Worker* also claimed that Gordon and Drake had been financed by Ralph Horr (a mayoral hopeful, like Hanson), Bert Sweazy (who operated the competing Pioneer Printing Plant), and Mrs. F. H. Jackson (who ran the Clear Lake Lumber Company, and could be presumed to fear IWW organizing efforts).[54]

The arrest of Gordon and Drake proved to be a very small triumph for freedom of the press. The arrests had been made only with the rare insistence of federal potentates; no investigation was made into the involvement of local business leaders, though Drake and Gordon admitted to being paid $1,000 by the Chamber of Commerce; the accused were promptly bailed out and went to work with the government's Spruce Division (basically a federally organized quasi-military corps of union-busters); when brought to trial the defendants pleaded a "temporary emotional insanity" brought on by reading the *Call* and *Industrial Worker* and were acquitted.[55] It seems clear that the judicial system in Seattle did not consider mobbing a printer who worked for radicals a crime worth taking notice of.

Oddly, Pigott, the chief aggrieved party, framed the riot as the work of business rivals. In a published statement in the *Industrial Worker*, Pigott declared that the mob attack had been "inspired by malice, envy, and other motives directed personally at the owners," not the IWW or the Socialists. He insisted that he was largely unconcerned with the politics of what he printed, except insofar as it might be "of a treasonable or seditious character." Echoing Benjamin Franklin's "Apology for Printers," Pigott insisted that "the officers and stockholders of the Pigott Printing Concern have no sympathy with some of the ideas and principles advocated in the Industrial Worker, but we do not set ourselves up to censor the beliefs and opinions of others any more than we allow others to censor our own beliefs and opinions."[56] By framing himself as a disinterested businessman, Pigott was defending himself from arguments that his own disloyalty justified the mobbing.

But in fact there is little doubt that the true targets of the attack were the *Call* and the *Industrial Worker*. And motivation for the attack was not simple disloyalty, though that was a handy justification, and the participation of uniformed sailors made it picturesquely believable. Rather, the attack seems to have been intended to stifle the voices of the left elements of Seattle's labor movement. It was occasioned by the ongoing turmoil in the lumber industry—for which the IWW was blamed—and the fascination with the Soviet model in the shipyards.

If the attack was not punishment for disloyalty, it was also not an expression of wartime hysteria. The attack was not a simple act of the popular will. In fact, it was planned by members of an elite, carried out by hired operatives, and excused by several layers of entrenched officeholders. Whether "the public" approved or not is hard to gauge. The Central Labor Council made its disapproval explicit, but there is no clear indication that Seattle's shopkeepers and professionals found the attack to be a regrettable infringement on the freedom of the press. And even if they did, they seemed to forget quickly enough when the perpetrators were pardoned. The victims, of course, insisted that the public was on their side: the *Industrial Worker* remarked that "the Worker, the Call, and the Pigott Concern never realized what a host of friends they had until this mob aroused the people of Seattle to show their true feelings." But the public remained quiescent when the *Call* failed a few months later—partly a victim of postal censorship—and when an explosion at the Pigott Concern in May followed by threats to any printer that handled IWW material forced the *Worker* to take an eleven-month holiday.[57]

The Red Scare of 1919

The Armistice did not end the outbreak of antiradicalism. Instead, with fear of Bolshevism running high, and with labor planning a new offensive—especially in steel and coal—attacks on radicals expanded in 1919 into what has become known as the Red Scare. Again with the federal government taking a leading role, this time under Attorney General Palmer, the Red Scare left a legacy of criminal syndicalism laws—passed in thirty-five states—and rump left-wing parties. By 1920 the IWW had been crippled (though it would experience a resurgence among agricultural workers in the 1920s), the Socialist party had been fragmented, the membership of the two Communist parties had declined from seventy to ten thousand, and the great national strikes in coal and steel were being defeated by appeals to anticommunist hysteria.[58]

The Red Scare also saw the continuation of violence against the radical press. With the end of the war and the relaxing of some wartime restrictions, there was a brief resurgence in the number of radical papers. But the pattern of "popular" action established during the war persisted. The activities of the American Legion are well known, and radical publications were frequently included as targets in attacks on Socialist, Communist, and IWW halls.[59]

Following the Red Scare, radicalism was not much of a threat through the 1920s. There were occasional cases of radical-influenced strikes, especially in textiles, and these would prompt overt repression and often violence. On the whole, however, the 1920s belonged to the KKK, not the IWW. Moreover, the legal machinery to cripple any radical movement remained in place after the Red Scare.

Consequently, antiradical violence did not reemerge in full force until the rise of the Communists in the 1930s. Then, responding to the Great Depression, Communists began organizing unemployment marches. These became targets for assault. The ACLU counted half a dozen and more such confrontations monthly in the early half of 1930 alone, reaching a climax on May Day, when dozens of marches in different cities were attacked. Such incidents remained common until Franklin Delano Roosevelt's administration took office in 1933.[60] Communist activism sparked other occasions of violence as well, most notably in California, where Communists trying to organize agricultural and maritime workers were targets of vigilante action by Red Squads.[61]

The Sacking of the *Western Worker*

The *Western Worker* was a weekly newspaper published in San Francisco. It was the official organ of the Communist Party USA in the West, and as such was a propagandist for labor militancy among agricultural workers and, especially in 1934, workers on the waterfront. To understand how the *Worker* came to be attacked by vigilantes, it is important to understand both the contemporary context of labor organizing on the waterfront and the crisis of 1934.

Workers on the waterfront in San Francisco and elsewhere had long been officially represented by the AFL-affiliated International Longshoremen's Association (ILA).[62] But the ILA, with its comfortable relationship to shipping interests, faced vigorous competition in the 1930s from the Marine Workers' Industrial Union (MWIU). The MWIU appealed to increasing frustration with work conditions on the docks, especially the detested "blue-book" system of recruiting workers. Growing discontent on the docks in San Francisco was registered in the appearance of the *Waterfront Worker*, a small mimeographed sheet, in December 1932, run mainly by rank-and-file longshoremen and directed at pushing the dockworkers toward a more radical course. Meanwhile, the *Western Worker* urged dockworkers to support the MWIU.

The labor situation in general exploded in June 1933 with the passage of the National Industrial Recovery Act (NIRA). Of particular importance was section 7(a) of the NIRA, guaranteeing the right to unionize; taking encouragement from this provision, workers in various industries began forming unions almost spontaneously. On the docks in San Francisco, there was an attempt to channel organizing activity into the largely moribund ILA, a move that received a paradoxical boost when the editors of the *Waterfront Worker* held a public meeting at which they announced that they'd joined the ILA. Thereupon the ILA was pushed leftward by the *Waterfront Worker* group and its following among the rank and file, who looked forward to striking when the current operating contract with shippers was to expire in May, rejecting meanwhile the bargaining posture of the old-line leadership.

The "Big Strike" of 1934 began on 9 May with a coastwide walkout of longshoremen; seamen and other maritime workers followed shortly after. Federal officials tried to reach agreement with AFL officials, but two agreements, in late May and mid-June, were voted down by the membership, which was becoming increasingly militant. The shipping interests then decided to open the ports with scabs and sluggers on 3 July. The result of this provocative move was a widespread outbreak of hand-to-hand combat on the waterfront as strikers tried to prevent the opening of the docks. The shippers' men responded with escalating force, resulting in the deaths of two strikers on 5 July.[63] One of the targets of violence during these days was the *Western Worker*.

The *Worker* had been harassed since the start of the strike. Its newsboys had been arrested on a variety of charges, including vagrancy, and vigilante groups had menaced the *Worker*'s office. Then a gang of Legionnaires (according to the *Worker*) attacked the office, breaking windows and trying to get inside to destroy the machinery, but a "defense committee" drove them off before they could do major damage. The police were not moved to punish the attackers—the *Worker* quoted a policeman as saying, "This should be expected nowadays." The *Worker* also noted with scorn the *Examiner*'s retailing of a police theory that the attack was an inside job done to gain sympathy.[64] This was a prelude to more serious violence, both against strikers and against the *Worker*.

Four days after the two strikers were killed in street fighting, a gigantic funeral procession was held. The march, carried out in ominous and impressive silence, catalyzed sentiment for a general strike, which commenced in Oakland and San Francisco on 16 July under the direction of AFL regulars. The conservative labor leadership had not wanted a general strike, of course, but changed direction in the hope of co-opting grass-roots militants. This strategy was successful; San Francisco's labor regulars managed to end the general strike just four days after it had begun. In the meantime, labor's opponents—including shipping and other business interests, the American Legion, and the local police—mounted a campaign of mob assault, climaxing in a spasm of violence on 17 July. Shortly after, the strikers were forced to accept federal mediation; the strike ended in a stalemate.

The police, the shipping interests, and elected officials had done much to encourage the rampage of the seventeenth. On that day, Hugh Johnson, who headed the NRA, spoke in the Bay Area and demanded that subversives in the labor movement be "run out like rats"; that afternoon, a wave of vigilante and police terror was unleashed on labor headquarters and workers' halls,[65] including an attack on the offices of the *Western Worker*, in which rioters tossed bricks through the windows of the building and caused significant damage.[66] The vigilantes, dressed as dockworkers, were as convincing as the Indians at the Boston Tea Party; the rioting was in fact stage-managed. The participation of police was demonstrated in several ways. There was the timing of police action: they'd show up after a vigilante raid and arrest the victims; it seemed clear that they'd been informed in advance of the plans of the attackers. Yet more damning was the fact that several specific policemen were identified as rioters, as for instance when the *Western Worker* published the license plate numbers of the cars of the people who raided its office.[67]

Why was the *Western Worker* a target of attack? One obvious answer is that it was important to the militant organization of the strikers. During the strike the *Worker* had published a series of extras, circulating as many as four thousand copies on the waterfront; the *Worker* claimed that such extras were responsible for defeating AFL-backed proposals for ending the strike.[68] As the strike progressed, the paper prepared to go to twice-weekly publication, asserting that "the capitalists know the powerful influence this little paper can wield, especially when they see the strikers accepting it as their voice."[69] After the strike, the paper continued to insist that it was the "only means of counter-attack against the treacherous lies and slanders of the capitalist press. The paper is a weapon in your hand. Use it."[70]

Another reason for attacking the *Western Worker* was the simple logic of anticommunism. One of the strategies of the shipping interests and their allies in the strike was to depict the workers as being seduced by the Communists. Raids on Communist targets heightened the perception that labor militancy was an artificial product of foreign indoctrination rather than a reasonable response to intolerable conditions. Of course, the success of this strategy hinged on a consensus that Communism was outside the bounds of the arena of public discussion. Attacking Communists could discredit the strike in the public mind because the Communist party was not considered a legitimate player.

The mainstream press in the Bay Area implemented this anticommunist strategy before the general strike began. The publishers of the main San Francisco and Oakland papers met to coordinate their news and editorial coverage. In this they had the active support of Mayor Rossi and of the leaders of the conservative wing of the local labor movement, who had a natural interest in seeing labor militancy discredited as the result of a Communist conspiracy. The publishers were able to persuade a balking Hugh Johnson in a late-night session that the general strike was in actuality a revolution against constituted authority—hence his inflammatory remarks on the seventeenth.[71]

The anticommunist strategy of the publishers produced some remarkable distortions in reporting. What follows is excerpted from the *Chronicle*'s coverage of the vigilante raids of the seventeenth, headlined "Unionists Smash Radical Hangouts in Purging Move":

> Aroused by the discovery that Communist groups had been parading as union strikers and flaunting banners and placards completely at variance with union tenets, conservatives quickly took the situation into their own hands.
>
> They organized 35 separate vigilante squads, equipped them with fast automobiles, and started on a city wide cleanup of 'red' centers and known Communist headquarters, wrecking several meeting places, destroying equipment and severely beating the asserted Communists.
>
> At the same time the Police Department began an independent drive to rid the city of communist-inspired terrorism.
>
> [Targets included] the plant of the Western Worker, communist newspaper, 37 Grove street. Here 25 vigilantes pulled up in five automobiles, threw rocks through the windows and stormed inside, completely demolishing everything in sight. Police arrived to find the raiders gone and the opposite plaza crowded with grinning spectators. Officer Mervin Pratt suffered laceration of the hands in the melee that followed.
>
> Although the raids were made under cover of militia machine guns and bayonets, the National Guardsmen had no part in them.[72]

The rhetorical and ideological nub of this strategy was the location of the people. If the wave of repression that ended the general strike was seen as the work of the police, under the direction of the shipping interests, and with the (passive or active) support of the city government and the mainstream press, then the victims could claim that the people had not acted and were themselves victims of this action, sharing in the deprivation of civil rights. So the fiction of a popular outburst was constructed. If union men had acted to purge their own organizations with members of the general public looking on approvingly, as the *Chronicle* and the other local papers reported, then it was the people who had acted, with the shipping interests entirely uninvolved and the authorities responding belatedly to keep order. But even the details that the *Chronicle* reported make this fiction hard to believe. How were the police able to respond in such a timely fashion to thirty-five separate incidents? Why did the police arrest only Communists and not vigilantes? Why were the national guardsmen looking on? How did Officer Pratt lacerate his hands?

But the fiction of popular action did not have to stand up to especially strict scrutiny to be effective. Although these newspaper reports seem to have been disbelieved by many in San Francisco and were contradicted by informed observers nationally, the unanimous voice of the area's press establishment lent enough credibility to the explanations of the raids that the raiders and the responsible authorities went unpunished.

World War II and Antiradicalism

World War II was a rare war in U.S. history for its domestic harmony. There was only an anemic antiwar movement, and the country's largest leftist organization, the Communist party, became actively prowar when the Soviet Union was attacked, and was relatively smiled upon by the government because it was then linked with a major U.S. ally.[73] Instead, the ideological opposition consisted of a very small group of active fascists, strongly rejected by the bulk of their natural ethnic cohorts, Italian- and German-Americans, and of a somewhat larger group of religious nonparticipants.

Fascists were handled with more orderliness than the opponents of earlier wars. Mobbings were rare. Partly this was because fascists were not highly visible, unlike, say, antidraft activists during World War I. But even more so it was because an effective system of legal surveillance and suppression was in place. The relevant World War I–era legislation was still in place, and early in the war, at a conference of governors and state-level law enforcement officials, Attorney General Robert Jackson achieved a consensual agreement that loyalty enforcement would be left in the hands of the federal government. Furthermore, once the war began, old-line liberals declined to engage the federal government on civil liberties issues. This lowered the level of conflict involved in the control of domestic fascism, and perhaps prevented the resort to extralegal means of suppression.[74]

More dramatic were the actions taken against groups that were only tangentially "disloyal." The most famous of these was the internment of West Coast Japanese-Americans. Less well known today is the wave of violence against Jehovah's Witnesses, beginning before the war in 1940 and continuing for several years thereafter. The Witnesses were odious to many Americans because they opposed "organized" religion and refused to participate in the rituals of patriotism, most notably the Pledge of Allegiance to the flag. In the fall of 1940, the ACLU counted hundreds of acts of violence against Witnesses, including "beatings, shootings, burning of literature, destruction of headquarters and equipment, demolition of trailers and physical force to compel Jehovah's Witnesses to salute the American flag. Some have been tarred and feathered." This wave diminished after the fall, but renewed violence against the Witnesses mounted to some three hundred more attacks between December 1941 and December 1943.[75]

The World War II–era moratorium on antiradicalism was to be short-lived. Quickly after peace, the federal government commenced a major drive against the Communist party and any political group associated with it. The drive was successful. With the support of a public energized by a successful war effort and convinced of the seriousness of the new cold war, the government managed to isolate radicals from their supporters in the labor movement and among intellectuals and to cripple the key radical political parties. The cold war ended the Old Left. A different problem was presented by the New Left.

The New Left

The New Left differed from the Old in several ways. It was youth-based rather than class-based; its constituency thus came from a more empowered sector of society. It received its impetus from a range of issues not associated with the workplace: first racism and the bomb, then the war in Vietnam, then the environment and women's issues, and throughout the politics of culture—drugs, sex, and rock and roll. It fought its battles on college campuses more often than in factories.

Perhaps because of its constituency, the New Left produced a more vibrant and various, but less specifically politicized, range of media than the Old. Much of the energy of the movement went into its music, for instance. In terms of print media, the New Left quickly produced a thriving underground press. By 1969 five hundred underground papers had a combined circulation of up to 4.5 million copies; by 1971 they claimed a circulation of between 10 and 20 million.[76]

The underground press was not strictly political. Its readers were drawn to psychedelia, record reviews, material that would be considered lewd by mainstream standards, and other content that had little to do with fighting racism or opposing the war. Much of this was intended simply to shock. Subtending it all was an attitude of derision toward the "normal" order of things, including business as usual, politics as usual, and the institutions of mainstream culture, including the media.

The underground press voiced contempt for the mainstream press. The *Black Panther* called the press "a conscious tool of the police"; Julius Lester of the Liberation News Service remarked that "in present-day America, the media can be nothing but an enemy of revolution."[77] Hence the underground papers showed little interest in entering the "marketplace of ideas" that the mainstream media supported and defined. Instead, they sought to present a different and competing marketplace, one with different actors, different events, and a different agenda. At the same time, the New Left tried to drive the press. Activists developed tactics of exploiting the media's values to force items onto the mainstream agenda.[78] Starting perhaps with the freedom rides, which drew national attention to southern racism, and continuing through demonstrations against the war, campus sit-ins, and other crowd actions, organizers were always conscious of the attention of the mainstream media and the general public.

Both the creation of a competing public sphere and the assault on the existing one prompted repression. A diverse array of official and unofficial actors set about policing the borders of discourse. FBI counterintelligence programs (COINTELPROs) directed at leftist political organizations and starting officially in the mid-1950s are now well known.[79] Noam Chomsky has pointed to the irony in the fact that the Nixon administration was toppled by the aftermath of the Watergate break-in, a relatively benign abuse of governmental powers compared with the sweeping surveillance and sabotage of leftists that Watergate-era investigations brought to the attention of the general public (the left had been aware of it all along, of course).[80] This irony points up a salient fact: the boundaries of the mainstream arena of public discussion also demarcate the frontiers of official repression. Within these boundaries, harassment is not tolerable—hence Nixon's forced resignation. Outside these boundaries, harassment is routinely tolerated and often encouraged: some Democrats may have considered the targets of COINTELPRO as fellow victims, but not that many.

In addition, underground newspapers were frequent targets of violence.[81] Actions ranged from vandalism—throwing bricks through windows, for example— to bombings; perpetrators ranged from local youths to vigilante organizations to the police. In most cases, because underground papers had already made themselves obnoxious to the local police, violence directed against those papers did not prompt the police to urgent action. Considering the passive attitude of the authorities, it is surprising that violence against the underground press was not more common. At the same time, police were known to harass and occasionally attack reporters for mainstream media covering movement activities. The most notorious case was the beating of reporters during the police riot at Chicago's 1968 Democratic national convention.[82]

It is difficult to say whether the New Left succeeded in changing the contours of the arena of public discussion. Despite a great deal of policing of various sorts, the national agenda did change, and in the process new speakers were given voice. But it is hard to judge just what role the New Left played in all of this. Its apologists say that its role was revolutionary; others point to the long prehistory of the "accomplishments" of the New Left by way of arguing for the significance of other actors.

Whatever the New Left did to the mainstream arena of public discussion, its attempt to create a competing public sphere must be considered a failure. The underground press did not die, it simply ceased to be underground. Now it is referred to as the alternative press, and in numbers and circulation it is larger than ever, but it does not constitute a public sphere. Instead, alternative papers generally seem to perform one of two functions: either they cater to a group with a specific interest—for example, fanzines—or they serve as the periphery to the mainstream press, offering some jarring material, perhaps, but in a supplementary rather than a competing fashion. The contents of the *Village Voice*, for instance, or the Chicago *Reader* presuppose a reader's knowledge of the local mainstream dailies.

It seems unlikely that violence was responsible for the failure of the alternative public sphere. The end of the underground press was the result of the success of the alternative press, not the demolition of underground papers. Accommodation to viable markets sapped the underground papers of whatever revolutionary potential they might have had.

Newspaper Workers and Violence

The level of violence associated with the economic operations of newspapers has occasionally been quite high. Rival newspapers have literally battled for newsstand space—most notoriously when Hearst moved into the Chicago market to challenge McCormick's *Tribune*, sparking a full-scale war, with both sides engaging gunmen and sluggers.[83] Often newsboys were the targets of such violence. And sometimes such violence had a political dimension, for instance, when newsboys from the Socialist Milwaukee *Leader* were attacked, or when unionizing newsboys were attacked.[84]

Similarly, violence has often adorned the efforts of newspaper workers to unionize or bargain collectively. Sometimes this violence has been directed against unionists, as when the Newspaper Guild began organizing newsroom employees in the 1930s. Sometimes violence has been directed against the newspaper. Often in the past a newspaper strike would produce a competing "strike" newspaper, and in some cases the competition between the strike newspaper and the struck newspaper has turned violent. The most celebrated case of recent years occurred in Wilkes-Barre, Pennsylvania.

The Wilkes-Barre *Times-Leader* had been a family-owned paper for many years when it was put up for sale in the mid-1970s. Secure as a monopoly paper and in a region with a rich tradition of labor organizing, it had negotiated reasonably with its own unions. But the paper's new owner, Capital Cities, a national media conglomerate that now owns the ABC television network, wanted to make changes, including modernizing the plant and reporting more aggressively. It also looked to modify union contracts.

Cap Cities quickly began hardball negotiations with the *Times-Leader*'s unions. When they balked, Cap Cities prepared for a strike, hiring an outside security agency, enclosing its offices and plant in barbed wire, sending signals that it expected violence.[85] Predictably, the strike came, and it was violent: on its first night, 6 October 1978, strikers gathered outside the barbed-wire fence, broke windows, destroyed delivery trucks, and attacked whatever guards came within reach. Violence continued at a high level for weeks, until local police, who were sympathetic to the strikers, showed signs of cracking down, and Cap Cities switched to a local security firm. Even so, "guerrilla" violence—destroying newspaper bundles, slashing tires on "scab" reporters' cars—continued, and the strikers maintained a picket until 1982.[86]

The violence did not deter Cap Cities, of course. Far more threatening was the strikers' establishment of a successful competing daily. The *Citizen's Voice* has maintained a circulation equal to or surpassing the *Times-Leader*'s since the late 1970s, and as a result Cap Cities has never made the money it expected in Wilkes-Barre.[87]

Wilkes-Barre was a prelude to developments in the 1980s and 1990s. The climate in government and business turned decidedly antiunion, new press technologies challenged old workplace habits, and new corporate giants in the media world refined techniques to cripple unions. When unions struck to prevent workplace changes, newspapers moved to break the unions, using permanent replacement workers, a tactic certified as legal by the Supreme Court in the 1930s but generally considered unacceptable until legitimated by the Reagan administration's reaction to the air traffic controllers' strike in 1981. The hiring of permanent replacements effectively broke the unions at the Chicago *Tribune*'s new printing plant in 1985 in a strike that featured a low level of picket-line violence.[88]

The most dramatic example of this kind of violence in recent years has been the 1990 strike at the New York *Daily News*. The *News* was also a property of the Tribune Company of Chicago. As contracts were set to expire in 1990, unions negotiated gingerly, aware that the Tribune Company was prepared to take advantage of a strike to replace union workers with permanent nonunion replacements. No contract was achieved, and after working for several months without a contract, the unions were effectively coerced into striking by deliberate provocation. Replacement workers were bussed in within an hour of what may or may not have been a walkout by drivers, and the newspaper's other workers walked out in sympathy.

The Tribune Company was determined to continue normal publication; the unions were determined to prevent that. The unions' acknowledged strategies included encouraging advertisers to boycott the *News* and vendors to refuse to carry it. Management declared that the unions also engineered a campaign of violence against vendors and replacement workers. Violence was certainly evident, but it is not clear that there was an organized campaign, despite a lawsuit filed by James Hoge, publisher of the *News*, to that effect.[89] The lawsuit was eventually dropped. At the same time, it was revealed that the *News* (with remarkable insincerity) had hired a firm called Securex to supply strikebreakers who would deliberately provoke violence—in earlier days, they would have been called sluggers. Coverage of the strike by mainstream news organizations probably gave a heightened impression of prounion violence, partly because it fit their definition of "news," but also because they had an economic interest in discrediting the striking newspaper unions. The *New York Times*, for instance, was itself about to open a new printing plant, and anticipated difficult negotiations with unions over staffing levels. The strike ended when the Tribune Company reached agreement to sell the *Daily News* to British press mogul Robert Maxwell, who quickly reached agreement with the unions on wages, benefits, and staffing levels.

It is questionable that violence actually played a role in determining the outcome of the *Daily News* strike. It worked to the advantage of both sides: reinforcing vendors' and advertisers' boycotts for the strikers, and discrediting the strikers for the *News* management. But violence seems much less salient in the resolution of such disputes than law, the legality of hiring permanent replacement workers, for instance, or than market forces, which made it cheaper for the Tribune Company to close the *Daily News* than to negotiate with its unions in good faith.

The deep lesson of the *Daily News* strike is the declining power of the newsworkers' unions. As contracts expire, unions increasingly find themselves in a suppliant position; as new technologies are introduced, workers find themselves exercising less autonomy. At the horizon, technologies promise a transformation of the craft structure of the newspaper; already, for instance, the division between copyediting and layout has been blurred, and there is no reason to imagine that the old craft structure of production will be appropriate in the future. But then who will have control in newspaper production?

Clearly, it is not the press workers who determine the content of the newspaper. An exception proves the rule: in 1919, the Seattle *Post-Intelligencer* published as an advertisement a screed by Edwin Selvin, editor of the *Business Chronicle*, calling for the legal and extralegal suppression of leftist groups, including "the IWW, the Nonpartisan League, . . . the pro-German Socialists, the Closed Shop Labor Unions, the agitators, malcontents, anarchists, syndicalists, seditionists, traitors." The ad provoked an immediate response by the printing trades, who of course were involved in the production of the *Post-Intelligencer*. They met and passed resolutions aimed at the newspaper's management, acknowledging that "we have even meekly witnessed your unfair and reprehensible campaign of falsehood and ruin," but insisting that this ad had gone too far, and that

> if your editorial directing heads must remain blind to the thing they are bringing us to; if together you cannot see the abyss to which you are leading us—all of us; if you have no more love for our common country than is manifested in your efforts to plunge us into anarchy, then as loyal American citizens . . . we must, not because we are unionists but because we are Americans, find means to protect ourselves from the stigma of having aided and abetted your campaign of destruction.[90]

The ad was dropped from subsequent editions.

What is impressive about this incident is the rare move of press workers imposing a limit on editorial control of a newspaper. The oddity of it is underscored by the nebulous nature of the threat attached to it. Does "find means to protect ourselves" mean walking off the job? Or does it mean sabotaging the press? Or does it mean actually taking over the paper? That the workers found themselves in uncertain terrain is also apparent from the fact that they said they acted as citizens and not as workers—they in effect denied that they had a particular interest at heart, and claimed to be acting only in the common interest of all Americans.

Press workers have not had a lot to do with the editorial composition of news media in recent history. Instead, editorial control has been concentrated in the hands of workers who are professionalized, and hence resistant to unionization; the Newspaper Guild is a much less powerful labor organization than the International Typographical Union precisely because many of its target workers are self-styled professionals.

One might argue, then, that the conflicts between management and press workers have little to do with the contours of the arena of public discussion. This is true in a specific sense, but more generally, it seems that the cordoning off of press workers from press content corresponds to the embargoing of the language of class from the media more generally. One might argue that the division of labor within the news industry is expressed as well in the absence of a working-class voice in the public sphere.

Conclusion

Labor-related violence and antiradical violence have been frequent and consistently patterned in U.S. history. At times violence has been a direct agent of silencing a working-class or radical voice, of policing the boundaries of the arena of public discussion. But violence itself has not determined that there will be no competing public sphere. Rather, violence might be most usefully studied to illuminate how the boundaries have been policed by other instrumentalities: by law, by government agencies, and by ideological forces, often working through mainstream media.

Appeals to class are rare in U.S. public discourse. The absence is not caused simply by the actions of interests that would find such rhetoric disadvantageous. Rather, class appeals are not allowed for in the very vocabulary of public discussion because that vocabulary is constructed around classical liberal ideology.

8

Recent Violence Against the Mainstream Press

In the latter part of the nineteenth century, the combative Wilbur Storey was known as the "fighting editor of the Chicago *Times*." True to his reputation, his career was littered with violent confrontations, the most notorious being a horsewhipping by the ladies of the Lydia Thompson Burlesque Troupe, remembered as the "Battle of the Blondes"; it is anyone's guess whether the dancers or the editor milked that one for more publicity.[1] Although Storey was more flamboyant than most of his colleagues, his habits still left him within the newspaper fraternity.

One would be amused to hear a contemporary newsperson referred to as "the fighting editor of the *Sun-Times*"; one would entertain the possibility that a "fighting editor" was a person who directed the coverage of wrestling and boxing. The term *fighting editor* never connoted only physical fighting, nevertheless it was assumed that a fighting editor would regularly find occasion to fight. Editors and other newspeople no longer find any more occasion to fight than anyone else.

The decline in the level of violence involving mainstream media has had a long history. In Chapter 3, we noted the disappearance in the early nineteenth century of overtly political majoritarian violence against mainstream political organs. After the War of 1812, "loyal opposition" became a normally accepted journalistic style; violence was reserved for nonmainstream groups like abolitionists or for wartime. But the disappearance of this type of political violence still left a whole range of violent behavior that newspeople were subjected to or participated in, from dueling to bombings during labor disputes.

Violence suited the volatile world of journalism. Before World War I, the newspaper industry was highly competitive; journalists were supposed to be aggressive, and the point of journalism was supposed to be confrontation, always of course of the most public sort. The metaphors applied to journalistic work were pugilistic: hard-hitting reporters wrote for their fighting editors.

196

Since World War I, and especially since World War II, the media have been far less confrontational. Newspapers are likely to be local monopolies, journalists are likely to be college-trained, and the metaphors that are used to describe journalism come from the professions rather than from the military or the prize-fighting ring. The media collectively are thought of as constituting a public institution; they take their place alongside other institutions, like government and organized religion, while journalists group themselves with doctors, lawyers, and clergy as public servants.

This institutionalization of the media came about in the period between the World Wars for a number of reasons. Two that we've already mentioned are the turn to monopoly and the rise of journalism education. Institutionalization and professionalism require monopoly to operate convincingly. The medical profession, for instance, maintains its professional status through a system of regulated entry and certification, sanctioned by legislatures of various sorts but really run by the profession itself. Doctors train doctors; doctors set the standards by which doctors will be licensed. Journalism in the United States by both tradition and law has lacked the barriers to entry that the other professions have enjoyed; the First Amendment rules out licensing arrangements of the sort that have been constructed for medicine and law. Consequently, the professionalization of journalism was retarded by competition until around 1920. At that time, conditions of monopoly became widespread.

By the end of World War II, monopoly conditions had reached the point where people both inside and outside the industry were demanding that standards of a professional sort be applied to the media. The best known of the documents of this period is the report of the Hutchins Commission on Freedom of the Press.[2] Beginning with the proposition that freedom of the press was endangered by increasing consolidation in media businesses, the commission concluded that to remain free from government interference (which an outraged populace might demand) and to continue to serve democracy, the media must assume certain responsibilities. Among the responsibilities were, first, a truthful, comprehensive, and intelligent account of the day's events in a context that gives them meaning; second, a forum for the exchange of comment and criticism; third, a means of projecting the opinions and attitudes of the groups in the society to one another; fourth, a method of presenting and clarifying the goals and values of the society; and fifth, a way of reaching every member of the society by the currents of information, thought, and feeling that the press supplies.[3]

Implicit in these media responsibilities is an entire repositioning of the media. Earlier, media were expected to be contenders within a marketplace of ideas. Now, according to the commission, the media were supposed to be themselves the marketplace of ideas. Each medium would have to represent the marketplace of ideas within its own content. The media's responsibilities in turn required professionalism from media operators. The responsibility to represent the "goals and values of the society," to take one example, requires the abilities of expert and unbiased observation and reportage: the stance of the professional. Thus the commission powerfully connected the appearance of actual monopoly with the demand for an ideal of professional behavior.

The Hutchins Commission report was not uncontroversial.[4] Publishers and journalists disputed the existence of monopoly, repudiated the assertion that the press was not already performing all the public services that the commission called for, and expressed wariness at the use of the responsibility concept as an entering wedge for government regulation. In the controversy, however, both sides accepted the notion that the modern media exert considerable power over the shape of public discourse, and that the media therefore could and should act professionally.

Subsequently, responsibility has become part of the common sense of the professional communicator. The language of responsibility has also penetrated the culture of the press among insiders and the public. Professional behavior is expected from journalists.

The expectation of professionalism has been inscribed in the very structure of the printed newspaper. Specifically, the appearance in the twentieth century of the op-ed page and the political column, and the frequent use of the byline, along with the creation of a highly designed front page,[5] indicate that the media are now taking it upon themselves to separate values and opinions from "news," and also structuring the news so that it forms a coherent pattern. The media have assumed the responsibility of explaining a complicated world to a challenged public.

Monopoly and professionalism have increased the distance between the media and the public. One aspect of this distance is the role definition involved in professionalism, both as practice and as ideology. As practice, professionalism insists on barriers between qualified practitioners and everyone else. Nonprofessionals are excluded from the media in practice by a set of codes and cues that only insiders can master; these markers of professional status may or may not have any serious content.[6] Ideologically, professionalism models the public as dependent in much the same way as patients depend on doctors for their health. Just as medical knowledge is so vast and complicated that it must be entrusted to a trained caste, so is the news of the day so full of competing truth claims and just simple noise that the public needs trained experts to tell them what is significant and what isn't. You wouldn't let a cabdriver deliver a baby; why should a cabdriver deliver the news?

The rise of the electronic media furthered monopoly and professionalism. Radio and television were introduced under slightly different rules from those for print media: although both were predominantly privately owned, with the broadcast media the federal government claimed an oversight role on the grounds that the First Amendment specified freedom of the *press* and *speech*, but included no prohibition on regulating other communications technologies. The presence of a licensing body encouraged controls on competition that approximated monopoly, especially after the rise of the network system.[7] At the same time, both licensing and the reliance on advertisers for all direct income encouraged broadcasters to avoid controversy. The very structure of broadcasting as an industry, then, cultivated a professional stance among broadcasters.

Meanwhile, broadcast technology as it was constructed widened the gulf between media and public. There is a great deal of irony to this because the great advantage of broadcast over print media is immediacy. Radio and television allow the creation of an impression of immediate presence: the voice or face of an actual person seems to come into one's presence; furthermore, that apparition enacts a performance in actual time. But the illusion of immediacy only emphasizes the absence of the possibility of answering. Only the looney believe that they have a personal relationship with Dan Rather simply by watching the CBS Evening News. In fact, the disparity between how well the audience knows the broadcast personality and how well the broadcast professional knows individual audience members can only heighten the impression that the people on *that* side of the microphone or camera are fundamentally different from the people on this side of the speaker or tube; this impression is enhanced by the exaggerated vocal styles that broadcast news people employ.

The entire conjuncture of twentieth-century changes in the media set this era off from the age of the fighting editor. Increased monopoly, professionalism as an ideology, the rise of electronic media (especially broadcasting but also cable), and the public's sense of these changes combine to make the media more remote from the public. At the same time, just on a physical level, media businesses are better protected from the public. They are more likely than previously to be situated in buildings with security personnel, and, in the case of broadcast media, quite often operate out of offices that are almost entirely unnoticed by the public; at the same time, police protection from violence is more readily available to the media than in the past. It is not surprising, and quite significant, that the level of antipress violence has fallen. Still, the types of antipress violence tell a lot about the contours of the media-public relationship.

Patterns of Violence

I made two systematic attempts to gauge the types and intensity of antipress violence in recent times. The first was a simple content analysis of the trade weekly *Editor & Publisher*[8] at five-year intervals starting in 1944. The second was a mail survey of a thousand managing editors and news directors.[9] In addition, I have regularly browsed mainstream news reports over the past ten years.

In the course of this research I've run across several hundred incidents involving mainstream media since World War II. The overall level of violence doesn't seem to be high—no year of the *Editor & Publisher* survey turned up more than a dozen or so instances—but some patterns emerge that underline what I think are key trends in the positioning and significance of the media in U.S. culture, society, and politics.

It will be well to begin with a snapshot of the level of contemporary violence. Let's turn to the survey results.

Survey Results

To complement the material gathered from published sources, I conducted a humble mail survey of managing editors and news directors. Survey forms were mailed to news executives at a thousand different media outlets, randomly chosen from the

1990 *Editor & Publisher Yearbook*, and divided representatively among daily news-papers, weekly newspapers, African-American newspapers, ethnic newspapers, student newspapers, radio stations, television stations, and national news organizations like the Associated Press. There were 347 responses, proportionately spread among the categories surveyed.

The survey was designed to do two things. First, it was supposed to give a glimpse of the level of violence experienced by the media today. Second, it was designed to test the attitudes of news executives about public actions and attitudes toward the press, including but not limited to violence.

The survey revealed the level of violence to be rather low. Few news organizations reported regular violence, and of the violent activities reported, most tended to be threatening phone calls or acts of vandalism. Thirteen percent reported regular vandalism, for instance,[10] and only .3 percent reported regular assaults.

As a result, questions about the effect of violence on news reporting and editorial positions turned out to be negative. On a 7-point scale, reponses to the statement "Threats or assaults have had a chilling effect on our editorial positions" averaged 6.2, where 7 meant "strongly disagree." When the same statement was posed about news coverage, the response was an even stronger 6.3.

There is some evidence that news organizations tend to underreport the threats and violence they encounter. When asked whether a news organization "should report as news the threats it receives" and "minor assaults on its property or personnel," responses averaged 5.0 and 4.9, where 4 would represent a neutral response and 7 would signal strong disagreement. Likewise, most respondents agreed with the statement "Reporting threats and assaults as news encourages imitators." The average response here was 3.5, with a little over half agreeing to some extent and only 24 percent disagreeing.

News executives seemed ambivalent about the level of public hostility toward the media. On three items designed to measure their sense of public opinion, the responses fell into a standard curve, indicating a more or less random distribution.[11] Apparently, news executives on the whole don't think that their public is especially alienated.

Similarly, most news executives don't believe that journalists are in any particular danger. When asked whether "a good journalist should expect to encounter violence," the responses averaged 4.7, indicating moderate disagreement. When asked whether "journalism properly practiced is *not* a dangerous profession," responses averaged 3.6, indicating mild agreement.

On the other hand, news executives feel that things are getting worse in this regard. There was moderate disagreement (4.5) with the statement "Journalism used to be more dangerous than it is today," and moderate agreement (3.7) with the statement "Journalism is becoming more dangerous."

There is some irony here. If one were to judge simply by news reports, one would suppose that journalism was becoming safer. And, compared with past generations, contemporary journalists seem to experience little violence. Then why do news executives look upon journalism as becoming more dangerous? One explanation is that they are echoing a fear of violent crime that is general to the society. Everyone, not just news executives, senses a rise in the societal level of violence, and when news executives agree that journalism is becoming more dangerous, they may simply be expressing the widely shared attitude that everything is becoming more dangerous. A second explanation is that news executives think in rather short time spans when they talk about change. Thus they may agree with the statement that journalism is becoming more dangerous by placing current experience within a five-year time span, whereas deep change within the system of news reporting, I have argued, occurred some fifty to seventy years ago. Few news executives would deploy that type of institutional memory.

On further analysis, the survey results yield some more revealing findings. First, a medium's likelihood of encountering threats and vandalism correlates strongly with the type of medium. Media that are primarily "news" media—daily newspapers, network television affiliates in large markets, urban talk radio stations, and urban weeklies—are far more likely to encounter violence than other media.[12] This clearly indicates that what violence these media experience is violence about news. It is news media, not all media, that experience violence.[13] Likewise, news media are far more likely to employ security personnel.[14]

The written responses that accompanied returned survey forms were also of interest. More than a few expressed an opinion that journalists are "easy targets" for frustrated people. Many remarked that they had little personal experience of violence, even though they expected these things might happen elsewhere.

But some reported more strategic campaigns. One respondent remarked that "we are sometimes victimized by well-thought-out letter-writing campaigns, angry, intimidation-minded phone calls and pressure to get rid of tough reporters."[15] Likewise, the editor of the Port Angeles, Washington, *Peninsula Daily News* notes violence—threats and newsboxes blown up—in response to its reporting on the troubled timber industry.

More commonly, respondents attributed threats and violence to "crazies." The news director of KTVL-TV in Medford, Oregon, wrote, "All of our threats come from mentally unstable people, many of whom believe we are in league with the devil!" The news director of KARK-TV in Little Rock, Arkansas, agreed: "Nut cases (i.e.: "Stop-beaming-into-my-living-room" stuff) have gone up. Nuts just don't get put away like they used to."

Some, like the editor of the Arvin, California, *Tiller*, blamed the media. "The problems many news organizations and journalists get themselves into today stem from their desire to exploit the news, or sensationalize it for all it is worth. Most claim to be objective, but are they really?"[16] But the news director of KMVT-TV in Twin Falls, Idaho, strongly objected to the "portrayal of the news business and the people in it as a pack of unruly, idiotic bastards who'll do anything to get the story before the next guy does. . . . It's no wonder that with no provocation whatsoever, people often want to take a swing at one of our reporters or photographers before they've shot a frame of video or asked a single question."

Others scoffed at the image of combative reporting. The news director of KFAI-FM in Minneapolis put it this way: "Physical intimidation of the press is an insignificant factor affecting coverage. Kowtowing to power and obedience to intellectual norms are the issues worthy of examination. . . . Our whole society is getting more violent, the press should stop whining."

News executives disagree about public attitudes and about violence, but they share a way of thinking about these things. News executives see the public as external to the news process, a big and loosely reasoning collection of receivers. The public depends on the media, and would be helpless without them. But, like any classroom full of students, the public can be unruly, underdisciplined, and not too bright. Judging from the record of recent violent actions against the press, the public too feels its dependency. In that regard, it has the same notion of the press-public relationship that news executives have. But the public tends to accentuate the media's inadequacies.

Violent Actions

I have divided the patterns of violence into three main categories: Exclusionary, Inclusionary, and Noise. Exclusionary violence is meant to prevent media attention toward certain people or events or notions. Inclusionary violence is meant to force media attention toward people, events, or notions that are considered under-reported; the appearance of inclusionary violence is, I think, the most significant difference between recent and older patterns of antipress violence. Noise refers to violence that has no clear intention: attacks by "crazies," for instance, or violence incidental to other violent activity, as for instance when a reporter is robbed while covering looters during a riot.

The bulk of the incidents reported in recent years has been exclusionary in nature. These are in turn evenly divided between those involving individuals, which are basically personal in nature, and those involving groups, which tend to be political.

Incidents of exclusionary violence involving individuals often have to do with a dispute over the definition of what is private and what is public. In turn, the private/public distinction underscores the professional status of newspeople. Both of these points require a little explanation.

The distinction between private and public is basic to any notion of newsworthiness. It arises continually in discussions of routine journalism ethics, especially in "delicate" cases, the most familiar probably being the publication of the names of rape victims or of juvenile offenders. Newspeople who identify themselves as professional or serious (to distinguish themselves from the tabloid journalism of the *National Enquirer* or Geraldo) generally maintain that respect for the private is crucial to responsible professional behavior. The public, meanwhile, seems to feel quite often that newspeople do not respect privacy but are interested only in getting stories or pictures that will sell newspapers or commercial time.[17]

Sometimes a news organization's violation of privacy prompts violent retaliation. This can range from the fairly common harassment of photographers and camera people at accident scenes[18] to more direct action. The most dramatic recent case occurred in Mesa, Arizona, when an irate reader drove a bus into the lobby of the *Mesa Tribune* building, causing $20,000 damage, to protest that newspaper's publication of a photograph of a tree trimmer who had been electrocuted. The bus was driven by the tree-trimmer's brother, who felt that publishing the picture was ghoulish and insensitive; *Tribune* managing editor John Genzale responded in professional terms: "We have a duty to our readers to cover the news of the day."[19]

An especially common form of "invasion-of-privacy" violence involves professional athletes. Athletes are by calling competitive, and the presence of an inquisitive journalist—especially one who's not a familiar face—in a losers' locker room is sometimes provocation enough for some form of violent response, usually in the form of verbal harassment or a punching out.[20] Sometimes such confrontations have been heightened by other factors. The most notorious recent case has been the harassment of Lisa Olson, a female sports reporter for the *Boston Herald*, by members of the New England Patriots football team—an incident with a striking sexual component. After Olson's harassment, other female sportswriters came forward with similar stories, sparking an investigation by National Football League Commissioner Paul Tagliabue.[21]

Personal violence often has a more political dimension. Lawmakers have been known to brawl with reporters and editors, though less now than ever before.[22] Members of the general public will also attack newspeople over political matters, as when a cabdriver in Anchorage, Alaska, attacked the publisher of the *Anchorage Times* for canceling a $1,000 ad attacking U.S. Senator Frank Murkowski.[23]

More often personal violence will have a criminal dimension. People who do not want allegations of criminal behavior reported will attack reporters and editors. A number of journalists in recent years have been murdered while pursuing investigations of, especially, organized crime. The most celebrated victim has been Don Bolles, a reporter for the *Arizona Republic*, who died after a bomb exploded under his car. Bolles had been investigating organized crime in Arizona. Likewise, Charles DeVetsco, a reporter for the Sunbury, Pennsylvania, *Harrisburg Patriot-News*, was murdered in 1980 by a man he was scheduled to testify against.[24] Less dramatic examples are numerous.[25] Sometimes the attacker is a public official with a reputation to protect, as when a county administrator "slugged" Kit Wagar of the Lexington, Kentucky, *Herald-Leader* while investigating property valuations.[26]

Personal violence of this sort always involves some kind of dispute over public and private. Either a private person resists or resents the publication of personal information or representations, or a public figure strikes out in an attempt to protect reputation. In most cases, including celebrity attacks on photographers, personal violence reasserts the realm of privacy in the face of encroaching publicity. Underlying this kind of violence is a deep disagreement over privacy, one that will probably remain acute for some time, though it may cease to spark violence.

A wider variety of contemporary antipress violence involves groups rather than individuals. Violence springs up along the dividing lines between racial groups and between religious groups; violence accompanies social movements on the left and on the right; and violence is deployed by embattled establishment groups, especially in small towns and rural communities.

Racial violence has been pronounced since World War II. Chapter 6 dealt with this style of violence in some detail, especially as it involved attacks on African-American media, noting that it has not disappeared. Likewise, racially motivated violence against mainstream media has been common and has not disappeared. Reporters were attacked while covering the civil rights movement in the South,[27] while covering race riots in the North,[28] and while covering school desegregation and bussing disturbances, in both the North and the South.[29] In these cases violence was an expression of anger with the way the media represented a group; in each case the violent act was an attempt by a group to control its own representation.

A good recent example of a group acting to control its representation involved Cubans in Miami, Florida. The Cuban American National Federation, led by the mercurial Jorge Mas Conosa, began a campaign against the *Miami Herald* shortly after its Spanish-language edition published an editorial criticizing Cuban leaders in Miami. Mas Conosa accused the paper of biased coverage, comparing it to *Granma*, the newspaper of the Cuban Communist party. The federation threatened a boycott and put up billboards in Spanish that said "I don't believe The Herald." Accompanying this campaign was a series of threats against the *Herald*'s personnel and vandalism of *Herald* property, including dozens of newsboxes.[30]

Routinely, in cases of group violence against mainstream media, the attackers believe that the media attacked are part of an oppressive power structure. When irate Bostonians attacked the *Globe* or Louisvillers attacked the *Courier-Journal* during those cities' bussing crises, they were saying in effect that the papers were among the actors imposing bussing on neighborhoods. The newspaper personified oppressive bureaucracy or oppressive liberalism, acting from outside actual communities (which is how antibussing activists characterized their constituencies). A similar logic seems to have been at work in a recent race riot in Shreveport, Louisiana. An African-American neighborhood erupted after an African-American was slain by a white woman; police cordoned off the riot area while several stores were looted and rocks and bottles were thrown at whites. Police and fire vehicles were specific targets, and a car from the KTBS-TV news department was burned.[31] Of course, because the news media define themselves as an institution serving a universal public, there is some inevitable truth to the perception that their interests are linked to the status quo. Mainstream media by definition stand at a distance from nonmainstream groups.

Religious passions have sparked more than a few recent cases of violence against media. The most dramatic cases have been connected to the Muslim condemnation of Salman Rushdie's *Satanic Verses*. In the Bronx, New York, *The Riverdale Press*, a weekly that has been noted for strong editorial positions and attention to controversial issues, was firebombed after running an editorial on the Rushdie affair.[32] Similarly, followers of guru Baghwan Sri Rajneesh planned to assassinate Portland *Oregonian* reporter Les Zaitz, who had authored a series of exposés on the Rajneeshi commune in Oregon.[33] In cases like these, the mainstream media are again seen as instruments of establishment repression; this impression is deepened by an accompanying sense of unholiness, one supposes.

Religious and racial themes are often combined in attacks on the media by movements on the extreme right of the political spectrum. Most notorious here have been the actions of the white supremacist group known as The Order or the Silent Brotherhood, members of which murdered Denver talk-show host Alan Berg, an outspoken Jew, in 1984.[34] At a 1989 meeting of another white supremacist group, the Aryan Nations, reporters and photographers covering the event were photographed by members (in an obvious attempt to intimidate them), and Harley Soltes, a photographer for the *Seattle Times*, was singled out for abuse—kicked and spat at—after members identified him as a Jew.[35] Anti-Semitism is a constant theme in the media criticism of right-wing extremists, drawing strength from the high visibility of Jews in some key elite media.

Right-wing media criticism has been mirrored by the left. Movements on the left have been equally suspicious of mainstream media, though violence from the left has been far less common in recent years—perhaps because the left has traditionally adopted freedom of expression as a cause. During the turbulence of the 1960s, there were occasions on which activists attacked newspeople, especially during demonstrations (presumably to prevent being identified at a later date). Activists also performed acts of symbolic violence on opposing media, like public burnings of copies of offending newspapers.[36] Since the end of the Vietnam era, relatively little of this sort of activity has been apparent.

Police forces have a traditional tendency to dislike journalists. They are naturally prone to believe that journalists have an interest in printing certain kinds of news that can only make life difficult for the police. On the whole, journalists who have worked on the police beat for any length of time dispel this hostility by assimilating, at least partly, to the attitudes of the police, an accommodation that is encouraged by the fact that news media generally rely on the cooperation of the police for a significant amount of their content. The rules of the beat are well enough established, and there are enough legal means of harassment available to the police, that violence is rarely seen. Only in rare cases—most notoriously the 1968 Chicago Democratic national convention—will the police actually beat reporters. Recently, the members of the Norfolk, Virginia, Sheriff's Department picketed that city's *Virginian-Pilot* and *Ledger-Star*; they were offended by articles about the way the department had operated the city's jail.[37]

A more common type of violence has involved editors of local weeklies. In small communities, a weekly often exercises a degree of monopoly on local news presentation far more notable than does an urban daily, which will compete to a limited extent with local broadcast outlets and other media. As a result, most small-town weeklies are somewhat cozy with local elites, with whom they have a symbiotic relationship in terms of news content and advertising revenue. Local merchants and officials need the paper as an outlet to the citizenry, and the paper—often owned by a local merchant—needs the merchants for ads and the officials for news. The newspeople who work at small-town papers, though, share the professional ideology of newspeople in general, including from time to time a notion of news media as the adversaries of government. When small-town editors muckrake, violence often results. Cases of embattled small-town editors are common in *Editor & Publisher*, each issue of which profiles a "weekly editor."[38]

The most dramatic example of an embattled small-town editor in recent years has been Ken Fortenberry of the *McCormick Messenger* in South Carolina.[39] Fortenberry had been executive editor of the *News Chief* in Winter Haven, Florida; he moved to McCormick County and bought the *Messenger* in 1985 to "leave the rat race of a daily newspaper." But he brought a more combative notion of journalism than McCormick County was accustomed to. After running a series of damning reports on the local sheriff's office, Fortenberry became the target of a series of violent acts, starting with harassment and culminating in the explosion of two bombs at his home.

Local citizens gave a series of reasons why Fortenberry ran into trouble. Some cited his attitude: he projected an arrogance unbecoming in a local editor. Others remarked on the attention he drew to their locality, saying he was giving the place a bad reputation.[40] It was clear that his notion of journalism was too confrontational for that particular rural community, which didn't have a high level of tolerance for criticism of leading citizens, even when justified, by an outsider who seemed to lack the proper loyalties.

The harassment of small-town editors seems quaint. The sense of community invoked in these instances seems rooted in nineteenth-century ideals and values that no longer match the reality of a metropolitan society. One is tempted to categorize these cases as relics of a bygone era. Alternately, one's instinct is to question the sincerity of those who proclaim the interests of the community as justification for curbing probing journalists; one suspects that this rhetoric is just a smokescreen for corrupt self-interested parties. One should resist both these tendencies. To dismiss small-town violence as an anachronism is to cut it off from the broad currents of contemporary society; and to dismiss communitarian rhetoric as intentionally deceptive is to deny the real identification of people with communities. A more fruitful approach to these small-town incidents is to view them as samples in isolation of forces and tendencies that are usually checked by other forces and tendencies in metropolitan situations. In other words, people who live in big cities also live in imagined small towns, but they can't always act that way because of the confines imposed by the simultaneous existence of numerous other imagined small towns. Hence the contradictory contours of tolerance and intolerance in actions and behavior in the contemporary United States. People think in terms of the small town, and their attitudes are often quite intolerant; but at the same time they are obliged to live in the big city, and their behavior will have to be more tolerant. People thus assent semiconsciously to laws that guarantee toleration of behavior and expression that they find generally intolerable. The result is a society where an individual can get away with wild behavior but at the same time sense intolerance all around. We will return to this point later; for now it will suffice to insist that the small-town mentality not be looked upon as simply quaint.

Inclusionary Violence

Recent years have seen the appearance of a broad category of antipress violence that I've called inclusionary. These are violent acts, ranging from kidnappings to simple vandalism, that are designed to force media attention toward neglected or obnoxious issues or movements. The rise of inclusionary violence complements the development of a whole array of nonviolent tactics for imposing a news agenda on the media, ranging from press conferences and press releases to dramaturgic displays, like demonstrations, mass meetings, and publicity stunts.[41] All of this action should be looked upon as a struggle over editorial control of the media.

Implied in all of these tactics is a conviction that the media are the market-place of ideas. Instead of being a simple conveyor of public expression, the media now are thought to define and constitute the public sphere. Whereas in the nine-teenth century a political meeting was often thought of as a primary means of political communication, and the reporting of it was secondary, now the political meeting is often thought of as being simply a means of getting media attention. This transposition of means and ends is familiar to anyone who has attended a speech and heard audience members afterward defer judgment over the significance of the event until they watch the evening news. The speech itself was less of a contribution to public discourse than the report of the speech.

It is customary to attribute the substitution of media reportage for public action to the electronic media, especially television. Although it seems clear that broad-casting as it's been constructed as a news medium enhances the shift from speeches to sound bites and from face-to-face communication to mediated communication, still the history of this shift preceded radio and television. Michael McGerr has vividly described the shift from campaigning by spectacle (where a diverse public would physically gather) to campaigning by mediated education and advertising at the turn of the century, well before broadcast media became significant players in campaigns.[42] The shift should not be looked upon as technologically determined.

But the shift to mediated campaigning became much more significant as the news media institutionalized in the twentieth century. Control of the boundaries of public discourse was reconstrued: instead of the conflict of mainstream parties, the supposedly neutral judgment of news professionals defined the limits of pub-lic discourse. Granted, the boundaries stayed in roughly the same places, with main-stream partisans and officials granted newsworthiness and outsiders denied the same. But now access was to be achieved by making news. Indeed, the rules of entry to public debate stipulate that making sense is secondary to making news.

The result is that individuals or movements who believe that the agenda of public discourse needs to be altered begin by trying to make news. Sometimes this is done by violent means. Rioting is one violent way of making news. Two facts that emerged clearly about the race riots of the 1960s is that rioters tended to be more politically aware than the average citizen, and that rioters tended to have a low estimation of coverage of social issues affecting them in the mainstream media.[43] It is not an exaggeration to say that recent rioting has been among other things an exercise in media criticism.

In addition, sometimes individuals or movements resort to direct action to wrest editorial control from a medium. The kidnapping of Patty Hearst is one well-known example. In Cincinnati in 1980, an armed man entered the studios of WCPO-TV, demanding to go on the air live in order to focus attention on social issues.[44] More recently, in Lumberton, North Carolina, two Tuscarora Indians occupied the offices of the *Robesonian*, an afternoon daily, to protest discrimination and corruption in Robeson County.[45] Such instances do not happen often, probably because all but the smallest media organizations are well protected, both by private security and by police; because few people care deeply enough about public discourse; and because there remain numerous outlets for voicing nonmainstream concerns, though few of these reach a wide constituency. Given a choice between occupying a television station and producing a spot for a public access channel on a local cable system, few people would choose the former, even though the latter is virtually guaranteed to escape the notice of the mainstream public.

A very recent tactic for gaining access to the mainstream media through unconventional means involves vandalizing newsboxes. In 1989 a wave of phony front pages appeared in at least a dozen cities. These were wrapped around the regular editions of those cities' major newspapers and called attention to U.S. activities in Central America. The phony front page for the *Arizona Daily Star*, for instance, carried a major headline that read "U.S. at war in El Salvador—70,000 Killed."[46] This tactic has a twofold usefulness. First, it promises to shock regular newspaper readers by first presenting them with a convincing facsimile of their familiar paper, then becoming apparent as a hoax. This should cause the readers to wonder why this news wasn't printed in this form in their newspaper, which in turn might cause them to ponder and criticize the premises by which their newspaper determines newsworthiness and processes or constructs "the news." Second, the phony-front-page ploy can itself become a news event, forcing newspapers to call attention to their own editorial processes by reporting these attempts to challenge them. The success of this tactic in actually reaching the public is questionable, but it certainly upsets the targeted media, who don't know whether to press charges, which would serve to generate more publicity, or to ignore the event, which would confirm their unwillingness to devote attention to the issues concerned, and might encourage the perpetrators to repeat their action. Of course, to regularly print a front-page wraparound would be rather expensive, especially because unlike the target newspaper, the vandals derive neither sales nor advertising revenue from the wraparound's readers.[47]

At the extreme, inclusionary violence can shade over into the kind of violence that I've categorized as "noise," when the cause involved is clearly off the political spectrum altogether. The most telling recent example is when an apparently armed man (it turned out that his gun wasn't loaded) forced his way into a news studio at the KNBC station in Burbank, California, and forced famed consumer reporter David Horowitz to read a statement over the air. The statement concerned aliens and the CIA, and is extraordinary enough to bear quotation at length:

> The man who has appeared on KNBC for the last 3 years is not my biological father. He is a clone, a double created by the CIA and alien forces. It is only a small part of a greater plot, to overthrow the U.S. government, and possibly the human race itself.
>
> The CIA has replaced and tried to destroy my family, and those of my friends. Although I have known about this since 1981, I have not taken any action about it, for fear of the lives of my family. I have been forced into CIA-run mental hospitals since that time, where I have seen nightmares no human being could imagine. . . .
>
> I heard an interview a few weeks ago . . . in which a former CIA official . . . spoke of secret teams that were created after World War II. I say that the CIA

assassinated John F. Kennedy and the 22 material witnesses that day, who all died within 2 years of each other, a mathematical impossibility. What they are capable of, I know only too well.

I demand the public release of all secret Air Force files concerning UFOs. . . .

I demand the release of information concerning the objects contained in Hangar 18 at Wright Patterson Air Force Base, now obscurely referred to as the Environmental Control Building, the most highly guarded building in the world. . . .

These people, or whatever they are. are taking over the phone services right now. The CIA is either doing this themselves, or are helping them.

I was warned by someone with connections to the CIA to stay off of computers, that they didn't trust people on computers.[48]

The gunman might be dismissed as a "crazy," but his statement displays continuity with some fairly widespread themes in public attitudes toward the media. Immediately obvious is his tendency to think in terms of conspiracies. The statement touches on two of the more common motifs in contemporary conspiracy thinking, the CIA and the Kennedy assassination. It also dwells on UFOs, another very common though less respectable staple among conspiracy theorists. The mention of these themes underscores their dismissal by mainstream news organizations. The reporting of UFO stories is a simple index for determining the level of professionalization of a news medium: the *Weekly World News*, a supermarket tabloid, is full of UFO stories; local newspapers, occasionally confronted with what seem like mass sightings of UFOs, are obliged to print a few stories; and elite national media report none at all. It is neither here nor there whether UFOs exist at all. UFO sightings are quite common, and the definition of them as nonnews is only partly a judgment based on fact. Rather, UFO news is clearly out of bounds for the professionally defined news world because it cannot be made to make sense; news that can't be explained is of no use to people who identify themselves as professional explainers.

Conspiracy theories about the Kennedy assassination(s) are another index of professionalism. The most remarkable testimony of the salience of the Kennedy assassination is the reaction to Oliver Stone's *JFK*, a film that dramatizes evidence (some fictional) pointing to a conspiracy. Professional newspeople have reacted to the film with a barrage of criticism unparalleled in recent memory, and I suspect easily eclipsing the criticism of *Birth of a Nation* in 1916 or *Gone with the Wind* in 1939, both far more fanciful and pernicious Hollywoodizations.[49] The animus behind this reaction can be explained only partly by appeals to historical accuracy. Another ingredient is the need for professional journalists to claim mastery over this area of public discourse, and this necessitates driving out an element that threatens to overturn a generation of sense-making about the age of Camelot.[50]

Finally, the gunman's statement returns over and over again to the motif of the dissipation of identity in a society brought closer together by new communications technologies. One does not have to believe in flying saucers to see the force of this sentiment in contemporary culture, especially as it involves the media.

Attacks by "crazies" are similar to more politically coherent acts of inclusionary violence. Whether the motivation is criticism of U.S. policy in Central America or distress about strange visitors from other planets, the target is control by news professionals over the boundaries of public discourse. Inclusionary violence seeks to disrupt a perceived monopoly in the public sphere. Although political extremists are the ones likely to take action, they seem to share the perception of monopoly with a large segment of the general public.

Recent Surveys of Public Opinion Regarding the News Media

In the 1980s, following the Reagan administration's invasion of Grenada, news organizations became alarmed at public attitudes regarding the media. The administration had effectively muzzled the press during the invasion, resulting in serious distortions in the information that the public received; the public, however, seemed undisturbed. News professionals had been riding a wave of high self-esteem, convinced that the public shared an image of heroic journalists ending the unpopular war in Vietnam and toppling the corrupt Nixon administration. Now they came to suspect that the public did not share their sense of the value of critical reporting of government activities. As a result, a series of polls was commissioned to study the apparent "credibility crisis."

There is more than a little irony to the media's perception of a credibility crisis. In a libertarian marketplace of ideas, citizens should be continually critical of contestants for their support; the news media themselves value their mission of challenging governmental authority. Why should newspeople be hurt if the public doubts the media in the same fashion that they are encouraged by the media to doubt elected officials? The desire of media professionals to be above public skepticism implies a sense that they are *not in* the marketplace of ideas, which is in effect a covert assertion of the monopoly status that the media tend to deny in other settings.

In any case, the polls turned up a considerable level of press criticism, though no real crisis of credibility.[51] One area where the public is highly suspicious regards media claims to independence. They feel that the press frequently succumbs to commercial pressures (the need to appeal to large numbers of readers or viewers) and pressure from special interests, including political interest groups and advertisers.[52]

A more significant area in which public attitudes deviate from what media professionals hope for involves tolerance. Survey researchers have found widespread intolerance for the rights of nonmainstream groups—communists, socialists, homosexuals, atheists—for many years.[53] The latest confirmation of this tendency comes from Robert Wyatt's comprehensive two-part survey of public opinion on free expression, commemorating the 1991 bicentennial of the Bill of Rights. Wyatt concludes that freedom of expression is a right cherished by Americans, "but it is cherished far more in the abstract than in the specific. . . . Americans assert their dedication to freedom of expression only when asked in general terms."[54] But when asked whether they supported the right to free expression in specific cases, like promoting homosexual behavior or making unauthorized disclosures about national security or even editorializing during a campaign, respondents are as likely to support regulating expression, at least some of the time.[55] Wyatt summarizes his findings aptly: "Americans do *believe that they believe* in free expression. But, in fact, those same Americans most often believe in regulating, limiting, or suppressing expression."[56]

It follows that there is a wide difference between what media professionals believe about the rights of the media and what the public believes. Simply put, the people believe in a right to free expression, but they hold it as a personal right. They do not perceive the media to be persons exercising a personal right to free expression; rather, they see the media as an institution, like governments and churches, that have rights mostly in relation to other institutions but, in relation to the people, have only responsibilities. Thus people consistently express a belief that the press should be generally free from government interference except in cases involving legitimate governmental responsibilities (like national security), but they don't agree with legal protections that the press currently enjoys from libel prosecutions by individuals, nor do they condone press interference with privacy.[57]

Within these bounds, the press seems to be relatively popular compared with other institutions. In a 1988 Gallup Times-Mirror survey, the "daily newspaper you are most familiar with" and "network TV news" achieved a higher percentage of "highly favorable" ratings—22 percent and 21 percent, respectively—than any other institution, including the military (17 percent), the Supreme Court (13 percent), Congress (10 percent), lawyers (7 percent), and the CIA (4 percent).[58]

These polls are as interesting for what they reveal about news professionals as for what they tell us about the public. The news media involved express great concern for the safety of a democracy in a land where the people have no confidence in the information they receive, but also pronounced is a sense of professional and institutional anxiety: the media fear that the public will condone the curtailment of the traditional prerogatives of the press. Moreover, the media fear that such curtailment will come because the public fails to accept a "social-responsibility" justification for media rights. A subtext behind the construction of the questionnaires used is a fear that the public thinks of the media in the same category as automobile manufacturers and other big businesses rather than in the category of medicine, law, and the other professions or the category of Congress, the judiciary, and other public institutions. Because freedom of the press has become in practice a right for corporate entities and not for individuals, it is important that the public view the media as corporate entities of the sort that deserve special protection, instead of simply as profit-making businesses.

Conclusion

The level of violence against the press currently is as low as it's ever been. Journalists and news executives consider violence to be a rather unimportant feature of their work environment. Far more significant, judging from written responses to my survey and published remarks, is the fear of legal action, especially libel suits. In addition to being violent, Americans have always been litigious.

But the violence that does exist underscores a particular set of developments in the structure and ideology of the media in the twentieth century. Seen in the light of recent public opinion surveys, it suggests a powerful and perhaps accurate perception of a shrinking and increasingly monopolized public sphere. The number of violent people is small, but the number of alienated people is large and growing. There is more than a little cause for concern.

9

Conclusion

Our ways of thinking and talking about communicating place it in an entirely different category than, say, economics. On a commonsense level, we posit a fundamental difference between the stuff of communication—call it information or opinion or images or discourse or truth—and the stuff of the economy, which is thought of as material and tangible, as things that can be dropped on your foot. Only the ill-informed continue to think that economics is about things that can be dropped on your foot, of course. When the stock market crashed in 1987, half a trillion dollars disappeared from the U.S. economy. Where did it go? Well, the better question is, where was it in the first place? The shortest answer is that it existed as information. It's a truism to say that modern economies are more and more information-based; it's truer to say that information has always been central to economic production.

If economics tells us that the dichotomy between communications and the material world is false (or at least outmoded), what can we learn from the other part of the equation? We've inherited an apparatus of thinking about the intellectual world as essentially different from the material world. We tend to assume, for instance, that "truth" has power fundamentally different from other kinds of power, that information is a resource that can be used without being used up, that ways of thinking can be autonomous from other ways of being in the world: these are all notions embedded in Western liberal traditions. A contrary tradition of materialism, which denies the (actual or potential) autonomy of the intellectual, appeals mainly to intellectuals and hasn't won wide adherence. Let's leave aside the question of whether the intellectual itself is material. Not only can't we answer it, but the question is so abstract as not to be all that interesting. The question we can answer is whether the *media* are material. The answer is yes. And, if the history of violence against the press in the United States demonstrates anything, it is that people have always understood the materiality of the press. Violence is always an assertion of materiality.

This is not to say that the press is only material. As I've already remarked, we tend to distinguish, both in law and in common sense, between "speech acts" or acts of expression and belief and other kinds of acts, say, commercial acts. Such a distinction is basic to legal protections for speech acts: if we believed that expression had the same material reality as theft or assault, then we would have to regulate the use of expressive force in the same way that we regulate the use of physical force. We don't, and I think that's a good thing. Instead, we posit that expression will be regulated by rules of its own—the power of truth, for instance. Because the media are vehicles for expression, they too are privileged by this thinking.

But the media *are* material. They are produced industrially and marketed commercially (in most of the world) and cannot function without all sorts of things that can be dropped on your foot. Moreover, and this must be emphasized, the power they exercise is not just the power of truth. And you don't have to deny the existence of the power of truth to see that. The media exercise power *prior to* the power of truth. They empower groups by their very existence, as we've seen in the history of violence against nonmainstream media. They have been the instruments of political power. They police the boundaries of the public sphere. All of these functions, whether one believes in the power of truth or not, are material functions.

The material functions of the media have a history. Most obviously, the conditions of production of the media have changed over time, and the ways they're made always affect (though they don't determine) the things they do. Current conditions of monopoly or near-monopoly allow the media to police the public sphere; previous conditions of competition didn't, and future conditions might not. (History doesn't end.) Media production involves a lot more than economics and technics, however; it also involves institutions and ideologies. This returns us to a point I made in the introduction: the media aren't things in themselves; they are networks of relationships. They're always embedded in their social world, and are always carriers of powers other than the power of truth. The networks of relationships that constitute the media are extensive; they embrace political parties and markets and so forth. And they change partly in response to the ways they're imagined—hence my recurrent emphasis on ideology.

But I needn't have written such a long book to say this. These grand points could easily have been made without going into much detail about actual events and persons. Other points emerge only from the buzz of occurrences. Here are some less grand conclusions.

The first, and least ambitious, is that acts of violence against the press say something. Acts of violence have rarely been just noise—senseless explosions of passion, bestial reactions from bestial people. On the contrary, most of the acts of violence discussed here were quite strategic. Furthermore, they might all be usefully considered as statements, often in dead languages, about the commonly agreed upon proprieties and boundaries of public discourse.

That public discourse always has boundaries is a second fairly obvious point. Violence was both a way of declaring some public expression illegitimate and a way of expressing the illegitimate—the boundaries of speech can themselves be unspeakable. The United States has had an ideological allergy toward the open suppression of expression by governmental authority, but at the same time U.S. citizens have also had serious qualms about the public expression of certain ideas (atheism, communism, and the like), about certain types of public expression (personal attacks, for example), and about the prerogatives of some groups of people (racial and ethnic minorities, for instance, or the working class). These limits are articulated reluctantly because of the general commitment to freedom of expression. Absent more explicit policing, people have relied on silent regulators, like the marketplace, or direct violent action.

Violence has declined *pari passu* with the rise of a widely accepted metaphor of public discourse as a marketplace. At present, U.S. citizens seem to be satisfied that their marketplace is wide open, that anyone can get anything one wants in it. There is no question that heterodox ideas circulate freely in the mail and in bookstores. At the same time, few people fear that mass political movements will arise from all of this available stuff. Rather, it seems that the things most people fear from free discussion are moral rather than political. They fear the corrosion of family and Christian values; they fear outbursts of criminal behavior. The flashpoints of these anxieties are adult bookstores, not "the press" as it has been traditionally denoted. Mass political movements, it is believed, have always withered in the marketplace; the U.S. public is thought of as pragmatic, immune to the influence of ideology. If there be people in the United States who have been insulated from the purifying effects of the marketplace, they might be fit tools for the designs of corruption, and hence might need some correction beyond that offered by the invisible hand. Most people see few such "unmeltables" today.

As a corollary, we might suppose that people are no longer as impressed with the power of ideas as they once were. In modern times, people have become accustomed to being bombarded with ideas, and they consider this situation to be normal. They know that they will not be affected by the bombardment, though they still suspect that others are not as immune.

Likewise, violence has declined in step with the rise of legal and judicial means of regulating "abuses" of public discourse. The standard history of Supreme Court First Amendment decisions gives a misleading impression of the continual triumph of liberalism over authoritarianism. In fact, judgments that protect free expression from government interference should also be read upside down as evidence of vigorous campaigns to regulate expression. There is an immense legal apparatus designed to prevent dangerous or damaging expression; its growth in the twentieth century has made some of the older, violent tactics superfluous.

But the absence of violence does not necessarily indicate the triumph of tolerance. On the contrary, survey research has demonstrated repeatedly that citizens don't condone legal protection for certain kinds of expression: the seditious, the obscene, and the blasphemous, especially. Expression of these sorts survives without public outcry only inasmuch as it cordons itself off from the general public. Hence what seems to be tolerance is often nothing more than ignorance.

Patterns of violence against the press have changed as the press has changed. The character of the media as networks of relationships has changed over time; in the twentieth century, "the media" are constituted as an institution among other institutions; their relationship to the public is refracted by their mass circulation and by the ascendance of an ideology of professionalism. In relation to the media, the public is modeled as markets and as clients. I argued in Chapter 8 that contemporary violence against the press might be seen as an expression of this dependent relationship of the public to the media. In more than a few cases, violent acts might be looked upon as frank acts of protest against media that seem imperial.

This raises a more general question. Is violence against the press actually a form of press criticism? One would not argue, for instance, that robbery is a form of criticizing capitalism. On the contrary, a robber deprives a person of property by taking it for oneself; a robber appropriates property but by no means criticizes ownership in general or in the abstract. Is violence against the press like robbery?

In some cases, the comparison to robbery is apt. Sometimes someone strikes out against the press with the simple intention of personal gain. Some labor-related violence has been of this sort, as well as much of the personal violence motivated by a desire to protect reputation. But these cases are a minority of the cases that I've described.

In most cases, violence against the press expresses some kind of judgment about the proprieties of public discourse. Antipress violence is and has been political in the deepest sense: it has been about the definition of polity.

One feels an embarrassed sadness about the diminution of violence against the press. Although one never wants to hear of an editor's being lynched or a newspaper or broadcast station's being bombed, still activities of this sort have always indicated a liveliness of attention. The perpetrators are showing intolerance of the most extreme sort, but they deem it appropriate because they imagine an attentive public. Intolerance has outlived the age of violence and will no doubt soon produce new types of violence, but the lively public seems to be a thing of the past in the United States.

Commentators have often discerned a malaise in U.S. political culture. One thing all persuasions seem to agree on is that the citizenry is moribund. Citizens no longer vote in great numbers, and seem to be spending less time paying attention to the news. There is an obvious explanation for this malaise. Americans today have no experience in recent memory of active political discourse. Parties and candidates share a sameness and rely on the blandest media representations to make their points, and elections are run and perceived as sporting events. Any substantive opposition has been embargoed by institutional factors and by a long tradition of suppression of various sorts. What remains for the average citizen is a passive role as witness to a mediated spectacle. The poverty of political discourse as it actually exists is obvious from any consideration of what happens when it's disrupted. David Duke's candidacy for the governorship of Louisiana in 1991 was hardly a triumph for a reinvigorated public sphere, but voters turned out in record numbers, apparently because they felt that their engagement in the political process had serious substance. How lamentable that professional politicians wage subtantive campaigns only as rear-guard actions against Klansmen and Nazis, real or imagined.

The primitive sense of republican government of the eighteenth century called for citizens to be the actors in the arena of public discourse. When people imagined a *mediated* public sphere, they imagined it in terms of an artificially extended town meeting, a place where individuals addressed their peers. The mediated public sphere as it developed was something else altogether. Through several permutations, it became a site for contests over representing the public to itself; in the process of being spoken for, the public found less opportunity to speak for itself. Should we be surprised if it no longer has anything to say?

This will sound like a familiar point to the reader. After all, haven't I quoted critics from the eighteenth century onwards about the failures of public discourse? But such commentators have always lamented the death of rationality in public discourse, and yes, there's no novelty there. U.S. politics, I think, has always used "irrational" means, especially violence. I differ in pointing out the disappearance of a particular form of *irrationality* from public discourse. It is ironic that, in an age of escalating violence, the United States should experience a decline in *political* violence. This decline isn't lamentable in itself—I abhor violence—but it might indicate a lamentable change. People and groups of people have always fought over power in the United States. Perhaps they've stopped fighting because they've become more civilized or mature, but if this were the case, one would expect violence of every sort to decline. Why have they stopped fighting over politics and not over money or sex? Is it that there's nothing worth fighting over in politics anymore?

Violence is often a means of public expression, but it is not a good one. It has often accompanied and warred against more desirable forms of public expression; in fact, there has been no great national debate in U.S. history without a significant level of violence. The waning of violence against the media is an index of the evisceration of public debate. When there is vigorous debate, violence is often its companion. There is a worse alternative, though: In the absence of public debate, violence may become its substitute.

Appendix A:
Survey Questionnaire

If your news organization has experienced any of the
following over the past twelve months, please check the
appropriate space indicating frequency:

	daily	weekly	monthly	less
Threatening letters or phone calls	—	—	—	—
Acts of vandalism (directed against newsboxes, advertisements, or any other kind of property)	—	—	—	—
An actual physical assault	—	—	—	—

Does your news organization employ security guards or take similar security measures?	YES	NO
If you answered yes to the previous question: Are your security measures designed primarily to prevent information leaks?	YES	NO

If you answered yes to any of the above, please respond
to the following by checking the appropriate space:

	strongly disagree				strongly agree
People who threaten or assault a news organization are terrorists.	1	2	3	4	5
People who threaten or assault a news organization tend to be crackpots.	1	2	3	4	5
People who threaten or assault a news medium are motivated by disagreement with editorial positions.	1	2	3	4	5
People who threaten or assault a news medium are usually motivated by a personal grudge.	1	2	3	4	5
Threats or assaults have had a chilling effect on our editorial positions.	1	2	3	4	5
Threats or assaults have had a chilling effect on our news reporting.	1	2	3	4	5
A news organization should always report threats to the police.	1	2	3	4	5

	strongly disagree				strongly agree
A news organization should always report minor assaults and vandalism to the police.	1	2	3	4	5
A news organization should report as news the threats it receives.	1	2	3	4	5
A news organization should report as news minor assaults on its property or personnel.	1	2	3	4	5
Reporting threats and assaults as news encourages imitators.	1	2	3	4	5
A large part of the public feels hostility toward the media.	1	2	3	4	5
The public would *not* condone legal restrictions on freedom of the press.	1	2	3	4	5
A large part of the public feels that some journalists deserve a beating.	1	2	3	4	5
A good journalist should expect to encounter violence.	1	2	3	4	5
Journalism properly practiced is not a dangerous profession.	1	2	3	4	5
Journalism used to be more dangerous than it is today.	1	2	3	4	5
Journalism is becoming more dangerous.	1	2	3	4	5
Much of the violence or threats of violence news organizations encounter is motivated by racial tensions.	1	2	3	4	5
Much of the violence or threats of violence news organizations encounter is motivated by economic tensions.	1	2	3	4	5
Much of the violence or threats of violence news organizations encounter results from labor disputes within the organization.	1	2	3	4	5

COMMENTS: Please use the back of this form to add any comments you feel are appropriate. Are there questions you feel should be addressed? Are there any specific incidents you would like to report? Please indicate whether you would like your remarks to be confidential.

Appendix B:
The Flow of Antiabolitionist Violence

Benjamin Lundy beaten by slavetrader Austin Woolfolk	Baltimore, Md.	Autumn 1827
Jocelyn's school harassed by mob	New Haven, Conn.	Summer 1831
Arthur Tappan's home mobbed *re* support for S. Jocelyn's school	New Haven, Conn.	Summer 1831
Anti-Slavery Society organizing meeting mobbed	New York	Fall 1833
Antislavery convention mobbed	Twinsburg, Ohio	Spring 1834
Antislavery convention mobbed	Middletown, Conn.	Spring 1834
Week-long antiabolitionism rioting, including mobbing of Lewis Tappan's home	New York	Summer 1834
Antiabolitionism rioting	Newark, N.J.	Summer 1834
Riot at Miami University	Oxford, Ohio	Summer 1834
Three-night-long antiabolitionism riot	Philadelphia	Summer 1834
Antislavery convention mobbed	Lockport, N.Y.	Summer 1834
O. S. Murray lecture mobbed	Burlington, Vt.	Summer 1834
Prudence Crandall's house, school mobbed	Canterbury, Conn.	Summer 1834
George Thompson mobbed	Augusta, Maine	Fall 1834
George Thompson mobbed	Lowell, Mass.	Fall 1834
George Thompson mobbed	Concord, N.H.	Fall 1834
O. S. Murray lecture mobbed	Woodstock, Vt.	Winter 1835
O. S. Murray lecture mobbed	Randloph, Vt.	Winter 1835
O. S. Murray lecture mobbed	Windsor, Vt.	Winter 1835
Antislavery meeting stoned	Cincinnati, Ohio	Spring 1835
T. D. Weld mobbed	Oldtown, Ohio	Spring 1835
T. D. Weld mobbed	Circleville, Ohio	Spring 1835

Abolition lecture attacked by mob led by Levi Lincoln, Jr., son of Mass. governor	Worcester, Mass.	Summer 1835
Attempted mobbing of alleged abolitionist David Paul Brown	Philadelphia	Summer 1835
Integrated academy mobbed	New Canaan, N.H.	Summer 1835
Mob gathers at jail as Prudence Crandall's brother is arrested	Washington, D.C.	Summer 1835
Mob gathers at jail as three alleged abolition agents arrested	New York	Summer 1835
Mob at the Reverend May lecture	Haverhill, Mass.	Summer 1835
Vermont Anti-Slavery Society meetings mobbed	Montpelier, Vt.	Fall 1835
T. D. Weld mobbed	Chester, Ohio	Fall 1835
T. D. Weld mobbed	Painesville, Ohio	Fall 1835
George Thompson mobbed	Abington, Vt.	Fall 1835
Mob at A. A. Phelps lecture	Farmington, Conn.	Fall 1835
J. W. Alvord mobbed	Middlebury, Ohio	Winter 1836
S. W. Streeter threatened with tar and feathers by mob	Grafton, Ohio	Winter 1836
J. A. Thome egged by mob	Hanover, Ohio	Winter 1836
J. A. Thome egged by mob	Cadiz, Ohio	Winter 1836
Antislavery convention mobbed	Granville, Ohio	Spring 1835
Abolition lecturer mobbed	Mt. Vernon, Ohio	Spring 1836
J. G. Birney lecture egged	Xenia, Ohio	Spring 1836
Purdy's print office egged	Xenia, Ohio	Spring 1836
T. D. Weld mobbed	Lockport, N.Y.	Spring 1836
A. W. Kitchell tarred and feathered	Hillsborough, Ga.	Summer 1836
Mob prevents celebration of British emancipation anniversary	Boston	Summer 1836
C. C. Burleigh mobbed	Mansfield, Mass.	Fall 1836
Antiabolitionism mob	New Canaan, N.H.	Fall 1836
Yale students riot at lecture by Boston abolitionist, the Reverend Rand	New Haven, Conn.	Fall 1836
Marius Robinson severely beaten	Berlin, Ohio	Spring 1837
J. G. Birney egged	Dayton, Ohio	Winter 1837
Antiabolitionism mob	Mt. Vernon, Ohio	Winter 1837
Antiabolitionism mob	Hartford, Ohio	Winter 1837
The Reverend A. T. Rankin mobbed	Dayton, Ohio	Winter 1837
J. G. Birney lecture mobbed, broken up	Hartford, Conn.	Spring 1837
Marius Robinson mobbed	Berlin, Ohio	Spring 1837
Abolitionist lecturer mobbed	Mount Liberty, Ohio	Spring 1837
Abolitionism debate threatened by mob	Blendon, Ohio	Summer 1837

S. L. Gould lecture mobbed	Poughkeepsie, N.Y.	Winter 1838
Baltimore Religious Magazine publicly burned	Parkersburg, Va.	Spring 1838
Mob throws "filth" at antislavery lecture	Norwich, Conn.	Spring 1838
Hall burned, including offices of *Pennsylvania Freeman*	Philadelphia	Summer 1838
Abolition lecture mobbed	Wareham, Mass.	Fall 1838
Postmaster leads mob against meeting of antislavery society	Tarentown, Pa.	Fall 1838
Abolitionist debate mobbed	Barnsville, Ohio	Fall 1838
Abolitionist tarred and feathered	Guyandott, Va.	Winter 1839
Suspected abolitionist beaten	Jackson, Ohio	Winter 1839
Mob frees arrested African-American man	Sardinia, Ohio	Spring 1839
Attempted bombing of antislavery depository	Hartford, Conn.	Spring 1839
Harassment of Ohio Anti-Slavery Society meeting	Zanesville	Spring 1839
Gerrit Smith egged	Eastern towns	Summer 1839
Two abolitionist lecturers tarred and feathered	Vincennes, Ind.	Summer 1839
J. M. McKim lecture egged	Gettysburg, Pa.	Summer 1839
D. Putnam, Jr., and A. Stone thrown into Ohio River by crowd	Parkersburg, Va.	Summer 1839
Abolitionist tarred and feathered	Georgetown, Ky.	Spring 1840
Daniel Neall (traveling with wife Lucretia Mott) tarred and feathered	Smyrna, Del.	Spring 1840
Dr. A. Brooke mobbed after trial to free slaves	Waynesville, Ohio	Autumn 1840
Dr. Jewett's house mobbed	Dayton, Ohio	Winter 1841
Fugitive slave riot	Oberlin, Ohio	Winter 1841
Abolitionist lecturers egged	Sharon, Ohio	Spring 1841
James Boyle lecture egged	Sharon, Ohio	Summer 1841
The Reverend Edward Smith egged by mob	Steubenville, Ohio	Summer 1841
Church trashed by mob over rumored abolition lecture	Pittsburgh	Summer 1841
Whitehead, a fugitive slave's lawyer, mobbed	Kaskaskia, Ill.	Summer 1841
Mob attacks, tries to burn barn of the Reverend J. Rankin	Ripley, Ohio	Fall 1841
Thomas Hicklin lecture mobbed	Lancaster, Ind.	Fall 1841
C. C. Burleigh lecture mobbed	Cincinnati	Fall 1841
Antislavery convention mobbed	Washington, Ill.	Summer 1842
W. L. Garrison lecture egged, mobbed	Syracuse, N.Y.	Fall 1842
Antiabolition mob	Pendleton, Ind.	Summer 1843
Antiabolitionism mob	Richmond, Ind.	Summer 1843
"Scanlan Mob" riots over a fugitive slave	Cincinnati	Summer 1843

Antislavery meetings mobbed	Cleves, Ohio	Summer 1843
Samuel Davis suspends *Register* under threat	Peoria, Ill.	1843
Rioting over S. S. Foster lecture	Providence, R.I.	Spring 1844
Fugitive slave raid	Red Oak, Ohio	Fall 1844
S. S. Foster and Charles L. Remond lecture mobbed	Newtown, Pa.	Spring 1845
Abby Kelley and Jane Hitchcock lecture egged	Harrisburg, Pa.	Spring 1845
Fire set to office of *Anti-Slavery Standard*	New York	Spring 1845
African-American abolitionist stoned	Newark, N.J.	Spring 1845
Attempted mobbing of antislavery meeting	Cincinnati	Spring 1845
Parker Pillsbury silenced by crowd at New England Antislavery Society Convention	Marlboro, Mass.	Spring 1845
DePuy, antislavery editor of *Indiana Freeman*, attacked by mob	Indianapolis	Summer 1845
Isaac S. Flint egged	Paris, Ohio	Summer 1845
Isaac S. Flint egged	Hanover, Ohio	Summer 1845
Isaac S. Flint egged	Massillon, Ohio	Summer 1845
Antislavery meeting egged, broken up	Peoria, Ill.	Spring 1846
African-American abolitionist A. Baer, Jr., mobbed	Ohio (several towns)	Summer 1846
Parker Pillsbury pelted with rocks and eggs	Sterling, Mass.	Summer 1846
S. S. Foster and Abby Kelley Foster egged, meeting broken up	Abington, Mass.	Winter 1847
M. R. Hall's *Clarion of Freedom* trashed	Cambridge, Ohio	Fall 1847
Frederick Douglass/William Lloyd Garrison lecture mobbed, egged	Harrisburg, Pa.	Fall 1847
Parker Pillsbury et al. mobbed	Harwich, Mass.	Summer 1848
Editor Ordway of the *Advertiser* assaulted	Portland, Maine	Fall 1848
Frederick Douglass's *North Star* files trashed by mob	Rochester, N.Y.	Fall 1848
L. Moody lecture mobbed	East Bridgewater, Mass.	Summer 1850
Mob besets Frederick Douglass lecture	Columbus, Ohio	Summer 1850
L. F. W. Andrews suspends *Georgia Citizen* under threat	Macon, Ga.	Summer 1850
Tammany leader Isaiah Rynders et al. break up American Anti-Slavery Society Meeting	New York	Summer 1850
George Thompson and other abolitionists jeered off stage at Faneuil Hall	Boston	Fall 1850
George Thompson threatened by crowds, hung in effigy	Springfield, Mass.	Winter 1851
Mob at antislavery/nativism lecture	Quincy, Ill.	Fall 1855

Virginians attack Ohio anti-Fugitive Slave Law meeting	Quaker Bottom, Ohio	Spring 1856
Crowd fires cannon at home of E. C. Goodwin, editor of pro-Fremont *Enquirer*	Litchfield, Conn.	Fall 1856
"Dead Rabbits" trash *Anti-Slavery Standard* office	New York	Summer 1859
Massachusetts Anti-Slavery Society meeting mobbed	Boston	Winter 1861

The 124 actions listed above do not include ten actions described in chapter four: the Utica mob, the two Philanthropist riots, the Garrison mob, the four Lovejoy riots, and the crowd actions involving Cassius Clay's *True American* and Gamaliel Bailey's *National Era*. Of the 134 actions, 24 directly involved the press. Chronologically, the actions break down thus:

Period	Number of Actions
pre-1840	79
post-1840	55
1840–1845	34
1846–1861	21

Appendix C:
Civil War Newspaper Mobbings

Target	Date
Allentown, Pa. *Democrat*	22 August 1861
Allentown, Pa. *Republikaner*	22 August 1861
Austin, Texas *Southern Intelligencer*	? 1861
Baltimore *Die Wecker*	20 April 1861
Bangor, Maine *Democrat*	12 August 1861
Beaver, Pa. *Western Star*	? May 1861
Bellefontaine, Ohio *Gazette*	n.d.
Belleville, Ill. daily *Volksblatt*	? March 1863
Belleville, Ill.daily *Volksblatt*	19 May 1864*
Bloomington, Ill. *Times*	22 August 1862
Bluffton, Ind. *Banner*	? April 1865
Boonville, Mo. *Observer*	18 June 1861*
Bridgeport, Conn. *Advertiser and Farmer*	24 August 1861*
Brooklyn, N.Y. *Eagle*	17 April 1861
Brooklyn, N.Y. *News*	17 April 1861
Brooklyn, N.Y. *Standard*	17 April 1861
Brooklyn, N.Y. *Star*	17 April 1861
Brookville, Ind. *Democrat*	? 1864
Brown County (Ohio) *Argus*	? August 1863
Bucyrus *Forum*	8 September 1861
Butler, Pa. *Democratic Herald*	? 1863
Cadiz, Ohio *Sentinel*	? September 1863
Canton, Ohio *Stark County Democrat*	22 August 1861*
Carbon, Pa. *Democrat*	31 August 1861

Target	Date
Carlisle, Pa. *American Volunteer*	24 October 1864*
Chambersburg, Pa. *Valley Spirit*	? July 1864*
Chester, Ill. *Picket Guard*	Fall 1864
Chicago *Times*	3 June 1863*
Columbus, Ohio *Crisis*	5 March 1863*
Columbus, Ohio *Ohio Statesman*	5 March 1863*
Concord, N.H. *Democratic Standard*	8 August 1861*
Covington, Ind. *People's Friend*	20 August 1861
Dayton, Ohio *Daily Journal*	5 May 1863
Dayton, Ohio *Empire*	3 March 1864*
Easton, Pa. *Sentinel*	19 August 1861
Easton, Pa. *Argus*	19 August 1861
Ebensburg, Pa. *Democrat and Sentinel*	? 1863
Evansville, Ind. *Daily Times*	1 March 1864*
Fairfield, Iowa *Constitution and Union*	8 February 1864*
Franklin, Ind. *Herald*	early 1864*
Fremont, Ohio *Messenger*	14 April 1864*
Galveston, Texas *Die Union*	3 January 1861
Greenville, Ohio *Democrat*	29 February 1864*
Greensburg, Pa. *Argus*	Spring? 1864
Hartford, Conn. *Times*	? August 1861*
Haverhill, Mass. *Essex County Democrat*	20 August 1861
Huntingdon, Pa. *Monitor*	20 May 1863
Indianapolis, Ind. *State Sentinel*	1 September 1861
Indianapolis, Ind. *State Sentinel*	? 1863
Jackson, Ohio *Iron Valley Express*	? August 1861
Jackson, Ohio *Iron Valley Express*	17 July 1863*
Jackson, Ohio *Standard*	17 July 1863*
Junction City, Kans. *Kansas Frontier*	10 March 1862*
Keokuk, Iowa *Daily Constitution*	19 February 1863*
Kittaning, Pa. *Mentor*	? May 1863
LaCrosse, Wis. *Democrat*	Fall 1864
Lafayette, Ind. *Argus*	Fall 1861*
Lancaster, Ohio *Eagle*	28 January 1864*
LaPorte, Ind. *Democrat*	16 February 1864*
Leavenworth, Kans. *Inquirer*	11 February 1863
Leavenworth, Kans. *Western Sentinel*	27 August 1863*
Lebanon, Ohio *Citizen*	12 August 1862

Target	Date
Lebanon, Pa. *Advertiser*	Early 1864
Logan, Ill. *Sun*	n.d.
Louisiana, Mo. *Union*	10 June 1864
Marietta, Ohio *Democrat*	27 March 1863
Marion, Ohio *Mirror*	? August 1861
Maysville, Kans. *Constitutional Gazetteer*	20 August 1863
Meadville, Pa. *Crawford Democrat*	5 February 1864
New York *Day Book*	15 April 1861
New York *Herald*	15 April 1861
New York *Journal of Commerce*	15 April 1861
New York *News*	15 April 1861
New York *Tribune*	? July 1863
Newark, N.J. *Mercury*	? July 1863
Newark, N.J. *Daily Journal*	? 1862
Nicholasville, Ky. *Democrat*	? May 1861
Northumberland, Pa. *Democrat*	7 February 1864
Olney, Ill. *Herald*	30 August 1863*
Oskaloosa, Iowa *Times*	n.d.
Paris, Ill. *Times*	22 February 1864*
Parkersburg, W.V. *News*	20 May 1861
Philadelphia *Age*	8 May 1863
Philadelphia *Palmetto Flag*	14 April 1861
Portsmouth, N.H. *States and Union*	10 April 1864
Princeton, Ind. *Union Democrat*	1 March 1864*
Raleigh *North Carolina Standard*	? September 1863*
Raleigh *State Journal*	? September 1863
Richmond, Ind. *Jeffersonian*	15 March 1863*
Rockport, Ind. *Democrat*	? January 1863*
Saint Clairsville, Ohio *Gazette*	n.d.
Saint Clairsville, Ohio *Citizen*	n.d.
San Francisco *Democratic Press*	16 April 1865
San Francisco *Monitor*	16 April 1865
San Francisco *News Letter*	16 April 1865
San Francisco *Occidental*	16 April 1865
San Francisco *L'Union Franco Americaine*	16 April 1865
Selinsgrove, Pa. *Times*	? 1862
Somerset, Ohio *Union*	? March 1864*
South-Tier, Iowa *Democrat*	n.d.

Target	Date
Sunbury, Pa. *Northumberland County Democrat*	18 January 1864
Sunbury, Pa. *Northumberland County Democrat*	? March 1864*
Terre Haute, Ind. *Journal and Democrat*	21 October 1861*
Troy, N.Y. *Times*	? July 1863
Vincennes, Ind. *Western Sun*	1 March 1864
Visalia, Calif. *Equal Rights Expositor*	? 1862*
Wauseon *Ohio Democratic Press*	18 February 1864*
West Chester, Pa. *Jeffersonian*	19 August 1861
Westminster *Western Maryland Democrat*	16 April 1865
Wilmington *Delaware Gazette*	24 August 1861
Youngstown, Ohio *Mahoning Sentinel*	28 January 1864*

Summary

State	Number
California	6
Connecticut	2
Delaware	1
Illinois	8
Indiana	14
Iowa	4
Kansas	4
Kentucky	1
Maine	1
Maryland	2
Massachusetts	1
Missouri	2
New Hampshire	2
New Jersey	2
New York	10
North Carolina	2
Ohio	23
Pennsylvania	22
Texas	2
(West) Virginia	1
Wisconsin	1
Total	111

Time of Year

January	5
February	9
March	12
April	19
May	8
June	3
July	6
August	22
September	5
October	2
November	-
December	-
Spring	1
Fall	3
Early	2
None	14
Total	111

Year

1861	36
1862	6
1863	28
1864	28
1865	7
none	6
Total	111

Note: Includes cases of mob intimidation; "n.d." indicates that the date of the action is unavailable.

*Indicates soldiers participated.

Notes

Chapter One

1. Edwin McDowell, "Book Notes: A Canceled Contract," *New York Times*, 19 July 1989, p. C20; V. M., "Collins Cancels 'Rushdie Dossier,'" *Publishers' Weekly* 19 May 1989. *Publishers' Weekly* reports that "Collins CEO Socia Land and Barry Winkleman, newly appointed managing director of the general division, disagreed with the book's editors at Fontana that it had attained the promised objectivity." There was also pressure within the British publishing industry to let the Rushdie controversy die a natural death. Subsequently, both books were published, though by different houses. Daniel Pipes, *The Rushdie Affair: The Novel, the Ayatollah, and the West* (New York: Carol Publishing, 1990); Lisa Appignanesi and Sara Maitland, eds., *The Rushdie File* (Syracuse: Syracuse University Press, 1990). Ironically, Pipes is rather critical of Rushdie and his writing, even while condemning Khomeini's edict.

2. Salman Rushdie, "Is Nothing Sacred?" in Rushdie, *Imaginary Homelands: Essays and Criticism, 1981–1991* (New York: Viking, 1991), pp. 416, 420.

3. *Satanic Verses* is a novel about the postcolonial experience of Indians and Pakistanis, among other things; it was unfair to Rushdie that his work would seem to many to be just another colonialist humiliation.

4. The following discussion is drawn from Jürgen Habermas, *The Structural Transformation of the Public Sphere: An Inquiry into a Category of Bourgeois Society*, Thomas Burger, trans. (Cambridge, Mass.: MIT Press, 1989).

5. This is not to say that law is lax, only that it seems lax to most people. To mention only the most familiar legal restrictions on expression is to compose a long list: obscenity and indecency; sedition and treason; incitement; libel, slander, and defamation; patent and copyright; and immigration regulation. In addition, there are numerous governmental and procedural restrictions on the flow of information that are justified by national security, and the range of secrecy continues to grow.

6. Alexis de Tocqueville, *Democracy in America*, ed. J. P. Mayer (Garden City, N.Y.: Doubleday, 1969), chap. 15, "The Unlimited Power of the Majority in the United States."

7. All documented in Ben Bagdikian, *The Media Monopoly*, 2d ed. (Boston: Beacon Press, 1987). See also Bagdikian, "The U.S. Media: Supermarket or Assembly Line?" *Journal of Communication* 35 (1985): 97–109, along with the dissenting view in Benjamin Compaine, "The Expanding Base of Media Competition," ibid., pp. 81–96.

8. The most revealing work on press economics in the nineteenth century has been done by Carolyn Stewart Dyer: "Economic Dependence and Concentration of Ownership among Antebellum Wisconsin Newspapers," *Journalism History* 7 (1980): 42–46, and "Political Patronage and the Wisconsin Press, 1849–1860: New Perspectives on the Economics of Patronage," *Journalism Monographs*, no. 109, February 1989.

9. Mill, *On Liberty*, in *Utilitarianism, Liberty, and Representative Government*, Everyman's Library ed. (New York: Dutton, 1951), pp. 124–26.

10. Gaye Tuchman, *Making News: A Study in the Construction of Reality* (New York: Free Press, 1978); Herbert J. Gans, *Deciding What's News: A Study of CBS Evening News, NBC Nightly News, Newsweek, and Time* (New York: Pantheon, 1979); Edward Jay Epstein, *News from Nowhere: Television and the News* (New York: Random House, 1973).

11. For a compelling discussion of the way in which Joseph McCarthy used the conventions of journalistic professionalism to manipulate press coverage, see Edwin R. Bayley, *Joe McCarthy and the Press* (Madison: University of Wisconsin Press, 1987).

12. Mark Twain, "Journalism in Tennessee," in Twain, *Writings of Mark Twain*, 37 vols. (New York: G. Wells, 1922–1925), vol. 8, *Sketches New and Old*, pp. 35–43. The piece was originally written in 1871, and is meant to depict a time in Twain's young manhood, probably the 1850s or 1860s.

13. See, for instance, Twain, "A Duel Prevented," in Twain, *The Works of Mark Twain: Early Tales and Sketches*, ed. Edgar Marquess Branch and Robert H. Hirst, 2 vols. (Berkeley: University of California Press, 1979), vol. 1, *1851–1864*, pp. 262–66; Twain, "Old Nevada Days (1906)," in Twain, *Mark Twain at His Best*, ed. Charles Neider (Garden City, N.Y.: Doubleday, 1986), pp. 415–22.

14. Benjamin Franklin, "An Account of the Supremest Court of Judicature in Pennsylvania, viz., the Court of the Press," *Federal Gazette*, 12 September 1789, reprinted in *The Writings of Benjamin Franklin*, ed. Albert Henry Smyth, 10 vols. (New York: Macmillan, 1907), vol. 10, *1789–1790*, pp. 36–40.

15. This is Russell Nye's argument in "Freedom of the Press and the Antislavery Controversy," *Journalism Quarterly* 22 (1945): 1–11. See also his *Fettered Freedom: Civil Liberties and the Slavery Controversy, 1830–1860* (East Lansing: Michigan State University Press, 1946).

16. De Tocqueville, *Democracy in America*, pp. 254–59.

17. A newspaper consumes its audience by selling it to its advertisers, of course.

Chapter Two

1. The preceding discussion is based on the classic works of the republican synthesis: Bernard Bailyn's *The Ideological Origins of the American Revolution* (Cambridge: Harvard University Press, 1967); J. G. A. Pocock's *Politics, Language, and Time: Essays on Political Thought and History* (New York: Atheneum, 1971); Gordon Wood's *Creation of the American Republic, 1776–1787* (Chapel Hill: University of North Carolina Press, 1969).

2. Historiographically, liberalism is a less unified camp than republicanism. Some of the key works in the emergent liberal synthesis are rooted in republicanism and push forward. Among these are Drew McCoy's *The Elusive Republic* (Chapel Hill: University of North Carolina Press, 1980); Joyce Appleby's *Capitalism and a New Social Order: The Republican Vision of the 1790s* (New York: New York University Press, 1984). Others are written in more or less direct refutation of republican readings of Revolutionary-era thought. See Robert Webking, *The American Revolution and the Politics of Liberty* (Baton Rouge: Louisiana State University Press, 1988); John Patrick Diggins, "Comrades and Citizens:

New Mythologies in American Historiography," *American Historical Review* 90 (1985): 614–38; Thomas Pangle, *The Spirit of Modern Republicanism: The Moral Vision of the American Founders and the Philosophy of Locke* (Chicago: University of Chicago Press, 1988). For a useful summary of the debate over republicanism, see Joyce Appleby, "Introduction: Republicanism and Ideology," *American Quarterly* 37 (1985): 461–73, as well as the other articles in that issue. A more recent summary of the career of republicanism as an organizing theme in U.S. history is Daniel Rodgers, "Republicanism: The Career of a Concept," *Journal of American History* 78 (1992): 11–38. Rodgers concludes that republicanism has lost much of its effectiveness because it's been used to explain too many things and because the concept of ideology that made it so appealing is no longer convincing. I think he's wrong on both counts: the multiple meanings of republicanism all share a suspicion of the marketplace as the master metaphor for social and public life, as well as a notion of community or society as naturally human. Although it is true that evidence of this persuasion can be found all over in U.S. history, still it retains some unity. And, although one must recognize that as an ideology, republicanism seemed to mix well with other ideologies, still it did exclude a range of characteristically liberal positions by the very way it structured political expression—one of the points of this chapter and the next.

3. There have been two great moments of class-dominated history writing on the topic of the Revolution. The first was the flowering of the Progressive historians. See especially Carl Lotus Becker, *The History of Political Parties in the Province of New York, 1760–1776* (Madison: University of Wisconsin Press, 1909); Arthur Schlesinger Sr., *The Colonial Merchants and the American Revolution, 1763–1776* (New York: Columbia University Press, 1918); and Charles Beard, *An Economic Interpretation of the Constitution of the United States* (New York: Macmillan, 1913). The second grand moment was the appearance of New Left revisionism in the 1960s, a movement that remains quite vital. Basic works in the New Left tradition include the essays in Alfred Young, ed., *The American Revolution: Explorations in the History of American Radicalism* (DeKalb: Northern Illinois University Press, 1976), and Gary Nash, *The Urban Crucible: Social Change, Political Consciousness, and the Origins of the American Revolution* (Cambridge: Harvard University Press, 1979), as well as numerous studies of individual colonies and cities, many of which are cited below. I use the term "typographical" culture in reference to Harry Stout's provocative article "Religion, Communications, and the Ideological Origins of the American Revolution," *William and Mary Quarterly*, n.s., 34 (1977): 519–41. In it, Stout argues that the culture that ideological historians have examined has been limited to printed material that was important to only an elite. The mass movements of the period were centered on the spoken word, and much of the ideology that emerged from the period was an expression of the oral style of popular meetings, rituals, and crowd actions.

4. Levy's signature book was *Legacy of Suppression: Freedom of Speech and Press in Early America* (Cambridge: Harvard University Press, 1960). This book has been enlarged and revised as *Emergence of a Free Press* (New York: Oxford University Press, 1985). See also his *Jefferson and Civil Liberties: The Darker Side* (New York: Quadrangle, 1963). Another recent book that is congruent with Levy's interpretation of colonial and Revolutionary law and attitudes is Norman L. Rosenberg's *Protecting the Best Men: An Interpretive History of the Law of Libel* (Chapel Hill: University of North Carolina Press, 1986).

5. This point is made in Mary Ann Yodelis Smith and Gerald Baldasty, "Criticism of Public Officials in the New Nation," *Journal of Communication Inquiry* 4 (1979): 53–74, and in Jeffery A. Smith, *Printers and Press Freedom: The Ideology of Early American Journalism* (New York: Oxford University Press, 1988). Smith also argues, *contra* Levy, that printers indeed formulated an ideology of public expression based on the marketplace-of-ideas concept that was quite modern.

6. Rosenberg points out that "no single view, and certainly not a Blackstonian one as Leonard Levy once claimed, dominated colonial dicussion about free expression. If there were agreement that public officials should, and could, limit political criticism, this consensus shattered when discussion turned to consideration of what these limits were, and how restraint should be applied in actual cases" (*Protecting the Best Men*, p. 44). Rosenberg sees several different positions: an orthodox Blackstonian view; a moderate Whig view, following Trenchard and Gordon in *Cato's Letters*, justifying criticism of officials in the interest of preventing corruption, a role for the press that few colonials disputed; and an "open-press" view, which held that the press should be free to all but licentious or scurrilous publications.

7. Stephen Botein, "'Meer Mechanicks' and an Open Press: The Business and Political Strategies of Colonial Printers," *Perspectives in American History* 9 (1975): 127–225.

8. Jeffery Smith disagrees: "Impartiality and Revolutionary Ideology: Editorial Policies of the *South Carolina Gazette*, 1732–1775," *Journal of Southern History* 49 (1983): 511–26. But printer Timothy's partisanism seems precisely the sort that I describe: transitory and well fortified.

9. Clinton Rossiter, *Seedtime of the Republic: The Origin of the American Tradition of Political Liberty* (New York: Harcourt-Brace, 1953), p. 141; *Boston Evening Post*, 6 March 1769, also discussed Cato.

10. John Phillip Reid, *Constitutional History of the American Revolution: The Authority of Rights* (Madison: University of Wisconsin Press, 1986), pp. 7–8.

11. Arthur M. Schlesinger, Sr., *Prelude to Independence: The Newspaper War on Britain, 1764–1776* (New York: Knopf, 1957), p. 189.

12. "Novanglus" (John Adams), "III: To the Inhabitants of the Colony of Massachusetts-Bay," in John Adams, *The Adams Papers*, ed. Robert J. Taylor, ser. 3, *General Correspondence*, 6 vols. (Cambridge: Harvard University Press, 1977), 2:245, 6 February 1775.

13. The salience of virtue is argued by Richard Buel, "Freedom of the Press in Revolutionary America: The Evolution of Libertarianism, 1760–1820," in Bernard Bailyn and John B. Hench, eds., *The Press and the American Revolution* (Worcester: American Antiquarian Society, 1980). See also William Bollan, *The Freedom of Speech and Writing upon Public Affairs, Considered, with an Historical View* (London, 1766), p. 137; Lawrence Leder, "Newspapers in Defense of Their Own Liberty," *Huntington Library Quarterly* 30 (1966): 1–16; Isaiah Thomas, *The History of Printing in America*, 2 vols. (New York: Burt Franklin, 1967), 2:17, 132; and no. 3 of the *Dougliad* (New York: 1771). On the plasticity of this notion and the opportunism with which it could be applied, see letter of Edward Sexby, *Boston Gazette*, 12 October 1772. Because Whig thought was dominated by ideas of conspiracies, Revolutionaries would have been unlikely to consider opponents as virtuous citizens, and were prone to believe them to be tools of factions or cabals. Clark Rivera, "Ideals, Interests and Civil Liberty: The Colonial Press and Freedom, 1735–1776," *Journalism Quarterly* 55 (1978): 53.

14. *Pennsylvania Journal*, 8 September 1766; also printed in *Boston Gazette*, 29 September 1766.

15. Letter of "SON OF LIBERTY," *Boston Gazette*, 5 September 1768.

16. See, for instance, letter of "A," *Boston Gazette*, 8 December 1766; letter of "Freeborn American," ibid., 9 February 1767; letter of "True Patriot," ibid., 14 March 1768. John Adams (Novanglus) was concerned to defend the patriot press from charges of partiality and to brand loyalist publicists as paid "scribblers" and ministerial hirelings: "III: To the Inhabitants of the Colony of Massachusetts-Bay," *Adams Papers*, ser. 3, 2:243–44, 6 February 1775. See also letter of "Britannicus," *Boston Chronicle*, 13–17, 20–24 July 1769. "Pro Aris et Focis," in a letter that cites such significant Whig images of repression as the Court

of Star Chamber and the Spanish Inquisition, writes, "Whenever the right of delivering opinions and arguments, touching political transactions, is restrained by any thing, but the *common good* of the whole, the natural, the just claim of freemen, is so far *unnecessarily* infringed" (emphasis in original). *Boston Gazette*, 11 September 1769. Also "D," "For the Pennsylvania Evening Post," reprinted in *Maryland Gazette*, 19 September 1776.

17. *Boston Gazette*, 9 May 1774. Likewise, the Anne Arundel (Maryland) County Committee of Observation on 10 April 1775 condemned an item in a London paper about riotous events in Maryland as being inimical "to the liberties of this Province." In Peter Force, comp., *American Archives: . . . A Documentary History of the Origin and Progress of the North American Colonies . . .* (projected as six series, though only 4 and 5 published; Washington: Peter Force, 1833–1840), ser. 4, vol. 2, p. 309.

18. "Independant [*sic*]," *Boston Gazette*, 12 February 1770. Much of this account of colonial press ideology is similar to Michael Warner's account of republican notions of the public sphere. See *The Letters of the Republic: Publication and the Public Sphere in Eighteenth-Century America* (Cambridge: Harvard University Press, 1990). Warner, though, tends to explain republicanism as a creature of the grammatology of print discourse rather than as an ideological or cultural persuasion that extended well beyond the realm of print. As a result, he does not and perhaps cannot explain the decline of republicanism in the post-Revolutionary press.

19. "Not until the rise of the troubles with Britain did the editor come to think of himself as a maker of opinion as well as a transmitter of news and literary offerings." Schlesinger, *Prelude*, p. 61.

20. Gary Nash, *Urban Crucible*, abridged ed. (Cambridge: Harvard University Press, 1985), pp. 93–95.

21. Zenger, "From my Prison," *New York Journal*, 20 December 1734; Thomas, *History of Printing*, 1:297.

22. Smith, "Impartiality," p. 520.

23. On intimidation, see Bill F. Chamberlin, "Freedom of Expression in Eighteenth-Century Connecticut: Unanswered Questions," in Donovan H. Bond and W. Reynolds McLeod, eds., *Newsletters to Newspapers: Eighteenth-Century Journalism* (Morgantown: School of Journalism, West Virginia University, 1977), p. 255; William F. Steirer, "Hobby-Horse," ibid., p. 267; Rollo G. Silver, "Aprons instead of Uniforms: The Practice of Printing, 1776–1787," *Proceedings of the American Antiquarian Society* 87 (1977): 191.

24. See especially Edmund Sears Morgan and Helen Morgan, *The Stamp Act Crisis: Prologue to Revolution* (Chapel Hill: University of North Carolina Press, 1953); Richard Maxwell Brown,"Violence and the American Revolution," in Stephen G. Kurtz and James H. Hutson, eds., *Essays on the American Revolution* (Chapel Hill: University of North Carolina Press, 1973), pp. 81–120; Pauline Maier, *From Resistance to Revolution: Colonial Radicals and the Development of American Opposition to Britain, 1765–1776* (New York: Knopf, 1972); Dirk Hoerder, *Crowd Action in Revolutionary Massachusetts, 1765–1780* (New York: Academic Press, 1977); Edward Countryman, *A People in Revolution: The American Revolution and Political Society in New York, 1760–1790* (Baltimore: Johns Hopkins University Press, 1981); Paul Gilje, *The Road to Mobocracy: Popular Disorder in New York City, 1763–1834* (Chapel Hill: University of North Carolina Press, 1987). Much of this was inspired by the attack on Gustav LeBon's seminal sociological treatise, *The Crowd: A Study of the Popular Mind* (London, 1896), in which he argues that a mob has a consciousness of its own, quite distinct from the individual consciousnesses of its members, and that the actions of a crowd thus spring from its own irrational impulses. The gist of recent research has been to show that crowd behavior is rational and goal-directed, and that the crowd has been a recognized, quasi-legitimate political instrument throughout Anglo-American

history. In the European context, see especially George Rude, *Wilkes and Liberty: A Social Study of 1763–1774* (Oxford: Clarendon Press, 1962) and *The Crowd in History: A Study of Popular Disturbances in France and England, 1730–1848* (New York: Wiley, 1964), and E. P. Thompson's famous essay, "The Moral Economy of the English Crowd in the Eighteenth Century," *Past and Present* 50 (February 1971): 76–136.

25. On which, see Morgan and Morgan, *Stamp Act Crisis*; Donna Jane Spindel, "The Stamp Act Riots" (Ph.D. diss., Duke University, 1975).

26. "A Mourner," Newport, October 28, in *Boston Gazette*, 4 November 1765. Likewise, see letter of "Populus," ibid., 14 March 1768: "NO MOBS—NO CONFUSIONS—NO TUMULTS."

27. The perceived strategic importance of the press helps explain an anomaly of the Stamp Act crisis. The Stamp Act included a tax on newspapers, and one might expect the protests to have included vigorous defenses of freedom of the press. But freedom of the press was hardly mentioned. Far more frequent were cries of alarm over the shortage of hard currency in the colonies. Currency drainage was a more immediate concern to patriots than press regulation; they were more concerned with using the press as a means than protecting it as an end in itself.

28. Schlesinger, *Prelude*, pp. 78–79; Alfred Lawrence Lorenz, *Hugh Gaine: A Colonial Printer-Editor's Odyssey to Loyalism* (Carbondale: Southern Illinois University Press, 1972), pp. 43–44; Philip Ranlet, *The New York Loyalists* (Knoxville: University of Tennessee Press, 1986), p. 17; Walter H. Conser, "The Stamp Act Resistance," in Conser et al., *Resistance, Politics, and the American Struggle for Independence, 1765–1775* (Boulder, Colorado: Lynne Rienner, 1986), p. 66. See also "To the Printer," *New-York Gazette*, 30 October 1765, reprinted in *Boston Gazette, Supplement*, 18 November 1765.

29. Steirer, "Hobby Horse," pp. 266–67.

30. For examples, see *Boston Gazette*, 23, 30 December 1765, 10 February 1766; Schlesinger, *Prelude*, p. 80.

31. "Extract of a Letter from Portsmouth [N.H.], January 13," *Boston Gazette*, 20 January 1766. This type of symbolic action was persistent. In 1770, when the merchants of New York City abandoned the nonimportation agreement, students at Princeton and merchants in Boston symbolically destroyed copies of the letter announcing this step. *Boston Gazette*, 30 July 1770.

32. "Extract of a Letter from a Gentleman at Newport, Rhode Island," *Boston Gazette*, 2 September 1765.

33. Ibid.; Spindel, "Stamp Act Riots," pp. 80–90. Howard remained a notorious target for patriot hostilities. Two years later, while passing through Boston, he was mobbed again, and cryptic newspaper accounts called attention to his role in the Stamp Act crisis. *Boston Gazette*, 13 July 1767; *Massachusetts Gazette and Boston Newsletter*, 9, 16 July 1767.

34. Rosenberg, *Protecting the Best Men*, chap. 1.

35. This account is based on descriptions in the *Boston Gazette*, 11, 18, 25 September 1769; *Massachusetts Gazette, and Boston Weekly Newsletter*, 7 September 1769; *Boston Evening Post*, 11 September 1769; *Boston Chronicle*, 7–11, 14–18 September 1769; *Boston Chronicle Supplement*, 9 October 1769; *Boston Gazette*, 29 July 1771, 14 September 1772. The fight is recounted in Schlesinger, *Prelude*, pp. 99–100; Hoerder, *Crowd Action*, p. 206; Robert Middlekauf, *The Glorious Cause: The American Revolution, 1763–1789* (New York: Oxford University Press, 1982), pp. 199–201. Similarly, "Mr. Irving," another customs official, attacked Richard Draper, printer of the *Massachusetts Gazette*, for printing an obnoxious advertisement signed by William Palfrey, one of John Hancock's clerks. See *Boston Gazette*, 28 August 1769; *Boston Evening Post*, 28 August 1769.

36. Ward L. Miner, *William Goddard, Newspaperman* (Durham: Duke University Press,

1962), pp. 74–77; Steirer, "Hobby Horse," p. 268; Schlesinger, *Prelude*, pp. 119–20; Smith, *Printers*, pp. 140–41.

37. *Boston Gazette*, 25 January 1768; John E. Alden, "John Mein: Scourge of Patriots," *Colonial Society of Massachusetts Publications* 34 (1943): 583–86; Stephen Botein, "Printers and the American Revolution," in Bailyn and Hench, *Press and Revolution*, p. 36. Mein was later found guilty of assault and fined £130, reduced to £75 on appeal. Alden, "Mein," pp. 585–86.

38. Letter of "Populus," *Boston Gazette*, 1 March 1768.

39. Letter of "Q. A.," *Boston Gazette*, 11 December 1769.

40. Ranlet, *Loyalists*, pp. 30–31; Countryman, *People*, p. 42.

41. For reports of customs informers tarred and feathered, see *Boston Gazette*, 16, 23 October 1769; *Boston Evening Post*, 19 June, 25 September, 5, 16, 23 October 1769. For general discussions of the significance of tar and feathers, see R. S. Longley, "Mob Activities in Revolutionary Massachusetts," *New England Quarterly* 6 (1933): 112–16; Brown, "Violence and the American Revolution," pp. 103–8; Peter Shaw, *American Patriots and the Rituals of Revolution* (Cambridge: Harvard University Press, 1981); Ann Fairfax Withington, *Toward a More Perfect Union: Virtue and the Formation of American Republics* (New York: Oxford University Press, 1991) chap. 8.

42. Letter to "Messrs. Fleets" in *Boston Evening Post*, 25 September 1769.

43. Alden, "Mein."

44. *Boston Chronicle Supplement*, 30 May–6 June 1768.

45. *Boston Gazette Supplement*, 5 June 1769.

46. *Boston Gazette*, 14 August 1769.

47. *Boston Chronicle*, 14–17 August 1769.

48. *Boston Gazette*, 21, 28 August 1769; *Massachusetts Gazette and Boston Weekly Newsletter*, 24, 31 August 1769.

49. *Boston Chronicle*, 21–25 September, 28 September–2 October 1769.

50. Ibid., 31 August–4 September 1769.

51. "A MAN," "To J--- M---," *Boston Evening Post*, 18 September 1769.

52. "Humanus," "J--n M--n!" *Boston Gazette*, 18 September 1769.

53. Minutes of the Boston town meeting, in *Boston Gazette*, 9 October 1769.

54. 4 September 1769.

55. 8 January 1770.

56. *Boston Gazette*, 28 August 1769.

57. *Boston Chronicle*, 31 August–4 September, 4–7 September, 2–5 October, 14–21 November 1769.

58. In a display ad that ran continually on the *Chronicle's* front page after the 23–26 October 1769 issue.

59. 11–15 January 1770.

60. *Chronicle*, 8–12 February 1770.

61. *Chronicle*, 18–21 September 1769. The Merchants' Committee was linked to the Jesuits also in the mock "Letter of P. Debelloy, of the Society of Jesuits, to Mr. W[illiam] M[olineux]," *Chronicle*, 1–5 March 1770.

62. *Chronicle*, 27–30 November 1769.

63. *Boston Gazette*, 28 August 1769.

64. See, for example, ibid., 3 July, 2, 9, 30 October 1769; *Boston Evening Post*, 30 October 1769.

65. Schlesinger, *Merchants*, p. 225.

66. *Boston Gazette*, 28 August 1769.

67. Ibid., 2 October 1769.

68. Hoerder, *Crowd Action*, p. 236.

69. *Boston Gazette*, 25 September 1769.

70. Letter of Nathaniel Sartell Prentice, *Boston Gazette Supplement*, 26 February 1770.

71. Thomas, *History of Printing*, 1:151.

72. See controversy with D. Bayley, *Boston Evening Post*, 16 October 1769; *Chronicle*, 23–26 October 1769.

73. For examples, see *Massachusetts Gazette and Boston Weekly Newsletter*, 21 September, 5, 12, 26 October, 2 November 1769.

74. *Massachusetts Gazette and Boston Weekly Newsletter*, 27 July 1769; John Phillip Reid, *In a Rebellious Spirit: The Argument of Facts, The Liberty Riot, and The Coming of the American Revolution* (University Park: Pennsylvania State University Press, 1979).

75. Peter Oliver, *Origin and Progress of the American Rebellion*, Douglass Adair and John Schutz, eds. (San Marino, Calif.: Huntington Library, 1961), p. 62.

76. *Boston Evening Post*, 9 October 1769; letter of "Pacificus," *Boston Gazette*, 9 October 1769.

77. George Mason to Joseph Harrison, Boston, 20 October 1769, in Alden, "Mein," pp. 586–87.

78. This account is based on accounts in *Boston Evening Post*, 30 October 1769; *Massachusetts Gazette and Boston Weekly Newsletter*, 2 November 1769; *Boston Gazette*, 30 October 1769; *Boston Chronicle*, 23–30 October 1769; Thomas Hutchinson, *The History of the Colony and Province of Massachusetts-Bay*, ed. Lawrence Shaw Mayo, 3 vols. (Cambridge: Harvard University Press, 1936), 3:186–87; Alden, "Mein," pp. 587–89; Bernard Bailyn, *The Ordeal of Thomas Hutchinson* (Cambridge: Harvard University Press, 1974), pp. 133–34; Levy, *Emergence*, pp. 67–68.

79. Letter of A TORY, *Boston Evening Post*, 6 November 1769.

80. *Boston Chronicle*, 6–9 November 1769; *Massachusetts Gazette and Boston Weekly Newsletter*, 9 November 1769; *Boston Evening Post*, 13 November 1769; Longley, "Mob Activities," pp. 116–17; Peter Shaw, *Rituals*, pp. 98–101.

81. *Massachusetts Gazette and Boston Weekly Newsletter*, 17 November 1769; *Boston Gazette*, 20 November 1769.

82. Alden, "Mein," pp. 590–98.

83. See, for instance, the metaphorical account of the harassment of the *Chronicle* in the *Boston Gazette*, 1 January 1770.

84. Manifests reappeared in the 7–11 December 1769 issue of the *Chronicle*. For threats, see letter of "Detector," *Boston Gazette*, 18 December 1769; Mary Ann Yodelis, "Courts, Counting House and Streets: Attempts at Press Control, 1763–1775," *Journalism History* 1 (1974): 14.

85. *Boston Gazette*, 25 December 1769.

86. *Boston Chronicle*, 12–16 October 1769; letter of "An Honest Bostonian," *Boston Gazette*, 19 February 1770; letter of "Liberus," *Boston Chronicle*, 19–22 February 1770.

87. Mary Ann Yodelis, "Who Paid the Piper? Publishing Economics in Boston, 1763–1775," *Journalism Monographs*, no. 38 (February 1975).

88. Adams (Novanglus), "III: To the Inhabitants of the Colony of Massachusetts-Bay," 6 February 1775, *Adams Papers*, ser. 3, 2:244.

89. Gage to Dartmouth, Salem, 5 July 1774, in Force, *Archives*, ser. 4, 1:515.

90. "To the People of Pennsylvania," Philadelphia, 17 August 1774, ibid., ser. 4, 3:718–22.

91. Janice Potter, *The Liberty We Seek: Loyalist Ideology in Colonial New York and Massachusetts* (Cambridge: Harvard University Press, 1983), p. 5. On the flood of Tory

literature, see John Adams (Novanglus), "III: To the Inhabitants of the Colony of Massachusetts-Bay," 6 February 1775, *Adams Papers*, ser. 3, 2:245.

92. Agnes Hunt, *The Provincial Committees of Safety of the American Revolution* (1904; reprint, New York: Haskell House, 1968); Henry J. Young, "Treason and Its Punishment in Revolutionary Pennsylvania," *Pennsylvania Magazine of History and Biography* 90 (1966): 288–89. George Washington, dissatisfied with the action of the committees, urged governors Trumbull of Connecticut and Cooke of Rhode Island to take more direct action. Washington to Trumbull, Washington to Cooke, 15 November 1775, in Force, *Archives*, ser. 4, 3:1562–63.

93. See, for example, Committee of Kent County, Pa., 15 February 1775, letter to Philadelphia Committee of Correspondence, in Force, *Archives*, ser. 4, 1:1232; New Windsor, N.Y., Committee of Observation, ibid., 2:132–33; Orange County, Va., Committee, ibid., pp. 234–35.

94. Brookhaven, N.Y., 6 March 1775, in Force, *Archives*, ser. 4, 2:37.

95. See, for example, *Boston Gazette*, 16 March 1772, 8 November 1773.

96. See, for example, *New York Journal*, 8 December 1774; Claude H. Van Tyne, *The Loyalists in the American Revolution* (New York: Macmillan, 1902), p. 60; Schlesinger, *Prelude*, p. 223; Leroy Hewlett, "James Rivington, Loyalist Printer, Publisher, and Bookseller of the American Revolution, 1724–1802: A Biographical-Bibliographical Study" (Ph.D. Diss., University of Michigan, 1958), pp. 63, 66; Ranlet, *Loyalists*, p. 53.

97. Oscar Zeichner, *Connecticut's Years of Controversy, 1750–1776* (Chapel Hill: University of North Carolina Press, 1949), pp. 198–204; Alexander C. Flick, *Loyalism in New York during the American Revolution* (New York, 1901), pp. 48, 58–61; Robert M. Calhoon, *The Loyalists in Revolutionary America, 1760–1781* (New York: Harcourt Brace Jovanovitch, 1973), p. 168. For a partial list of loyalists mobbed between August 1774 and February 1775, see Oliver, *Origin*, pp. 152–57.

98. See "Reverend Samuel Peters of Hebron CT" in Force, *Archives*, ser. 4, 1:711–12; Peters to his mother, to Rev. Dr. Auchmuty, ibid., 3:715–16; Report to Gov. Trumbull, ibid., pp. 712–14; Samuel Peters, *A General History of Connecticut*, ed. Samuel Jarvis McCormick (New Haven, 1829; reprint, New York: D. Appleton, 1877), pp. 262–63; Zeichner, *Connecticut*, p. 175; Calhoon, *Loyalists*, pp. 191–93. Peters blamed Connecticut's Governor Jonathan Trumbull for his mobbing: Peters, *General History*, p. 141n.

99. For crowd action against Samuel Seabury, see Potter, *Liberty*, pp. 30–31. On Dr. John Kearsley, see Steven Rosswurm, *Arms, Country, and Class: The Philadelphia Militia and the 'Lower Sort' during the American Revolution, 1775–1783* (New Brunswick: Rutgers University Press, 1987), pp. 46–47.

100. "New-London," *Pennsylvania Evening Post*, 28 February 1775.

101. Van Tyne, *Loyalists*, p. 48.

102. Colden to General Thomas Gage, Spring Hill, N.Y., 31 May 1775, in *Colden Letter Books*, 2 vols. (*New York Historical Society Collections*, vols. 9–10, 1876–1877), 2 (1877): 414. See also Lorenz, *Gaine*, pp. 94–95.

103. I have found evidence of the following printers being harassed or threatened by patriots: Richard Draper ("Speculator," "To Mr. Draper," *Boston Gazette Supplement,* 22 February 1773); Ezekial Russell of Boston and Salem (Timothy M. Barnes, "Loyalist Newspapers of the American Revolution: A Bibliography," *Proceedings of the American Antiquarian Society* 83 [1974]: 224); Robert Luist Fowle of New Hampshire (Ralph Adams Brown, "New Hampshire Editors Win the War: A Study in Revolutionary Press Propaganda," *New England Quarterly* 12 [1939]: 36); Daniel Fowle of New Hampshire (New Hampshire House of Representatives, 17 January 1776, in Force, *Archives*, ser. 4, 5:11);

Enoch Story of Philadelphia (Schlesinger, *Prelude*, p. 238; Dwight Teeter, "Benjamin Towne: The Precarious Career of a Persistent Printer," *Pennsylvania Magazine of History and Biography* 89 [1965]: 318). Other cases will be discussed below.

104. Samuel Loudon to the Committee of Safety of the Colony of New York, 20 March 1776, in Force, *Archives*, ser. 4, 5:438–40; recounted also in Sidney I. Pomerantz, "The Patriot Newspaper and the American Revolution," in Richard B. Morris, ed., *The Era of the American Revolution* (New York: 1939), p. 321; Lorenz, *Gaine*, p. 100; Dwight Teeter, "'King Sears,' the Mob, and Freedom of the Press in New York, 1765–1776," *Journalism Quarterly* 41 (1964): 543; Levy, *Emergence*, p. 175; Gilje, *Mobocracy*, p. 64.

105. Samuel Loudon, "To the Public," in Force, *Archives*, ser. 4, 5:439–40. For Loudon's appeal, see "Petition of Samuel Loudon" and "Reflections on the Crime of Pamphlet Burning," New York State Petitions, 32:110, 147, in New York (State) *Calendar of Historical Documents Relating to the War of the Revolution in the Office of the Secretary of State*, 2 vols. (Albany: Weed, Parsons & Co., 1868), 1:273, 281. Loudon claimed losses of £150, a serious sum of money: New York Committee of Safety, 20 March 1776, in Force, *Archives*, ser. 4, 5:1389.

106. New York Provincial Congress, in Force, *Archives*, ser. 4, 6:1393.

107. Hugh Hughes to John Adams, New York City, 31 March 1776, *Adams Papers*, ser. 3, 4:98–99.

108. Isaiah Thomas, for instance, was threatened with tar and feathers in Boston: Thomas, *History of Printing*, 1:liv–lv, 2:63. John Holt in New York City was also reported to be a target: "Extract of a Letter to a Gentleman in Philadelphia," London, 8 July 1775, in Force, *Archives*, ser. 4, 2:1607.

109. The British framed this action as a blow for freedom of the press: "They say they want to print a few papers themselves; that they looked upon the press not to be free." "Extract of a Letter," Norfolk, 1 October 1775, in Force, *Archives*, ser. 4, 3:923. Holt referred to this accusation of partiality when he remarked in a notice "To the Publick" that "as his paper has hitherto been free and open to all parties, he intends to observe the same caution and impartiality in his future publications." 12 October 1775, ibid. p. 1031. For accounts of the Dunmore raid, see Fred Siebert, "The Confiscated Revolutionary Press," *Journalism Quarterly* 13 (1936): 179–81; Victor H. Palsits, "John Holt—Printer and Postmaster," *Bulletin of the New York Public Library* 24 (1920): 487; Schlesinger, *Prelude*, p. 239; Calhoon, *Loyalists*, p. 463; Carl Berger, *Broadsides and Bayonets: The Propaganda War of the American Revolution*, rev. ed. (San Rafael, Calif.: Presidio Press, 1975), p. 106.

110. Oliver, *Origin*, p., 105.

111. Joseph Galloway, *A Candid Examination of the Mutual Claims of Great-Britain and the Colonies: With a Plan of Accommodation, on Constitutional Principles* (New York: James Rivington, 1775; reprint, New York: Research Reprints, 1970), p. 1. See also Daniel Leonard (Massachusettensis), "To the Inhabitants . . . ," in Bernard Mason, ed., *The American Colonial Crisis: The Daniel Leonard-John Adams Letters to the Press, 1774–1775* (New York: Harper & Row, 1972), p. 3; Potter, *Liberty*, p. 29.

112. Hewlett, "Rivington," pp. 4–43.

113. Pomerantz, "Newspaper," p. 315.

114. James Parker, "Letters for James Parker," ed. Worthington C. Ford, *Massachusetts Historical Society Proceedings*, 2d ser., 16 (1902): 220–21; Hewlett, "Rivington," p. 35; Lorenz, *Gaine*, pp. 59–60.

115. "To the Subscribers," *New-York Gazetteer*, 22 April 1773; "To the Committee of Inspection for the City and County of New York," ibid., 23 March 1775; ibid., 20 April 1775. Some scholars have deemed Rivington true to his claim of impartiality: Van Tyne,

Loyalists, p. 13n; Robert M. Ours, "James Rivington: Another Viewpoint," in Bond and McLeod, *Newsletters*, p. 219.

116. For discussions of New York loyalism, see John Shy, "The Loyalist Problem in the Lower Hudson Valley: The British Perspective," in Robert A. East and Jacob Judd, eds., *The Loyalist Americans: A Focus on Greater New York* (Tarrytown, N.Y.: Sleepy-hollow, 1975), pp. 3–13; Esmond Wright, "The New York Loyalists: A Cross-Section of Colonial Society," ibid., pp. 74–94; Milton M. Klein, "Why Did the British Fail to Win the Hearts and Minds of New Yorkers?" *New York History* 64 (1983): 357–76. Ranlet argues that New York loyalism was far weaker than has been portrayed: *Loyalism*.

117. *Gazetteer*, 13 April 1775.

118. *Gazetteer*, 8 December 1774; also in Potter, *Liberty*, p. 34.

119. *Gazetteer*, 19 April 1775; also in Force, *Archives*, ser. 4, 2:348–49.

120. See Ours, "Rivington."

121. See especially letter of "Poplicola," *Gazetteer*, 2 December 1773; Van Tyne, *Loyalists*, pp. 12–13; Ours, "Rivington."

122. Charles Lee to Benjamin Rush, 15 December 1774, in *The Lee Papers*, 4 vols., in *New York Historical Society Collections*, vols. 4–7, 1871–1874), 1:143–44.

123. Hewlett, "Rivington," pp. 55–56.

124. Ebenezer Hazard to Silas Deane, New York, 25 February 1775, in *The Deane Papers*, 5 vols. (*New York Historical Society Collections*, vols. 19–23, 1886–1890), 5 (1890): 541. King's College had been a focus of controversy between New York's political clans for years, since its initial chartering, when Presbyterians tried to prevent it from falling under the direction of Anglicans. The Presbyterian party tended to merge directly into patriot politics in the 1760s and 1770s.

125. Hewlett, "Rivington," pp. 69, 79; Governor Josiah Martin (North Carolina) to Earl of Dartmouth, New Bern, N.C., 23 March 1775, in K. G. Davies, ed., *Documents of the American Revolution, 1770–1783*, 21 vols. (Shannon: Irish University Press, 1972), 7:287; John Pownall to Rivington, Whitehall, 5 April 1774, New-York Papers S.P.O., in E. B. O'Callaghan, ed., and John Romeyn Brodhead, comp., *Documents Relative to the Colonial History of the State of New York*, 11 vols. (Albany: Weed, Parsons & Co., 1857), 8:568.

126. See, for instance, Committee of Correspondence of Philadelphia to Committee of Correspondence of New York, 16 February 1775, in Force, *Archives*, ser. 4, 1:1243; Newport, R.I., Committee of Inspection, ibid. 2:12–13.

127. Freehold, N.J., Committee of Observation and Inspection, in Force, *Archives*, ser. 4, 2:35–36; Shawangunk, N.Y., Committee, 26 June 1775, ibid., 1:1183.

128. Hanover, N.J., Committee of Observation, ibid., 1:1240–41; Newark, N.J., Committee, ibid., 1:1029–30; Newport, R.I., Committee of Inspection, ibid., 2:12–13; Elizabethtown, N.J., Committee, 19 December 1774, ibid., 1:1051–52; *New-York Gazetteer*, 2 March 1775.

129. Calhoon thinks so: *Loyalists*, pp. 250–51.

130. "Coriolanus" (John Vardill), "The Case of Mr. James Rivington, Printer at New York," *Gentlemen's Magazine* XLVI (November 1776), pp. 510–11, claimed that this attack on anonymity was the real reason behind Rivington's troubles with the patriots. A patriot correspondent using the pseudonym "An Occasional Remarker" did encourage "the Committee of Safety, the Congress, and other friends of the rights and liberties of *America*" to discover and silence the authors of loyalist items in Rivington's and Gaine's papers: "To the Inhabitants of New York," 14 November 1775, in Force, *Archives*, ser. 4, 3:1552–54.

131. Letter from a Gentleman now at New York to the Committee of Correspondence in Portsmouth, N.H., Force, *Archives*, ser. 4, 2:448–49.

132. Morris County, N.J., meeting, 9 January 1775, ibid., 1:1106.

133. As early as September 1774 Silas Deane reported a boycott in Philadelphia and was writing to committees in Hartford and New Haven, Conn., to promulgate it: Deane to Mrs. Elizabeth Deane, Philadelphia, 8 September 1774, in *Deane Papers* 1 (1886): 16; Hewlett, "Rivington," pp. 62, 66.

134. Hewlett, "Rivington," pp. 75–76; New York *Journal*, 17 November 1774; *New-York Gazetteer*, 20 April 1775.

135. Pauline Maier, *The Old Revolutionaries: Political Lives in the Age of Samuel Adams* (New York: Knopf, 1980), pp. 51–100; Teeter, "Sears"; Countryman, *People*, p. 144.

136. Teeter, "Sears," p. 541; Hewlett, "Rivington," pp. 57–58; Ours, "Rivington," p. 225.

137. *New-York Gazetteer*, 20 April 1775; Teeter, "Sears," p. 542.

138. Sears to Roger Sherman and others, 28 November 1775, quoted in Ranlet, *Loyalists*, p. 62.

139. *New-York Gazetteer*, 2, 16 March 1775; *New-York Gazette, and Weekly Mercury*, 20 March 1775; New York City Committee of Observation, in Force, *Archives*, ser. 4, 2:50; Lorenz, *Gaine*, p. 99; Bernard Mason, *The Road to Independence: The Revolutionary Movement in New York, 1773–1777* (Lexington: University of Kentucky Press, 1966), p. 54.

140. *New-York Gazetteer*, 23 March 1775.

141. See, for example, Massachusetts Provincial Congress, 21 October 1774, in Force, *Archives*, ser. 4, 3:839.

142. William Smith, *Historical Memoirs*, ed. William H. W. Sabine, 2 vols. (New York: Colburn and Tegg, 1956), 2:222–23; "Minutes of the Council of New York," 1 May 1775, in Cadwallader Colden, *Colden Letter Books*, 7 vols. (*New York Historical Society Collections*, 1917–1923), 7 (1923): 288–89; Colden to Lord Dartmouth, New York City, 3 May 1775, *Colden Letter Books*, 2 (1877): 402; Colden to Lord Dartmouth, New York City, 4 May 1775, ibid. p. 406; Roger J. Champagne, *Alexander McDougall and the American Revolution* (Schenectady: 1975), pp. 82–84; Leopold Launitz-Schürer, Jr., *Loyal Whigs and Revolutionaries: The Making of a Revolution in New York, 1765–1776* (New York: 1980), pp. 155 *et seq.*; Ranlet, *Loyalists*, pp. 52–53.

143. Colden to Lord Dartmouth, 7 June 1775, in *Colden Letter Books*, 2 (1877): 421–22.

144. Ibid.; Gilje, *Mobocracy*, pp. 61–62.

145. *New-York Gazetteer*, 18 May 1775.

146. "Petition of James Rivington to the Continental Congress," 20 May 1775 (Petitions, 31:214) in New York (State) *Calendar* 1:88.

147. James Rivington to the New York Provincial Congress, 2 June 1775, in Force, *Archives*, ser. 4, 2:899–90; New York Congress Proceedings, 7 June 1775, ibid., p. 1284.

148. Richard Henry Lee to Gouvernour Morris, Philadelphia, 28 May 1775, in Force, *Archives*, ser. 4, 2:726. See also Morris to Charles Lee, New York, May 1775, in *Lee Papers*, 1(1871): 178–79.

149. Hewlett, "Rivington," pp. 84–85; Schlesinger, *Prelude*, pp. 222–27.

150. Mason, *Road*, pp. 54–56.

151. For newspaper accounts of the raid, see Hartford *Connecticut Courant*, 27 November 1775; *Boston Gazette*, 4, 11 December 1775.

152. Tryon to Earl of Dartmouth, on board HMS *Dutchess of Gordon*, New York Harbor, 6 December 1775, in O'Callaghan, *Documents*, pp. 645–46.

153. *Pennsylvania Evening Post*, 25 November 1775; Mason, *Road*, pp. 56–60.

154. Pomerantz, "Newspaper," p. 318; Champagne, *McDougall*, pp. 95–96; Maier, *Old Revolutionaries*, pp. 87–88; Gilje, *Mobocracy*, pp. 61–64.

155. Pomerantz, "Newspaper," p. 318.

156. Hamilton to John Jay, New York City, 26 November 1775, in *The Papers of Alexander Hamilton*, ed. Harold C. Syrett, 27 vols. (New York: Columbia University Press, 1961–1987), 1:176–78.

157. Jay to Nathaniel Woodhull, Philadelphia, 26 November 1775, in Force, *Archives*, ser. 4, 4:410.

158. Ibid., pp. 185–86.

159. Philadelphia, 5 January 1776, ibid., pp. 1033–34.

160. 12 December 1775, ibid., p. 401.

161. Governor Trumbull to New York Provincial Congress, 10 June 1776, ibid., pp. 1398–99.

162. "Coriolanus" (John Vardill), "Rivington," p. 502.

163. Force, *Archives*, ser. 4, 4:335.

164. Like New Hampshire: See R. A. Brown, "Editors."

165. Lorenz, *Gaine*, p. 100.

166. For example, in Philadelphia in November 1776; see Young, "Treason," p. 291.

167. See, for example, "To the Printer," *Pennsylvania Packet*, 12 August 1780; resolutions of "A respectable number of the inhabitants of Philadelphia," *Maryland Gazette*, 29 May 1777.

168. "Mr. Gzxythins, N. York" sarcastically praised lawyers' mercenary motives: *Pennsylvania Packet*, 8 July 1779.

169. Note, for instance, the trials of the German printers of the Sauer family. The senior Sauer, Christopher, Jr., had his valuable stock of German religious books and tracts confiscated. The younger Sauers became Tories (under the influence of Joseph Galloway). Christopher III was captured by the Continental Army and swapped to the British. He found a wartime home in New York, working on the *Royal Gazette*: Thomas, *History of Printing*, 1:275–78, 282–84.

170. In 1780, for instance, a writer in the *Pennsylvania Packet* recalled that he'd kept his silence regarding "the finances of America" earlier in the war because of the "epidemical madness of the times." "An American," "To the Inhabitants of America," 17 February 1780.

171. Van Tyne, *Loyalists*, pp. 60–86, 198–203, 327–30, 333–35; Jackson Turner Main, *The Sovereign States, 1775–1783* (New York: New Viewpoints, 1973), chap. 8. Pennsylvania's Treason Act of 1777 included a crime called misprision of treason, defined as writing or speaking in opposition to the public defense. Eighty-one men were prosecuted under this law during the war, a relatively small number because of the strictness of the law: Young, "Treason," pp. 293–95. Under all loyalty statutes, 1,402 accusations—a much heftier number—were filed during the war years in Pennsylvania: Anne M. Ousterhout, "Controlling the Opposition in Pennsylvania during the American Revolution," *Pennsylvania Magazine of History and Biography* 105 (1981): 3–34.

172. Hunt, *Committees*; Main, *Sovereign States*, p. 276.

173. See the protest of the New York Provincial Congress to Major General Charles Lee, 6 March 1776, over the arrest of Samuel Gale in New York City: Force, *Archives*, ser. 4, 5:342–43.

174. Lorenz, *Gaine*, pp. 125–26.

175. See, for instance, printer Frederick Green's protestation of his "diligence" in attributing his failure to publish the proceedings of Maryland's Constitutional Convention to "their extraordinary length": *Maryland Gazette*, 12 December 1776.

176. Steirer, "Hobby Horse," p. 268; Thomas, *History of Printing*, 1:263, 2:141.

177. Silver, "Aprons," pp. 149–52.

178. *Royal Gazette*, 27 December 1777, 7 October 1778; see also "TO THE PRINTER," ibid., 10 October 1778.

179. Statement of Peter Edes of Boston, Watertown, 13 March 1776, in Force, *Archives*, ser. 4, 5:168–70; Hewlett, "Rivington," pp. 152–63; Charles Lee, in *Pennsylvania Packet*, 6 April 1779.

180. Junius, "For the Pennsylvania Packet," *Pennsylvania Packet*, 3 August 1779; Teeter, "Towne," pp. 326–28; Eric Foner, *Tom Paine and Revolutionary America*, p. 173; John Cadwalader, "To the Citizens of Philadelphia," *Pennsylvania Packet*, 31 July 1779.

181. Miner, *Goddard*, pp. 1–66. Katherine Goddard was herself attacked on 25 May 1776, by George Somerville, "on account of a late publication in her paper," an incident serious enough to require the attention of the Baltimore County Committee of Safety: Baltimore County Committee, 3 June 1776, in Force, *Archives*, ser. 4, 6:1460.

182. Hunt, *Committees of Safety*, pp. 105–9.

183. On Whig Club banishments, see Council of Safety to Committee of Observation for Baltimore County, Annapolis, 9 January 1777, in "Journal and Correspondence of the Council of Safety, Jan. 1 to Mar. 20, 1777," *Archives of Maryland* (Baltimore: Maryland Historical Society) 16 (1897): 31; minutes of Council of Safety in *Maryland Gazette*, 19 December 1776.

184. *Maryland Journal*, 25 February 1777; also in William Goddard, *The Prowess of the Whig Club* (Baltimore, 1777), appendix 2.

185. See Whig Club's account of the affair, reprinted as appendix 1 in Goddard, *Prowess*.

186. Goddard, *Prowess*, p. 6.

187. Goddard, "Mr. David Rusk!" (broadside, Evans #15314, Baltimore, 25 March 1777).

188. Charles G. Steffen, *The Mechanics of Baltimore: Workers and Politics in the Age of Revolution, 1763–1812* (Urbana: University of Illinois Press, 1984), pp. 63–72.

189. See William Galbraith to Maryland Council of Safety, 26 March 1777, in *Archives of Maryland*, 16 (1897).

190. *Maryland Gazette*, 17 April 1777.

191. Ibid.; see also State Council of Maryland to Worshipfull Justices of Baltimore County, Annapolis, Md., 23 April 1777, in *Archives of Maryland*, 16 (1897): 224–25.

192. Charles Lee to Goddard, Needwood, Md., 7 June 1779, in *Lee Papers*, 3 (1873): 339; *Maryland Journal*, 6 July 1779.

193. Miner, *Goddard*, pp. 168–70; Steffen, *Mechanics*, pp. 72–75; Schlesinger, *Prelude*, p. 299; Levy, *Emergence*, p. 74.

194. *Maryland Journal*, 14 July 1779; also in *Pennsylvania Packet*, 29 July 1779.

195. Council to William Goddard, Annapolis, 17 July 1779, in "Journal of Correspondence of the Council of Maryland, 1778–9," *Archives of Maryland*, 21 (1901).

196. Miner, *Goddard*, pp. 170–72.

197. *Pennsylvania Packet*, 29 July 1779; *Maryland Gazette*, 25 July 1779. While the battle simmered locally, Joseph Reed, president of the Continental Congress, published a rebuttal to Lee's "Queries." See Reed, "To The Public," Philadelphia, 14 July 1779, in *Lee Papers*, 3 (1873): 348–50.

198. *Maryland Journal*, 27 July 1779; J. S. Eustace to "Philadelphia Editors," undated, in *Lee Papers*, 3 (1873): 345–48; Lee to Eustace, Philadelphia, 24 August 1779, ibid., p. 362; Lee to President Joseph Reed, undated, ibid., p. 365.

199. William F. Steirer argues for a shift from a passive to an active style of press management in "Hobby Horse." Pomerantz, "Newspaper," pp. 330–31, argues that the printer became "an influential member of the new Revolutionary society," an opinion leader rather than a mere mechanic. Botein makes much the same argument in "Printers and the American Revolution."

200. According to Pomerantz, "Newspaper," p. 330.

201. Steirer, "Hobby Horse," p. 269, attributes this to "an echo chamber-like effect in which printers seemed able to hear only their own words and those of their supporters."

202. "Calamus" in *Pennsylvania Packet*, 23 December 1780; "B," ibid., 7 September 1782. See also the satirical exchange between the *Packet*'s printer David Claypoole and "Calumniator," 2, 8 April 1782.

203. The "Recantation" was first printed in the *New York Packet*, 1 October 1781; see also Thomas, *History*, 1:410–14.

204. *Pennsylvania Packet*, 20 November 1781.

205. For examples of threats against Tories, see *Pennsylvania Packet*, 4 March, 19 April, 31 May 1783; more generally see Van Tyne, *Loyalists*, pp. 296–97; Pauline Maier, "The Charleston Mob and the Evolution of Popular Politics in Revolutionary South Carolina, 1765–1784," *Perspectives in American History*, 4 (1970): 171–96. Rosswurm records militia attacks on the unilluminated houses of Philadelphia Quakers after the patriot victory at Yorktown: *Arms*, p. 246.

206. Hewlett, "Rivington," pp. 176–87; Ranlet, *Loyalists*, pp. 169–70; Gilje, *Mobocracy*, pp. 76–77.

207. Hamilton to Robert R. Livingston, New York, 18 March 1789, in *Hamilton Papers*, 5:300–301.

Chapter Three

1. In another regard, press freedom better fits the catalog. All of the liberties mentioned are intended as safeguards against government tyranny, and the entire amendment is framed as a prohibition on congressional action. Implied here is an image of government as tending by nature to seek power at the expense of citizens' rights, an image quite consistent with traditional Whig ideology and congruent with patriot depictions of the tendencies of British institutions. The First Amendment is, then, among other things, a hedge against a repeat of imperial tyranny.

2. Jefferson is usually understood as a classical liberal, and the Declaration of Independence as a popularization of—one might say the Cliff's Notes to—Locke's Second Treatise on Government. This view is presented most lucidly in Carl Becker's classic *The Declaration of Independence*. A recent and important dissent from that understanding of Jefferson was presented by Garry Wills in *Inventing America: Jefferson's Declaration of Independence* (Garden City, N.Y.: Doubleday, 1978). Wills sees Jefferson as less a disciple of Locke than of the Scottish common-sense philosophers, especially Francis Hutcheson, and argues that Jefferson's "republican vision" was less individualistic and more corporate, less rational and more emotional than has been traditionally thought. Wills has been roundly criticized by Jefferson scholars for his heterodoxy. There is no doubt that the Declaration as it was promulgated was a Lockean document. Still, in the discussion to follow, it will be apparent that I construe Jefferson to be something other than a classical liberal.

3. On Jefferson and the press, the standard positive view is capably represented in Josephus Daniels, "Jefferson and the Free Press," the introductory essay in vol. 18 of *The Writings of Thomas Jefferson*, ed. Andrew A. Lipscomb, 20 vols. (Washington, D.C.: Thomas Jefferson Memorial Association, 1903). For the strongest statement of a critical interpretation of Jefferson's actions toward the press, see Leonard Levy, *Jefferson and Civil Liberties: The Darker Side* (New York: Quadrangle, 1961). For a more moderate view, see Frank Luther Mott, *Jefferson and the Press* (Baton Rouge: Louisiana State University Press, 1943).

4. On the Alien and Sedition Acts generally, see James Morton Smith, *Freedom's Fetters: The Alien and Sedition Laws and American Civil Liberties* (Ithaca: Cornell University Press, 1956); John Chester Miller, *Crisis in Freedom: The Alien and Sedition Acts* (Boston: Little, Brown, 1951).

5. Jefferson to Edward Carrington, Paris, 16 January 1787, in Julian P. Boyd et al., eds., *The Papers of Thomas Jefferson* (Princeton: Princeton University Press, 1950) 11:49.

6. Jefferson to Mr. Pictet, Washington, D.C., 5 December 1803, in Lipscomb, *Writings*, 10:357.

7. Jefferson to Dr. Walter Jones, Monticello, 2 January 1814, ibid., 14:46.

8. Jefferson to James Monroe, Monticello, 5 May 1811, ibid., 13:59.

9. Jefferson to Elbridge Gerry, Washington, D.C., 29 March 1801, ibid., 10:254–55.

10. Jefferson, "First Inaugural, 1801," ibid., 3:317–23. Likewise, he wrote to Count Volney that "the two parties which prevailed with so much violence when you were here, are almost wholly melted into one." Washington, D.C., 8 February 1805, ibid., 11:68.

11. Even though some of his key supporters were partisan printers, Jefferson insisted to Washington that his association with Philip Freneau, editor of the *National Gazette*, and translating clerk in the State Department while Jefferson was secretary of state, was entirely innocent of partisan politics: Jefferson to George Washington, Monticello, 9 September 1792, ibid., 8:394–408. Likewise, he distanced himself daintily from Thomas Callendar and from William Duane's *Aurora*: Jefferson to James Monroe, Washington, D.C., 17 July 1802, ibid., 10:333–34, and Jefferson to Paine, Washington, D.C., 5 June 1805, ibid., 11:81–83. Jefferson read newspapers regularly through most of his career but frequently repeated— especially while president—a pledge that he would never contribute to the battles of opposing pseudonyms that were so frequent in the national partisan papers of his day, quite unlike Hamilton, whose newspaper sponsorships were numerous, and John Adams, who delighted in publishing his political disquisitions under assumed names, especially "Davila."

12. Publius (James Madison), *The Federalist, or The New Constitution* (New York: Heritage Press, 1945), No. 10. Much is made of this argument in Gordon Wood, *Creation of the American Republic, 1776–1787* (Chapel Hill: University of North Carolina Press, 1969), where Madison's essay is seen as signaling the end to the Revolution's obsessive concern with civic virtue: chap. 15, "A New Science of Politics."

13. Jefferson to Thomas Seymour, Washington, D.C., 11 February 1807, in Lipscomb, *Writings*, 11:154–56; to William Short, Monticello, 6 September 1808, ibid., 12:159–61.

14. See, for instance, his commiseration with John Jay over the latter's treatment at the hands of the press in the 1780s: Jefferson to John Jay, Paris, 25 January 1786, in Boyd, *Papers*, 9:125; to James Currie, Paris, 28 January 1786, ibid., 9:239–40.

15. For support of Bill of Rights, see Jefferson to William Carmichael, Paris, 15 December 1787, ibid., 12:423–27; to James Madison, Paris, 20 December 1787, ibid., 12:438–43. On the Alien and Sedition Acts, see "Kentucky Resolutions," in Lipscomb, *Writings*, 17:379–91. On state regulation of the press, see Jefferson to Abigail Adams, Monticello, 11 September 1804, ibid., 11:49–52, and Levy, *Jefferson and Civil Liberties*, *passim*.

16. Hence Jefferson to Thomas Seymour, Washington, D.C., 11 February 1807, in Lipscomb, *Writings*, 1:154–56.

17. Jefferson to Hogendorp, Paris, 13 October 1785, ibid., 5:180–84. See also letter to Francis Hopkinson, Paris, 1 August 1787, ibid., 6:205–9.

18. Jefferson expresses this sentiment most notably in *Notes on Virginia*, "Query XIX: The Present State of Manufactures . . . ," ibid., 11:228–30, where he attributes the debasement of the masses in Europe to a lack of economic independence. See also Jefferson to George Wythe, Paris, 13 August 1786, ibid., 5:394–98. The preservation of the independence of U.S. citizens was one of the recurrent themes in Jefferson's political career, as

was the extension of the intelligence of the people—consider his educational proposals, for example, letter to Peter Carr, Monticello, 7 September 1814, ibid. 19:211–21.

19. Thus Jefferson's comments to John Norvell, Washington, D. C., 14 June 1807, ibid., 17:379–91.

20. "Albemarle County Instructions," in Boyd, *Papers*, 6:284–91.

21. Jefferson to Madison, Paris, 31 July 1788, ibid., 12:440–43.

22. But falsity was a very delicate judgment in the communicative system of early national politics. Most newspaper copy was reprinted from other papers obtained through a system of mutual free exchanges among editors through the mails, a practice that was recognized in the creation of a special postal category for exchange papers. This style of information diffusion did not make it easy for printers to check their facts. And, indeed, the more important a story seemed, the more likely a printer would be to print it without time-consuming verification. The papers were bound to be full of falsehoods, a fact that Jefferson came more and more to recognize (on which, see the above-cited letter to Norvell). And this meant that a law punishing printers for falsehoods could be enforced in such a manner as to gag virtually any newspaper, as Jeffersonians were to realize during the crisis over the Alien and Sedition Acts.

23. William Cobbett, "To the Public," *Porcupine's Gazette*, 4 March 1797.

24. Though rooted in a fantasy about citizens, politicians, and the medium of print, "rational liberty" nevertheless inspired certain varieties of press conduct, like the usual absence of outright editorials and the frequent verbatim reprinting of speeches and legislation, the raw material of politics. And, although the most famous, and probably most important, papers of the period were partisan papers that were roundly denounced as violators of rational liberty, other papers maintained at least an appearance of impartiality, impersonality, and lack of editorial interference. Most particularly, a class of papers I've called country weeklies adhered to a policy of rational liberty throughout most of the early national period. Their behavior can be explained by exigency as well as ideology: being local, they were less likely to serve a public divided on issues of national politics; being local monopolies, they had an incentive to seem impartial; being run by printer-editors, they lacked the personnel to editorialize like the partisan press. I've written about this at length in *The Culture of the Press in the Early Republic: Cincinnati, 1793–1848* (New York: Garland, 1989), chap. 3.

25. On this period of theorizing, see especially Lance Banning, *The Jeffersonian Persuasion: Evolution of a Party Ideology* (Ithaca: Cornell University Press, 1978), pp. 251–64; Leonard Levy, *Emergence of a Free Press* (New York: Oxford University Press, 1985), pp. 282–308.

26. On the ratification struggle in New York, see Linda Grant De Pauw, *The Eleventh Pillar: New York State and the Federal Constitution* (Ithaca: Cornell University Press, 1966); John P. Kaminski, "New York: The Reluctant Pillar," in Stephen L. Schechter, ed., *The Reluctant Pillar: New York and the Adoption of the Federal Constitution* (Troy, N.Y.: Russell Sage College, 1985).

27. De Pauw contends that "a third of both Federalist and Anti-Federalist articles were devoted to *ad hominem* attacks" in New York: *Eleventh Pillar*, p. 100.

28. On economic pressure, see Robert Rutland, "The First Great Newspaper Debate: The Constitutional Crisis of 1787–1788," *Proceedings of the American Antiquarian Society* 97 (1987): 507. De Pauw attributes complaints about postal service in New York (see *New York Journal*, 25 February, 10 March 1788) to that state's recent switch from stagecoaches to express riders for mail delivery; lapses were due to unfamiliarity with the new system, not political persecution (*Eleventh Pillar*, pp. 95–96).

29. The account of the Philadelphia procession, which took place on 4 July, is taken

from the *Massachusetts Spy*, 7 August 1788; that of the New York procession of 21 July is from the *Massachusetts Centinel*, 9 August 1788.

30. De Pauw counts 130 of the total 160 antifederalist essays as appearing in the *Journal*: *Eleventh Pillar*, pp. 102–3.

31. Ibid., pp. 123–24.

32. *Journal*, 1 January 1788. Federalist No. 23 appeared in the *Journal* on 18 December 1787; it had been sent to Greenleaf in manuscript: De Pauw, *Eleventh Pillar*, p. 110.

33. *Journal*, 24 July 1788; Philadelphia *Independent Gazetteer*, 1 August 1788.

34. *New-Haven Gazette*, 31 July 1788.

35. According to the correspondent of the Philadelphia *Independent Gazetteer*. See "Extract of a letter from a Gentleman in New York, to his friend in this city, July 31," printed 7 August 1788. The initial account from New York, printed in an "extra" edition of the *Independant Journal* on 28 July, said the crowd was "headed by a number of the first characters." (Note: This account was reprinted widely. See *Pennsylvania Packet*, 30 July 1788; Hartford, Conn., *American Mercury*, 4 August 1788; Hartford *Connecticut Courant*, 4 August 1788; Providence, R.I., *United States Chronicle*, 5 August 1788; *Massachusetts Spy*, 7 August 1788; *Norwich Packet*, 7 August 1788.) The "first characters" may have led the crowd through its initial celebrations, but it seems likely that they had dropped off before it visited Greenleaf's residence and office.

36. For accounts of the crowd action, besides those mentioned above, see Philadelphia *Independent Gazetteer*, 30 July 1788; *Massachusetts Gazette*, 1 August 1788; *Massachusetts Centinel*, 2 August 1788. For Greenleaf's own account, reprinted from the *Journal*, see Philadelphia *Independent Gazetteer*, 12 August 1788. See also Rutland, "First Great Newspaper Debate," p. 57; Alfred Young, *The Democratic-Republicans of New York: The Origins, 1763–1797* (Chapel Hill: University of North Carolina Press, 1967), p. 120; Paul A. Gilje, *The Road to Mobocracy: Popular Disorder in New York City, 1763–1834* (Chapel Hill: University of North Carolina Press, 1987), pp. 97–99.

37. Greenleaf's account is quoted in full in the Philadelphia *Independent Gazetteer*, 12 August 1788.

38. *New-Hampshire Gazette*, 14 August 1788.

39. Ronald P. Formisano, "Deferential-Participant Politics: The Early Republic's Political Culture, 1789–1840," *American Political Science Review*, 58 (1974): 473–87. For a similar argument on the decentralized and underorganized nature of the so-called first party system, see James Sterling Young, *The Washington Community, 1800–1828* (New York: Columbia University Press, 1966); Ralph Ketcham, *Presidents above Party: The First American Presidency, 1789–1828* (Chapel Hill: University of North Carolina Press, 1984). Formisano presents a revised version of his argument in "Federalists and Republicans: Parties, Yes—System, No," in Paul Kleppner, ed., *The Evolution of American Electoral Systems* (Westport, Conn.: Greenwood Press, 1984). For an argument to the contrary, based largely on studies of congressional voting patterns, see John F. Hoadley, *Origins of American Political Parties, 1789–1803* (Lexington: University Press of Kentucky, 1984). Descriptions of the press in this period have usually emphasized partisan connections; Frank Luther Mott titled his chapter on the years to 1830 as "The Dark Ages of the Party Press." See *American Journalism, 1690–1960* (New York: Macmillan, 1960). I have argued against this view on the grounds that partisanism was characteristic of only a class of newspapers, and that the prevailing ideology of printers and public opposed partisan practices: see especially chap. 3 of *The Culture of the Press*. For the argument that the first party system lacked a coherent ideology of partisan competition, see Richard Hofstadter, *The Idea of a Party System: The Rise of Legitimate Opposition in the United States, 1780–1840* (Berkeley: University of California Press, 1972).

40. On the emotional tenor of Federalist-era politics, see two classic essays by Marshall Smelser: "The Jacobin Phrenzy: Federalism and the Menace of Liberty, Equality, and Fraternity," *Review of Politics*, 13 (1951): 457–82, and "The Federalist Period as an Age of Passion," *American Quarterly*, 10 (1958): 391–419. On the salience of British-French competition in U.S. politics, see Robert Wiebe, *The Opening of American Society: From the Adoption of the Constitution to the Eve of Disunion* (New York: Random House, 1984), chap. 4.

41. Bache organized one such protest in Philadelphia that six thousand people attended; a few days later another crowd burned a copy of the treaty and attacked the residence of the British ambassador, breaking windows. Bernard Fay, *The Two Franklins: Fathers of American Democracy* (Boston: Little, Brown, 1933), pp. 248, 252.

42. Boston *Independent Chronicle*, 30 March 1797. These remarks were directed specifically against Noah Webster's *American Minerva*, William Cobbett's *Porcupine's Gazette*, and John Fenno's *Gazette of the United States*.

43. *Boston Independent Chronicle*, 6 April 1797.

44. Abigail Adams to Mercy Otis Warren, Philadelphia, 26 April 1798, in Adams, *Letters of Mrs. Adams*, Charles Francis Adams, ed. (Boston: 1848), p. 375.

45. Hamilton to King, 6 June 1798, in Hamilton, *The Papers of Alexander Hamilton*, Harold C. Syrett, ed., 27 vols. (New York: Columbia University Press, 1974), 21:490–91.

46. Thus Seymour Martin Lipset and Earl Raab: "The cause of distress was a group of evil and conspiratorial—therefore politically illegitimate—men; the remedy was to suppress such men by any means, as a matter of high morality." *The Politics of Unreason: Right-Wing Extremism in America, 1790–1977*, 2d ed. (Chicago: University of Chicago Press, 1978), pp. 34–35. Likewise, Michael Stohl notes "a persistent pattern of American violence, a pattern that is concerned with the utilization of violence for the maintenance of the American political system." *War and Domestic Political Violence: The American Capacity for Repression and Reaction* (Beverly Hills: Sage, 1976), p. 95.

47. William David Sloan, "Party Press and Freedom of the Press," *American Journalism*, 1988, pp. 91–92; Smith, *Freedom's Fetters*, pp. 178, 214–15, 338; Fay, *Two Franklins*, p. 292; Eugene Perry Link, *Democratic-Republican Societies, 1790–1800* (New York: Columbia University Press, 1942), p. 187; "To Tredwell Jackson," *Porcupine's Gazette*, 13 March 1797, is a sarcastic rejoinder to the Democratic Society of New York, which had recently consigned Peter Porcupine to the flames.

48. Smith, *Freedom's Fetters*, pp. 9, 192–93; Fay, *Two Franklins*, 317–18, 337; *Aurora*, 6 April 1797; *Independent Chronicle*, 20 April 1797; Abigail Adams to Mercy Otis Warren, 17 June 1798, in Adams, *Letters*, pp. 377–80.

49. Like Bache, who had been educated in France during his grandfather Benjamin Franklin's stay in that country in the 1780s, and William Cobbett, who had grown up in England, Duane came from outside the ideological stew of the Revolution. These partisan editors were not typical of U.S. press ideology, and gave the press at the nation's capital a unique flavor.

50. Harry Marlin Tinkcom, *The Republicans and Federalists in Pennsylvania, 1790–1801: A Study of National Stimulus and Local Response* (Harrisburg: Pennsylvania Historical and Museum Commission, 1950), p. 190; Kim T. Phillips, "William Duane, Philadelphia's Democratic Republicans, and the Origins of Modern Politics," *Pennsylvania Magazine of History and Biography*, 101 (1977): 368; Sloan, "Party Press," p. 91; *Columbian Centinel*, 20 February 1799.

51. Much of this account is based on documents from the 1804 trials of Duane's attackers. See "Supreme Court of Pennsylvania, Sat., December 9 1804—Duane vs. Dunlap," and "Deposition of Robert Oliphant," *National Intelligencer*, 21 December 1804; "Testimony of

John Massey," ibid., 24 December 1804. A verdict of $600 against Peter Miercken, one of the attackers, was announced in the summer of 1806: ibid., 21 July 1806. See also Tinkcom, *Republicans in Pennsylvania*, pp. 215–20.

52. The strongest account of the Federalist party's behavior in these years is David Hackett Fischer's *The Revolution of American Conservatism: The Federalist Party in the Era of Jeffersonian Democracy* (New York: Harper, 1965).

53. Ronald Formisano, *The Transformation of Political Culture: Massachusetts Parties, 1790s-1840s* (New York: Oxford University Press, 1983), pp. 10–11.

54. Though Kim Phillips argues that William Duane and his colleagues in Philadelphia did construct a notion of party politics as being a necessary component of governance, a notion that set them apart from their contemporaries, who put their stock in constitutions as the ideal and complete embodiment of government, and believed that party politics was an unnecessary intrusion. See Phillips, "Duane."

55. *National Intelligencer*, 29 June 1803; the editor insists that he keeps his paper open to all contributions except those that are unsuitable because of inadmissable personal invective and so forth.

56. Joseph Gales, inaugural editorial address, *National Intelligencer*, 31 August 1810.

57. Ibid., 26 September 1810.

58. Ibid., 2 August 1809.

59. The winter of 1808–1809 previewed the partisan violence of 1812. Following the naval confrontation between the *Leopard* and *Chesapeake*, mass meetings were held throughout the states to protest, and opponents of the anti-British fervor were condemned as Tories and threatened with tar and feathers, in imitation of the patriot actions of 1774–1776. For examples of meetings and resolutions, see *National Intelligencer*, 30 November 1808, 25 January, 3 February 1809. The most famous crowd action of that season was the tarring and feathering of an English-born journeyman shoemaker named Beattie (variously spelled) in Baltimore, ibid., 21, 28 October 1808; John Thomas Scharf, *The Chronicles of Baltimore* (Baltimore: Turnbull, 1874), p. 303. Leading rioters were indicted and convicted, fined and sentenced to three months' imprisonment: *National Intelligencer*, 1 February 1809.

60. A classic study of political ideology in the period is James M. Banner, Jr., *To the Hartford Convention: The Federalists and the Origins of Party Politics in Massachusetts, 1789–1815* (New York: Knopf, 1970). Fischer in *The Revolution of American Conservatism* and Shaw Livermore in *The Twilight of Federalism: 1815–1830* (Princeton: Princeton University Press, 1962) argue for the durability of the Federalist party, despite its failure to capture national power in the nineteenth century. On the ideological centrality of the War of 1812, see Roger H. Brown, *The Republic in Peril: 1812* (New York: Columbia University Press, 1964), and, more recently, Steven Watts, *The Republic Reborn: War and the Making of Liberal America, 1790–1820* (Baltimore: Johns Hopkins University Press, 1987), where it is argued that the war climaxed a shift from republicanism's emphasis on civic virtue to liberalism's emphasis on the individual.

61. Donald Robert Hickey, "The Federalists and the War of 1812" (Ph.D. diss., University of Illinois, 1972), pp. 18–19; L. Marx Renzulli, *Maryland: The Federalist Years* (Rutherford, N.J.: Fairleigh Dickinson University Press, 1972), p. 248; Brown, *Republic in Peril*, pp. 96–97, quotes a letter from Hanson to Francis J. Jackson urging Britain to adhere to the Orders in Council in 1812.

62. For accounts of the riot, see Baltimore *Federal Register*, 24 June 1812; Scharf, *Chronicles*, pp. 309–10; Hickey, "Federalists," pp. 104–19; Renzulli, *Maryland*, pp. 264–66; Noel B. Gerson, *Light Horse Harry: A Biography of Washington's Great Cavalryman, General Henry Lee* (Garden City, N.Y.: Doubleday, 1966), p. 232; Thomas Boyd, *Light-Horse Harry Lee* (New York: Scribner, 1931), pp. 308–9; Paul A. Gilje, "The Baltimore

Riots of 1812 and the Breakdown of the Anglo-American Mob Tradition," *Journal of Social History*, 13 (1980): 547–64, passim; John Lofton, *The Press as Guardian of the First Amendment* (Columbia: University of South Carolina Press, 1980), pp. 49–56.

63. Quoted in Gilje, "Baltimore Riots," p. 549.

64. *Federal Republican*, 27 July 1812.

65. Gilje, "Baltimore Riots," pp. 550–52; Charles G. Steffen, *The Mechanics of Baltimore: Workers and Politics in the Age of Revolution, 1763–1812* (Urbana: University of Illinois Press, 1984), p. 244; Charles Royster, *Light-Horse Harry Lee and the Legacy of the American Revolution* (New York: Knopf, 1981), p. 159.

66. For discussions of Hanson's supporters, see Renzulli, *Maryland*, p. 264; Gerson, *Lee*, pp. 232–33. That Hanson represented an extreme faction of Federalists is shown by J. H. Thomas's remark to Hanson in a letter of 20 July 1812, quoted in *Niles' Weekly Register*, 8 August 1812: "Until the Fed. Rep. revives, we have no press in Maryland." The *Federal Gazette* was also published in Baltimore at the time, but it had avoided the extreme criticism of the war effort that Hanson had engaged in.

67. Some of their correspondence was published after the ensuing riot, much to Hanson's embarrassment. A letter from John Lynn to J. H. Thomas (Cumberland, 19 July) listed the armaments to be purchased: muskets, bayonets, pistols, "plenty of buckshot provided for close work," tomahawks and hatchets. Thomas warned Hanson (Mt. Philip, 20 July) not to use force until "the attempts of the assailants will justify you in the eyes of the law." A. Toney (to Hanson, Frederick-Town, 24 July) feared "this will seem too much like a plan to provoke an attack, that we may take into our own hands the sword of justice, and you know that this the law will not allow." All are reprinted in *Niles' Weekly Register*, 8 August 1812.

68. This account of the riot is based on the contemporary accounts of a committee appointed by the city to investigate the riot, printed in *Niles' Weekly Register*, 8 August 1812, and of Alexander Hanson and his colleagues, printed in Scharf, *Chronicles*, pp. 313–26. See also Renzulli, *Maryland*, pp. 264–85; Hickey, "Federalists," pp. 104–19; Boyd, *Lee*, pp. 309–27; Royster, *Lee*, pp. 154–68.

69. Though Gilje, "Baltimore Riots," argues that this riot marked a break in the Anglo-American mob tradition.

70. The action also followed the recognized pattern of lynching. The defenders of the house were judged guilty of murder in the death of Dr. Gale; they were taken from the jail and given what the crowd adjudged to be the appropriate punishment.

71. Hanson et al., in Scharf, *Chronicles*, p. 324; Royster, *Lee*, p. 157; Steffen, *Mechanics*, p. 247; Boyd, *Lee*, p. 315; Narrative of John Thompson, in Scharf, *Chronicles*, p. 334.

72. Hanson et al., in Scharf, *Chronicles*, pp. 318–19, 322–23; Royster, *Lee*, pp. 160–61.

73. Thus, for instance, the vigorous action of Baltimore's police and militia in preventing mobs from taking the post office when, a week after the riot, Hanson mailed copies of the still-active *Federal Republican* to Baltimore. Crowds besieged the post office nightly for a week: Gilje, "Baltimore Riots," p. 556.

74. Rioters and defenders were both brought to trial for the events of the two days; there were no convictions.

75. Renzulli, *Maryland*, pp. 281–88; Royster, *Lee*, pp. 164–65; Hickey, "Federalists," pp. 120–21; Scharf, *Chronicles*, p. 337.

76. Irving Brant, *James Madison*, 6 vols. (Indianapolis: Bobbs-Merrill, 1948–1961), vol. 6, *The Commander-in-Chief, 1812–1836*, p. 31. Hickey asserts that Madison's main concern in this characterization was with political damage control: "Federalists," pp. 122–23.

77. Alexis de Tocqueville, *Democracy in America*, ed. J. P. Mayer, trans. George Lawrence (New York: Doubleday Anchor, 1969), pt. 2, chap. 4: "Freedom of the Press."

78. This statement is based on an unscientific sample of fights I've found in my research. I ran across only a few—excluding formal duels—in each of the decades before 1830, then counted eleven in the 1830s; eight in the 1840s; and twenty-seven in the 1850s. These fights represent a slight fraction of all the fights that occurred in those years. An editorial fight would not be reported nationally unless it had some unique appeal as a story— something of a man-bites-dog quality. The occurrence of such fights was so regular as to be cliché.

79. See *Courier and Enquirer*, 10 April 1833; *Herald*, 18, 21 January, 10 May, 5, 19 July 1836; Lambert A. Wilmer, *Our Press Gang: Or, A Complete Exposition of the Corruptions and Crimes of the American Newspapers* (Philadelphia: J. T. Lloyd, 1860), p. 312; Frank M. O'Brien, *The Story of the Sun: New York, 1833–1928* (New York: Appleton, 1928), p. 16.

80. The best study of conscious image-creation in this period remains John William Ward's *Andrew Jackson: Symbol for an Age* (New York: Oxford University Press, 1962).

81. On the nature of the second party system, see Richard P. McCormick, *The Second American Party System: Party Formation in the Jacksonian Era* (Chapel Hill: University of North Carolina Press, 1966).

82. Hamilton Cochran gives 1621 as the date of the first North American duel but argues that dueling peaked in the years 1770–1860: *Noted American Duels and Hostile Encounters* (Philadelphia: Chilton, 1963), chap. 1. Dueling's popularity during the Federalist era is indicated by a list in Claypoole's Philadelphia *Daily Advertiser*, 12 June 1800, of twenty-one duels fought in the United States in a six-week period.

83. Mathew Carey, *Autobiography* (1833–1834; reprint, Brooklyn: Eugene Schwaab, 1942), pp. 12–16; Smith, *Printers and Press Freedom*, p. 151; Fay, *Two Franklins*, pp. 77–78.

84. Anthropologist Julian Pitt-Rivers defines honor as "the value of a person in his own eyes, but also in the eyes of his society. It is his estimation of his own worth, but it is also the acknowledgment of that claim, his excellence recognized by his society, his *right* to pride. . . . Honour, therefore, provides a nexus between the ideals of a society and their reproduction in the individual through his aspiration to personify them. . . . The claimant to honor must get himself accepted at his own evaluation, must be granted reputation, or his claim becomes mere vanity, an object of ridicule or contempt." *The Fate of Shechem, or, The Politics of Sex: Essays in the Anthropology of the Mediterranean* (Cambridge: Cambridge University Press, 1977), p. 1. For similar discussions of honor in a specifically southern setting, see Elliott J. Gorn, "'Gouge and Bite, Pull Hair and Scratch': The Social Significance of Fighting in the Southern Backcountry," *American Historical Review* 90 (1985): 39–42, and Bertram Wyatt-Brown, *Southern Honor*.

85. Rhys Isaac, *The Transformation of Virginia: Community, Religion, and Authority, 1740–1790* (Chapel Hill: University of North Carolina Press, 1982); Gorn, "Gouge," pp. 21–22; 27.

86. Guion Griffis Johnson, *Antebellum North Carolina: A Social History* (Chapel Hill: University of North Carolina Press, 1937), pp. 42–47; Dickson D. Bruce, Jr., *Violence and Culture in the Antebellum South* (Austin: University of Texas Press, 1979), pp. 7–18.

87. Johnson, *Antebellum North Carolina*, p. 45; Bruce, *Violence*, p. 29; Gorn, "Gouge," p. 22.

88. Bruce, *Violence*, p. 27. See James Moss, *Duelling in Missouri History* (Kansas City, Mo.: privately published, 1966), on Missouri's antidueling laws.

89. Cochran, *Duels*, pp. 139–41; Don Carlos Seitz, *Famous American Duels* (New York: Crowell, 1929), pp. 251–82; Benjamin Perley Poore, *Perley's Reminiscences of Sixty Years in the National Metropolis*, 2 vols. (Philadelphia: Hubbard Bros., 1886), 1:207–8.

90. Twenty-one such petitions were presented to the House of Representatives on one day alone: *Congressional Globe*, 25th Cong., 2d sess., 9 April 1838, 6:280, House of Representatives, 4 April 1838.

91. Ibid., pp. 282–83; Senate, 5 April 1838.

92. Senator Franklin Pierce of New Hampshire, ibid., p. 284.

93. Ibid., p. 283.

94. Ibid., p. 285.

95. Ibid., p. 284.

96. Ibid., p. 282.

97. Ibid. A similar argument was put forward by the Philadelphia *Public Ledger*, 26 February 1838: Webb "may challenge with impunity to himself, as he is considered personally beneath the notice of any member of that body [Congress]." The editorialist recommended a traditional punishment for Webb: "a coat of tar and feathers, and a public invitation to leave town on a wheelless vehicle, with the usual accompaniment of appropriate music."

98. As recounted by Thomas Ritchie, Sr., in a letter to his daughter, Mrs. Isabella Harrison, Richmond, Va., 22 January 1843, in Barbara J. Griffen, ed., "Thomas Ritchie and the Code Duello," *Virginia Magazine of History and Biography* 92 (1984): 81–88. In the account that follows, page numbers in parentheses will refer to this letter. For additional accounts, see *Full Report of the Commonwealth of Virginia vs. Thomas Ritchie, Jr.* (Richmond, 1846); Clement Eaton, *Freedom of Thought in the Old South* (Durham: University of North Carolina Press, 1940), pp. 179–80.

99. Of seventy-one duels involving newspapermen I found in my research, five occurred before 1830, nine in the 1830s, thirteen in the 1840s, and forty-four in the 1850s. These numbers represent a small fraction of all such duels because antidueling laws encouraged duelists to avoid publicity, newspapers were unlikely to publish news of routine (that is, nonfatal) duels, and relatively few duels qualified as "national" news. Nevertheless, the increase in dueling is undeniable.

100. James T. Moore, "The Death of the Duel: The *Code Duello* in Readjustor Virginia, 1829–1883," *Virginia Magazine of History and Biography* 83 (1975): 259–76. Moore concludes that participants were "only keeping up appearances, acting out a charade. Sabotaged by its own adherents, therefore, the *code* had become little more than a parody of itself" (p. 276).

101. Lipset and Raab, *Politics of Unreason*, pp. 41–43; Paul Goodman, *Towards a Christian Republic: Antimasonry and the Great Transition in New England, 1826–1836* (New York: Oxford University Press, 1988), pp. 3–4, 7–8, 26–28; *Liberator*, 2 November 1833.

102. Carl E. Prince cites the breakdown of a "facade" of American republicanism in this period as the cause for the rash of riots in 1834–1835: "The Great 'Riot Year': Jacksonian Democracy and Patterns of Violence in 1834," *Journal of the Early Republic* 5 (1985): 17–18.

103. See, for example, Browne, *Baltimore*, p. 199.

104. Michael Feldberg, *The Turbulent Era: Riot and Disorder in Jacksonian America* (New York: Oxford University Press, 1980).

105. *Liberator*, 18 August, 22 September 1854, 17, 24 August 1855, 17 October 1856, 5 June 1857; Browne, *Baltimore*, pp. 209–13.

106. *Liberator*, 17 November 1848.

107. Richard Maxwell Brown describes vigilantism as a technique of "social reconstruction" used by upper- and middle-class groups to recreate advantageous social situations, characterized generally by respect for property and elite dominance. He counts "at least 210" such movements in the West between 1849 and 1902: "The American Vigilante

Tradition," in Roger Lane and John J. Turner, eds., *Riot, Rout, and Tumult: Readings in American Social and Political Violence* (Westport, Conn.: Greenwood Press, 1978), pp. 80–111.

108. *Liberator*, 28 July 1854.

109. William Tecumseh Sherman was the most famous of these bankers. In his memoirs he records the financial squeeze that bankers felt: though they were charging interest at 3 percent *per month* on loans, they still could fail to turn a profit after payments to eastern bankers and to steamship companies. As a result, rumors of insolvency flew from time to time, leading to a series of dramatic runs on the banks: *Memoirs of General William T. Sherman* (Bloomington: Indiana University Press, 1957), pp. 103–16.

110. Robert M. Senkiewicz, *Vigilantes in Gold Rush San Francisco* (Palo Alto: Stanford University Press, 1985).

111. Ibid., pp. 104–5. Sherman agrees that charges of corruption were exaggerated and opportunistic: *Memoirs*, pp. 118–19.

112. Discussed in Mary F. Williams, *History of the San Francisco Vigilance Committee of 1851: A Study of Social Control on the California Frontier in the Days of the Gold Rush* (New York: Da Capo Press, 1969).

113. Senkiewicz, *Vigilantes*, p. 161; Sherman, *Memoirs*, p. 119. His tone was offensive also to rivals within the Democratic party. In one noteworthy clash, Casey engaged in a shootout with U.S. Marshal John Bagley over a Democratic primary in 1855: Senkiewicz, *Vigilantes*, p. 7.

114. During an earlier residence in Washington, to distinguish himself from others of the same name, King added the patronymic "of William," and thereafter called himself James King of William.

115. Senkiewicz, *Vigilantes*, p. 161. Sherman recalls King as "a man of fine manners and address, he at once constituted himself the champion of society against the public and private characters whom he saw fit to arraign." *Memoirs*, p. 119.

116. Senkiewicz, *Vigilantes*, pp. 7–8, 167; Sherman, *Memoirs*, pp. 119–20.

117. *Memoirs*, p. 124. Sherman also records the angry denial of the leader of the Vigilance Committee, William T. Coleman, that his movement was a "mob": p. 122.

118. Senkiewicz, *Vigilantes*, pp. 177–78; Sherman, *Memoirs*, p. 131.

119. John A. Lent, "The Press on Wheels: A History of the *Frontier Index*," *Journal of the West* 10 (1971): 665, 687–92; Thomas H. Heuterman, "Assessing the 'Press on Wheels': Individualism in Frontier Journalism," *Journalism Quarterly* 52 (1976): 425.

120. Robert Wiebe, *The Search for Order: 1877–1920* (New York: Hill & Wang, 1967), pp. xiii and elsewhere. On localism, see the compelling argument in John P. Roche, "American Liberty: An Examination of the 'Tradition' of Freedom," in M. R. Konvitz and Clinton Rossiter, eds., *Aspects of Liberty: Essays Presented to Roger E. Cushman* (Ithaca: Cornell University Press, 1958), pp. 129–62.

Chapter Four

1. John L. Thomas, *The Liberator, William Lloyd Garrison: A Biography* (Boston: Little, Brown, 1963), pp. 252–53.

2. On the "anti-ideological" character of the second party system, see Richard P. Hofstadter, *The Idea of a Party System: The Rise of Legitimate Opposition in the United States, 1780–1840* (Berkeley: University of California Press, 1972); Richard P. McCormick, *The Second American Party System: Party Formation in the Jacksonian Era* (Chapel Hill: University of North Carolina Press, 1966).

3. I use the term *antislavery* to refer to the broad movement against slavery or its expansion; *abolition* refers to the more specific and radical demand for abolishing slavery altogether. I generally use *abolitionism* when discussing the attitudes of critics of the antislavery movement to reflect their rhetorical posture—*abolitionism* was a charged term; *antislavery* less so.

4. Gilbert Hobbs Barnes, *The Antislavery Impulse: 1830–1844* (New York: Harcourt Brace, 1933).

5. Thomas L. Haskell, "Capitalism and the Origins of the Humanitarian Sensibility," *American Historical Review* 90 (1985) pp. 339–61, 547–66. C. B. MacPherson, *The Political Theory of Possessive Individualism: Hobbes to Locke* (Oxford: Clarendon Press, 1962).

6. Eric Foner, *Free Soil, Free Labor, Free Men: The Ideology of the Republican Party before the Civil War* (New York: Oxford University Press, 1970); Louis Gerteis, *Morality and Utility in American Antislavery Reform* (Chapel Hill: University of North Carolina Press, 1987).

7. On the contradictions between slavery and market relations, see Eugene Genovese, *The Political Economy of Slavery: Studies in the Economy and Society of the Slave South* (New York: Pantheon, 1965). The *locus classicus* for the argument that capitalism first made slavery necessary and then made it obsolete is Eric Williams, *Capitalism and Slavery* (Chapel Hill: University of North Carolina Press, 1944).

8. Ira Berlin, "The Revolution in Black Life," in Alfred F. Young, ed., *The American Revolution: Explorations in the History of American Radicalism* (DeKalb: Northern Illinois University Press, 1976), pp. 349–82.

9. Lorman Ratner, *Powder Keg: Northern Opposition to the Antislavery Movement, 1831–1840* (New York: Oxford University Press, 1968), pp. 131–34.

10. William J. Rorabaugh, *The Craft Apprentice: From Franklin to the Machine Age in America* (New York: Oxford University Press, 1986).

11. Roy Allen Billington, *The Protestant Crusade: 1800–1860* (New York: Macmillan, 1938).

12. Vincent Harding, *There Is a River: The Black Struggle for Freedom in America* (New York: Vintage, 1981, 1983), pp. 81–94; Dwight L. Dumond, *Antislavery: The Crusade for Freedom in America* (Ann Arbor: University of Michigan Press, 1961), p. 115; "A Colored Bostonian," "Death of Walker," *Liberator*, 22 January 1831.

13. "The Insurrection," *Liberator*, 3 September 1831.

14. Garrison and some of the other abolitionists habitually used the term *agitation* to describe their activities. The use of *agitation* in a positive sense was, I think, somewhat novel.

15. Quoted in *Liberator*, 3 October 1835.

16. Some historians seem to view the antislavery press as just such a huge, technically innovative propaganda machine; see Leonard Richards, *"Gentlemen of Property and Standing": Anti-Abolitionist Mobs in Jacksonian America* (New York: Oxford University Press, 1970), pp. 71–73, 150, 162.

17. Barnes, *Antislavery Impulse*, pp. 59–61; Dumond, *Antislavery*, pp. 183, 189.

18. Wright to T. D. Weld, New York City, 16 September, 9 January 1835, in *Letters of Theodore Dwight Weld, Angelina Grimke Weld, and Sarah Grimke* (New York: Macmillan, 1934), 1:231, 194–97. Richards gives a figure of 1,100,000 pieces distributed in 1835: *"Gentlemen"*, pp. 50–52.

19. David Paul Nord, "The Evangelical Origins of Mass Media in America, 1815–1835," *Journalism Monographs* 88 (May 1984); Walter Sutton, *The Western Book Trade: Cincinnati as a Nineteenth-Century Publishing and Book Trade Center* (Columbus: Ohio State University Press, 1961), pp. 151–59.

20. *American Antislavery Almanac, 1839*, p. 14.

21. Barnes, *Antislavery Impulse*, pp. 100–102.

22. *Liberator*, 26 September 1835.

23. James Brewer Stewart, "Peaceful Hopes and Violent Experiences: The Evolution of Reforming and Radical Abolitionism, 1831–1837," *Civil War History* 17 (1971): 293–309.

24. [James G. Birney], *Narrative of the Late Riotous Proceedings against Liberty of the Press in Cincinnati* . . . (Cincinnati, 1836), p. 12; William G. Birney, *James G. Birney and His Times* (New York: Appleton, 1890), p. 221; *Philanthropist*, 24 March 1840.

25. Barnes, *Antislavery Impulse*, pp. 50–51; Edwin Emery and Michael B. Emery, *The Press and America: An Interpretive History of the Mass Media*, 6th ed. (Englewood Cliffs, N.J.: Prentice-Hall, 1988), pp. 147–48.

26. Birney, *Birney*, p. 221.

27. Barnes, *Antislavery Impulse*, pp. 50–51.

28. Gordon S. Wood, "Evangelical America and Early Mormonism," *New York History* 61 (1980): 366; David Grimsted, "Rioting in its Jacksonian Setting," *American Historical Review* 71 (1972): 393–94.

29. *Liberator*, 4 April 1835; William Archer Baughin, "Nativism in Cincinnati Before 1860" (Ph.D. diss., University of Cincinnati, 1963), pp. 240–51.

30. *Philanthropist*, 28 October 1836.

31. *Liberator*, 26 June, 24 July, 1838, 9 July 1841, 12 July 1844, 9 May 1845.

32. For examples of antitemperance crowd actions, see *Liberator*, 1 February, 27 September, 4 October 1834, 14 February, 21 March, 4 April, 4 July 1835, 14 July 1848, 29 May 1850, 8 June 1855.

33. Dumond, *Antislavery*, pp. 87–88, 92–93, 95, 168. On the tolerance of the South in general, see Clement Eaton, *Freedom of Thought in the Old South* (Durham: University of North Carolina Press, 1940).

34. Russell Nye, *Fettered Freedom: Civil Liberties and the Slavery Controversy, 1830–1860* (East Lansing: Michigan State University Press, 1949), p. 175. John M. McFaul, "Expediency vs. Morality: Jacksonian Politics and Slavery," *Journal of American History* 62 (1975): 26–27, notes that the movement to pass laws against abolitionist discussion *preceded* Turner's rebellion, having been promoted in the *National Intelligencer* as early as 1830.

35. See Carl N. Degler, *The Other South: Southern Dissenters in the Nineteenth Century* (New York: Oxford University Press, 1974).

36. *New York Daily Sentinel*, 17 September 1831; *Liberator*, 24 September 1831, 29 August, 26 September 1835; *Philanthropist*, 1 January 1836; Dumond, *Antislavery*, pp. 186, 205–67; *Cincinnati Daily Gazette*, 4, 7 July 1836. For other examples, see *American Antislavery Almanac, 1838*, p. 29; "The Abolition Paper at Macon," *Liberator*, 18 October 1850; "Excitement in Maryland—an Outrage," ibid., 23 July 1858.

37. *Liberator*, 19 December 1856.

38. On lynching in the Old South, see Eugene D. Genovese, *Roll, Jordan, Roll: The World the Slaves Made* (New York: Vintage, 1976), pp. 32–34; W. J. Cash, *The Mind of the South* (1941; reprint, New York: Vintage, 1960) pp. 43–46.

39. Nye, *Fettered Freedom*, pp. 176–93; *Liberator*, 3 October 1851.

40. Dumond, *Antislavery*, p. 105; Defensor [William Thomas], *The Enemies of the Constitution Discovered* . . . (Utica and New York, 1835), pp. 11–32; *Liberator*, 15 August 1835. Abolitionist literature was also confiscated and burned in Richmond, Va. (ibid., 26 September 1835), and again in Charleston in 1849 ("Abolition Pamphlets," ibid., 31 August 1849).

41. *Philanthropist,* 22 May 1838, 24 May 1843; a similar burning took place in Parkersburg, Va., in 1852: *Liberator,* 19 November 1852.

42. Dumond, *Antislavery,* p. 109.

43. See, for example, "Great Meeting in Philadelphia," *Liberator,* 29 August 1835; "Public Meeting at New York," ibid., 12 September 1835.

44. It was possible, of course, to intervene in a public meeting—to pass a resolution over the opposition of the meeting's planners. Antislavery activists often adopted the strategy of proposing an affirmation of the right to freedom of speech, press, and petition, for instance.

45. As resolved in Clinton, Mich., on 5 September 1835: *American Antislavery Almanac, 1838,* p. 22.

46. Vernon L. Volpe, "The Anti-Abolitionist Campaign of 1840," *Civil War History* 32 (1986): 325–39. Note how the antislavery *Philanthropist* ridiculed the attempts of Harrison supporters to make public meetings seem nonpartisan: "The Anti-Abolition Meeting," 19 March 1839.

47. Streeter to Weld, Oberlin, Ohio, 25 February 1840, in *Weld-Grimke Letters,* 2:825.

48. "Extract of a Letter from Jonathan Walker, Claremount, N.H., August 30, 1846," *Liberator,* 2 October 1846.

49. "Pennsylvania Hall Burnt," *Philanthropist,* 29 May 1838. Likewise, John Thomas notes, "There lay in the silent hostility of the many and the compulsive hates of the few a major threat to free institutions": *Liberator,* p. 206.

50. In one extreme case, the "people" of Litchfield, Conn., in the wake of the 1856 presidential election, fired two cannon shots at the home of E. C. Goodwin, the editor of the pro-Fremont *Enquirer:* "Ruffianism in Connecticut," *Liberator,* 28 November 1856.

51. Two full-length books have been written on the subject: Ratner, *Powder Keg,* and Richards, *"Gentlemen".*

52. Antiabolitionist activists were fond of comparing themselves to the Revolutionary generation—for instance, "Public Sentiment" pointed out that the Revolutionaries "did not deem themselves the slaves of the law. . . . Such was the reasoning of our revolutionary fathers—may we not thus reason now?" (Cincinnati Daily *Whig,* 19 July 1836). Defensor was keen to refute such comparisons in his account of the 1835 Utica riot: *Enemies,* pp. 27–28.

53. Dumond, *Antislavery,* pp. 204–5.

54. Letter of "Public Sentiment," Cincinnati *Whig,* 19 July 1836.

55. As early as 1805, the *National Intelligencer* had used fear of slave insurrection as a reason to refuse to print a contribution arguing against slavery: *National Intelligencer,* 18 December 1805. Still, one might accuse antiabolitionists of using the slave insurrection bogey cynically, especially in the North. On antiaboltitionist fears of slave rebellion, see Ratner, *Powder Keg,* pp. 74–80; Dumond, *Antislavery,* p. 206.

56. Gerald L. Henig, "The Jacksonian Attitude toward Abolitionism in the 1830s," *Tennessee Historical Quarterly* 28 (1969): 42–56.

57. Richards, *"Gentlemen",* pp. 61–62, argues that, at the root of antiabolitionist sentiment was fear of centralized control enforcing uniform patterns of behavior, supplanting autonomous local groups and leaders. Although somewhat believable, this ill consists with the same people's knack of violently punishing deviant behavior and beliefs. Ratner, *Powder Keg,* pp. 42–46, points out that northern suspicion of the exercise of federal power against the peculiar institution was reinforced by northerners' romantic and pastoral image of southern life. See also Henig, "Jacksonian Attitudes."

58. Ratner, *Powder Keg,* pp. 51–62.

59. Letter of "Public Sentiment," Cincinnati Daily *Whig*, 19 July 1836; see also Henig, "Jacksonian Attitudes"; Ratner, *Powder Keg*, pp. 28–42; Richards, *"Gentlemen"*, pp. 62–71.

60. Adrian Cook, *The Armies of the Streets: The New York City Draft Riots of 1863* (Lexington: University Press of Kentucky, 1974) p. 24.

61. "The 'Refuge of Oppression,'" *Liberator*, 8 January 1847.

62. Leon Litwack, *North of Slavery: The Negro in the Free States, 1790–1860* (Chicago: University of Chicago Press, 1961), pp. 159–68; as examples, consider rioting between black and white railroad laborers near New Market, Md., in 1831 (*Liberator*, 10 September 1831), and the Fourth of July riot between blacks and Irish in New York City in 1838 (ibid., 17 July 1838).

63. Race riots were frequent in antebellum northern cities. Curry records twenty between 1800 and 1850, and his list is not by any means exhaustive, leaving out numerous riots over runaway slaves like the Scanlan Riot in Cincinnati in 1843 (*Weekly Liberty Hall and Cincinnati Gazette*, 3, 10 August 1843; Patrick Allen Folk, "The Queen City of Mobs: Riots and Community Reactions in Cincinnati, 1788–1848" [Ph.D. diss., University of Toledo, 1978], pp. 330–38; William Birney to James G. Birney, Cincinnati, 7 August 1843, in Birney, *Letters*, pp. 750–52) and similar riots in Detroit (*Liberator,* 29 June 1833), Albany (*Liberator*, 3 May 1834) and most dramatically, Christiana, Pa. (*Liberator*, 26 September 1851), in which blacks rioted to free fellow blacks from slave bounty hunters. Incidents like these multiplied after passage of the stiff federal Fugitive Slave laws in the 1850s.

64. See Linda K. Kerber, "Abolitionists and Amalgamators: The New York City Race Riots of 1834," *New York History* 48 (1967): 28–39.

65. Richards, *"Gentlemen"*, pp. 30–42; Ratner, *Powder Keg*, pp. 3–22; Henig, "Jacksonian Attitudes."

66. Louis Gerteis, *Morality and Utility in American Antislavery Reform* (Chapel Hill: University of North Carolina Press, 1987), p. 4 and elsewhere; John B. Jentz, "The Antislavery Constituency in Jacksonian New York City," *Civil War History* 26 (1981): 101–22; Richards, *"Gentlemen"*, pp. 26–30, chap. 5; Ratner, *Powder Keg*, pp. 62–64; *Liberator*, 2 August 1834; O. Scott, "A Watchword for Mobs," *Liberator*, 21 March 1835; William Goodell, "To the Laboring People of the Free States," *American Anti-Slavery Almanac, 1838*, p. 42.

67. Volpe, "Anti-Abolitionist Campaign of 1840"; McFaul, "Expediency," p. 27.

68. See, for instance, *Philanthropist*, 16 December 1836; *Liberator*, 6 November 1846; *American Anti-Slavery Alamanac, 1838*, p. 40; Defensor, *Enemies*, pp. 46–47, 55.

69. "Editors and Magistrates," *Liberator*, 30 August 1834; T. D. Weld to the Reverend Ray Potter, Troy, N.Y., 11 June 1836, *Weld-Grimke Letters*, 1:309–10.

70. McFaul, "Expediency," p. 34; see also Ronald P. Formisano, "Political Character, Antipartyism, and the Second Party System," *American Quarterly* 21 (1969): 683–709.

71. Thus Barnes argues that the 1842 congressional attempt to censure John Quincy Adams for repeatedly defying the gag rule was primarily aimed at restoring party discipline. It failed: *Antislavery Impulse*, pp. 185–87.

72. "Editors and Magistrates," *Liberator*, 30 August 1834; Lewis Tappan to T. D. Weld, New York, 10 July 1834, in *Weld-Grimke Letters*, 1:153–56; Weld to Judge James Hall, Cincinnati, 20 May 1834, ibid., 1:145; "Democracy in Ohio," *Philanthropist,* 22 September 1841; Richards, *"Gentlemen"*, pp. 26–30; *Liberator*, 2 August 1834, 21 March 1835; Jeffrey Rutenbeck, "Partisan Press Coverage of Anti-Abolitionist Riots" (Paper presented at Association for Education in Journalism and Mass Communication (AEJMC) convention, 1987, San Antonio).

73. Richards, *"Gentlemen"*, pp. 73–81.

74. "Mr. Birney's Answer," *Philanthropist*, 1 January 1836; see also "The Reign of

Terror," *Liberator*, 15 August 1835; *Anti-Slavery Almanac, 1839*, p. 11. In the same fashion, abolitionists made a great deal out of the congressional gag rules that called for the automatic tabling of antislavery petitions. See Barnes, *Antislavery Impulse*, chap. 11.

75. Cincinnati *Whig*, 13 August 1836.

76. Cincinnati antiabolitionist meeting's resolutions, as reported in *Philanthropist*, 29 January 1836. See also "Thoughts on Slavery & c.," *Daily Cincinnati Republican*, 17 February 1836; "Abolitionism," *Cincinnati Daily Gazette*, 2 August 1836; "Mind Your Own Business," *Cincinnati Daily Evening Post*, 2 August 1836.

77. "Appeal to Our Fellow Citizens," *Liberator*, 22 August 1835.

78. *Liberator*, 11 February 1832.

79. "Portraits of Reformers," *National Era*, 17 June 1847.

80. "Spirit of Intolerance," *Philanthropist*, 4 November 1836; see also *Liberator*, 5 January 1833.

81. *Philanthropist*, 7 October 1836.

82. Weld to S. Webb and William H. Scott, New York, 3 January 1838, in *Weld-Grimke Letters*, 2:511–12.

83. Birney, "Freedom of the Press," *National Era*, 15 July 1847. Linda Kerber agrees: "Abolitionists and Amalgamators."

84. "Mobs—Free Discussion—Rights of the People Peaceably to Assemble—Things to be Thought of," *American Anti-Slavery Almanac, 1840*, p. 4.

85. Weld to Judge James Hall, Cincinnati, 20 May 1834, in *Weld-Grimke Letters*, 1:145.

86. *Utica Elucidator*, 14 January 1834; *Liberator*, 25 January, 1 February 1834.

87. *Liberator*, 17, 24 October 1824.

88. The following account is based on Howard Alexander Morrison, "Gentlemen of Proper Understanding: A Closer Look at Utica's Anti-Abolitionist Mob," *New York History* 62 (1981); Benjamin Sevitch, "The Well-Planned Riot of October 21, 1835: Utica's Answer to Abolitionism," *New York History* 50 (July 1969): 251–63; Thomas, *Liberator*, p. 198; Richards, *"Gentlemen"*, pp. 85–92; and Dumond, *Antislavery*, p. 221.

89. Defensor, *Enemies*, p. 58.

90. Defensor, *Enemies*, pp. 64–67.

91. Defensor, *Enemies*, pp. 76–87; Richards, *"Gentlemen"*, p. 91.

92. Defensor, *Enemies*, pp. 93–94; *Philanthropist*, 8 January 1836.

93. Defensor, *Enemies*, pp. 61, 74.

94. Especially by Robert P. Forbes: "Setting the Imps to Work: The Politics of Anti-Abolitionism and the Election of 1836," *Journal of the Early Republic* (forthcoming).

95. *Philanthropist*, 8 January 1836; Defensor, *Enemies*, p. 60. See also editorial on southern concern with the convention in Dauby's *Observer*, 20 October 1835.

96. Morrison, "Utica," pp. 64, 70–82; McFaul, "Expediency," pp. 29–34; Defensor, *Enemies*, pp. 46–47, 55, 101.

97. "Training of the Utica Mob," *Philanthropist*, 8 January 1836.

98. Senate, Tuesday, 19 January 1836, 24th Cong., 1st sess., in *Register of Debates in Congress*, vol. 12 (Washington, D.C.: Gales and Seaton, 1836), pp. 203–8.

99. Martin Van Buren to W. C. Rives, 17 January 1836, in Rives Collection, Library of Congress, quoted in Morrison, "Utica," p. 81.

100. Thomas, *Liberator*, pp. 67–69; *Liberator*, 12 October 1833.

101. Thomas, *Liberator*, pp. 38–39; *Liberator*, 5 January, 16 February 1833.

102. Barnes, *Antislavery Impulse*, p. 63; Ratner, *Powder Keg*, pp. 28–42.

103. "Meeting at Faneuil Hall," *Liberator*, 29 August 1835.

104. "A Heavy Present," *Liberator*, 19 September 1835.

105. Thomas, *Liberator*, p. 201.

106. This account of the riot is taken from Thomas, *Liberator*, pp. 99–205; Nye, *Fettered Freedom*, pp. 201–2; and two accounts printed in the *Liberator* itself: one by C. C. Burleigh in the issue of 24 October, and the other entitled "Triumph of Mobocracy in Boston" in the issue of 7 November.

107. Theodore M. Hammett, "Two Mobs of Jacksonian Boston: Ideology and Interest," *Journal of American History* 62 (1976): 845–68.

108. Betty L. Fladeland, *James G. Birney: Slaveholder to Abolitionist* (Ithaca: Cornell University Press, 1955), pp. 1–107; Birney, *Birney*, pp. 3–128.

109. J. A. Thome to T. D. Weld, Cincinnati, 8 January 1835, in *Weld-Grimke Letters*, 1:191; "James G. Birney," *Liberator*, 22 August 1835; Fladeland, *Birney*, pp. 113–22; Birney, *Birney*, pp. 180–87; Dumond, *Antislavery*, p. 201.

110. Richards, *"Gentlemen"*, p. 41; Fladeland, *Birney*, p. 96; Birney, *Birney*, pp. 128–29, 204; editorial address, *Philanthropist*, 1 January 1836; Fladeland, *Birney*, pp. 128–29; "Mr. Birney's Answer," *Philanthropist*, 1 January 1836; Birney, *Narrative*, pp. 11–13; *Philanthropist*, 29 January 1836; Cincinnati *Whig and Commercial Intelligencer*, 25 January 1836.

111. Fladeland, *Birney*, p. 133; Folk, "Queen City", pp. 66–68; "The Philanthropist," *Philanthropist*, 13 May 1836; "Lynch Law in Cincinnati," *Republican*, 13 April 1836; *Philanthropist*, 22 April 1836.

112. Birney, *Narrative*, pp. 12–14; Birney, *Birney*, pp. 241–42; *Republican*, 22 July 1836; "Midnight Outrage on the Press," *Philanthropist*, 15 July 1836; advertisement signed "Mayor's Office," *Gazette*, 16 July 1836.

113. Address of the Ohio Anti-Slavery Society, *Philanthropist*, 22 July 1836; "Abolitionism," *Cincinnati Daily Evening Post*, 14 July 1836; *Gazette*, 20 July 1836; "Efforts to Raise a Mob," *Philanthropist*, 22 July 1836. The Presbyterian *Cincinnati Journal and Western Luminary* likewise predicted a mob outburst but blamed it in advance not on proslavery forces but on "the licentiousness and disrespect for order wrought by the doctrines of Robert Owen, Frances Wright, Abner Kneeland and the like.": "Spirit of the Times," 21 July 1836.

114. Letter of "Cincinnati," *Whig*, 14 July 1836; letter of "Public Sentiment," ibid., 19 July 1836.

115. The published call for the meeting was signed by four dozen of the city's leading men: *Republican*, 23 July 1836. Charles Hammond, editor of the *Gazette*, asserted that not all of these men had actually consented to the use of their names: *Gazette*, 2 August 1836.

116. The resolutions of the Market House meeting are in *Gazette*, 25 July 1836; *Republican*, 26 July 1836; *Philanthropist*, 29 July 1836. The resolution invoking the Boston Tea Party drew special attention: *Journal and Luminary*, 28 July 1836; Clarissa Gest to Erasmus Gest, Cincinnati, 2 August 1836, in Charles Schultz, ed., "Glimpses into Cincinnati's Past: The Gest Letters," *Ohio History* 73 (1964): 165–66; Birney, *Narrative*, p. 25.

117. Richards, *"Gentlemen"*, pp. 92–100; Daniel Aaron, "Cincinnati, 1818–1838: A Study of Attitudes" (Ph.D. diss., Harvard University, 1945), pp. 454–76; Gerteis (*Morality and Utility*, pp. 27–28) discerns a conflict between the established elite and "new men—the merchants, artisans, and manufacturers recently arrived from England, New York, and New England—who threatened the established order with their independent commercial ties and their aggressive free labor and antislavery faith."

118. Hammond's editorial condemning the tendency of meetings like the Market House meeting to undercut the rights of minorities—precisely the rights that constitutions were enacted to protect—is a model of liberal argument: "Abolitionism—Mobocracy," *Gazette*, 22 July 1836. His editorial brother, James F. Conover of the *Whig*, was also less enthusiastic about the Market House meeting than most editors but was, in the final analysis, supportive.

119. For example, "Abolition Society in Cincinnati," *Republican*, 18 January 1835: The city, heedful of the "interests of her merchants, her capitalists, and her tradesmen" would not tolerate a break with the South. See also Vernon David Keeler, "The Commercial Development of Cincinnati to the Year 1860" (Ph.D. diss., University of Chicago, 1935), pp. 48–51.

120. "Cincinnati and Charleston Rail-Road," *Post*, 3 February 1836; *Philanthropist*, 29 January 1836; William Sherman Savage, *The Controversy over the Distribution of Abolition Literature, 1830–1860* (Washington, D.C.: Association for the Study of Negro Life and History, 1938), pp. 95–96; Edward Deering Mansfield, *Personal Memories, Social, Political, and Literary* . . . (Cincinnati: Robert Clarke, 1879), p. 303; "Cincinnati and Charleston Rail Road," *Republican* 20 April, 23 May, 27 May, 24 June 1836; letters from Daniel Drake, ibid., 12, 15, 16, 17, 18, 19 July 1836.

121. *Gazette*, 22 July 1836; *Philanthropist*, 30 September 1836.

122. See, for instance, *Republican*, 13 February 1836.

123. Including Burnet, Spencer, and Burke from the meeting's officers; as well as Nicholas Longworth, the city's richest man; leading bankers Josiah Lawrence and Robert Buchanan; leading merchants Thomas Bakewell and David Loring; the city's foremost lawyers, Timothy Walker and Morgan Neville; and David Disney, former speaker of the Ohio House of Representatives: Birney, *Narrative*, pp. 23–27; Birney, *Birney*, p. 244; *Republican*, 26 July 1836; Folk, "Queen City," pp. 120–23.

124. *Whig*, 1 August 1836; *Gazette*, 1 August 1836.

125. "Destruction of Property," *Gazette*, 2 August 1836; *Republican*, 1 August 1836; Birney, *Birney*, pp. 245–48; Dumond, *Antislavery*, pp. 221–23; Richards, *"Gentlemen"*, pp. 92–100; Stanley Harrold, *Gamaliel Bailey and Antislavery Union* (Kent, Ohio: Kent State University Press, 1986), pp. 17–18; "More Mob Spirit," *Whig*, 2 August 1836; Folk, "Queen City," pp. 57–147; Fladeland, *Birney*, pp. 136–42; *Western Messenger*, 2 (September 1836): 142–43.

126. "Great Meeting—Great Discomfiture," *Gazette*, 3 August 1836; "Great Meeting," *Post*, 3 August 1836; "Great Meeting!" *Whig*, 3 August 1836; "Great Meeting," *Republican*, 4 August 1836; Birney, *Narrative*, p. 42; Birney, *Birney*, p. 248.

127. In a curious footnote, a meeting of Cincinnati's free African-Americans was also arranged to express disapproval of the *Philanthropist* and blame the abolitionists for the riot. This meeting was quickly repudiated by a more legitimate meeting of the Union Society: "Cincinnati Union Society of Colored Persons," *Post*, 2 August 1836; "People of Color," *Gazette*, 6 August 1836.

128. "Abolitionism," *Gazette*, 2 August 1836; note that this reversal was written and published before the hijacking of the Court House meeting.

129. For typical examples of comment by Cincinnati papers, see "Mind Your Own Business," *Post*, 2 August 1836; *Whig*, 13 August 1836. For comments on the behavior of the press, see *Journal and Luminary*, 4 August 1836; *Gazette*, 5 August 1836; Birney, *Birney*, pp. 205–6; Folk, "Queen City," pp. 123–29; *Philanthropist*, 4 November 1836.

130. He went so far as to argue that "the effect of the violence, on the mass of the population through the country" had been "most happy": "The Reign of Terror," *Philanthropist*, 23 September (5 August) 1836. See also "Notices of the Recent Riotous Proceedings," *Philanthropist*, 21 October 1836; Birney, *Narrative*, p. 46; Birney, *Birney*, pp. 248–49.

131. "Triumph of Justice in Cincinnati," *Philanthropist*, 23 July 1839; Fladeland, *Birney*, p. 146.

132. John Gill, *Tide Without Turning: Elijah P. Lovejoy and Freedom of the Press* (Boston: Starr King, 1958); Merton P. Dillon, *Elijah P. Lovejoy, Abolitionist Editor* (Urbana: University of Illinois Press, 1961).

133. Richards, *"Gentlemen"*, pp. 100–102; *Philanthropist*, 13 May 1836; *Republican*, 3 June 1836; *Gazette*, 1 August 1836.

134. Richards, *"Gentlemen"*, pp. 102–3; "The Character of the City," *Gazette*, 5 August 1836.

135. Richards, *"Gentlemen"*, pp. 103–11; *St. Louis Bulletin*, 23 August 1837; *Philanthropist*, 1, 8, 22, 29 September, 14, 21, 28 November 1837.

136. Dumond, *Antislavery*, pp. 223–26.

137. See, for instance, letters of Sarah and Angelina Grimke to T. D. Weld, Fitchburg, Mass., 20 September 1837, in *Weld-Grimke Letters*, 1:447–48, and Brookline, Mass., 30 November 1837, ibid., pp. 485–86.

138. Abraham Lincoln, "The Perpetuation of Our Political Institutions," ed. Roy P. Basler, in *Papers of the Abraham Lincoln Association* 6 (1984): 7–14.

139. Nye, *Fettered Freedom*, chap. 8; Richards, *"Gentlemen"*, chap. 6. The periodicals Richards studied were *Niles' Weekly Register*, the *Emancipator*, the *Liberator*, and the *Philanthropist*: pp. 1–19.

140. Barnes, *Antislavery Impulse*, p. 161.

141. One of the key opponents of this move was Gamaliel Bailey, who had taken over editorship of the *Philanthropist*. He called Birney's candidacy "an altar on which to sacrifice a few votes." *Philanthropist*, 21 April 1840.

142. In Ohio in 1848–1849, two independent legislators agreed to vote with the Democrats in the statehouse in return for repeal of the black laws, provision of funds for public education of African-American children, and selection of Salmon P. Chase as U.S. senator: Frank U. Quillem, *The Color Line in Ohio: A History of Race Relations in a Typical Northern State* (Ann Arbor: George Wahr, 1913), pp. 35–43.

143. Volpe, "Anti-Abolitionist Campaign." For examples of antiabolitionist meetings arranged by Harrison supporters, see "The Great Anti-Abolition Meeting," *Philanthropist*, 12, 19 March 1839.

144. Rutenbeck, "Partisan Press Coverage."

145. "Reign of Terror in Cincinnati," *Philanthropist*, 8 September 1841; "Riot at Cincinnati," ibid., 17 September 1841; "Affairs in Cincinnati," ibid., 8 October 1841; Harrold, *Bailey*, pp. 42–43; Richards, *"Gentlemen"*, pp. 122–29; Folk, "Queen City," pp. 212–26; "Causes," *Philanthropist*, 6 October 1841; "The Philanthropist," ibid., 9 February 1842.

146. David L. Smiley, *The Lion of White Hall: The Life of Cassius M. Clay* (Madison: University of Wisconsin Press, 1962), pp. 82–83, 90–99, 103–4, 111, 133–42, 145; *Liberator*, 29 August, 5, 12, 19 September, 5 December 1845.

147. Nye, *Fettered Freedom*, p. 152n; *Liberator*, 8 August 1845; *National Era*, 23 September, 14 October 1847.

148. Harrold, *Bailey*, pp. 88–89, 125–27; Benjamin Perley Poore, *Perley's Reminiscences of Sixty Years in the National Metropolis*, 2 vols. (Philadelphia: Hubbard Bros., 1886), 1:398–99; *National Era*, 20, 27 April 1848; *Liberator*, 28 April 1848.

149. Nye, *Fettered Freedom*, p. 170; *Liberator*, 18 July 1856, 28 August 1857, 19 February 1858, 4 November 1859, 27 January 1860.

Chapter Five

1. See James A. Rawley, *Race and Politics: "Bleeding Kansas" and the Civil War* (Lincoln: University of Nebraska Press, 1979), pp. 32–78. This account has relied on Rawley and on Jay Monaghan, *Civil War on the Western Border, 1854–1865* (Lincoln: University of Nebraska Press, 1955), for the chronology of the Kansas-Nebraska controversy.

2. Rawley, *Race and Politics*, pp. 83–88.

3. Charles Robinson, *The Kansas Conflict* (New York: Harper & Bros., 1892), p. 181. Robinson was a free-stater associated with Thayer's Emigrant Aid Society, and was later elected Governor by the free-state faction.

4. Robinson, *Kansas Conflict*, pp. 181–82.

5. David W. Johnson, "Freesoilers for God: Kansas Newspapers Editors and the Anti-slavery Crusade," *Kansas History* 2 (1979): 76; Noble L. Prentis, "Kansas Journalists—Men of '57," in Noble Lovely Prentis, *Kansas Miscellanies* (Topeka, Kans.: Kansas Publishing House, 1889), pp. 92–95.

6. See, for example, the arrests of George W. Brown, editor of the *Herald of Freedom*, and Josiah Miller, one of the editors of the *Free State*: *New York Times*, 26 May 1856. Some of the enactments of the legislature were clearly aimed at newspapers. For instance:

> If any person print, write, publish, or circulate, or cause to be brought into, printed, written, published, or circulated, or shall knowingly assist in bringing into, printing, publishing, or circulating within this Territory, any book, magazine, handbill, or circular, containing any statements, arguments, opinions, sentiments, doctrine, advice, or innuendo, calculated to promote a disorderly, dangerous, or rebellious disaffection among the slaves in this Territory, or to induce such slaves to escape from the jurisdiction of their masters, or to resist their authority, he shall be guilty of a felony, and be punished by imprisonment and hard labor for a term not less than five years. (Robinson, *Kansas Conflict*, p. 157)

And again:

> If any person, by speaking or writing, assert or maintain that persons have not the right to hold slaves in this Territory, or shall introduce into this Territory, print, publish, write, circulate, or cause to be introduced into this Territory, written, printed, published or circulated in this Territory, any book, paper, magazine, or circular, containing any denial of the right of persons to hold slaves in this Territory, such person shall be deemed guilty of felony, and punished by imprisonment at hard labor for a term of not less than two years. (Robinson, *Kansas Conflict*, p. 157).

It was thus illegal for an emigrant to cross the Missouri River with a copy of the New York *Tribune* in his pocket. Such laws were on the books throughout the South, of course, but there they were mostly ceremonial because few southerners opposed slavery. In Kansas they were designed to rule over half the population out of the bounds of political discourse.

7. Not including the Parkville mobbing and the sack of Lawrence, to be discussed below, the following attacks occurred: "Missouri Ruffians" attack Joseph Speer, editor of the Kansas *Tribune*, November–December 1855 (*Liberator*, 14 December 1855); Leavenworth *Territorial Register* mobbed for free-soil sentiments, 22 December 1855 (*Liberator*, 20 June 1856); "Missouri ruffians" threaten Lawrence *Register*, 15 January 1856 (New York *Tribune*, 16 January 1856); New York *Tribune* reporter forced to flee Leavenworth, 3 June 1856 (*Liberator*, 20 June 1856); destruction of Ossawotomie printing office, 10? June 1856 (*Liberator*, 20 June 1856). I have not included a number of attacks on personnel because it cannot be determined whether these were intended as attacks on them as communicators.

8. *National Anti-Slavery Standard*, 28 April 1855; *Platte Argus Extra*, quoted in *Liberator*, 4 May 1855; Robinson, *Kansas Conflict*, pp. 130–31; Alice Nichols, *Bleeding Kansas* (New York: Oxford University Press, 1954), p. 27; Monaghan, *Civil War on the Western Border*, p. 20; Paul McCandless, *A History of Missouri*, vol. 2: *1820–1860* (Columbia: University of Missouri Press, 1972), p. 273. The Lawrence *Kansas Free State* closed its

account with the memorably droll quip "Sic transit gloria Saturdi": 7 May 1855. In a curious postscript, editor George Park returned to Parkville in November. On his return, a town meeting appointed a committee to order him to leave town, apparently fearing a renewed assault from the countryside. Park refused, and organized a group of townsmen to protect him. The conflict simmered, then apparently faded: *Liberator*, 30 November, 14 December 1855.

9. "Letter from Mr. Park," *Liberator*, 1 June 1855.

10. Platte, Mo., *Argus*, quoted in Robinson, *Kansas Conflict*, p. 131.

11. New York *Times*, 27 May 1856; correspondence of "Randolph," ibid., 30 May 1856; *Liberator*, 30 May 1856; Rawley, *Race and Politics*, pp. 129–34; Robinson, *Kansas Conflict*, pp. 231–64. The *Herald of Freedom* was reestablished later in 1856 with the help of northern donations collected by Mrs. George Brown, the wife of the editor: *Liberator*, 21 November 1856.

12. Robert S. Harper, *Lincoln and the Press* (New York: McGraw-Hill, 1951), p. 152. The mobbings were the Junction City *Kansas Frontier*, by soldiers, 10 March 1862; the Leavenworth *Enquirer*, 11 February 1863; the Marysville *Constitutional Gazetteer*, 20 August 1863; and the Leavenworth *Western Sentinel*, by soldiers, 27 August 1863.

13. James G. Randall, *Constitutional Problems Under Lincoln*, rev. ed. (Urbana: University of Illinois Press, 1964), pp. 492–93, lists twenty-five newspapers that were suppressed. For an example of a newspaper suppression that Randall does not include, see Stanton's order to seize the office and arrest the personnel of the Washington, D.C., *Sunday Chronicle*, 17 March 1862, in *The War of the Rebellion: A Compilation of the Official Records of the Union and Confederate Armies* (hereafter *Official Records*) (Washington D.C.: 1880–1901) ser. 2, vol. 2. Stanton's general policy was stated thus: "All newspaper editors and publishers have been forbidden to publish any intelligence received by telegraph or otherwise respecting military maneuvers." Stanton to General Dix et al., 25 February 1862, *Official Records*, ser. 2, 2:246. Randall argues that such suppressions were lenient, given the circumstances.

14. It was criticized by the House Judiciary Committee for using this system improperly, censoring "numberless" dispatches of a "political, personal, and general character." Quoted in "Freedom of the Press," *American Annual Cyclopedia and Register of Important Events of the Year*, vol. 2 (New York: Appleton, 1862), pp. 480–81.

15. Raymond A. Schroth, *The Eagle and Brooklyn: A Community Newspaper, 1841–1955* (Westport, Conn.: Greenwood Press, 1974), pp. 64–65.

16. Harper, *Lincoln and the Press*, pp. 114–15, 125. The legal status of a "presentment" remains unclear; it is certainly not an indictment, and the New York jury seemed to think that an indictment was not possible because there was no existing law to indict under. It should be noted that both of these actions were broader than the War Department's policy in that they were not restricted to publishing military information but also identified hostile *opinion* as an offense.

17. Joe Skidmore, "The Copperhead Press and the Civil War," *Journalism Quarterly* 16 (1939): 348–50; John F. Marszalek, *Sherman's Other War: The General and the Civil War Press* (Memphis: Memphis State University Press, 1981), p. 13.

18. In one appeal to Secretary of War Simon Cameron to suppress Fernando Wood's New York *Daily News*, U.S. Marshal David H. Carr remarked that it was "quite evident to me that our citizens as a body do not desire its circulation nor will they longer allow it." Carr to Cameron, New Haven, Conn., 3 September 1861, in *Official Records*, ser. 2, 2:54.

19. *Official Records*, ser. 1, vol. 2, pt. 2, pp. 894–95; Thomas Guback, "General Sherman's War on the Press," *Journalism Quarterly* 36 (Spring 1959): 176. Oddly, Napoleon was defeated without a free press.

20. A sentiment that Randall argues was justified: pp. 486–88. As a result, he expresses surprise at the restraint used by northern military commanders in applying martial law to the press: pp. 506 et seq.

21. Justin E. Walsh, *To Print the News and Raise Hell! A Biography of Wilbur F. Storey* (Chapel Hill: University of North Carolina Press, 1969), pp. 145–99; Craig D. Tenney, "To Suppress or Not to Suppress: Abraham Lincoln and the Chicago *Times*," *Civil War History* 27 (1981): 248–59. Tenney argues cogently that Lincoln's motives in this affair were more mercenary than Randall and others have long assumed. He cites a neglected telegram from Lincoln, sent after an initial order to rescind the suspension of the *Times*, ordering the postponement of the rescindment if it had not yet been announced. Lincoln's agenda seems to have been primarily political.

22. Among the newspaper casualties of Sherman's successful campaigns were the *Jackson* (Miss.) *Mississippian*, and the Fayetteville, Ga., *Telegraph* and *Observer*: J. Cutler Andrews, *The South Reports the Civil War* (Princeton: Princeton University Press, 1970), pp. 271, 498. On Sherman and the press generally, see Marszalek, *Sherman*.

23. Andrews, *The South Reports the Civil War*, pp. 61, 81, 235, 528–33, 540. For an example of a newspaper conductor imprisoned under suspicion of espionage, see letter of Arnold Harris to R. W. Johnson et al., Richmond, Va., 18 August 1861, *Official Records*, ser 2, vol. 2. Ron Synovitz remarks, "The notion of a free Confederate press is a myth that originated from public relations efforts of that government." "Freedom of the Press in the Southern Confederacy: A Study of Press Values in the Confederate States of America" (Paper presented at the American Journalism Historians Association convention, Charleston, S.C., October 1988), p. 45.

24. Skidmore, "Copperhead Press," pp. 352–54.

25. Andrews, *The South Reports the Civil War*, pp. 531–33. The meeting of New York editors took place on 8 June 1863; its resolutions were reported in "Freedom of the Press," *American Annual Cyclopedia*, vol. 3 (1863), p. 425.

26. This is the conclusion that Mark Neeley reaches after an exhaustive consideration of federal records: *The Fate of Liberty: Abraham Lincoln and Civil Liberties* (New York: Oxford University Press, 1991).

27. Schroth, *Eagle*, p. 64; Douglas Fermer, *James Gordon Bennett and the New York Herald: A Study of Editorial Opinion in the Civil War Era, 1854–1867* (New York: St. Martin's Press, 1986), pp. 187–89, argues convincingly that the crowd outside the New York *Herald* was quite hostile, and actually forced a change in editorial policy, though Bennett himself denied that he came to support the Lincoln administration out of any but the most principled motives. A mob also demanded a flag display by the Philadelphia *Palmetto Flag*: Harper, *Lincoln*, p. 109. For other examples of mobs forcing displays of loyalty, see ibid., pp. 154, 156; Alan A. Siegel, *For the Glory of the Union: Myth, Reality, and the Media in Civil War New Jersey* (Rutherford: Fairleigh Dickinson University Press, 1984), pp. 52–53.

28. The equipment was restored after Millward failed to secure an indictment; eventually, he was successfully sued for damages, illustrating one disadvantage to legal action as opposed to outright mobbing: Ray H. Abrams, "The *Jeffersonian*: Copperhead Newspaper," *Pennsylvania Magazine of History and Biography* 57 (1933): 260–83; Harper, *Lincoln*, p. 112.

29. Frank L. Klement, *Dark Lanterns: Secret Political Societies, Conspiracies, and Treason Trials in the Civil War* (Baton Rouge: Louisiana State University Press, 1984), p. 93.

30. The best account, though a self-serving one, is in P. T. Barnum, *Struggles and Triumphs* (1869 ed.; reprint, New York: Arno Press), pp. 611–14.

31. The *American Annual Cyclopedia* article on "Freedom of the Press" for 1862 (vol. 2)

remarked: "There has been no interference with the usual publications of the press during 1862, beyond the orders to abstain from publishing information of intended military movements" (p. 480). Likewise, Jon Paul Dilts, in his case study of Indiana, found no incidents of violence in 1862, after two in 1861, and before six in 1863, six in 1864, and one in 1865: "Testing Siebert's Proposition in Civil War Indiana," *Journalism Quarterly* 63 (1986): 365–68.

32. Ironically, according to Reed W. Smith, this action enhanced Medary's prestige among Ohioans: "The Paradox of Samuel Medary, Copperhead Newspaper Publisher" (Paper presented at Association for Education in Journalism and Mass Communication [AEJMC] convention, Minneapolis, August 1990).

33. Harper, *Lincoln*, pp. 195–96, 241; Harper, *The Ohio Press in the Civil War* (Columbus: Ohio State University Press, 1961), pp. 12, 20.

34. Harper, *Lincoln*, p. 349; Dilts, "Testing Siebert"; Arnold M. Shankman, *The Pennsylvania Anti-War Movement, 1861–1865* (Rutherford, N.J.: Fairleigh Dickinson University Press, 1980), pp. 213–17.

35. Harper, *Lincoln*, p. 147; Marilyn McAdams Sibley, *Lone Stars and State Gazettes: Texas Newspapers Before the Civil War* (College Station: Texas A&M University Press, 1983), pp. 276–77.

36. See, for instance, the mobbings of the Galveston *Die Union*, a German paper, and the San Antonio *Express*: Sibley, *Lone Stars*, p. 326; Harper, *Lincoln*, p. 70. The Austin, Texas, *Southern Intelligencer* was forced out of business without a mobbing: Sibley, *Lone Stars*, p. 304. Also folding was the Wilmington, N.C., *Daily Herald*: Andrews, *South Reports the Civil War*, pp. 540–41.

37. William Hurlbert, who was known to have written for the New York *Times*. See J. L. Petigree to Mr. Morton, Charleston, 17 July 1861; Hurlbert to Confederate Congress, Richmond, 26 July 1861, *Official Records*, ser. 2, 2:1491–95; Harper, *Lincoln*, p. 64.

38. For a good case study of Harrison County, Texas, see Randolph Campbell, "Political Conflict within the Southern Consensus: Harrison County, Texas, 1850–1880," *Civil War History* 26 (1980): 218–39.

39. Andrews, *South Reports the Civil War*, pp. 104–5. E. Junius Foster of the Sherman, Texas, *Patriot* was "killed in 1862 as a result of his editorial comments on the violence that wracked north Texas at that time": Sibley, *Lone Stars*, p. 368.

40. Donald L. Shaw and Stephen W. Brauer, "Press Freedom and War Constraints: Case Testing Siebert's Proposition II," *Journalism Quarterly* 46 (Summer 1969): 244.

41. New York *Times*, 6 July 1863; Adrian Cook, *Armies of the Streets: The New York City Draft Riots of 1863* (Lexington: University Press of Kentucky, 1974), p. 53.

42. The *Times* reported that "the feeling of the crowd was, on the whole, singularly happy. Occasionally some ill-natured fellow would blurt out his profane expression of opinion concerning the injustice of the affair, . . . others would make small puns upon inviting names, and others would stare with vacant stupidity as name after name was given out, and person after person in his acquaintance was put down upon the list of the 'soldiery.'" "The Draft," 12 July 1863.

43. New York *Times*, 15 July 1863; Cook, *Armies of the Streets*.

44. New York *Times*, 14 July 1863; Cook, *Armies of the Streets*, pp. 87–90.

45. New York *Times*, 16 July 1863; Ellen Leonard, *Three Days' Reign of Terror, or the July Riots in 1863, in New York* (New York: 1867), pp. 4–5; Cook, *Armies of the Streets*, pp. 66, 91, 105–8, 123–25.

46. New York *Times*, 14, 16 July 1863; Siegal, *Glory of the Union*, p. 51; Harper, *Lincoln*, pp. 274–75.

47. Editorial, "The Mob and the Press," New York *Times*, 14 July 1863.

48. For attacks on African-Americans, see Cook, *Armies of the Streets*, pp. 77–85, 97–100, 133–36, 139–45. For attacks on $300 men, see ibid., p. 117.

49. There is an interesting dispute on this question of incorporation, that is, whether the Fourteenth Amendment specifically was intended to incorporate the Bill of Rights (apply it to state governments), or whether its subsequent incorporation was an act of judicial legislation that could and should be rolled back. The argument against incorporation has been popular among political conservatives recently, and has been stated most influentially in scholarly form by Raoul Berger in *Government by Judiciary: The Transformation of the Fourteenth Amendment* (Cambridge: Harvard University Press, 1977). Berger's thesis downplays the antislavery origins of the post–Civil War amendments, a history recounted in Jacobus ten Broek's classic *Equal Under Law* (New York: Collier, 1965). An understanding of the antislavery mentality of the amendments' framers supports the notion that they intended incorporation, as is argued forcefully in Michael Curtis, *No State Shall Abridge: The Fourteenth Amendment and the Bill of Rights* (Durham: Duke University Press, 1986), and in Harold M. Hyman and William M. Wiecek, *Equal Justice Under Law: Constitutional Development, 1835–1875* (New York: Harper & Row, 1982), pp. 386–438. See also Eric Foner, *Reconstruction: America's Unfinished Revolution, 1863–1877* (New York: Harper, 1988), pp. 231–36.

50. This is Eric Foner's phrase: *Reconstruction: America's Unfinished Revolution.*

51. Dan T. Carter, *When the War Was Over: The Failure of Self-Reconstruction in the South, 1865–1867* (Baton Rouge: Louisiana State University Press, 1985), pp. 6–23.

52. Barry Crouch, "A Spirit of Lawlessness: White Violence, Texas Blacks, 1865–1868," *Journal of Social History* 18 (1984): 217–32.

53. Foner, *Reconstruction*, pp. 119–23; William E. Parrish, Charles T. Jones, Jr., and Lawrence O. Christensen, *Missouri: The Heart of the Nation* (St. Louis: Forum Press, 1980), pp. 106–7; W. E. B. Dubois, *Black Reconstruction* (Millwood, N.J.: Kraus-Thompson Organization, 1976), pp. 674–84; Allen W. Trelease, *Reconstruction: The Great Experiment* (New York: Harper & Row, 1971), pp. 161–74.

54. Melinda Meek Hennessey, "Racial Violence during Reconstruction: The 1876 Riots in Charleston and Cainhoy," *South Carolina Historical Magazine* 86, no. 2 (1985): 100–101. See also Michael Perman, *Reunion Without Compromise: The South and Reconstruction, 1865–1868* (Cambridge: Cambridge University Press, 1973), pp. 192, 230; Trelease, *Reconstruction*, pp. 153–60.

55. Foner, *Reconstruction*, pp. 340–45; Trelease, *Reconstruction*, p. 176; Michael Perman, *Road to Redemption: Southern Politics, 1869–1879* (Chapel Hill: University of North Carolina Press, 1984), pp. 159–70; Melinda Meek Hennessey, "Political Terrorism in the Black Belt: The Eutaw Riot," *Alabama Review* 33, no. 1 (1980): 35–48.

56. Foner, *Reconstruction*, p. 350. Foner also notes that although government printing contracts were available as long as Republican governments were in power, a single electoral defeat ended this means of support. On African-American illiteracy, note the remarks of Robert Flournoy, editor of the Pontotoc County, Miss., *Equal Rights*, to the select committee investigating the activities of the Ku Klux Klan in 1870: "They cannot read. Many of them would have taken my paper, and said to me that they wanted to do so, but neither themselves or their children could read it. I said to them it would be foolish to take the paper when they could not read it." Apparently, even unlettered African-Americans saw supporting the Republican paper as a significant political act. Joint Select Committee to Inquire into the Condition of Affairs in the Late Insurrectionary States, 42d Congress, 2d session, 1872 (hereafter KKK Committee), *Hearings*, Mississippi, pt. 1, 2:90.

57. See Flournoy's testimony, KKK Committee *Hearings*, Mississippi, pt. 1, 2:82–85, 88, 91–93. The attack on *Equal Rights* is attributed to Flournoy's advocacy of integrated schooling in Foner, *Reconstruction*, p. 303.

Chapter Six

1. The rise of a Darwinian mentality is the theme of George M. Frederickson, *The Inner Civil War: Intellectuals and the Crisis of the Union* (New York: Harper & Row, 1965). The demise of island communities is the theme of Robert Wiebe, *The Search for Order, 1877–1920* (New York: Hill & Wang, 1967).

2. This analysis of the ideology of social mobility is presented cogently in Stephan Thernstrom, *Poverty and Progress* (Cambridge: Harvard University Press, 1973). Sean Wilentz describes the reactions of artisans to the collapse of republican notions of a just economy: *Chants Democratic: New York City and the Rise of the American Working Class, 1789–1850* (New York: Oxford University Press, 1984).

3. With the exception of a minority of thinkers like Franz Boas. See George W. Stocking, Jr., *Race, Culture, and Evolution: Essays in the History of Anthropology* (Chicago: University of Chicago Press, 1982).

4. John Higham, *Strangers in the Land: Patterns of American Nativism, 1860–1925*, 2d ed. (New York: Atheneum, 1972).

5. Alfred D. Chandler, Jr., *The Visible Hand: The Managerial Revolution in American Business* (Cambridge: Harvard University Press, Belknap Press, 1973).

6. Despite the perceptions of conservative commentators. Note, for instance, the grouping of the NAACP, one of the more conservative African-American groups, with left-wing news sources in L. Brent Bozell and Brent H. Baker, eds., *And That's The Way It Isn't: A Reference Guide to Media Bias* (Alexandria, Va.: Media Research Center, 1990).

7. Eric Foner, *Reconstruction: America's Unfinished Revolution, 1863–1877* (New York: Harper, 1988), p. 350; Henry Louis Suggs, Jr., "Introduction: Origins of the Black Press in the South," in Suggs, ed., *The Black Press in the South, 1865–1979* (Westport, Conn.: Greenwood Press, 1983), pp. 3–4; Julius E. Thompson, *The Black Press in Mississippi, 1865–1985: A Directory* (West Cornwall, Conn.: Locust Hill Press, 1988), p. xiii; I. Garland Penn, *The Afro-American Press and Its Editors* (New York: Arno Press, 1969), pp. 100–104; testimony of Robert Flournoy, Joint Select Committee to Inquire into the Condition of Affairs in the Late Insurrectionary States, 42d Congress, second session, 1972 (hereafter KKK Committee) *Hearings*, Mississippi, pt. 1, 2:90.

8. Emma Lou Thornbrough, comp., *Black Reconstructionists* (Englewood Cliffs, N.J.: Prentice-Hall, 1972), pp. 124, 173–74, 176.

9. Quoted in Henry Clay Warmoth, *War, Politics, and Reconstruction: Stormy Days in Louisiana* (New York: Macmillan, 1930), p. 45.

10. Foner, *Reconstruction*, pp. 63–66; Warmoth, *War, Politics, and Reconstruction*, pp. 51–58.

11. Roger Shugg, *Origins of Class Struggle in Louisiana: A Social History of White Farmers and Laborers During Slavery and After* (Baton Rouge: Louisiana State University Press, 1939), p. 343.

12. "The Bag to Hold," *Opelousas Courier*, 16 May 1868; Foner, *Reconstruction*, p. 282; *Progress*, 7 September, 3 August 1867.

13. Barry Crouch, "A Spirit of Lawlessness: White Violence, Texas Blacks, 1865–1868," *Journal of Social History* 18 (1984), pp. 217–32.

14. Melinda Meek Hennessey, "Racial Violence during Reconstruction: The 1876 Riots

in Charleston and Cainhoy," *South Carolina Historical Magazine* 86, no. 2 (1985), counts thirty-three "major" riots, that is, riots in which more than one death occurred. Over a third of these took place within two weeks of an election, and over half "began with an attempt by whites to break up a black political meeting or to keep blacks from voting" (pp. 100–101). For more on Reconstruction-era race riots, see Melinda Meek Hennessey, "Political Terrorism in the Black Belts: The Eutaw Riot," *Alabama Review* 33, no. 1 (1980): 35–48; Allen W. Trelease, ed., *Reconstruction: The Great Experiment* (New York: Harper, 1971), pp. 153–74; Michael Perman, *Reunion Without Compromise: The South and Reconstruction, 1865–1868* (Cambridge: Cambridge University Press, 1973), pp. 192, 230.

15. W. E. B. DuBois, *Black Reconstruction* (New York: Harcourt Brace, 1935), pp. 674–84; Foner, *Reconstruction*, pp. 119–23; Dan T. Carter, *When the War Was Over: The Failure of Self-Reconstruction in the South, 1865–1867* (Baton Rouge: Louisiana State University Press, 1985), pp. 6–23; William E. Parrish, *Missouri Under Radical Rule, 1865–1870* (Columbia: University of Missouri Press, 1965), pp. 106–7.

16. Foner, *Reconstruction*, pp. 340–45.

17. Ibid., pp. 425–59; George C. Rable, *But There Was No Peace: The Role of Violence in the Politics of Reconstruction* (Athens: University of Georgia Press, 1984), pp. 95–97. On the Civil War–era popularity of secret political societies, see Frank L. Klement, *Dark Lanterns: Secret Political Societies, Conspiracies, and Treason Trials in the Civil War* (Baton Rouge: Louisiana State University Press, 1984).

18. On targets of Klan violence, see Herbert Shapiro, *White Violence and Black Response: From Reconstruction to Montgomery* (Amherst: University of Massachusetts Press, 1988), pp. 8–10; Wyn Craig Wade, *The Fiery Cross: The Ku Klux Klan in America* (New York: Simon & Schuster, 1987), pp. 62–79. For Klan attacks on specifically preachers and members of the Methodist Episcopal Church, see KKK Committee *Hearings*, pt. 1, pp. 70–73, 8:111–45. For attacks against the Mississippi free schools for blacks, see ibid., pt. 1, 73–80. On election-related Klan violence, see Trelease, *Reconstruction*, pp. 176, 181–82, 183–85; Wade, *Fiery Cross*, pp. 48–49, 83–85; Shapiro, *White Violence*, pp. 11–13. On reluctance of law enforcement and especially federal officials, see ibid., pp. 14–16; Foner, *Reconstruction*, pp. 343–45.

19. Wade, *Fiery Cross*, p. 90; Michael Perman, *The Road to Redemption: Southern Politics, 1869–1879* (Chapel Hill: University of North Carolina Press, 1984), pp. 159–70.

20. Figures taken from Foner, *Reconstruction*, pp. 425–59.

21. Examples of Reconstruction-era violence against black and black-allied Republican papers. New Orleans *L'Union* threatened: Jean-Charles Houzeau, *My Passage at the New Orleans Tribune: A Memoir of the Civil War Era*, ed. David C. Rankin, trans. Gerard F. Denault (Baton Rouge: Louisiana State University Press, 1984), p. 71; Charles Vincent, *Black Legislators in Louisiana During Reconstruction* (Baton Rouge: Lousiana State University Press, 1976), pp. 16–24. Memphis rioters threaten the *Memphis Post* (1866): James H. Robinson, "A Social History of the Negro in Memphis and Shelby County" (Ph.D. diss., Yale University, 1934) p. 73. *Maryville* (Tenn.) *Republican* editors prevented from voting, harassed: Samuel Shannon, "Tennessee," in Suggs, ed., *Black Press*, pp. 316–18. Norfolk, Va., *True Southerner* smashed by a mob: Suggs, "Virginia," in Suggs, ed., *Black Press*, p. 379. Decatur, Ala., *Republican* editor chased out of town: Allen William Trelease, *White Terror: The Ku Klux Klan Conspiracy and Southern Reconstruction* (New York: Harper, 1971), p. 87. Robert W. Flournoy, editor of the Pontotoc, Miss., *Equal Rights*, in gunfight with the Klan: KKK Committee *Hearings*, Mississippi, pt. 1, 74–75, 2:82–85; Trelease, *Terror*, 294–95. Klansmen harass B. F. Sawyer, editor of the Rome, Ga., *Courier*: Trelease, *Terror*, p. 326. Pro-Klan editor Ryland Randolph of the Tuscaloosa, Ala., *Monitor* brawls with the editors of the local Republican *Reconstructionist*: Trelease, *Terror*, p. 86. Pierce

Burton, editor of the Demopolis, Ala., *Southern Republican*, beaten and chased out of town by the "Knights of the Black Cross": KKK Committee *Hearings*, Alabama; Trelease, *Terror*, p. 304. Klansmen mob Rutherford, N.C., *Star*: Trelease, *Terror*, pp. 343–47; KKK Committee *Hearings*, pt. 1, pp. 22–3.

22. Ted Tunnell, *Crucible of Reconstruction: War, Radicalism, and Race in Louisiana, 1862–1877* (Baton Rouge: Louisiana State University Press, 1984) p. 157.

23. Trelease, *Terror*, pp. 95–98, 129, 130; *Opelousas Courier*, 24 October 1868; Warmoth, *War, Politics, and Reconstruction*, pp. 65–66.

24. *New Orleans Republican*, 17 February 1868; *Opelousas Courier*, 22 February 1868; *Progress*, 22 February 1868.

25. Resolutions reprinted in *Opelousas Courier*, 29 February 1868.

26. "An Outrage" (editorial), ibid.

27. Ibid.

28. *Progress*, 29 February 1868.

29. See, for example, *Opelousas Courier*, 11 July 1868—references to Bentley's reports as "carpet-bagger mendacity and effrontery"; ibid., 22 August 1868—references to Bentley et al. as "unscrupulous mountebanks and renegade scalawags."

30. "A Grand Republican Rally," *Progress*, 19 September 1868. A couple of weeks earlier, the *Opelousas Courier* had carried a report of a similar rally at which Bentley had spoken, prompting "that frenzied and indecent applause which characterizes him and his disciples" ("Let Us Have Peace," 5 September 1868). It seems that Democrats sought to portray Republican organizing as a threat to political and social order, thus playing upon perhaps understandable, though certainly exaggerated, fears of armed insurrection by blacks. In an article reprinted from the *New Orleans Bee*, it was acknowledged that "measures have been taken for self-defense . . . , but those measures may never be put into operation unless the Radicals themselves give the provocation" (*Opelousas Courier*, 15 August 1868).

31. *Opelousas Courier*, 26 September 1868.

32. "Intimidation," *Progress*, 5 September 1868.

33. The resolutions were printed in both the *Progress* and the *Opelousas Courier* of 26 September 1868.

34. KKK Committee *Hearings*, pt. 1, p. 22, 14:73–94; *Opelousas Courier*, 3 October 1868; Warmoth, *War, Politics, and Reconstruction*, p. 67; DuBois, *Black Reconstruction*, p. 681; Trelease, *Terror*, pp. 128–29; Rable, *No Peace*, pp. 75–76; Carolyn E. Delatte, "The St. Landry Riot: A Forgotten Incident of Reconstruction Violence," *Louisiana History* 17 (Winter 1976): 41–49; Tunnell, *Crucible of Reconstruction*, p. 156; Joseph G. Dawson III, *Army Generals and Reconstruction: Louisiana, 1862–1877* (Baton Rouge: Louisiana State University Press, 1982) pp. 86–87.

35. Franklin, La., *Planter's Banner*, 10 October 1868. The New Orleans *Picayune* headlined its article on the riot, in the multiple-deck convention of the time, NEGRO RISING IN ST. LANDRY/PROGRAM OF SPOLIATION, RAPINE, CONFLAGRATION, AND MURDER/ THE RADICAL EDITOR A SOCIAL FIREBRAND/CONCILIATORY POLICY OF THE WHITES/OPELOUSAS INVESTED BY THE NEGROES/THEY ARE DRIVEN BACK AND DISARMED. Joe Gray Taylor, *Lousiana Reconstructed: 1863–1877* (Baton Rouge: Louisiana State University Press, 1974) pp. 168–69.

36. KKK Committee *Hearing*, pt. 1, p. 22; *Opelousas Courier*, 24 October 1868; Foner, *Reconstruction*, p. 282.

37. James Elbert Cutler pointed out as early as 1905 the "statistics, however, cannot be made to show that more than thirty-four per cent of the negroes lynched in the South during the last twenty-two years have been lynched for the crime of rape, either attempted, alleged, or actually committed.": *Lynch Law: An Investigation into the History of Lynch-*

ing in the United States (New York: Longmans, 1905), pp. 177–78; Arthur F. Raper, "Lynching and Racial Exploitation," in Frank Shay, ed., *Judge Lynch: His First Hundred Years* (Montclair, N.J.: Patterson Smith, 1969), p. xxi; Walter Francis White, *Rope and Faggot* (New York: Arno Press, 1969), chap. 4, esp. p. 76. More recently, Michael R. Belknap has argued that lynching was primarily a tool used by whites "to maintain their traditional dominance over blacks," a form of terrorism: "The brutality often associated with this form of murder was a consequence of its purpose." In addition, lynching was "a means of reuniting whites across class lines." *Federal Law and Southern Order: Racial Violence and Constitutional Conflict in the Post-Brown South* (Athens: University of Georgia Press, 1987), pp. 6–8.

38. Thornbrough, "Negro Newspapers," p. 468.

39. On the rise of the Klan in the years following World War I and on the controversy surrounding *Birth of a Nation*, see Wade, *Fiery Cross*, esp. p. 165; Comer Vann Woodward, *Strange Career of Jim Crow*, 2d rev. ed. (New York: Oxford University Press, 1966), p. 87.

40. Charles Crowe, "Racial Violence and Social Reform: Origins of the Atlanta Riot of 1906," *Journal of Negro History* 53 (1968), esp. pp. 242, 254; Raper, in his introduction to Shay, *Judge Lynch*, contends that "it is by no means an accident that the same decades of Southern history which record the greatest decrease in the number of lynchings also record numerous statutes and ordinances and community practices directly and indirectly prescribing the Negro's working and living conditions" (p. xviii). J. Morgan Kousser notes that "disfranchisement was a typically Progressive reform": *The Shaping of Southern Politics: Suffrage Restriction and the Shaping of the One-Party South, 1880–1910* (New Haven: Yale University Press, 1974), p. 190.

41. Thornbrough, "Negro Newspaper," pp. 472–78, 87; Teresa C. Klassen and Owen V. Johnson argue for an early (late 1890s) birth of a small-town activist press: "Sharpening of the *Blade*: Black Consciousness in Kansas, 1892–97," *Journalism Quarterly* 63 (1986): 298–304; Martin E. Dann, ed., *The Black Press, 1827–1890: The Quest for National Identity* (New York: Putnam, 1970), p. 8, and Charlotte G. O'Kelly, "Black Newspapers and the Black Protest Movement: their Historical Relationship, 1827–1945," *Phylon* 43 (1982)," pp. 5–7, argue that the black press was activist from the start. E. Franklin Frazier in his classic *Black Bourgeoisie, 1894–1962* (Glencoe, Ill.: Free Press, 1957) and Gunnar Myrdal in *An American Dilemma: The Negro Problem and Modern Democracy* (New York: Pantheon, 1975) both characterize the black press as characteristically genteel, elitist, accommodationist, and noncontroversial. On partisanism, see Nudie E. Williams, "Black Newspapers and the Exodusters" (Ph.D. diss., Oklahoma State University, 1977), pp. 188–89. Thornbrough notes that in the Ayers newspaper directory of 1914, two-thirds of black newspapers claimed a Republican party affiliation: "Negro Press," 478–82. On the importance of northern-based national papers, see ibid., p. 476. On the importance of Booker T. Washington, see ibid., pp. 482–85; O'Kelly, "Black Newspapers," p. 3; August Meier, "Booker T. Washington and the Negro Press with Special Reference to the *Colored American*," *Journal of Negro History*, 39 (1953): 67–90; John Dittmer, *Black Georgia in the Progressive Era, 1900–1920* (Urbana: University of Illinois Press, 1980), p. 163; Abby Arthur Johnson and Ronald M. Johnson, "Away from Accommodation: Radical Editors and Protest Journalism, 1900–1910," *Journal of Negro History* 62 (1979): 325–38.

42. In 1888 editor John Mitchell of the Richmond, Va., *Planet* received death threats for investigating a lynching; in 1892 a mob stormed the Selma, Ala., *Independent* "because the editor said that Negroes were just as capable of governing as the white man." Suggs, "Virginia," in Suggs, *Black Press*, p. 395; Joseph Matt Brittain, "Negro Suffrage and Politics in Alabama Since 1870" (Ph.D. diss., Indiana University, 1958), pp. 69–70.

43. For a characteristic claim "to be the outspoken friend of the negro" except "when

the negro undertakes to control and run the Government, or to demand social admixture, as now and then one does," see "From Boston," *Montgomery Daily Advertiser*, 16 July 1887.

44. *Montgomery Daily Advertiser*, 16 August 1887.

45. The events that followed the editorial are described in Allen Woodrow Jones, "Alabama," in Suggs, *Black Press*, pp. 29–30, and Jones, "The Black Press in the 'New South': Jesse C. Duke's Struggle for Justice and Equality," *Journal of Negro History* 64 (1979): 221–25.

46. "Across the Line," *Montgomery Daily Advertiser*, 16 August 1887.

47. "Colored Citizens," ibid., 17 August 1887.

48. "A Card from Dr. Dorsette," ibid.

49. Jones, "Alabama," pp. 31–33; Jones, "Black Press: Jesse Duke," p. 225; also recently threatened were H. Thweat, editor of the Tuskegee *Black Belt*, and a Mr. Harvey, who edited a black paper in Columbus, Ga., according to an excerpt from the *Tuskegee News* reprinted in the *Montgomery Daily Advertiser*, 18 August 1887.

50. "The Duke Case," *Montgomery Daily Advertiser*, 17 August 1887.

51. Shapiro, *White Violence*, pp. 54–55; Thomas C. Holt, "The Lonely Warrior: Ida B. Wells and the Struggle for Black Leadership," in John Hope Franklin and August Meier, eds., *Black Leaders of the Twentieth Century* (Urbana: University of Illinois Press, 1982).

52. Ida B. Wells Barnett, *Crusade for Justice: The Autobiography of Ida B. Wells*, ed. Alfreda M. Duster (Chicago: University of Chicago Press, 1970), pp. 35, 38–41; Holt, "Lonely Warrior"; David M. Tucker, "Miss Ida B. Wells and the Memphis Lynchings," *Phylon* 32, no. 2 (1971): 112–13.

53. Holt, "Lonely Warrior"; Wells Barnett, *Crusade*, pp. 36–37; Tucker, "Wells," pp. 113–14; Samuel Shannon, "Tennessee," in Suggs, ed., *Black Press*, pp. 325–26.

54. Wells Barnett, *Crusade*, pp. 47–51; Tucker, "Wells," p. 116.

55. Stories of this sort in the Memphis *Appeal-Avalanche* from one week in May include "Three Dark Necks Snap," about a Birmingham, Ala., lynching tied to rape, 17 May; "Negro Necks Cracking," also rape, in Clarksville, Ga., 18 May; "Black Necks Cracking," about several rape-related lynchings, 20 May; "Weems is Wanted," about an alleged black rapist, 21 May.

56. See, for example, "The Logic of the Bigot," 4 April 1892, and "Justice to the Negro," 12 April 1892, ibid.

57. Shannon, "Tennessee," p. 326; Wells Barnett, *Crusade*, pp. 53–59.

58. Wells Barnett, *Crusade*, p. 64.

59. Shapiro, *White Violence*, p. 55; Holt, "Lonely Warrior"; Tucker, "Wells," pp. 116–17; Shannon, "Tennessee," p. 326.

60. Wells Barnett, *Crusade*, p. 66.

61. Ibid., pp. 66, 59–63; Tucker, "Wells," pp. 116–17; Shapiro, *White Violence*, pp. 56–58; Shannon, "Tennessee," pp. 326–27; Sharon Murphy, *Other Voices: Black, Chicano, and American Indian Press* (Dayton, Ohio: Pflaum/Standard, 1974), p. 27; [Williams], J. Helen Goldbeck, ed., *A Survey of Blacks' Response to Lynching* (Las Vegas, N.M.: Highlands Media Materials Center, 1973), p. 5.

62. Holt, "Lonely Warrior."

63. "The White and Colored Races," *Appeal-Avalanche*, 8 June 1892.

64. "Colored Folk Protest," *Appeal-Avalanche*, 30 June 1892.

65. Kousser notes that North Carolina's liberal election laws, the fairest in the South at the time, resulted in very high voting turnouts for statewide elections—85.4 percent of eligible voters in 1896: *Shaping of Southern Politics*, pp. 183–87.

66. The standard work on North Carolina Populism is Helen G. Edmonds, *The Negro*

and Fusion Politics in North Carolina, 1894–1901 (Chapel Hill: University of North Carolina Press, 1951). See also Dwight B. Billings, Jr., *Planters and the Making of a "New South": Class, Politics, and Development in North Carolina, 1865–1900* (Chapel Hill: University of North Carolina Press, 1979), pp. 156–191; William A. Mabry, "The Negro in North Carolina Politics since Reconstruction," *Historical Papers of the Trinity College Historical Society*, ser. 23 (1940), pp. 32–40; Eric Anderson, *Race and Politics in North Carolina: The Black Second, 1872–1901* (Baton Rouge: Louisiana State University Press, 1981).

67. 17 July 1898.

68. H. Leon Prather, *We Have Taken a City: Wilmington Racial Massacre and Coup of 1898* (Rutherford, N.J.: Fairleigh Dickinson University Press, 1983), pp. 22–26, 31–48; Mabry, "Negro in North Carolina Politics," pp. 52–53; Henry L. West, "The Race War in North Carolina," *Forum* 26 (January 1899): 578–91; Edmonds, *Negro and Fusion Politics*, pp. 163–64.

69. Prather, *We Have Taken a City*, pp. 22–26; Mabry, "Negro in North Carolina," pp. 44–46, 52–53; West, "Race War"; Josephus Daniels, *Editor in Politics* (Chapel Hill: University of North Carolina Press, 1941), p. 288. Kousser notes that business interests were also alarmed by the Populist legislative program that called for added funding for services and state ownership of railroads: *Shaping of Southern Politics*, pp. 186–87.

70. For general accounts of the white supremacy campaign, see H. Leon Prather, *Resurgent Politics and Educational Progressivism in the New South: North Carolina, 1890–1913* (Madison, N.J.: Fairleigh Dickinson University Press, 1979), pp. 133–72; J. G. de Roulhac Hamilton, *North Carolina since 1860*, vol. 3 of *History of North Carolina* (Chapel Hill: University of North Carolina Press, 1919), pp. 28–29.

71. All quotations are from *Star* editorials: "There Will Be More," 23 July 1898; 24, 26, 28, 30, 31 July, 3 August 1898; "The Color Line," 9 August 1898; "Will They Oust the White Man?" 7 September 1898.

72. For the general argument that white government was the best safeguard for African-Americans, see "A White Man's Country," *Star*, 18 August 1898; a typically sensationalized account of a run-in between an African-American deputy and a white streetcar conductor is "Outrageous Affair," ibid. 16 August 1898. In the two weeks between 9 and 23 August, the *Star* printed nine stories about lynchings.

73. "Opening the Campaign," *Star*, 16 July 1898.

74. "Politics in Robeson," 31 July; "White Men's Rally," 4 August, "White Supremacy," 27 August 1898.

75. Daniels, *Editor in Politics*, p. 302.

76. Prather, *Resurgent Politics*, pp. 151–53; Prather, *We Have Taken a City*, pp. 68–75; Henry Lewis Suggs and Bernardine Moses Duncan, "North Carolina," in Suggs, ed., *Black Press*, pp. 266–67.

77. The editorial first was reprinted under the headline "Vile and Villainous" in the *Star* on 23 August; it was reprinted daily thereafter. Edmonds argues that the editorial would not have attracted attention had Josephus Daniels not publicized it: *Negro and Fusion Politics*, p. 147.

78. Prather, *We Have Taken a City*, p. 73; Daniels, *Editor in Politics*, p. 287; "County Executive Committee," *Star*, 25 August 1898; "Riotous Negroes," ibid. As a result of this disturbance, Manly's landlord forced him to relocate the *Record* office: "Daily Record on the Move," ibid. 26 August 1898; Prather, *We Have Taken a City*, pp. 68–75.

79. "The Recent Outrage," *Star*, 24 August 1898.

80. The quotation is from an affidavit from W. L. DeRosset et al., printed in "A Horrid Slander," *Star*, 30 August 1898. The affidavit and the general strategy of pinning the editorial on the Republicans is discussed in Daniels, *Editor in Politics*, p. 289. On this and

other aspects of the Wilmington riot, the novel *Marrow of Tradition*, by African-American author Charles W. Chesnutt (1901; reprint, Ann Arbor: University of Michigan Press, 1969), is illuminating.

81. The front page of the *Star* for 25 August, for instance, carried both the qualified support of "The Negro Ministers of Wilmington" and the denunciation of the Republican County Executive Committee. See the stories "Getting Worse and Worse" and "County Executive Committee."

82. Daniels, *Editor in Politics*, p. 286; Prather, *We Have Taken a City*, p. 73. On the tactic of repudiation generally, an eloquent summary—albeit a partial one—is an editorial, "Standing by Their Organ," *Star*, 15 September 1898. In an interesting and somewhat related case, the African Methodist Episcopal *Church Quarterly*, edited by John Dancy, U.S. Customs collector for the Port of Wilmington, printed an article by Bishop Hood discussing and approving of racial intermarriage. The *Star* noted this in an article titled "Almost as Bad as Negro Manly," 9 October 1898. Dancy was forced to leave Wilmington in the aftermath of the riot of early November.

83. The Red Shirt stratagem first appeared in Mississippi in 1874 but was perfected in South Carolina by "Pitchfork" Ben Tillman, who imported it into North Carolina at a rally at Fayetteville on 21 October, where he addressed a crowd of seven to ten thousand: H. Leon Prather, Sr., "The Red Shirt Movement in North Carolina, 1898–1900," *Journal of Negro History* 62 (1977): 174–84. The Red Shirts are also discussed in Hamilton, *North Carolina*, p. 287; Daniels, *Editor in Politics*, p. 293; Raleigh *News and Observer*, 30 October, 3 November 1898, quoted in Hugh Talmage Leifler, ed., *North Carolina History: Told by Contemporaries*, 3d ed. (Chapel Hill: University of North Carolina Press, 1956) p. 398. Kousser cites evidence of gentry dominance among the Red Shirts: *Shaping of Southern Politics*, pp. 188–89.

84. Thad Stem, *The Tar Heel Press* (Southport: North Carolina Press Association, 1973), p. 124; Daniels, *Editor in Politics*, pp. 293, 307.

85. Mabry, "Negro in North Carolina Politics," pp. 52–53.

86. Quoted in Daniels, *Editor in Politics*, p. 301.

87. "Citizens Aroused: Large Mass Meeting of Business Men," *Star*, 10 November 1898; Hamilton, *North Carolina*, p. 294.

88. There is strong evidence that the rioters were motivated by class concerns as well as race. Rioters were led by members of the business class, who proudly lent their names to the mass meetings that preceded the fighting. Those who signed the resolutions of these meetings tended to come disproportionately from the ranks of professionals and businessmen: see Hayumi Higuchi, "White Supremacy in the Cape Fear: The Wilmington Affair of 1898" (Master's thesis, University of North Carolina, 1980); Shapiro, *White Violence*, pp. 65–75. The argument here is that African-Americans locally, like the alliance of poor whites and African-Americans statewide, threatened to displace the traditional white leadership class; the race argument was a mask for a program to recapture economic power. See Paul D. Escott, *Many Excellent People: Power and Privilege in North Carolina, 1850–1900* (Chapel Hill: University of North Carolina Press, 1985), xviii, 254–55; West, "Race War." Prather concedes that "it would, indeed, be a mistake to assume that the race riot of 1898 was only politically oriented" (*We Have Taken a City*, p. 26). Still, Eric Anderson insists that race was the central salient factor: *Race and Politics*, pp. 252–79. In any event, it is clear that the politics of race allowed whites to conceal or divert attention from the politics of class; although an economic agenda may have been central to (some) white leaders (see, for instance, the resolutions of Wilmington's Chamber of Commerce in "Strong Resolutions," *Star*, 7 October 1898), it was the specter of African-American power-holding and the even more emotionally charged issue of miscegenation that impelled the white

electorate, as well as the crowds at rallies and the ranks of Red Shirts and the body of the rioters in Wilmington.

89. Direct quotation from "Bloody Conflict with Negroes," *Star*, 11 November 1898. See also Edmonds, *The Negro and Fusion Politics*; Prather, *We Have Taken a City*; Hamilton, *North Carolina*, pp. 295–97; Michael Wallace, "The Uses of Violence in American History," *American Scholar* 40 (1970–1972): 87; Daniels, *Editor in Politics*, pp. 307–10; Mabry, "Negro in North Carolina Politics," pp. 54–56.

90. On the aftermath of the campaign and riot, see Prather, *Resurgent Politics*, pp. 173–96; voting statistics are taken from Billings, *Planters*, p. 198.

91. Crowe, "Racial Violence," p. 243.

92. On social Darwinism, see Richard Hofstadter, *Social Darwinism in American Thought, 1860–1915* (Philadelphia: University of Pennsylvania Press, 1944). On "scientific" racism, see Higham, *Strangers in the Land*; Thomas F. Gossett, *Race: The History of an Idea in America* (Dallas: Southern Methodist University Press, 1963).

93. Dittmer, *Black Georgia*, p. 187; Murphy, *Other Voices*, p. 56; Lee Finkle, *Forum for Protest: The Black Press During World War II* (Rutherford, N.J.: Fairleigh Dickinson University Press, 1975), pp. 64–65. For attacks on southern agents of northern papers, see Frederick Detweiler, *The Negro Press in the United States* (Chicago: University of Chicago Press, 1922), pp. 20, 139–40, 153–55; Roland E. Wolsely, *The Black Press U.S.A.* (Ames: Iowa State University Press, 1972) p. 38.

94. Dittmer, *Black Georgia*, pp. 123–31.

95. Ibid., pp. 166–67; Johnson and Johnson, "Away from Accommodation," pp. 331–32; "The Colored Magazine in America," *Crisis* 5 (November 1912): 33–34; "Opinion," ibid. (December 1912): 72; Penelope Bullock, *The Afro-American Periodical Press, 1838–1909* (Baton Rouge: Louisiana State University Press, 1981), p. 123.

96. Similarly, William Jefferson White, editor of the Augusta *Georgia Baptist*, was threatened during the riot by Klansmen. White had been threatened earlier and would be threatened again some years after the riot, when two hundred whites marched on his office after he'd called a lynched black man a "martyr in defense of female virtue." In that case, blacks defended the building, and the crisis passed after White issued a public apology: Dittmer, *Black Georgia*, pp. 164–65. In another similar case, in Onancock, Virginia, during rioting apparently rooted in black insistence on higher wages for agricultural labor, James D. Uzzle, publisher of the *Peninsula Times*, fired on a gang of whites who attacked him on the street, injuring one. In the aftermath, his printing office was burned to the ground by a mob: Brooks Miles Barnes, "The Onancock Race Riot of 1907," *Virginia Magazine of History and Biography* 92 (1984): 336–51.

97. Shapiro, *White Violence*, pp. 149–56.

98. Scott Ellsworth, *Death in a Promised Land: The Tulsa Race Riot of 1921* (Baton Rouge: Louisiana State University Press, 1982), pp. 25–33.

99. Ibid., pp. 7–14.

100. *Tulsa Star*, 25 September 1920, 20 January 1921; Williams, "Black Newspapers," pp. 23–24.

101. Shapiro, *White Violence*, pp. 180–85; Ellsworth, *Death in a Promised Land*, pp. 45–70, 104–6; Allen D. Grimshaw, "Three Cases of Racial Violence in the United States," in Grimshaw, ed., *Racial Violence in the United States* (Chicago: University of Chicago Press, 1969), pp. 105–8; Williams, "Black Newspapers," pp. 156–57. Two other noteworthy riots were sparked by African-American newspapers: one in Houston, Texas, and one in Longview, Texas: Detweiler, *Negro Press*, p. 152; Neil A. Wynn, *From Progressivism to Prosperity: World War I and American Society* (New York: Holmes and Meier, 1986) p. 189.

102. Fisk University, *Monthly Summary of Events and Trends in Race Relations* 1, no. 6 (January 1944), p. 2; Shapiro, *White Violence*, p. 337. Of these incidents, 46 percent were in the South and 42 percent in the North (the rest were on the West Coast); southern incidents frequently involved black soldiers and "social etiquette"; northern incidents often involved housing and labor.

103. Harvard Sitkoff, "Racial Militancy and Interracial Violence in the Second World War," *Journal of American History* 58 (1971): 661–81; Ralph N. Davis, "The Negro Newspapers and the War," *Sociology and Social Research* 27 (May–June 1943): 373–80. On federal action toward the African-American press generally, see Patrick Washburn, *A Question of Sedition: The Federal Government's Investigation of the Black Press during World War II* (New York: Oxford University Press, 1986).

104. Virginius Dabney, "Nearer and Nearer the Precipice," *Atlantic Monthly* 171 (January 1943): 91; Finkle, *Forum for Protest*, pp. 62–77.

105. Fisk University's *Monthly Summary* included a column reviewing the front-page contents of the nation's most important black newspapers, and remarked on several occasions in 1943 and 1944 that potentially divisive news was consistently downplayed: "The Front Page," vol. 1, no. 4 (November 1943): 22; vol. 1, no. 6 (January 1944): 22.

106. The black newspaper, after all, has generally been a conservative institution, often tied to white merchants and politicians, affiliated with black elites, and dedicated to a vision of race advancement as self-improvement along lines established by mainstream (white) society. Although black editors were often courageous, and thought of themselves as crusaders for justice, the black press as an institution came to supplement rather than supplant its white counterparts, and in the final analysis was reluctant to embrace bottom-up movements for change.

107. See Philip Gleason's essay in the *Harvard Encyclopedia of American Ethnic Groups*, ed. Stephan Thernstrom (Cambridge: Harvard University Press, 1980); Stephen Steinberg, *The Ethnic Myth: Race, Ethnicity, and Class in America*, rev. ed. (Boston: Beacon Press, 1989), p. 56; Andrew Hacker, *The End of an American Era* (New York: Atheneum, 1970), p. 14.

108. The most frequently mentioned examples of this "consensus" notion of the American character include Daniel Bell's *The End of Ideology* (Glencoe, Ill.: Free Press, 1962), and Daniel Boorstin's *The Americans*, 3 vols. (New York: Random House, 1973). Again, this is not a novel set of ideas—the gist of the myth of the American character can be found in Frederick Jackson Turner's writings on the frontier. What was new was the receptiveness to thinking about U.S. society that denied the salience of ethnic and, of course, class identity, matters that had stubbornly intruded in the official culture of the 1930s.

109. Julius Eric Thompson, "Mississippi," in Suggs, ed., *Black Press*, pp. 189–91; Henry Louis Suggs and Bernadine Moses Duncan, "North Carolina," ibid., pp. 271–72; Theodore Hemmingway, "South Carolina," ibid., pp. 302–3.

110. Calvin Smith, "Arkansas," ibid., p. 82.

111. Belknap, *Federal Law and Southern Order*, pp. 30, 138; Todd Gitlin, *The Sixties: Years of Hope, Days of Rage* (Toronto and New York: Bantam, 1987), pp. 128, 150–51. Attacks against sympathetic white media were not novel in the 1960s, of course. During the East St. Louis riot of 1917, policemen attacked white reporters and destroyed photographic equipment ("*East St. Luis Riots: Report of the Special Committee Authorized by Congress*," in Grimshaw, ed., *Racial Violence*, p. 69). In the 1920s, Julian Harris, son of Joel Chandler Harris of Uncle Remus fame, who won the Pulitzer Prize for his exposés of the KKK in his Columbus, Georgia, *Enquirer-Sun*, was repeatedly threatened with violence (White, *Rope and Faggot*, pp. 174–75; Wade, *Fiery Cross*, p. 202). A racist organization calling itself the Columbians made secret plans to flog editor Ralph McGill of the *Atlanta*

Constitution in 1946 (Shapiro, *White Violence*, p. 374). And in the late 1960s, news director Dick Sanders of television station WLBT in Jackson, Mississippi, a station famous for an FCC investigation into its failure to cover black issues fairly, received constant threats: "If I had put any more blacks on the air, those hotheads from Rankin County would have bombed the station." Fred W. Friendly, *The Good Guys, the Bad Guys, and the First Amendment: Free Speech vs. Fairness in Broadcasting* (New York: Random House, 1976), p. 94.

112. Networks were susceptible to such pressure because they relied in part on the loyalty of local station affiliates, including many in the South: Wade, *Fiery Cross*, p. 312.

113. This is one of the findings of the Kerner Commission: *Report of the U.S. National Advisory Commission on Civil Disorders* (New York: Dutton, 1968). Nor have these tensions disappeared, despite the post-1968 decline of rioting. Indeed, the objective conditions that sparked rioting have if anything intensified; the decline in actual collective violence is probably the result of improvements in policing and the erosion of the ghetto's "organizational infrastructure" as radical groups have been decimated and leaders either imprisoned or recruited into the middle class: Sandra J. Ball-Rokeach and James F. Short, Jr., "Collective Violence: The Redress of Grievance and Public Policy," in Lynn A. Curtis, ed., *American Violence and Public Policy: An Update of the National Commission on the Causes and Prevention of Violence* (New Haven: Yale University Press, 1985), pp. 159, 165–67.

114. On Los Angeles, see M. L. Stein, "No One Immune from Mob's Rage," *Editor and Publisher*, 9 May 1992, pp. 7–8; "LATS Hit by Rioting," ibid., 16 May 1992, pp. 45–46. In Atlanta, see Katherine Bishop, "Violence against Journalists Hampers Coverage of the Riots," New York *Times*, 1 May 1992. On Minneapolis, see Dirk Johnson, "When Rumor Mixes with Rage," ibid., 10 May 1992.

115. The Klan was especially active during Reconstruction, and then again during the 1920s, when Klansmen visited numerous black editors and papers, including the Birmingham, Alabama, *Baptist Leader* and the Houston, Texas, *Informer*: James Smallwood, "Texas," in Suggs, ed., *Black Press*, p. 363; Allen Woodrow Jones, "Alabama," ibid., p. 42. Ironically, in 1923, a bomb wrecked the offices of the Klan's own newspaper in Chicago: *New York Times*, 7 April 1923, p. 15; Higham, *Strangers in the Land*, p. 298.

116. Suggs, *Black Press*, p. ix; Wade, *Fiery Cross*, p. 395.

117. For example, see David Astor, "Columnist Is a 'Voice of the Opposition,'" *Editor and Publisher*, 6 December 1986, pp. 52–54 (about Les Payne of *Newsday*); James Hicks, "Missing Pages," *Gannett Foundation Magazine*, Summer 1989, pp. 12–15 (about Wallace Terry's forthcoming book of the same name).

118. *New York Times*, 26, 28 January 1991. Wade quotes a scoring system for members of The Order aspiring to the status of full "Aryan Warrior": one point is awarded for the assassination of the president, 1/5 of a point for a member of Congress, and 1/12 for journalists and local politicians: *Fiery Cross*, pp. 400–401.

119. See Doug McAdam, *Freedom Summer* (New York: Oxford University Press, 1988).

120. Commission on Freedom of the Press, *A Free and Responsible Press* (Chicago: University of Chicago Press, 1947), p. 26.

121. Especially during the Gulf War, Arab-Americans have experienced an increasing amount of hostility. During the events leading up to the war and during the war itself, Arab-Americans were threatened, businesses and homes were bombed. One target of threats was *Sada al-Watan*, based in Detroit, the nation's largest Arabic-language newspaper: Fox Butterfield, "Arab-Americans Report Increase in Death Threats and Harassment," *New York Times*, 29 August 1990; editorial, "Home-Grown Hatemongers," ibid., 27 February 1991.

122. Robert Justin Goldstein, *Political Repression in Modern America: 1870 to the Present* (New York: Schenkman, 1978), pp. 34–44. Goldstein notes that animosity in this

period was informed by a fear of anticapitalist labor groups, especially centering around the stereotype of the anarchist.

123. Sidney Fine, "Anarchism and the Assassination of McKinley," *American Historical Review* 60 (1955): 777–99; Higham, *Strangers in the Land*, p. 111; Goldstein, *Political Repression*, pp. 66–70.

124. Higham, *Strangers in the Land*, p. 213.

125. For instance, the American Protective Association (APA), which professed to protect against the conspiratorial nature of Roman Catholicism, flourished in the 1890s, claiming half a million active members in 1894–1895: Thomas J. Curran, *Xenophobia and Immigration, 1820–1930* (Boston: Twayne, 1975), pp. 93–108. Higham remarks that, despite its pervasiveness, "the amount of physical violence produced by the anti-Catholic hysteria of the nineties was not great," and that much of the violence was directed against APA lecturers by Catholics: *Strangers in the Land*, pp. 79–80.

126. Erik Kirschbaum, *The Eradication of German Culture in the United States, 1917–1918*, vol. 2 (1986) of *American German Studies* (Stuttgart), pp. 37–38; Frederick C. Luebke, "The German-American Alliance in Nebraska, 1910–1917," in Luebke, *Germans in the New World: Essays in the History of Migration* (Urbana: University of Illinois Press, 1990), pp. 14–30.

127. Kirschbaum, *Eradication*, pp. 39–43; Clifton J. Child, *The German-Americans in Politics* (New York: Arno Press, 1970), pp. 1–7, 27–32; Higham, *Strangers in the Land*, p. 188.

128. Kirschbaum, *Eradication*, pp. 75–76.

129. From a speech at the Columbia County Fair in Chatham, New York, 6 September 1917, quoted in Anna A. Linck, "Freedom of the Press in the United States in World Wars I and II" (M.A. thesis, Ohio State University, 1947), p. 106. Roosevelt's stand was not uncommon; Higham notes that "many patriots clamored for the suppression of all German-language newspapers, and in numerous areas local officials banned their sale." *Strangers in the Land*, p. 208.

130. Luebke, "Legal Restrictions on Foreign Languages in the Great Plains States, 1917–1923," in Luebke, *Germans in the New World*, p. 35.

131. *Final Report of the Missouri Council of Defense* (Jefferson City) (St. Louis: C. P. Curran, 1919), pp. 61–62. World War I was tremendously unpopular in Missouri, as in much else of the nation outside the Northeast: Christopher C. Gibbs, *The Great Silent Majority: Missouri's Resistance to World War I* (Columbia: University of Missouri Press, 1988).

132. Luebke, "Legal Restrictions," pp. 31–50; Higham, *Strangers in the Land*, pp. 208–12; Kirschbaum, *Eradication*, pp. 89–111.

133. Kirschbaum, *Eradication*, pp. 83, 115–17, 126–32; Luebke, "Legal Restrictions," pp. 39–40; American Civil Liberties Union, *Wartime Persecutions, 1919* (New York, 1919), tallies 164 cases of mob violence in 1918 alone, including a mob attack on the Sioux Falls, South Dakota, *Deutschen Herold*; most of the mob actions were directed at individuals for "personal disloyalty"; this tally does not include raids by the American Protective League on the Chicago *Arbeiter-Zeitung* and *Sozial Demokraten* and the Philadelphia *Tageblatt*: Kirschbaum, *Eradication*, p. 87.

134. The most prominent exception was George Sylvester Viereck, editor and publisher of *The Fatherland* and *The American Weekly*. As a result of his opposition to the war, Viereck became the object of congressional investigations; his offices were raided by police, his books confiscated; and, in August 1917, a mob in Mount Vernon, New York, threatened his family. Viereck was a singular figure, however—before U.S. entry, he had been a hired agent of the German government; this connection, though it ceased with the U.S.

laration of war, was no secret. Phyllis Keller, *States of Belonging: German-American Intellectuals and the First World War* (Cambridge: Harvard University Press, 1979), pp. 157–59.

135. Kirschbaum, *Eradication*, pp. 82–83, 87.

136. Ibid., pp. 27–31. Press endorsement of such action seemed to have significant effects, as did press encouragement of tolerance: see John D. Stevens, "Press and Community Toleration: Wisconsin in World War I," *Journalism Quarterly* 46 (1969): 255–59.

137. Kirschbaum, *Eradication*, pp. 37–38; Keller, *States of Belonging*, p. 175. The dropoff was closely tied to the war: the Missouri Council of Defense noted that since the beginning of the war, the number of German-language papers in Missouri had fallen from fifteen to ten, "that several of them were printing half English, and that others were preparing to cease publication or printing exclusively in the English language" (*Final Report*, p. 62).

138. Higham, *Strangers in the Land*, p. 188.

139. See, for instance, the argument in Robert Ezra Park's germinal *The Immigrant Press and Its Control* (New York and London: Harper & Bros., 1922).

Chapter Seven

1. Taft and Ross state simply: "The United States has had the bloodiest and most violent labor history of any industrial nation in the world." Philip Taft and Philip Ross, "American Labor Violence: Its Causes, Character, and Outcome," in Roger Lane and John J. Turner, Jr., eds., *Riot, Rout, and Tumult: Readings in American Social and Political Violence* (Westport, Conn.: Greenwood Press, 1978), pp. 218–50, quotation at p. 219.

2. Beecher's remarks are taken from a sermon delivered at New York City's Plymouth Church, 29 July 1877, as reported in the *New York Times*, 30 July 1877: Samuel Yellen, *American Labor Struggles, 1877–1934* (1936; New York: Monad Press, 1974), p. 37.

3. Mike Davis, *Prisoners of the American Dream: Politics and Economy in the History of the Working Class* (London and New York: Verso, 1986), p. 113. David Montgomery makes much the same point: "The ideology of acquisitive individualism, which explained and justified a society regulated by market mechanisms and propelled by accumulation of capital, was challenged by an ideology of mutualism, rooted in working-class bondings and struggles." *Fall of the House of Labor: The Workplace, the State, and American Labor Activism, 1865–1925* (Cambridge and New York: Cambridge University Press, 1987), p. 171.

4. See Paul K. Edwards, *Strikes in the United States, 1881–1974* (New York: St. Martin's Press, 1981), Appendix A, Table A.6, p. 260.

5. Justin Kaplan, *Lincoln Steffens: A Biography* (New York: Simon & Shuster, 1974), pp. 108–9.

6. Dan Schiller, *Objectivity and the News: The Public and the Rise of Commercial Journalism* (Philadelphia: Temple University Press, 1981); Sean Wilentz, *Chants Democratic: New York City and the Rise of the American Working Class, 1789–1850* (New York: Oxford University Press, 1984). Schiller and Wilentz both associate this press with the travails of craft labor; on the same note, see William J. Rorabaugh, *The Craft Apprentice: From Franklin to the Machine Age in America* (New York: Oxford University Press, 1986). In part, this argument adequately describes the papers in industrializing areas, but not all of these papers nationally were aimed at this class of worker. Many were aimed at farmers, for instance (e.g., Cincinnati's *Western Tiller*). It is fair to say that all of these newspapers shared an anxiety about the creation of a dominant national market economy, along with the institutions that accompanied it: banks, commodities exchanges, paper money.

7. They did distinguish between "producers," that is, those who actually made things in their work, and landlords and other proprietors, who themselves produced nothing. This distinction was not actually a class distinction because "producers" included many classes, nonproducers did not constitute an actual class but were merely parasites on producers, and the ideal republic would be composed entirely of producers (without necessarily being classless).

8. The figures in Table I show how many workers per thousand were on strike at any time during a particular year in the time periods listed. If we designate (somewhat arbitrarily) periods of high strike activity as those in which this figure totals thirty-five or higher (meaning more than 3.5 percent of the work force per year was on strike), we can isolate the following as peak periods of industrial conflict: 1886–1889, 1894–1897, 1912–1922, 1934–1957, and 1966–1972.

**Table 1 Ratio of Number of Workers on Strike
to Number of Employed Persons × 1,000**

Period	
1881–1885	19.5
1886–1889	35.7
1890–1893	27.0
1894–1897	35.5
1898–1901	32.6
1902–1905	34.5
1906–1908	19.0
1909–1911	26.7
1912–1915	38.9
1916–1918	53.5
1919–1922	80.4
1923–1926	19.0
1927–1929	10.3
1930–1933	19.7
1934–1937	46.7
1938–1941	37.6
1942–1945	51.4
1946–1949	68.2
1950–1953	55.0
1954–1957	36.4
1958–1961	31.5
1962–1965	23.1
1966–1969	37.2
1970–1972	38.6
1973–1974	32.4

Source: Figures from Paul K. Edwards, *Strikes in the United States, 1881–1974* (New York: St. Martin's Press, 1981), Appendix A, Table A.1, p. 254.

9. Paul A. Gilje, *The Road to Mobocracy: Popular Disorder in New York City, 1763–1834* (Chapel Hill: University of North Carolina Press, 1987), p. 198.

10. Robert J. Goldstein, *Political Repression in Modern America* (Cambridge, Mass.: Schenkman, 1978), p. 72; Taft and Ross, "Labor Violence," pp. 233–34, also note attacks on "union halls, newspapers, and cooperatives" in the 1901 preview to the "war" of 1903–1904. For more on manipulation—especially through the Associated Press wire—of news

from Colorado by the mining interests in this era, see Upton Sinclair's *The Brass Check: A Study of American Journalism* (Pasadena: The Author, 1919).

11. David Corbin, *The Socialist and Labor Star* (Huntington, W.V.: Appalachian Movement Press, 1971), pp. 16–24. Corbin notes that although martial law had been declared in parts of the state, Huntington was eighty miles from the martial law zone—nor would martial law have dictated that the raid take place at 2:00 A.M., nor that the printing equipment be destroyed.

12. James A. Lynch, *Epochal History of the International Typographical Union* (Indianapolis: ITU, 1925), pp. 37–44. Specifically on agitation for the eight-hour day in 1902–1906, see pp. 57–64. Ongoing revolutions in newspaper technology, from steam printing to stereotyping to the linotype and beyond, allowed proprietors to circumvent traditional craft restrictions on hiring higher-paid journeymen for tasks like compositing, instead hiring "rats" (as noncraft replacement workers were called) or women or children, who could generally be coerced into accepting lower rates of pay: William S. Pretzer, "'The British, Duff Green, the Rats and the Devil': Custom, Capital, and Conflict in the Washington Printing Trade, 1834–1836," *Labor History* 27 (1985–1986): 5–30; Justin E. Walsh, *To Print the News and Raise Hell* (Chapel Hill: University of North Carolina Press, 1968), pp. 224–26. Among editorial workers, the collectivism that unionization implied was often seen as fundamentally incompatible with the independence that journalism required—as one publisher remarked, "There's Bolshevism in it and if it ever forces open the sacred portals of journalism the freedom of the press which you and I have defended will be gone forever." Emil Gauvreau, *My Last Million Readers* (New York: Dutton, 1941), p. 89, quoted in Daniel J. Leab, *A Union of Individuals: The Formation of the American Newspaper Guild, 1933–1936* (New York: Columbia University Press, 1970), p. 20.

13. Bob Gottlieb and Irene Wolt, *Thinking Big: The Story of the Los Angeles Times, Its Publisher, and Their Influence on Southern California* (New York: Putnam, 1977), pp. 17–21; Mike Davis, *City of Quartz: Excavating the Future in Los Angeles* (London and New York: Verso, 1990), pp. 112–14; Jack R. Hart, *The Information Empire: The Rise of the Los Angeles Times and the Times Mirror Corporation* (Washington, D.C.: University Presses of America, 1981), pp. 20–24. Davis is perhaps hyperbolic when he writes, "For the half-century between the Spanish-American and Korean wars, the Otis-Chandler dynasty of the *Times* did preside over one of the most centralized—indeed militarized—municipal power structures in the United States. They erected the open shop on the bones of labor, expelled pioneer Jews from the social register, and looted the region through one great real-estate syndication after another." *City of Quartz*, p. 101.

14. Davis, *City of Quartz*, pp. 113–14; Gottlieb and Wolt, *Thinking Big*, pp. 45–47, 58.

15. Hart, *Information Empire*, pp. 33–36, 38; Gottlieb and Wolt, *Thinking Big*, pp. 32–43, 50, 51–52.

16. "The Wolves are Howling," editorial, *Times*, 3 September 1910, p. 4.

17. Gottlieb and Wolt, *Thinking Big*, pp. 23, 47–48; Davis, *City of Quartz*, p. 228.

18. Gottlieb and Wolt, *Thinking Big*, pp. 82–84; Hart, *Information Empire*, p. 39; for examples of hostile coverage of labor troubles in the *Times*, see "The Blight on San Francisco: City Cannot Prosper until Yoke of Labor Unions is Thrown Off," 6 September, p. 2:2; "Union Sluggers are Arrested," 8 September, p. 1:4; "Unions Reach End of Rope," 15 September, p. 1:5; "Make Union Brutes Flee," 16 September, p. 2:1; "Labor Unions are Hit Hard," 21 September, p. 2:1; "Labor Forces Rates Upward," 22 September, p. 2:5; "Oil Industry is Attacked: Union Gang Starts Reign of Terror," 27 September 1910, p. 2:1. Characteristically, these stories featured slender reports under big scare headlines that were often misleading about the content of the reports themselves. A front-page story of 29 Septem-

ber, for instance, featured a dizzying stack of tiered headlines that read DISCOVERY OF GRAFT/Pinhead and Tveitloe are Defied/SACRAMENTO UNIONISTS REFUSE TO DIG UP MORE FOR LOS ANGELES STRIKERS/Demand and are Refused Account of Distribution of Funds/BIG ROW STARTED IN NORTH OVER SUPPORT OF LOCAL LABOR LOAFERS. The story itself was about a relatively minor disagreement over whether relatively recent hires should qualify for strike pay. For an example of the *Times*'s baiting of the ironworkers, see editorial, "Can't Blame Corpse This Time," 30 September 1910, p. 2:4.

19. The best account of the actual blast is in Gottlieb and Wolt, *Thinking Big*, pp. 84–85; see also the coverage of the *Times* itself, 2 October 1910. Other local papers, including the *Herald*, offered their printing plants to the *Times*: "Hands to Help Offers Prompt," *Times*, 2 October 1910, p. 1:2.

20. *Times*, front-page headline, 2 October 1910; "Where the Blame Lies," 3 October 1910, p. 1:6.

21. Otis, "His Statement of the Case," *Times*, 2 October 1910, p. 1:2; see also, in the same issue, "The Inhumanity of It," p. 1:6, and "Burdette at the Bat XXIV," p. 1:6.

22. For accounts of the aftermath of the explosion and trial, see Gottlieb and Wolt, *Thinking Big*, pp. 82–104; Marshall Berges, *The Life and Times of Los Angeles: A Newspaper, a Family, and a City* (New York: Atheneum, 1984), pp. 20–25; and Selig Perlman and Philip Taft, *Labor Movements*, vol. 4 of John R. Commons et al., eds., *Trade Unionism and Labor Problems*, 2d ed. (Boston: Houghton Mifflin, 1921), pp. 318–25.

23. Quoted in Gottlieb and Wolt, *Thinking Big*, p. 97.

24. Gene Fowler, *Timber Line: A Story of Bonfils and Tammen* (Garden City, N.Y.: Garden City Press, 1933; reprint, 1947), pp. 101, 132, 155–59, 229–45.

25. Robert K. Murray, *Red Scare: A Study in National Hysteria, 1919–1920* (Minneapolis: University of Minnesota Press, 1955), remains the best treatment of the Red Scare.

26. "Talk Violence to Injure Streetcar Men's Cause," *Denver Labor Bulletin*, 24 July 1920, p. 1.

27. Details of the riot are taken from the 7 August strike issue of the *Denver Labor Bulletin*.

28. "Tramway Strike Riots," ibid., p. 1.

29. "Tramway Strike Riots," "A Question of a Living Wage," "The Cause of the Riots," ibid., 7 August 1920; "Strike at Source of Wrong," quoting the *Oklahoma Federationist*, ibid., 4 September 1920. For additional examples of criticism of the daily press, see the following articles in the special strike issue of the *Labor Bulletin*: "Truth about Tramway Strike: Daily Papers Tell Tramway Side Only," John E. Connelly, "What the Strike Indicates," "The Lying Press"; see also Charles M. Kelley, "The Harvest of the Open Shop," ibid., 21 August 1920.

30. Kelley, "The Harvest of the Open Shop," *ibid*. The sensitivity to propaganda noted in these comments is certainly a reflection of the recent experiences of World War I. Despite the criticisms that labor leaders voiced, I have not been able to find one endorsing violence against a news medium as an appropriate response. Kelley's article explicitly denounces violence and calls instead for workers to boycott antilabor newspapers. Likewise, the International Typographical Union, at its annual meeting, specifically denounced the sacking of the *Post* as a "violation of the principle of the constitution of the United States—freedom of the press and the preservation of life and property." ("Post Sacking is Denounced," ibid., 25 September 1920.) As in the case of the *Los Angeles Times*, it seems that labor had already made a great ideological investment in the cause of freedom of expression, while the antilabor dailies had made a similar investment in industrial liberty and property rights.

31. "Justice in Denver," *Denver Labor Bulletin*, 25 September 1920.

32. "Streetcar Strike Off," ibid., 6 November 1920.

33. Montgomery, *Fall of the House of Labor*, p. 156.

34. Herbert Gutman, "Class, Status, and Community Power in Nineteenth-Century American Industrial Cities: Paterson, New Jersey; A Case Study," and "A Brief Postscript: Class, Status, and the Gilded Age Radical: A Reconsideration," in Gutman, *Work, Culture, and Society in Industrializing America* (1966; reprint, New York: Vintage, 1977), pp. 234–92.

35. Milwaukee *Leader*, 14 December 1912.

36. Harvey O'Connor, *Revolution in Seattle, A Memoir* (New York: Monthly Review Press, 1964), p. 201; R. T. Ruetter, "Anaconda Journalism: The End of an Era," *Journalism Quarterly* 68 (1960): 3–12; *Butte Bulletin*, 1 July 1920.

37. ACLU, *Civil Liberties Quarterly*, June 1933, p. 1: "Act to Restore Rights of Illinois Miners." Similarly, "In May 1937, Henry Ford's private police mercilessly beat UAW organizers attempting to pass out leaflets near the Rouge plant." Robert H. Zeiger, *American Workers, American Unions, 1920–1985* (Baltimore: Johns Hopkins University Press, 1978), p. 55.

38. ACLU, *Civil Liberties Quarterly*, September 1931, p. 1: "Rule by Gun Dominates Harlan County"; *Workers' Defense*, October 1931, p. 1. Also reported attacked was Bruce Crawford, editor of a liberal weekly in Norton, Virginia. Similarly, note the beating of Esther Shemitz of the *World Tomorrow*, Sophie Shulman of the *New Masses*, and Sender Garlin, also a reporter, by police during a strike at Botany Worsted Mills in Passaic, New Jersey, in 1926: *ACLU Report*, July/August 1926, p. 5; and the kidnapping of Ellis O. Jones, a journalist, along with an ACLU representative by opponents of agricultural unionists in California in 1934: ACLU, *Civil Liberties Quarterly*, April 1934, p. 1.

39. *ACLU Reports*, April 1929, p. 4. In Passaic, according to Goldstein, "authorities even broke the cameras of newsmen covering the strike. Eventually the press corps took to wearing steel helmets and covering the strike from low-flying planes or automobiles which resembled tanks." A similar pattern was discernible in textile strikes in New Bedford, Massachusetts, in 1928 and Gastonia, North Carolina, in 1929: *Political Repression*, pp. 186–88.

40. The following table presents incidents representing antiradical violence:

Selected Violent Actions Against Radical Publications, 1900–1940 (excluding World War I)

Target	Date	Attacker and motive
Hearst newspapers: New York, Chicago, San Francisco	September 1901	Bundles burned by mobs after McKinley assassination
New York *Freie Arbeiter Stimme*	September 1901	Mobbed after McKinley assassination
Spring Valley, Ill., *L'Aurora*	September 1901	Mobbed after McKinley assassination
Prosser, Wash., *Record*	Fall 1908	George E. Boomer, printer, mobbed twice
Bremerton, Wash., *Kitsap County Leader*	1912	George E. Boomer, editor, beaten by a by a soldier
New York *Forward*	January 1915	Garment strikers; felt betrayed
Wewoka, Okla., *Capital-Democrat*	December 1922	Editor kidnapped by KKK
Oakland, Calif., *Free Press*	April 1922	Editor tarred and feathered
Labor Herald	August 1922	William Z. Foster, editor, kidnapped
Il Martello	March 1927	Carlo Tresca, editor, mobbed by fascists
David Weinberg, Miami, Fla.	September 1930	Tarred and feathered for distributing Communist literature to blacks

Selected Violent Actions Against Radical Publications, 1900–1940 (excluding World War I)

Target	Date	Attacker and motive
El Centro, Calif., San Bernardino Calif., Toledo, Ohio, radio stations	December 1936	Violence after Communist Party broadcasts
Austin, Texas, *Pension and Politics*	September 1937	Distributors "molested" by Texas Rangers
Aberdeen, Wash., Finnish Workers Hall	December 1939	Mobbed, probably over preparedness
Pekin, Ill., Communists	June 1940	Literature burned re election petitions

41. Emma Goldman, *Living My Life* (1931; reprint, New York: Da Capo, 1970), p. 312; Goldstein, *Political Repression*, pp. 66–70; Bernell E. Tripp, "The Decline of Yellow Journalism, 1901–1917" (Paper presented to the American Journalism Historians Association convention, Charleston, S.C., October 1988), pp. 9–13; M. J. Heale, *American Anti-Communism: Combatting the Enemy Within, 1830–1970* (Baltimore: Johns Hopkins University Press, 1990), p. 45; O'Connor, *Revolution in Seattle*, p. 7.

42. Sidney Fine, "Anarchism and the Assassination of McKinley," *American Historical Review* 60 (1955): 777–99.

43. James Weinstein, *The Decline of Socialism in America, 1912–1925* (New York: Monthly Review Press, 1967), pp. 143–44, 161; Richard Schwarzlose, "The Marketplace of Ideas: A Measure of Free Expression," *Journalism Monographs* 118 (December 1989), p. 28; Alfred McClung Lee, *The Daily Newspaper in America: The Evolution of a Social Instrument* (New York: Macmillan, 1937), pp. 722–23. There is some disagreement on the timing and steepness of the decline in Socialist newspapers. Daniel Bell, arguing that the decline was based on popular uninterest, asserts that publications dropped from 262 in 1912 to 42 in 1916—before U.S. entry into the war but not before the beginnings of the loyalty and preparedness campaigns. Weinstein argues convincingly that the appropriate numbers should be 170 for 1912 and 133 for 1916, a much slower decline, indicating the continued popularity of the Socialist press. Its later decline, according to Weinstein, is attributable to "wartime hysteria and government suppression." Weinstein, *Decline of Socialism*, pp. 84–93. In either case, by 1918 Socialist newspapers were becoming concentrated in cities and tended to depend on the mails for circulation, a situation that left them vulnerable.

44. John Higham, *Strangers in the Land: Patterns of American Nativism, 1860–1925* (New York: Atheneum, 1969), pp. 219–20; "Fighting for Democracy," *Seattle Union Record*, 28 July 1917; Neil A. Wynn, *From Progressivism to Prosperity: World War I and American Society* (New York: Holmes & Meier, 1986), pp. 51–52; *Milwaukee Leader*, 10 October 1917; Paul Buhle, *Marxism in the United States: Remapping the History of the American Left* (London: Verso, 1987), pp. 118–19.

45. Wynn, *Progressivism to Prosperity*, pp. 51–56, 59; Goldstein, *Political Repression*, pp. 110–12; H. C. Peterson and Gilbert Fite, *Opponents of War, 1902–1952* (Madison: University of Wisconsin Press, 1957), pp. 63, 148–51; Weinstein, *Decline of Socialism*, p. 91; David M. Kennedy, *Over Here: The First World War and American Society* (New York: Oxford University Press, 1980), pp. 78–83; Higham, *Strangers in the Land*, p. 224; William Pencak, *For God and Country: The American Legion, 1919–1941* (Boston: Northeastern University Press, 1989), pp. 145, 149–53.

46. Wynn, *Progressivism to Prosperity*, pp. 43–49, 96–103; Goldstein, *Political Repression*, p. 134.

47. W. A. Swanberg, *Citizen Hearst: A Biography of William Randolph Hearst* (New York: Scribner, 1961), pp. 371–75. Seventeen IWW members, including their printer, were kidnapped and tarred and feathered in Tulsa in 1917: Scott Ellsworth, *Death in a Prom-*

ised Land: The Tulsa Race Riot of 1921 (Baton Rouge: Louisiana State University Press, 1982), pp. 25–33. In Cleveland, Boy Scouts burned bundles of the *Wachter und Anzeiger*: Carl Wittke, *The German-Language Press in America* (New York: Haskell House, 1973), p. 271. The following table gives further examples:

Selected World War I–Era Antipress Actions

Date, 1918	Action
5 January	Mob attacks Pigott Printing Concern, Seattle, Wash.
23 March	Non-Partisan League *Madelia News* painted yellow by mob, Rock Creek, Minn.
3 April	Mob paints windows of the *Deutschen Herold*, Sioux Falls, S.D., yellow.
8 April	Norman M. Harris, editor, beaten by mob at Mounds, Ill.
21 April	Mob attacks man distributing literature condemning the suppression of "The Finished Mystery" in Firewater, Ore.
22 April	Mob attacks man distributing "Finished Mystery" circular in Pendleton, Ore.
30 April	Four men tarred and feathered for selling "Kingdom News," a publication of the International Bible Students Association. in Walnut Ridge, Ark.
June	*Madelia News* editor driven from town, Rock Creek, Minn.
16 September	Mob attacks newstand, burns Hearst papers in Eugene, Ore.

Sources: All except last item, The American Civil Liberties Union's annual reports, *Wartime Persecutions*, for 1918 and 1919; last item, W. A. Swanberg, *Citizen Hearst: A Biography of William Randolph Hearst* (New York: Scribner, 1961), pp. 374–75.

48. Gerald B. Nelson, *Seattle: The Life and Times of an American City* (New York: Knopf, 1977), pp. 51–62; Roger Sale, *Seattle: Past to Present* (Seattle: University of Washington Press, 1976), pp. 104–5.

49. O'Connor, *Revolution in Seattle*, pp. 90–94; Anna Louise Strong, *I Change Worlds: The Remaking of an American* (New York: Holt, 1935), pp. 62–70.

50. O'Connor, *Revolution in Seattle*, pp. 22–23; *Seattle Union Record*, 4 August 1917; *Industrial Worker*, 29 December 1917.

51. *Seattle Union Record*, 29 September 1917, editorialized on the Home Guards; for later incidents of violence against leftists, see ibid., 27 April 1918; O'Connor, *Revolution in Seattle*, pp. 171–72; Leo Huberman, "Introduction," in O'Connor, *Revolution in Seattle*, x.

52. "Lawless Mob Wrecks Huge Printing Office," *Industrial Worker*, 12 January 1918; "Plant of Seattle Socialist Newspaper Wrecked by Jackies," *Milwaukee Leader*, 7 January 1918; Strong, *I Change Worlds*, p. 66; Weinstein, *Decline of Socialism*, p. 91.

53. "Condemn Pigott Press Raiders," *Seattle Union Record*, 12 January 1918.

54. "'Mimic Men' Mob Leaders Arrested," *Industrial Worker*, 19 January 1918 (this story identifies G. Merle Gordon as "C. Murl"); "Authorities Lax in Riot Probe," *Seattle Union Record*, 26 January 1918.

55. O'Connor, *Revolution in Seattle*, pp. 95–96; Thomas McEnroe, "The IWW: Theories, Organizational Problems, and Appeals as Revealed Principally in the *Industrial Worker*" (Ph.D. diss., University of Washington, 1960).

56. "Statement from Our Printers," *Industrial Worker*, 12 January 1918.

57. O'Connor, *Revolution in Seattle*, p. 96; Thomas H. McEnroe, *The IWW* (Ann Arbor: University of Michigan Press, 1961).

58. For background, see Murray's *Red Scare*; Heale, *Anti-Communism*, pp. 60–75. State criminal syndicalism laws remained a key means of antiradical enforcement until the later 1930s, when the U.S. Supreme Court ruled against their constitutionality in overturning the conviction of Dirk de Jonge, an Oregon Communist.

59. Higham, *Strangers in the Land*, p. 225, cites fifty new radical newspapers follow-

ing the war. Examples of violent action against radical publications during the Red Scare include American Legion raid on the Oakland *World*, 14 November 1919; kidnapping of Tom Lassiter, radical news vendor, in Centralia, Wash., June 1919; mobbing by soldiers and sailors of the New York *Call*, August 1919. In 1919, according to Pencak, the American Legion attacked halls in such major cities as Columbus, Ohio, Cincinnati, and St. Louis—the attacks were "so numerous that the American Civil Liberties Union despaired of counting them." In the Cincinnati attack on Communist party headquarters, police looked on while a mob burned a huge pile of literature in the street: *Legion*, pp. 154–57. The instinct of authorities to attack the IWW became comical on occasion; for instance when Upton Sinclair was arrested for inciting a riot as he read the Bill of Rights at a meeting held on private property in San Pedro, Calif.: Goldstein, *Political Repression*, pp. 185–86.

60. See, for instance, *ACLU Reports*, February 1930, p. 2 (seven instances); March 1930, p. 5 (twenty-one instances); April 1930, p. 2 (eight instances). For May Day rioting, see ibid., May 1930, pp. 2–3. For the dropoff in 1933, see *Civil Liberties Quarterly*, June 1933.

61. For California examples, see "Red Squad Smashes John Reed Club Headquarters," *Western Worker*, 20 February 1933; "Raid Sacramento Workers Center," ibid., 7 August 1933; "Red Squad Threatens Life of John Diaz," ibid., 26 February 1934; "Legion Hoodlums Gang Up on Chico Workers Meeting," ibid., 19 March 1934; "Pedro Red Squad Attack Answered with More Militancy," ibid., 28 May 1934; "Minority Party Rights in Campaign Surveyed" (the bombing of three radio stations that had aired speeches by Communist candidates), *Civil Liberties Quarterly*, December 1936.

62. The best recent account of the labor history of the maritime workers in the 1930s and of the West Coast strike is Bruce Nelson, *Workers on the Waterfront: Seamen, Longshoremen, and Unionism in the 1930s* (Urbana: University of Illinois Press, 1988), esp. chaps. 4, 5.

63. The fighting of 3, 4, and 5 July, beginning with flying squads of strikers attacking strikebreakers and climaxing with the killing of two strikers in the counterattack that became known as the Battle of Rincon Hill, is recounted in *Western Worker*, 16 July 1934; see also Art Preis, *Labor's Giant Step: Twenty Years of the CIO* (1964; 2d ed., New York: Pathfinder Press, 1972), pp. 31–34.

64. "Freedom of the Press in California," *Western Worker*, 2 July 1934; "Legion Anti-Red Week," ibid., 9 July 1934.

65. Nelson, *Workers on the Waterfront*, pp. 147–48.

66. The *Western Worker* published a photograph on 29 October purportedly showing a policeman "a few seconds before the vigilant raid of July 17." The *Worker* asserted that the value of the property damaged during the police raid was $3,000, and sued for that amount. It listed the destroyed property as "seven desks, six typewriters, seven tables, 222 chairs used in the upstairs hall, literature in the Worker's Bookstore, electrical equipment, files of the Western Worker." "Western Worker Sues Police for $3000 Damages in Free Press Fight," *Western Worker*, 20 August 1934.

67. Goldstein, *Political Repression*, p. 227; "These Are the Cars of the Raiders," *Western Worker*, 3 September 1934.

68. "The Shipowners' Plan is a Boss-Controlled Hiring Hall," ibid., 4 June 1934.

69. "Freedom of the Press in California," ibid., 2 July 1934.

70. "Your Paper is a Weapon: Use It," ibid., 8 August 1934.

71. George Seldes, *Freedom of the Press* (Indianapolis and New York: Bobbs-Merrill, 1935), pp. 280–90.

72. *Chronicle*, 18 July 1934. In the same issue, see "Strike Bred in Moscow, AFL Avers," for more of that newspaper's strategy of discrediting the strike by portraying it as the work of a cabal.

73. Though up to the German attack on the Soviet Union and the change in the Communist party line, attacks remained common. See, for instance, "Riot at Communist Meeting," *Civil Liberties Quarterly*, September 1939; "Attacks on Communists Increasing," ibid., December 1939. The attention of a hostile federal government remained strong as well, with the formation of the Dies Committee and the campaign of the FBI to drive Communists out of CIO-affiliated unions: Heale, *Anti-Communism*, pp. 122–29.

74. Anna A. Linck, "Freedom of the Press in the United States in World Wars I and II" (M.A. thesis, Ohio State University, 1947), pp. 145–46; Goldstein, *Political Repression*, pp. 263–64; Richard Polenberg, *War and Society: The United States, 1941–1945* (Philadelphia: Lippincott, 1972), pp. 45–46.

75. "Sect Victim of Assaults in 44 States," *Civil Liberties Quarterly*, September 1940; Goldstein, *Political Repression*, p. 283.

76. Abe Peck, *Uncovering the Sixties: The Life and Times of the Underground Press* (New York: Pantheon, 1985), pp. 183, 267.

77. *Black Panther*, July 1967; Peck, *Uncovering the Sixties*, pp. 66–67.

78. See Todd Gitlin, *The Whole World Is Watching: Mass Media in the Making and Unmaking of the New Left* (Berkeley: University of California Press, 1980). Gitlin notes that media coverage also inflected the recruitment of new members for radical organizations.

79. Athan Theoharis, *Spying on Americans: Political Surveillance from Hoover to the Huston Plan* (Philadelphia: Temple University Press, 1978), pp. 133–95. On the underground press specifically, see Geoffrey Rips, *UnAmerican Activities: The Campaign Against the Underground Press* (San Francisco: City Lights, 1981); Peck, *Uncovering the Sixties*, pp. 176–85.

80. Edward S. Herman and Noam Chomsky, *Manufacturing Consent: The Political Economy of the Mass Media* (New York: Pantheon, 1988).

81. For examples, see Peck, *Uncovering the Sixties*, pp. 89, 115, 121–33, 136, 143, 158, 229–31, 239, 261; David Armstrong, *A Trumpet to Arms: Alternative Media in America* (Los Angeles, J. P. Tarcher, 1981), pp. 147, 156–57; Rips, *UnAmerican Activites*, 114–32; Todd Gitlin, *The Sixties: Years of Hope, Days of Rage* (New York: Bantam Books, 1987), pp. 237–38, 250.

82. Gitlin, *Sixties*, p. 327; Peck, *Uncovering the Sixties*, pp. 115–16.

83. "Hearst Slugger Stabs Newsboy," *Chicago Daily Socialist*, 25 September 1909; Swanberg, *Citizen Hearst*, pp. 321–25.

84. *Leader* newsboys were attacked often during December 1911: "Leader Newsboys are Driven from Streets by 'Huskies,'" 14 December 1911; "Two Leader Boys Forced from Street," 15 December 1912. See also Elmer Beck, "Autopsy of a Labor Daily: The Milwaukee *Leader*," *Journalism Monographs* 16 (1970), p. 4. The *Western Worker*, 20 November 1933, reported that sluggers from "four capitalist papers" attacked a newboy's meeting held at a Communist meeting hall in 1933: "SF Newspaper Thugs Attack Newsboys Meet; SF Examiner Circulation Head Reported Among Them."

85. Thomas J. Keil, *On Strike! Capital Cities and the Wilkes-Barre Newspaper Unions* (Tuscaloosa: University of Alabama Press, 1988), pp. 79–88. The security company hired, Wackenhut Security, was a big player in industrial disputes; Cap Cities was connected with Wackenhut through William J. Casey, later Director of Central Intelligence under Ronald Reagan, then a large shareholder in Cap Cities and a member of its board. Casey had handled Wackenhut's legal affairs in previous years: ibid., p. 112.

86. Ibid., pp. 88–105.

87. Both newspapers continue to publish, and occasionally the competition generates low-level violence—a *Times-Leader* reporter has had his tires slashed several times, for instance:

William Robbins, "Pennsylvania City Divided by 2 Newspapers' War," *New York Times*, 26 July 1983.

88. Mark Fitzgerald, "Violence Mars Chicago Tribune Strike Rally," *Editor and Publisher*, 11 January 1986, pp. 10–11. For another example of low-level violence in a labor dispute, see George Garneau, "Labor Dispute Gets Nasty at Southern NJ Daily," ibid., 1 March 1986, pp. 10–11. Similarly, Washington *Post* workers were fired and replaced when management determined they had sabotaged new presses in 1975: Howard Bray, *The Pillars of the Post: The Making of a News Empire in Washington* (New York: Norton, 1980), pp. 251–89.

89. The events and issues of the strike are usefully summarized and commented on in hearings held in New York on legislation barring the use of permanent replacement workers: Senate Committee on Labor and Human Resources, Subcommittee on Labor, *New York Daily News Strike and Permanent Replacements: Hearing . . . December 11, 1990* one hundred first Congress, second session, 1990 (Washington, D.C.: Government Printing Office, 1991).

90. Quoted in O'Connor, *Revolution in Seattle*, pp. 184–85.

Chapter Eight

1. Justin Walsh, *To Print the News and Raise Hell* (Chapel Hill: University of North Carolina Press, 1968), pp. 7, 220–24.

2. Robert D. Leigh, ed., *A Free and Responsible Press* (Chicago: University of Chicago Press, 1947).

3. Ibid., pp. 20–21.

4. A stern and comprehensive rebuttal to the Hutchins Commission is Frank Hughes, *Prejudice and the Press: A Restatement of the Principle of Freedom of the Press with Specific Reference to the Hutchins-Luce Commission* (New York: Devin-Adair, 1950).

5. See Kevin G. Barnhurst and John Nerone, "Design Changes in U.S. Front Pages, 1885–1985," *Journalism Quarterly* 68 (1991): 796–804.

6. On professionalism and news values, see Gaye Tuchman, *Making News: A Study in the Construction of Reality* (New York: Free Press, 1978); Herbert J. Gans, *Deciding What's News: A Study of CBS Evening News, NBC Nightly News, Newsweek, and Time* (New York: Pantheon, 1979).

7. On the rise of the network broadcast system, see especially Robert McChesney, *Telecommunications, Mass Media, and Democracy: The Battle for the Control of U.S. Broadcasting, 1928–1935* (New York: Oxford University Press, 1993). On the role of regulation in creating monopoly, both in general and specifically in telecommunications, see Robert Britt Horwitz, *The Irony of Regulatory Reform: The Deregulation of American Telecommunications* (New York: Oxford University Press, 1989).

8. Research assistance in retrieving incidents from *Editor and Publisher* was rendered by Fr. Britto Berchmanns.

9. Assistance on the mail survey was rendered by William Mueller and Gilbert Brinkley Rodman; a grant was provided by the Research Board of the University of Illinois at Urbana-Champaign.

10. This is interpreting "regular" to mean a frequency of "monthly" or more.

11. The precise items were "A large part of the public feels hostility toward the media," "The public would *not* condone legal restrictions on the press," and "A large part of the

public feels that some journalists deserve a beating." Average responses were 4.1, 3.9, and 4.4, respectively, with 1 meaning strong agreement and 7 strong disagreement.

12. Significance (measured by Pearson's *r*) = .006 and .000, respectively.

13. A weak correlation was also found between class of medium and perception of public hostility (measured by Pearson's *r* at .086). There was a stronger correlation between whether a medium experiences regular threats and whether it perceives public hostility: .009. Likewise, media that experience regular threats are somewhat more likely to agree that journalism is a dangerous profession (.042).

14. Significance (measured by Pearson's *r*) = .000.

15. Christine LaVigne of Topics Newspapers in Indianapolis, Indiana.

16. The editor of the Anchorage Alaska *Tundra Times* writes: "I believe that many people have become very disappointed with the media. They are really tired of much of the 'tabloid sensationalism' that has taken over many areas of reporting. Also, the obvious lack of care about the victims."

17. A Gallup survey commissioned by Times-Mirror found that 73 percent of the general public responded in the negative when asked whether the media "respect people's privacy." *The People and the Press: A Times-Mirror Investigation of Public Attitudes Toward the News Media*, pt. 1 (Los Angeles: Times Mirror, 1986), p. 30.

18. Michael Sherer, "Assaults on Photojournalists," *Newspaper Research Journal* (Spring 1991): 82–91.

19. The case of the *Mesa Tribune* is recounted in "Bus Deliberately Driven into Newspaper's Lobby," *Editor and Publisher*, 28 October 1989, p. 25. For similar cases, see "Enraged Reader Attacks City Editor at His Desk," ibid., 18 August 1979; "Shot at Cameraman Costs Housewife $5," ibid., 8 March 1969, p. 26; Arthur W. Geisleman, Jr., "Take Pictures of Tragic Scene or Flee from Irate Onlookers?" ibid., 15 August 1959, p. 13.

20. Recent examples from the world of baseball involved Dennis "Oil Can" Boyd, Danny Cox, and Darryl Strawberry; the all-time record holder is probably the late Billy Martin.

21. Gerald Eskenazi, "Tagliabue Looks Into Harrassment Charge," *New York Times*, 27 September 1990, p. B10.

22. For a few cases, see "Senator Hits Newsman, Later Apologizes," *Editor and Publisher*, 26 February 1949, p. 13; "Fla. Reporter Punched, Barred from Senate," ibid., 11 June 1949, p. 10; "Cheers Press after Melee," ibid., 21 November 1959, p. 2; "Mayor Has Reporter Arrested," ibid., 16 May 1959, p. 76; "Official Breaks Reporter's Nose," ibid., 26 September 1964, p. 52.

23. "Alaska Publisher Subdues Gunman," *Editor and Publisher*, 6 December 1986, p. 22; similarly, though this incident involved sports as much as politics, a reader attacked the publisher of the *Nashville* (Arkansas) *News*: see "Irate Reader Beat Up Publisher, Police Say," *Arkansas Democrat*, 22 May 1991, pp. 1B, 6B.

24. "Execution Set for Killer of Reporter," *Editor and Publisher*, 17 January 1987, p. 31. Similarly, see the shooting death of radio personality Bill Mason: "Bill Mason Pays with His Life to Close up Texas Hall of Sin," ibid., 6 August 1949, p. 6; and the conspiracy to kill *Gary* (Indiana) *Post Tribune* reporter Alan Doyle: "Indiana Couple Guilty of Reporter Death Plot," ibid., 27 January 1979, p. 13. In 1986 Ned Day of the *Las Vegas Review Journal* had his car firebombed while investigating organized crime: M. L. Stein, "Columnist's Car Firebombed," ibid., 19 July 1986, p. 9; and photographer Al Gutierrez was kidnapped and tortured by drug smugglers while on assignment for the *El Paso* (Texas) *Herald-Post*: Debra Gersh, "12 Hours of Torture," ibid., 17 May 1986, p. 15.

25. See, for instance, "Fla. Developer Charged with Assaulting Photogs," ibid., 25 January 1986, p. 28; "West Coast Reporter Vindicated in Kidnap Case," ibid., 1 December 1984,

p. 17; "Reporter Beaten and Stabbed," ibid., 8 December 1979, p. 2; "NY Post photogs, re-porters assaulted," ibid., 4 August 1979, p. 18; "Cameraman Floored But He Takes Pictures," ibid., 11 July 1959, p. 46; "Army Colonel Strikes Photog, Breaks Camera," ibid., 26 Febru-ary 1944, p. 66; "Photographer Assaulted in Philadelphia," ibid., 1 April 1944, p. 53; "Thugs Attack Another Phila. Newspaperman," ibid., 15 April 1944, p. 30.

26. "Ky Official Charged with Hitting Reporter," ibid., 19 August 1989, pp. 24, 56.

27. See, for instance, "Reporter Attacked on KKK Story; 2 Held," ibid., 25 June 1949, p. 11; "Newspaper Bombed, UPI Man Injured," ibid., 5 September 1964.

28. See, for instance, "Reporters Face Gas and Guns in Riot," ibid., 22 August 1964, p. 50; "Harlem Rioters Injure, Threaten Newsmen," ibid., 25 July 1964, p. 11; "Photogra-phers Attacked in Cleveland Race Riots," ibid., 8 February 1964, p. 9; "Reporter Beaten in Chester Riots," ibid., 2 May 1964, p. 55.

29. See, for instance, "Whites Vent Ire Against Reporters," ibid., 27 September 1969, p. 90; "Newsman Injured in Attack Calls Mob Action 'Justified,'" ibid., 6 September 1969, p. 47; Darrell Leo, "Pickets Protest News Coverage of School Squabble," ibid., 28 Sep-tember 1974, pp. 9, 67.

30. Larry Rohter, "When a City Newspaper is the Enemy," *New York Times*, 19 March 1992, p. A8; John Newhouse, "A Reporter at Large (Cuba)," *New Yorker*, 27 April 1992, pp. 52–83.

31. "Hundreds Go on Rampage After a Black Man is Slain in Shreveport," *New York Times*, 22 September 1988, p. 10.

32. David E. Pitt, "Weekly Newspaper's Office in the Bronx is Firebombed," *New York Times*, 1 March 1989, p. 13; Andrew Radolf and Mark Fitzgerald, "Weekly Firebombed, Support of Rushdie Is Suspected Reason," *Editor and Publisher*, 4 March 1989, pp. 13, 48; Debra Gersh, "Outspoken Weekly Paper Survives Bombing," ibid., 11 March 1989, pp. 9–10; Don Terry, "In Wake of Bombing, Paper Sticks to Its Values," *New York Times*, 14 March 1989, p. 15.

33. "Feds: Portland Reporter Was Targeted for Assassination," *Editor and Publisher*, 9 November 1985, p. 13.

34. Thomas J. Knudson, "Trial Opens in Slaying of a Denver Radio Host," *New York Times*, 31 October 1987, p. 8; "Two Killers of Denver Radio Host Sentenced to 150 Years in Prison," ibid., 4 December 1987, p. 13.

35. "Skinheads Berate Seattle Times Photographer," *Editor and Publisher*, 13 May 1989, p. 9.

36. See, for example, "Students Punished for Hitting Newsman," ibid., 28 June 1969, p. 45; Ludmilla Alexander, "Editors Stand Guard for the Campus Press," ibid., 5 July 1969, pp. 17–18.

37. John B. Gordon, "Police Officers Picket Paper," ibid., 4 March 1989, p. 29.

38. For some examples of antipress violence perpetrated by a small-town establish-ment being attacked by the local newspaper, see "Editor Charges Police Chief with Assault," ibid., 8 January 1944, p. 16; "Citation for Courage Goes to Dan Hicks Jr.," ibid., 12 July 1969, p. 14; Philly Murtha, "Plant Fire Draws Attention to Crusading Weekly Editor," ibid., 14 September 1974, p. 48; "Police Issue Warrants in Weekly Arson Case," ibid., 26 October 1974, p. 36; Debra Gersh, "Libel Suits, Death Threats, and Arson Have Not Stopped Homer Marcum from Publishing His Weekly Newspaper in Inez, Ky." ibid., 3 May 1986, p. 18.

39. Ken H. Fortenberry's story is told in his book *Kill the Messenger: One Man's Fight against Bigotry and Greed* (Atlanta: Peachtree, 1989). See also Debra Gersh, "Dream Turns into Nightmare," *Editor and Publisher*, 24 January 1987, pp. 12–13.

40. Debra Gersh, "Why McCormick County Rebelled against Publisher," *Editor and Publisher*, 31 January 1987, p. 12.

41. Terrorism is seen by many as a way of violently imposing editorial decisions on the media, hence much of the animus behind press coverage of terrorism. The media in turn are quite sensitive to public opinion concerning their coverage of terrorism—whether they have been too willing to give free publicity to terrorists: see, for example, Times-Mirror/Gallup, *The People and the Press* (pt. 1), for attention to how press coverage of terrorism affects public attitudes toward the media. *Terrorism* is a term applied too opportunistically for the scholarship on it to be of real use here. For a convincing critique, see Noam Chomsky, *The Culture of Terrorism* (Boston: South End Press, 1988).

42. Michael E. McGerr, *The Decline of Popular Politics: The American North, 1865–1928* (New York: Oxford University Press, 1986).

43. U.S. Commission on Civil Disorders, *Report* (New York: Dutton, 1968).

44. "Man Kills Himself after Holing up in Cincinnati Station," *Broadcasting*, 20 October 1980, p. 51.

45. In this case, the hostage taking was deemed newsworthy enough to place on the front page of the *New York Times*: Peter Applebome, "Behind Hostage Case, Issues of Rural Justice," 8 February 1988, pp. 1, 9.

46. M. L. Stein, "Copies of Phony Front Page Placed in Vending Machines," *Editor and Publisher*, 4 February 1989, p. 15. Other examples, all reported in *Editor and Publisher*, include "Another Newspaper Victimized with Phony Front Page," 11 February 1989, p. 31; Mark Fitzgerald, "Phony Front Pages Keep Surfacing," 25 March 1989, p. 18; "More Fake Front Pages Surface," 8 April 1989, p. 40; "Phony Front Pages Pop Up in Conn.," 5 August 1989, p. 36; and "More Phony Front-Page Wraparounds," 28 October 1989, p. 25. All these cases involved U.S. actions in Central America; the campaign seems to have been coordinated by the Committee in Solidarity with the People of El Salvador.

47. That this tactic has some attractiveness is clear from the fact that it has been copied by the extreme right. In August 1989, a racist tabloid, *Racial Loyalty*, was found inserted in news racks belonging to the *Austin* (Texas) *American-Statesman*: "Racist Tab Inserted in Five News Racks," *Editor and Publisher*, 25 November, 1989, p. 4.

48. Gary Stollman, "Gary Stollman's Statement," reprinted in *Off the Deep End*, no. 6/7 (June/July 1989), pp. 7–8.

49. See Garry Trudeau's satirical summary of press reaction to *JFK*: "Overkill," *New York Times*, 8 January 1992, p. A15.

50. See Barbie Zelizer, *Covering the Body: The Kennedy Assassination, the Media, and the Shaping of Collective Memory* (Chicago: Unversity of Chicago Press, 1992).

51. Asking whether people found the press to be believable or trusted in the accuracy of news reports, surveyers have found that a high percentage respond positively, and that there has been no serious change in believability since the 1930s: Gallup/Times-Mirror, *The People and the Press*, pt. 1, p. 20.

52. Ibid., pp. 31–32.

53. Two landmark surveys are Samuel Stouffer, *Communism, Conformity, and Civil Liberties: A Cross Section of the Nation Speaks Its Mind* (Garden City, N.Y.: Doubleday, 1955), and Herbert McClosky and Alida Brill, *Dimensions of Tolerance: What Americans Believe about Civil Liberties* (N.Y.: Russell Sage Foundation, 1983). For a summary of research on tolerance, see Michael Corbett, *Political Tolerance in America: Freedom and Equality in Public Attitudes* (New York: Longman, 1982).

54. Robert O. Wyatt et al., *Free Expression and the American Public: A Survey Commemorating the 200th Anniversary of the First Amendment* (Murfreesboro: Middle Tennessee State University and the American Society of Newspaper Editors, 1991), p. 35.

55. The table below presents responses to questions about whether individual or media rights "should be protected by law" in specific cases.

Opinions on Situation-Specific Legal Protection of Individual and Media Rights

Situation	All the Time %	Some of the Time %	Not at All %
"Taking God's name in vain and other sacrilege"	32	28	39
"Using words that might offend another religious group"	31	43	25
"Burning the flag to protest government action"	28	12	59
"Newspapers editorializing during a campaign"	34	38	28
"Journalists criticizing political leaders"	32	41	22
"Reporting national security stories without government approval"	17	37	45

Note: The above responses are from the first wave of surveys conducted by Wyatt et al. A second wave, conducted on the eve of the Persian Gulf War, found heightened support of some individual rights but on the whole less tolerance on these specific issues: *Free Expression and the American Public: A Survey Commemorating the 200th Anniversary of the First Amendment* (Murfreesboro: Middle Tennessee State University and the American Society of Newspaper Editors, 1981), pp. 13, 20, 23, 24.)

56. Wyatt et al., *Free Expression*, p. 6.
57. Gallup/Times-Mirror, *The People and the Press*, pt. 1, pp. 10–11.
58. Norman Ornstein et al., *The People, the Press, and Politics: The Times-Mirror Study of the American Electorate* (Reading, Mass.: Addison-Wesley, 1988), p. 32. In an earlier poll conducted for the American Society of Newspaper Editors, the media did much more poorly relative to other institutions. Responding to the question "As far as the people running these institutions are concerned, would you say you have a great deal of confidence, only some confidence, or hardly any confidence in them?" the following are the "great confidence" response percentages: U.S. Supreme Court, 44; education, 41; banks and financial institutions, 38; executive branch of the federal government, 37; organized religion, 33; newspapers, 26; Congress, 23; the press, 23; television, 21; and, finishing last, organized labor, 17. Interestingly, excepting banks and financial institutions, which have no doubt fallen a great deal in public esteem since the survey was conducted, the media finished ahead of all other private for-profit institutions, indicating some degree of public acceptance of an image of the media as public servants: MORI Research, *Newspaper Credibility: Building Reader Trust* (Minneapolis, 1985) p. 25.

Index